PELICAN BOOKS
A1020
A HISTORY OF THE COST OF LIVING

Born in 1925, John Burnett was educated in Nottingham and at Emmanuel College, Cambridge, where he was an Exhibitioner and Sizar; he graduated in 1946 with a part I History tripos and a part II Law tripos. He began his career by teaching in primary schools in Nottingham, then in 1948 he was appointed assistant lecturer at Guildford Technical College; later he became lecturer in economic history and law. In 1951 he took the Cambridge LL.B. by part-time study, specializing in the history of English law, and he subsequently researched at the London School of Economics on the history of food adulteration in Great Britain for a Ph.D., awarded in 1958. In the same year he was appointed head of the Division of Liberal Studies at the Borough Polytechnic, London, responsible for organizing courses in general studies for undergraduates in science and technology. He became head of the Department of General Studies at Brunel College in 1962 and, on its elevation to university status, Reader in Economic and Social History in the School of Social Sciences.

A History of the Cost of Living is John Burnett's second book. His previous publication, *Plenty and Want, A Social History of Diet in England from 1815 to the Present Day*, first appeared in 1966 and was published by Penguins in 1968. He is now editing a collection of nineteenth-century diaries and autobiographies on the general subject of the standard of living.

John Burnett is married and has a son. His interests, apart from food and the cost of living, include music, architecture and antiques.

A HISTORY OF
THE COST OF LIVING

John Burnett

PENGUIN BOOKS

Penguin Books Ltd, Harmondsworth, Middlesex, England
Penguin Books Inc., 7110 Ambassador Road, Baltimore, Maryland 21207, U.S.A.
Penguin Books Australia Ltd, Ringwood, Victoria, Australia

First published 1969
Copyright © John Burnett, 1969

Made and printed in Great Britain by
Hazell Watson & Viney Ltd, Aylesbury, Bucks

Set in Monotype Plantin

This book is sold subject to the condition
that it shall not, by way of trade or otherwise,
be lent, re-sold, hired out, or otherwise circulated
without the publisher's prior consent in any form of
binding or cover other than that in which it is
published and without a similar condition
including this condition being imposed
on the subsequent purchaser

Contents

Acknowledgements	7
Introduction	9
1. The Middle Ages	15
2. Tudor and Stuart England	55
3. The Eighteenth Century	128
4. The Nineteenth Century	189
5. The Last Fifty Years	282
Graph of Cost of Living 1266-1954	328
Note on Further Reading	329
Index	335

Acknowledgements

MY interest in the history of what people consume and the ways in which they spend their earnings derives from the teaching of two eminent scholars who, although they wrote commendably little themselves, have inspired a generation of social historians – the late E. Welbourne, formerly Master of Emmanuel College, Cambridge, and University Lecturer in Economic History, and H. L. Beales, formerly Reader in Economic History at the London School of Economics and Political Science. Countless students have been encouraged by their imaginative insight and immense knowledge of sources to explore areas of history that were, until recently, either unknown or unfashionable.

This book has drawn freely on the researches of many other scholars, past and present. It could not have been written without the pioneering studies into price history made by James E. Thorold Rogers in the latter part of the nineteenth century and by the late Lord Beveridge, who directed a Price and Wage History Research group in the 1930s: regrettably, only the first volume of what was to have been a large-scale study was published. Among contemporary scholars I am especially indebted to Professor E. H. Phelps Brown, whose price index from the thirteenth to the twentieth century has been used extensively in the text, to Dr G. E. Mingay and Dr F. M. L. Thompson for their illuminating studies of the structure of English landed society, and to Professor Guy Routh for his analysis of changes in occupation and earnings in the present century. The many other authorities I have used are cited in the Note on Further Reading at the end of the volume. I hope that their views have not been distorted by the compression which such a brief survey demands.

I am also grateful to Professor O. R. McGregor for many valuable references, and to D. J. Burningham for commenting on my drafts from an economist's viewpoint. Peter Wright, of

ACKNOWLEDGEMENTS

Penguin Books, gave the kind of informed interest and advice which authors hope to receive from publishers, but do not often find. Lastly, I am grateful to Annemarie Maggs, who typed my manuscripts and was often able to interpret my handwriting better than I could myself.

Brunel University J.B.
December 1967

Introduction

It is probably true that the one economic issue that concerns more people more directly and intimately than any other is the cost of living. Though few may be able to define it in precise terms, everyone – from the child in the sweet-shop to the Chancellor of the Exchequer – knows that if prices rise while income remains the same they get less for their money and the standard of life is depressed by that amount: conversely, if prices fall while income remains stationary, the money goes further and command over the necessaries and luxuries of life increases. Changes in the level of prices can therefore imply personal gain or personal loss, even personal tragedy if the hard-won savings of a lifetime become valueless in old age as a result of inflation. On a larger scale, price changes may affect the fortunes of entire classes of society, the fate of political parties, even the welfare and stability of the state as a whole. Especially since the second world war, the cost of living has been a major preoccupation of successive governments, culminating in the present unique experiment of a general prices and incomes policy.

The aim of this book is to show that prices and their movements have also been of interest and importance to our predecessors. The following chapters trace the history of the cost of living in England from the Middle Ages to the present day, not as an academic economic abstraction, but in the context of general economic developments of which changes in price have sometimes been the cause, sometimes the consequence. It may, for instance, be of intrinsic interest to know that the average price of a chicken in the year 1300 was 1d. (weight unspecified) or of a bottle of whisky in 1914 3s. 6d., but in themselves the figures tell us next to nothing about the times or the standard of life of the people who lived in them. They become more meaningful if they are compared over a period of time – if, for example, the medieval chicken is set against its modern counterpart at 3s. 6d. the pound. They take on another, even more important dimension when they are compared with average earnings: then, the penny chicken becomes dear when it is seen to represent half the daily wage of an agricultural labourer, whereas today it would take only about one-fifth. Comparison – with time on the one hand, and with earnings on the other – is, therefore, the essence of this study.

But the England of 1968 only remotely resembles that of 1300, and therefore whatever comparisons are made must take account of the fundamental changes that have altered the fabric of society in the last few hundred years. For one thing, the occupations of the people – and, hence, their earnings and ways of life – are quite different from those of the Middle Ages, when agriculture was the primary pursuit of the population: then, the great majority of people lived on the land and produced a substantial part of their own food and other needs, whereas today four out of every five people live in towns and are dependent on professional producers and retailers for almost everything. Our study must, therefore, place the history of the cost of living in the context of occupational changes which, in turn, have led to far-reaching changes in the social structure of the country. Just as the cost of living meant something very different to the medieval lord of the manor and to his serf, today it still has different implications for the company director and the unskilled worker.

Similarly, no absolute comparison of the cost of living over long periods of time can be made because people now spend their earnings in ways very different from those of their predecessors. It is obvious, for example, that while motoring now takes 2s. in every pound of personal expenditure, fifty years ago it took hardly anything and a century ago nothing at all: the same applies to washing-machines and refrigerators, radios, televisions and a hundred other products of modern technology. But throughout the centuries changes in the pattern of expenditure have gone on as new items have appeared and new tastes and fashions developed. Tea and coffee were unknown before the seventeenth century, fried fish and chips before the late nineteenth: in 1400 'bread' might be made of wheat, oats, barley, rye or a mixture of all of them, but by 1800 it was made almost everywhere in England exclusively of wheat. We cannot com-

INTRODUCTION

pare the cost of a medieval peasant's cottage with a modern council house, or of the Wife of Bath's habit with a mini-skirt, in any meaningful way: all are typical enough of their times, but the times have changed.

Each chapter of this book therefore contains an outline of the more important economic changes of the period, a discussion of the movement of prices, both in general and with respect to particular items, some account of changes in population, earnings, occupations and social structure, and, finally, an assessment of the cost of living as it was felt by different classes and sections of the people. This is a formidable task within the confines of a small volume, and it has compelled many omissions and many generalizations with which specialists in a particular period will almost certainly disagree.

It will be clear by now that the purpose of this kind of study is not merely to record a history of prices, but to examine over time the ways in which different strata of society have derived money and spent it. To the economist, prices are determined by the ratio between the supply of and the demand for money: the supply of money is the currency in circulation (which, until 1931, depended on the quantity of gold in circulation and in reserve) and the demand for it is represented by the quantity of goods and services available for sale. A reduction in the amount of currency would cause a fall in prices since, assuming the population to be stable, there would be less money per head: an increase in the supply of currency would cause a rise. Similarly, an increase in production of goods and services would result in a price-fall, and a reduction in production in a price-rise. Other factors obviously enter into the equation. An increase in the rapidity of circulation has the same effect as an increase in the volume of currency; an increase in population has the same effect as a reduction in the amount of money, since there will be less per head. If there are changes in the distribution of the population as between town and country this may also affect the level of prices, since town-dwellers tend to spend more money than country-dwellers. Many of these general principles of price-changes will be illustrated by reference to the historical environment in which they occurred.

The major difficulty for any student of the history of the cost

INTRODUCTION

of living is the paucity of data on past prices. Although scattered references to prices are to be found in almost any contemporary source – from household books and accounts to diaries, journals, letters and autobiographies – they usually relate to a particular place at a particular time only: the historian needs to be able to compare over a period of years, and there is no kind of certainty that the medieval barrel of beer was at all like its modern equivalent, in capacity or in strength, or that the meat and fish, the cloth, the shoes or the bread can be compared with their present-day counterparts in any very meaningful way. Even today prices vary from one part of the country to another, and in the past, before the development of an integrated economy, such variations were very much greater. Again, there is an obvious difference between wholesale and retail prices, but all too often in contemporary records it is not clear which is being quoted. What the historian would like are long series of retail prices of goods of a known and standard description, bought at various places at frequent and regular intervals, but these are almost non-existent. With the exception of wheat, bread and one or two other items, the price-series that have survived from early times relate either to wholesale prices, or to the prices paid by institutions such as schools and hospitals for goods supplied to them under long-term contracts: these often show a surprising rigidity over time, suggesting that they were to some extent insulated against ordinary fluctuations, and closer to wholesale than to retail prices. Thus, although such series have been used in the text for want of an alternative, it should be remembered that their chief value is in exhibiting trends rather than the exact price paid in the market-place.

If the prices of a large number of items are combined and reduced to a standard base, usually represented by 100 points, they are said to form an index number, and can be used to measure changes in the general level of prices by re-calculations at regular intervals. Index numbers are 'weighted' to allow for the differing importance of particular items in a supposedly 'typical' budget – thus, at any time before the twentieth century bread would have been allocated more points out of the total 100 than meat, clothing would receive more than transport, and so on. In very sophisticated index numbers, hundreds of items are

INTRODUCTION

taken into account and, nowadays, weighted on the basis of investigations into family expenditure. Clearly, if such index numbers were sufficiently wide, accurate and representative they could form a valid index of the cost of living which would be of immense value to economists and historians, as well as to government departments, employers and trade unions. But it will be obvious from what has been said earlier that such index numbers cannot be reliable for making comparisons of the general price-level over long periods of time, still less as an accurate measure of the cost of living for any particular individual or social class. Prices vary in different districts, quality varies from time to time: new products come into existence and existing ones drop out of use. One of the defects of the old cost of living index, in use between the two world wars, was that it was based on a pattern of expenditure calculated in 1914: it therefore overweighted the importance of food compared with other items, and paid undue regard to candles and oil, which had by then largely been replaced by gas and electricity. In times of rapid change, index numbers are out of date almost before they are compiled. Thus, like price-series, they are referred to here where they seem relevant, but should be read with caution, mainly as possible indicators of the directions of change.

All these limitations of the available data make the writing of a history of the cost of living, especially over a period of centuries, a hazardous venture. Yet the temptation to compare over time is irresistible. In the fourteenth century, the retail price of a pound of sugar would have bought 29 lb. of butter or 34 dozen eggs: in 1938 it would have bought only 3 oz. of butter or 2 eggs. The wages of the craftsmen who built Merton College in the fourteenth century were 3d. a day, of their successors who built Nuffield College in our own day about 450d. There can be no such thing as the value of money in the abstract. In the early fourteenth century wheat cost 5s. a quarter and steel 6d. a pound or £50 a ton: just before the second world war wheat cost 50s. a quarter and steel £10 a ton. We cannot say what was the 1938 equivalent of £1 in 1338, for it depends on what one wants to buy. What did the agricultural labourer's wage of around 10s. a week a hundred years ago buy when the (4 lb.) loaf of bread cost 10d., but oysters could still be had for a penny

INTRODUCTION

each? By what processes did tea, originally the luxury of the very rich and costing up to 50s. a pound in the middle of the seventeenth century, come to be the national drink of England little more than a century later? These are intriguing and important questions which the lay public has the right to ask the historian, and the historian a duty to try to answer. That the answers cannot be precise or final is no reason for abandoning the attempt, for this kind of history – the social history of consumption rather than production – is virtually unexplored territory. It is more than merely the history of prices, for it seeks always to relate prices to people: it is less than the history of the standard of living, though it throws some light on this still larger question. It may be called, in brief, the history of getting and spending, and these are by no means the least important, or least worthy, of human activities.

CHAPTER I

The Middle Ages

I

How far back in English history a concern for the cost of living can be traced is uncertain. Throughout the long period of time which lay between the Norman Conquest and the accession of the first Tudor in 1485 the great majority of English people lived and worked on the land, under a primitive economic system in which money played little part. To a considerable degree the medieval economy was a 'natural' one of services and exchange, rather than a 'monetary' one in which things are bought and sold. On the manorial estates which existed, in different forms, throughout the country, serfs enjoyed the use of land in return for periodic labour on the lord's demesne. They grew most, if not all, of their food, built their own cottages, made their own furniture and cooking utensils: their wives and daughters baked and brewed, spun and wove coarse cloth. Compared with the present day there was little specialization of labour, and although professional skills like those of the miller and the smith certainly existed, few could devote their time exclusively to such occupations.

Modern research has emphasized the diversity in what was once thought of as a standard 'manorial system'. Important regional differences were determined partly by geography and fertility, partly by racial and historical factors. We now know that the 3-field system and strip cultivation were by no means universal, that in some areas 'enclosed' farms of a recognizably modern form predominated, while in others, less fertile, land was worked for a few years and then left to recover: similarly, the status of villeinage was not universal, nor were its nature and incidents uniform. But the fact remains that a large part of midland and southern England was for many centuries farmed in a way which had certain well-defined characteristics. Essentially, the labourer was unfree and dependent. He was permitted the use of land in return for 'predial' services – his labour for 2 or

3 days a week on the lord's demesne, additional 'boon' work at harvest and other busy seasons, payments in kind such as eggs at Easter and fowls at Christmas. In addition there were numerous 'fines' to be paid in order to distinguish privileges from rights – on inheritance, on the apprenticeship or education of a son, on the marriage of a daughter outside the manor. A villein had rights enforceable against other villeins, though not generally against his own lord. He could not sell or devise his land, gather wood, pasture cattle, or leave the manor without the lord's consent. Though distinct in status from a slave, he was only in a limited sense a free man.

Difficulties of communication, and the fact that much of the land still consisted of uncleared forest or undrained marsh, meant that each manor, and, indeed, each household, aimed at a high degree of self-sufficiency. Again, it is likely that the extent to which this was achieved has, in the past, been exaggerated, and that there was always a sizeable list of articles that could not be supplied locally and had to be 'imported' from outside. Account rolls indicate that household needs included salt, wine, pepper, spices, knives and dishes, while requisites for the farm added iron, tar, rope and many other items.

Such things had to be paid for out of the surplus agricultural production of manorial demesnes. From the earliest times estates, both lay and ecclesiastical, sold corn, meat and wool in the scores of little market towns which dotted the countryside. The improved law and order, and the continental connexion which the Norman occupation brought, favoured the development of trade, industry and town life, and already by the thirteenth century London served as a market for the Thames Valley, Norwich for the whole county of Norfolk. A hundred or more smaller towns, some already incorporated as chartered boroughs free from feudal control, others still struggling for independence, were drawing together craftsmen and merchants, dealers and shopkeepers, all those whose daily business lay in the manufacture and exchange of goods, the use and the abuse of money.

2

Throughout the Middle Ages English currency was based on silver. Coining was not yet a royal prerogative, and there were numerous local mints. The standard was the penny, probably introduced from France in the eighth century, and originally the pound weight of silver was coined into 240 silver ones. 'Sterling', it seems, derived its name from the 'steorra' or star which was inscribed on the early coins. The silver penny acquired a good reputation at home and abroad because of its consistent fineness, and although other units, such as the pound, the shilling and the mark (13s. 4d.) were used as yardsticks, they were not generally employed as mediums of exchange.

The chief disadvantage of the penny was that it lost weight by use and was not infrequently clipped. New coins of full weight tended to be hoarded, leaving the old, light ones in command, and the only solution which the mints could devise was to make new issues at the average weight of coins in circulation. The result was that the actual weight of the silver penny progressively declined – from 22 grains troy in 1300 to 15 in 1412 and 10 by 1544.

At least from the thirteenth century, and probably earlier, manorial farming was carried on for profit, not merely for subsistence, and many estates kept meticulous accounts of their income and outgoings, their stock, implements and farm buildings. These accounts indicate that the professional farm servants who compiled them – bailiffs, stewards and reeves – were a remarkably literate and numerate body of men who regarded farming as a serious professional activity. Land values in the thirteenth century averaged about 7s. an acre, calculated on the basis of fourteen years' purchase of land yielding 6d. an acre in rent. To stock, equip and run a large estate required an outlay of capital which by the standards of the day was considerable: a calculation from an estate of 1,448 acres shows the livestock valued at £291, the dead stock at £200, farm buildings, mills and similar property £800, and floating balance £115 – a total approaching £1,500, or £1 an acre. By contrast, a small tenant farmer renting 20 acres on the manor of Cuxham in Oxfordshire made £3 10s. profit a year, out of which rent and other dues took

17

10s.: proceeds from pasture and common rights, and the occasional earnings of his wife and child, brought up the total to nearly £4 a year, sufficient to provide a not uncomfortable standard of life.

Walter of Henley, the first English writer on agriculture, sets out the costs of farming in the thirteenth century as follows: the land is ploughed 3 times at a cost of 6d. an acre; hoeing costs 1d. an acre; 2 bushels of seed at Michaelmas 1s.; a second hoeing ½d. an acre; reaping 5d. an acre; carriage 1d. an acre; and the straw will pay for the threshing. Labourers' wages in the thirteenth century were generally 2d. a day, women 1d. and boys ½d., although piece-work payments and yearly hirings of farm servants were more common. But heavy, non-recurrent expenses are met with throughout the manorial records. On one estate 200 sheep are hired for eight weeks to 'lie' on the land and manure it, at a charge of 8d. a week; on others, marling costs from 3s. 6d. to 8s. an acre. In 1331 Oldman, the bailiff of Cuxham, travels to London in search of five new mill-stones, which he eventually buys for the enormous sum of £15 16s. 8d.: the journey cost him 3 days' time, and the negotiations 5 gallons of Bordeaux wine. A return visit was necessary to arrange for the carriage of the stones by boat to Henley and the payment of dues for wharfage, murage and the maintenance of the river-bank.

Manorial rolls also contain details of the obligations of the tenants, from which it is clear that already in the thirteenth century these were paid partly in labour, partly in kind and partly in money. On one estate the villeins each hold half a 'virgate' of land (12 to 15 acres), for which they must plough, sow and till half an acre of the lord's land and give such other services as are required by the bailiff, pay a quarter of seed-wheat at Michaelmas, a peck of wheat, 4 bushels of oats and 3 hens on 12 November, and at Christmas a cock, 2 hens and twopennyworth of bread: there are also some cash payments – a halfpenny on 12 November and a penny whenever they brew. Each villein is also to reap 3 days at harvest time, but for this he is to have ale and a loaf of bread, and is entitled to carry home as large a sheaf of corn as he can lift on his sickle. On another manor at Ibstone in Buckinghamshire lives a privileged freeholder who holds his virgate by charter and pays only 1d. yearly at Christmas: his further liability, however, is to ride with his lord whenever there is war between England and Wales, to be armed with iron helmet, breastplate and lance, and to remain with him at his own expense for 40 days. Besides villeins, there are also at Ibstone a number of inferior cottars who, for their small holdings of a few acres, pay a rent of from 1s. 2d. to 2s. a year, and are required to work for only a few days at hay-making and harvest: for the rest of the year they are free labourers, available to be hired by the lord or by more prosperous villeins.

That money was in regular, if limited, use on thirteenth-century manors is certain. It is also clear that villeins were already beginning to commute their labour services for money payments and to become, in effect, rent-paying tenants. The practice was often mutually advantageous. The lord found that the money enabled him to employ bordars who were more efficient workers than unwilling villeins; equally, the villein preferred to spend all his time on his own acres and not to be called away precisely at those busy seasons when his strips required all his attention. A basis for calculation of rent existed in the system of fines for non-attendance at compulsory labour. If a villein was fined a penny or twopence for absence from a day's work, his total yearly 'works' could be added together to give a year's rent.

Commutation of this kind was proceeding in a piecemeal and irregular way when England was overtaken by the greatest of the medieval plagues, the Black Death, which swept over the country in 1348 and 1349. Although no reliable statistics of its incidence are available, it is likely that about a third of the whole population perished. In many areas it produced an acute shortage of labour, so much so that some manors were reported to be almost entirely depopulated, with the ungathered harvests rotting in the fields. Labourers were now in a bargaining position, lords bidding against one another for the scarce commodity. Wages rose steeply – never less than 50 per cent, in some cases by as much as 200 per cent – prices following more slowly. The Statute of Labourers, which was passed in 1351 and was an attempt by the government to compel payment of wages at the customary rates which must qualify as the earliest recorded attempt at a wage-freeze, had little or no effect. Rents had to be remitted or reduced, and the profits of farming slumped badly: one estate which had shown a yield of 20 per cent in 1332–3 realized a mere 4 per cent in 1350–1.

In particular, the Black Death precipitated two changes which ultimately brought to an end the medieval system of agriculture. The commutation of labour services for money rents had, as we have seen, begun before the plague; it accelerated greatly after it. Villeins made use of their bargaining power to demand their freedom, and lords, faced with the threat of desertion, often acceded. This was not achieved without a struggle, since labour was now more valuable than money, and the Peasants' Revolt thirty years later was an indication that commutation had not everywhere proceeded rapidly. But by the beginning of the fifteenth century villeinage had all but disappeared in England, and the serf had become a rent-paying copyholder free from the most onerous of feudal obligations, forced labour.

The second change affected the lord's demesne, the home-farm of the manorial estate, which had often occupied a third or more of the whole area. Because of the high cost of labour some lords now found it unprofitable to continue as practising farmers and more economical to let out the demesne to freeholders or wealthier copyholders, either as a single unit, or more often in a number of portions. These were generally 'stock-and-land' leases, since few tenants were able to command sufficient capital to equip a large farm. Where this happened, the demesne was broken up and the lord of the manor became an absentee landlord. Both events, which profoundly affected the system of agriculture and the lives of the majority of English people, were the result of changes in the level of prices induced by a natural though unprecedented disaster. The Black Death had brought the cost of living for the first time into the forefront of public consideration and concern.

3

Before the price revolution of the mid fourteenth century an income of £4 a year, such as might have been earned by a small tenant farmer of about twenty acres, would have ensured a

THE MIDDLE AGES

reasonably comfortable existence. The largest charge would be for bread, but an allowance of four quarters of wheat a year, costing £1 3s. 6d., would have been ample for a family. Two quarters of second-quality malt for brewing would cost 7s. 7d., sufficient to provide about four gallons of ale weekly; and 800 pounds of meat yearly, at a farthing a pound, the usual price in the thirteenth century, would add another 16s. 6d. The total is only £2 7s. 9d. a year, while another 12s. 3d. would provide for clothes, boots and other necessaries; much of the cloth was homespun russet, or hemp or linen shirting, and a pair of boots would not cost more than 2s. Such a budget still left £1 a year for luxuries or for saving; this sum could go towards increasing the holding, portioning a daughter or putting a son into the Church.

Such a man had the security of land and the possibility of supplementing his diet from the produce of his own garden, pigsty or hencoop. Few wage-earners would have fared as well, though the most skilled and highly paid approached this standard closely. Any consideration of wages at this period is complicated by the fact that many were paid partly in kind as well as in cash – they might, for instance, include board and lodging, or a daily meal, an allowance of ale or cider, or an annual gift such as clothes or shoes. It was commonly assumed in the thirteenth century that a man could live simply on a penny a day. This was what Brother William, described as the recluse of St Peter, who inhabited the bailey of the Tower of London, received, while in 1256 King Henry was supporting an anchoress at Dover Castle at the more comfortable rate of $1\frac{1}{2}$d. a day. The lowest-paid workers were at about this level. Petronilla, the laundress in the Countess of Leicester's household, received a 1d. a day and her keep, though she also had a present of shoes, valued at 12d., at Easter, and 15d. on 31 May for extra work. Women agricultural workers were paid at this rate, as were some female assistants to skilled male workers, such as thatchers.

The general rate for unskilled male labourers, whether in agriculture or industry, was 2d. a day without board, totalling about £2 10s. a year. On the land there was always extra employment at hay-making and harvest, which would bring in another 5s., while a labourer's wife could also earn as much in piece-work at such times. The earnings of a couple of boys might bring the joint family income to very much that of the small tenant farmer, though such a family would be entirely dependent on its wages, and without the additional benefits of land-holding. Wage rates also varied from region to region, being highest in the eastern counties and in the neighbourhood of London, lowest in the west and north: the reason seems to have been the competition of industrial employment in the former areas and the higher prices which even then prevailed in the capital. Single men were more often employed on a yearly contract than by the day, and in this case the wage was often paid mainly in goods – a hind, for instance, might receive a quarter of corn at 4s. every 8 weeks, and a cash payment of 6s., that is, about 32s. a year, but he was always boarded at harvest-time and other busy periods, so that his real wages were considerably more than this. In any case, some farm servants like shepherds, swineherds and dairy-maids frequently worked for more than one master.

The wages of artisans varied considerably with degrees of skill and responsibility, probably more so than today. The common labourer or assistant in the thirteenth century generally had 2d. a day, but a carpenter earned 3d. or 3½d. according to skill, and a pair of sawyers 7d. to 8d. Master carpenters and masons received up to 6d. a day, often with an annual gift in addition. When Newgate Gaol was built in 1281 one set of carpenters received 5½d., another 5d., a third 4d.; the sawyers had 9½d. a pair, and the masons 5d. each. These were of course London rates, which were anything from 25 per cent to 50 per cent above the average. The wage-rate for masons before the Black Death was 4d. or 4½d.; the hewers of freestone had 4d., and the servants of masons 3d.; but the interesting point is the diversity of rates in the same occupation. At Caernarvon Castle in October 1304 there were 53 masons on the payroll in receipt of 17 different rates. At Vale Royal Abbey in Yorkshire, in the summer of 1280, 51 masons were employed at 13 different rates. Such differences seem to point to the absence of any strong organization among workers, as well as to variations in skill due to the lack of any uniform or systematic method of training.

The best workers were always in demand and worth retaining

when they could be found. One method was to bind them by a yearly contract – 2s. a week and an annual robe was common – or even, exceptionally, for life; one such engagement made in 1359 between John of Evesham and the Dean and Chapter of Hereford Cathedral guaranteed him 3s. a week plus a white loaf daily, with what amounted to a pension of 12d. a week during protracted illness or infirmity. Similarly, household servants were almost always employed for long engagements, often remaining with the family or institution for years or even generations. Royal servants were sometimes paid handsomely – William Twici, the huntsman of Edward II, receiving the extraordinarily high wage of 7½d. a day, and a royal fowler 3s. 4d. a week. In Henry – Edward II's son's – household, cooks and tailors received 2d. a day with keep and the annual present of a robe worth 9s., while the clerk in charge of the household's daily affairs had 4½d. a day and a fine robe costing 30s. 8d.

Domestic servants had the great advantage of regular employment, while daily wage-earners were paid only for the days actually worked. A carpenter who worked under cover and was more or less independent of the weather might put in 312 days in a year, but a mason's year was sometimes reckoned as low as 235. Again, winter wages were always about 25 per cent lower than those for other seasons, though 'winter' seems to have included only November, December and January. Apart from Sundays, medieval holidays were generally few, and it would appear that not all the numerous Church festivals of the Catholic calendar were free of toil. Walter of Henley's treatise on agricultural practice reckons the working year as 328 days, which allows 5 holidays: on the other hand, masons on contract work at Beaumaris Castle and Vale Royal Abbey observed up to 27 festivals during which they received no wages. Their working day averaged 8 hours in winter and something over 12 in summer, for they were required to report at 5 a.m. and continue until 7 or 8 p.m., with intervals of half an hour for breakfast and an hour and a half for dinner and siesta.

Both wages and prices had been rising steadily before the Black Death of 1348–9. The growth of foreign trade, particularly the export of wool and cloth, had brought honest money into the country, while the spoils of the French Wars had added more of less legitimate origin. A monetary economy was already imminent when the great plague created an acute scarcity of labour and placed the labourer, perhaps for the first time in English history, in a strong bargaining position.

The effect on wages was immediate, though not always easy to determine with precision. Under the Statute of Labourers employers were supposed not to offer more than the customary pre-1348 rates, and in a number of manorial rolls there are clearly simulated erasures, a figure of 5d. being entered as the cost of threshing wheat, with a line drawn through and 3d. substituted: almost certainly, the higher amount was paid, if not in cash, in some covert way such as additional allowances or a more liberal concession of common rights. In general, it appears that the wages of unskilled and poorer-paid workers rose more than those of the higher-paid, a common phenomenon during periods of wage-inflation. Thus a thatcher's assistant (known as a 'homo', though it was generally a woman or young boy), who earned 1d. a day before the Black Death, got as much as 2½d. after it, the thatcher himself rising by only 50 per cent. The wages of carpenters increased between 42 per cent and 48 per cent, those of sawyers by 70 per cent and of tilers 34 per cent. Masons, who as we have seen averaged 4d. a day before the plague, received 6d. or 6½d. after it. The rise continued until about 1370, wages thereafter remaining remarkably stable until the opening of the sixteenth century. Thus the gains of the Black Death were permanent. Masons continued to receive 6d. a day throughout the 1400s, 7½d. or 8d. a day in London; the agricultural labourer's 2d. had risen to 4d. and even 6d. a day at harvest time, and, if he was boarded, the deduction amounted to no more than 1s. a week. For these and other reasons, the fifteenth century has sometimes been described as the Golden Age of the English labourer.

4

By contrast with the slender means of wage-earners, the incomes of the wealthy in medieval society seemed colossal. Richest of all were the earls like Richard of Cornwall, Henry III's brother, who had a yearly income of £4,000–5,000, though the Lord Edward, the King's son, had twice as much as this. Earl Walter Marshall had £3,350, and Isabella de Fortibus, heiress to the earldoms of Devon and Aumale, had £2,500. The Earl and Countess of Leicester ranked among the poorest with around £1,000 a year: they were always short of ready money and frequently in debt either to the king or to moneylenders, though this was not uncommon among those whose incomes were derived from land and who were obliged to wait for receipts from produce and rent. An idea of the value of these inheritances may be gathered from the fact that an estate worth only £20 a year was considered sufficient to subject its holder to the royal demand that he be knighted.

But men of relatively humble origin could, by ability, hard work and wise investment, rise to positions comparable with those of the landed aristocracy. Clement Paston, described as a 'good, plain husbandman' with 100 or 120 acres, borrowed money to send his son William to school and later to the Inns of Court; in 1429 William was a Judge of Common Pleas with a comfortable, though not princely, salary of 110 marks a year. But at his death he left in bullion alone £1,460 in London and £958 in Norwich, besides numerous manors and estates. In the next generation Margaret Paston and her household often moved from one estate to another, consuming the produce as a manorial lord might have done centuries before.

When one considers the vast heritage England possesses of cathedrals, churches and abbeys, of castles, city fortifications and manor houses, it is not remarkable that the greatest public expenditure in the Middle Ages went into building and construction. Of monastic establishments alone there were between 900 and 1,000, many of them of great size; of parish churches there were several thousands. What the total size of the building industry was in terms of masons, bricklayers, carpenters, joiners, plasterers and so on is impossible to tell, but we know that individual projects involved great numbers. In 1377, when the population of London numbered about 35,000, the building of Beaumaris Castle provided employment for 400 masons, 30 smiths and carpenters, 1,000 unskilled workers and 200 carters. The construction of Vale Royal Abbey in the late thirteenth century needed the labours of 15 quarrymen to provide stone and of 31 carters to transport it, while Eton College required in a single year, 1443–4, more than a million bricks.

The building industry was probably the first to be organized on a capitalist basis, in which the materials and tools were provided for a large body of work-people receiving daily or piece-work wages but having no financial interest in the ultimate product. Clerks of works, overseers, master masons, undermasters and guardians of the lodges in which the labour force was housed, provided the necessary administrative and executive hierarchy in a remarkably modern form. The costs of large enterprises were, by the standards of the day, immense. The building of Vale Royal Abbey cost in three years more than £1,500; Caernarvon, Conway and Harlech Castles cost in one year, 1291, over £14,000, while expenditure on York Minster during the period of thirty years for which records are available totalled £10,500. The construction of great cathedrals and abbeys often extended over many years, sometimes over centuries, and the ultimate costs were correspondingly higher; work on the nave of Westminster Abbey, for example, totalled some £25,000 between 1376 and 1532. The scale of these undertakings may be measured against the cost of a single, relatively small-scale operation like the building of the bell-tower of Merton College, Oxford, between 1448 and 1450, the total bill for which, including two cranes at £6 6s., was £142.

Large establishments, whether civil, clerical or military, also required constant repair and upkeep. To quote only one example, a survey of Clarendon Palace in Wiltshire in 1272 recites 24 different items needing renewal: it includes such comments as 'the kitchen of our lord the King requires roofing', 'the gutters of the chapel of our lady the Queen, together with the ceiling and painting of the same chapel, want repair and mending', 'the steps of the postern are broken and must be mended', 'the Strangers' Chamber wants one door, five windows, and floors – therefore it needs great repairs'. To save costs, and probably because of personal interest also, private persons often acted as their own clerks of works, directing building operations personally. In such a case they would rent a stone-quarry, hire labourers and carts by the day to dig and carry it, burn lime with their own wood, have trees felled from their forest or park, employ sawyers to prepare planks, and so on through the whole range of building operations. No doubt this economy in the profits of middlemen was one reason why medieval building costs were, for their scale, relatively low. Some materials were cheap by modern standards – with bricks at 18d. per thousand, the million used at Eton College would cost only £75, and glass, once a great luxury, was becoming more reasonable in the thirteenth century at 4d. a square foot. Two small windows and the necessary ironwork were erected at this time for 2s. 1d., while, under what must be one of the earliest of all maintenance contracts, the windows of Chichester Cathedral were to be repaired for 13s. 4d. a year, plus daily bread and ale. Lead, however, was not cheap, £100 being required in 1267 to roof a dormitory at St Augustine's Abbey, Canterbury. Transport was also a difficult and expensive matter, often costing substantially more than the materials themselves: thus, timber which cost 13s. to fell and prepare at Llanrwst Wood in 1330, cost 55s. 6d. to carry by land and water to Beaumaris, while sand used at Kirby Muxloe in 1480–4 cost a halfpenny a load to dig and 2d. a load to carry. The primitive state of roads, necessitating the extensive use of coastal shipping, river barges and even sleds, was the principal reason for this. But also expensive was work which demanded the skill of creative artists rather than that of mere masons or joiners. The Pastons spent over £100 on the choir-stalls of Brimholme parish church in the fifteenth century, and Peter the Mason of Nottingham, a renowned worker in alabaster, received the extraordinarily high sum of 300 marks for a great reredos which was transported to Windsor in ten carts.

The manor house was becoming a more comfortable place in which to live, less the fortified moated castle, more the richly ornamented and fenestrated country house which came into full flower in the Tudor period. Usually it was a collection of buildings, grouped round a courtyard and entered through a gatehouse: 2 sides would be occupied by living rooms, the other 2 by domestic offices such as bakehouse, brewhouse, slaughterhouse and occasionally a spinning-house. A chapel, with an upper chamber for the lady of the house or for principal guests, was an important feature, but the focal point was the hall, where the lord and his guests dined at a raised dais at one end, with the servants below. Halls were often of vast size – 90 feet long by 45 feet wide at Kenilworth Castle – and great houses might have two, as at Caister, where Sir John Fastolf had a Great Hall and a (presumably smaller) Winter Hall. From the screens which gave access to the hall, doors or passages led to kitchen, buttery, pantry and larder, while at its other end, behind the dais, was the lord's chamber, serving both as a private room where meals could be taken and as a bedroom. 'Parlours' are also mentioned by the late fifteenth century, when growing sophistication of manners was encouraging a greater desire for privacy and separation from the servants. Bedrooms, usually situated on an upper floor, still served as living rooms for receiving guests, nor was it considered indelicate for a lady to entertain male friends in one. A large house like Caister had 25 bedrooms, besides two 'draught-chambers' and numerous smaller 'wardrobes' in which clothes were kept.

The day-to-day running of a large house, ultimately the responsibility of the lady of the house, had already become a complex administrative operation by the thirteenth century, requiring a hierarchy of officials and considerable division of labour. A modern analogy might be the administration of an Oxbridge college or boarding school, though in some ways the problem was greater, since a medieval household was also the nucleus of a land-holding system and had the additional responsibility of administration of estates. A household like that of the Earl and Countess of Leicester had to provide for 60 servants besides the family; moreover, in a period of 7 months there were over 50 visitors, many of them accompanied by large retinues. Even in the household of a minor baron like the Lord of Eresby there was a steward who was a knight, a wardrober who was the chief clerical officer and examined the daily expenditure with the steward each evening, a wardrober's deputy who was clerk to the offices, a chaplain, an almoner, 2 friars with a boy clerk, a chief buyer, a marshal, 2 pantry-men and butlers, 2 cooks and larderers, a saucer, a poulterer, 2 ushers and chandlers, a potter, a baker, a brewer and 2 farriers; each had their own boy helpers.

Such a list indicates that feeding and provisioning was the major concern of a medieval household. The problem was complicated by the fact that food could not be bought in such quantities as were required from week to week or even from month to month, partly because fresh meat and fish were only available in winter at prohibitive cost, partly because communications and supplies of any kind were uncertain and liable to interruption in bad weather. Households large and small therefore laid in winter stores in the autumn, much as though preparing for a siege. In a household like that of the Leicesters' the daily consumption of grain alone varied from 5 bushels to as much as 44 bushels when the Earl and his retinue were at home: private stocks had usually become depleted in the weeks before the new harvest, and wheat had to be bought at prices ranging from 3s. 8d. to 8s. a quarter in the 1260s. Salt herrings costing 10d. the 100 (in fact 120) were consumed at the enormous rate of from 400 to 1,000 a day during Lent, while 3,700 eggs costing 3½d. to 4½d. the 100 were disposed of in a single week. Sturgeon was bought by the barrel (31s.), pears by the 100 (300 for 10d.), wine by the tun (equal to 252 gallons), earthenware dishes by the 1,000 (6s. 8d.), and wine pitchers by the same quantity (21s. 6d.). Two hundred years after this, in the 1460s, the Account of Expenses of Sir John Howard, Knight (later Duke of Norfolk) notes the purchase in September of 20 great oxen (£17), 20 cows (£10 10s.) and 10 bullocks (£6) from a butcher, besides 800 dried salt fish (£9 12s.) and quantities of salt, wine and spices purchased in Fenchestrete (Fenchurch Street).

Shopping on this scale was no simple matter. Margaret Paston at Caister could often not obtain what she wanted locally, or even in Norwich, the second city of the kingdom. In one letter she tells her husband that she has arranged to buy a horse-load of herring for 14s. 6d., but 'I can get no eels yet': in another, her bailiff offers good advice:

Mistress, it were good to remember your stuff of herring now this fishing time. I have got me a friend in Lowestoft to help to buy me 7 or 8 barrel and they shall not cost me above 6s. 8d. a barrel . . . you shall do more now [autumn] with 40s. than you shall at Christmas with 5 marks (66s. 8d.).

But foreign goods like spices and flavourings, silks and other cloths, were obtainable only in London or were available there in greater variety and at less cost than in the country. Margaret

Paston constantly pesters friends and relatives who happen to be in the capital to buy goods or send a note of prices: in one letter alone she asks her son to price pepper, cloves, mace, ginger, cinnamon, rice, almonds, saffron, raisins and galingale, while in others she asks for sugar loaves, pots of treacle, dates, oranges and other imported fruits.

It is clear that the provisioning of a large establishment, whether castle, manor house or monastery, was a major administrative problem, and although many of the basic foods like bread and meat could be supplied in part or in whole from the institution's own estates, a wide variety of other things had to be purchased from outside. Bread was the staple article in any household, rich or poor, and large establishments always kept their own baker who baked loaves of varying degrees of fineness from 'wastel' and 'manchet', the finest white bread, down to whole-wheat (the usual) and common wheat containing a high proportion of refuse. Under the Assize System, which dated back to 1266 and probably earlier, public bakers were obliged to sell every loaf at a standard ¼d. or ½d., the size depending on the degree of fineness and the current price of wheat. Meat of all kinds was plentiful in the Middle Ages, though pork seems to have had a more honoured place than later, probably because it was available fresh all the year. Beef, mutton and veal could generally only be obtained salted from autumn until spring because of the scarcity of winter feed for animals, which necessitated killing all but the strongest beasts. In the late thirteenth century oxen were generally sold at about 9s., pigs at 3s. 6d., sheep at 12d.; meat usually cost ¼d. a pound, though such things as venison and boars were more expensive delicacies. Poultry was widely eaten, and hens at ½d. each were cheap; properly fattened capons cost between 2d. and 3d., as did geese, but partridges at 4½d. a brace were already a luxury. Fish was consumed in great quantity not only during Lent, when meat was forbidden, but also on Wednesdays, Fridays and Saturdays, which were usually fish days all the year round. Red or white herring, depending on whether they were smoked or salted, were the great staples, and mackerel, stockfish and cod were also common, but on feast days in baronial households a wide choice of fish was served – pike (6s. 8d. for a three-foot one), lampreys, oysters, porpoise, sturgeon and whale, the last two being regarded as royal fish and very highly prized, as well as salmon, doreys, bream, eels and shellfish. The vast quantity of eggs eaten in medieval households has already been mentioned – the Countess of Leicester's account book shows 1,000 for Easter Sunday 1265, and nearly 4,000 for the week following. Many were used in cooking such dishes as frumenty, a gruel of hulled wheat, boiled with milk and flavoured with spices, which required 100 for each 8 pints of milk. Most other items of food, such as milk, butter and cheese, vegetables and fruit, were produced on estates as required, and their cost does not appear in the accounts. Of vegetables there was a limited range, since roots were not yet grown, the main ones being beans and peas, onions, garlic, cabbages and leeks, though many herbs were cultivated, both for culinary and medicinal use. Similarly, most of the fruit required was grown in the orchard – pears, the commonest of all, apples, medlars, quinces, cherries, strawberries, plums and peaches: when fruit was bought, it seems moderate in price.

By contrast, spices were always a heavy expense in medieval accounts, since their use for cooking was lavish. This was partly, no doubt, to make up for the restricted variety of flavours in medieval food, especially in winter when so much was salted, partly to disguise the fact that much food was tainted and decayed before it came to table. At all events, practically every medieval recipe required the use of numerous spices, herbs and flavourings, and many of these had necessarily to be imported at high cost from distant lands. Some of the commonest were pepper (10d.–2s. a lb.), ginger (10d.–2s. 6d. a lb.), galingale (1s. 6d. a lb.), zedoary (2s. a ½ lb.), saffron (10s.–14s. a lb.), cummin (2d.–10d. a lb.), anise and fennel (3d. a lb.), as well as mace, cloves, horse-radish, nutmeg, coriander and grains of paradise. Also included in the spice account because of their cost and rarity were sugar (1s.–2s. a lb.), rice (1½d. a lb.), almonds (5 lb. for 1s.), and exotic fruits such as pomegranates (2 for 1s.).

The common drinks were ale (not yet beer, as hops were unknown until the early fifteenth century), which varied according to the price of barley from ¼d. to ¾d. a gallon, and cider, especially in the West Country (5s.–9s. a tun of 252 gallons). But wines of all kinds were drunk by the better-off, and by all classes on festive occasions. Some white wine was still produced locally, but the great bulk came from Gascony, Bordeaux and Poitou, the total import rising to some 3 million gallons a year by the fifteenth century, a third of Britain's whole import trade. Prices varied greatly according to season and quality, but generally averaged about £2 a tun. The heavy consumption can be gauged from the fact that the Leicester's household consumed three-quarters of a tun each week, and the minimum siege ration allowed at Dover Castle was a quart per person per day.

Some idea of the daily fare of the wealthy can be gathered from the fifteenth-century Northumberland Household Book which, in effect, sets out sample menus for a large household:

This is the ordre of all such Braikfasts as shal be allowid daily in my Lordis hous Every Lent ... And what they shall have at theire Braikfasts ... Braikfast for the Nurcy for my Lady Margaret and Maister Ingeram Percy. Item a Manchet a Quarte of Bere a Dysch of Butter a Pece of Saltfisch a Dysch Sproitts or iij White Herryng. Braikfast for my Ladis Gentyllwomen. Item a Loof of Brede a Pottell of Bere a Pece of Saltfisch or iij White Herryng.

On flesh days, instead of fish 3 or 4 'Mutton Bonys or ells a Pece of Beif boiled' were substituted.

Such meals seem generous in quantity, though unexciting. The monks of St Swithun's appear to have been more lavishly fed, for an entry for one Sunday in 1492 gives 'molle' (bread warmed under the roasting meat and soaked in dripping), 162 eggs, 'nombles en pittance' (venison cut from the inner side of the thigh and regarded as a great delicacy – 'pittance' implying an extra portion), 'sew for supper' (pottage or broth), beef and mutton. Two carcases of meat were consumed a day, and each brother had an allowance of half a loaf and cheese for dinner and supper. The total food bill for a day at St Swithun's was 7s. 4d. But at the Priory of Durham an even more elaborate cuisine was maintained, a year's account showing that 65 kinds of fish were consumed, 21 of flesh, and 27 of fowl, besides 15 kinds of spices and 9 of fruit.

That some fared sumptuously there can be no doubt. In the 1460s Sir John Howard pays the very high price of 20d. for a salmon, and for 2 tuns of what must have been very good

Spanish wine, 16 marks. He evidently enjoyed his drink, for on another occasion he 'spent the same day at the tavern 16d.'. Another entry by the bailiff is unusually vague; 'My master has spent in London in the taverns at drinking and in another place £5'. 'A pot of treacle for my lady' costs him 4d., and while at Colchester he gives for plaice 2d., for whelks 1d. and for shrimps 1d. A quart of wine for 1d. seems cheap by comparison, though, like the shrimps, it represented half a day's pay for a workman. The Household Ordinances of Edward III allowed 13s. 4d. a day for the 'diette' of a duke and 6s. 8d. for that of an earl: the Black Book of Edward IV decreed 40s. for the queen's board, and in 1485 Henry VII generously allowed the same amount for the keep of his prisoner, the Earl of Surrey.

Expenditure of this order permitted banqueting rather than mere dining, and the accounts that have survived of medieval feasts suggest a length of two or three hours, innumerable dishes, many of them exotic, but a general lack of plan about the meal. Nominally there were three courses, but a 'course' consisted of up to a dozen different dishes, and each might contain many varieties of fish, flesh and fowl served indiscriminately together. Usually there would be a *pièce de résistance*, a boar's head, swans, herons or peacocks put back into their skins and feathers after being cooked – with many more delicately made 'devices' or 'subtleties' of sugar, pastry or jelly. Almost everything was heavily spiced and seasoned: often several meats would be blended together with the yolks of eggs to form 'mortrews', or many different kinds of fowl would be united in a pie. The food was taken with large quantities of wine, one banquet alone specifying 16 different kinds.

Next to food, clothing was the principal recurrent expenditure in medieval households, partly because materials themselves, whether home-grown wool or imported silk and other cloths, were expensive, partly because dress was a very precise indicator of social status, and different classes were socially obliged to dress accordingly. A sumptuary law of 1363, for example, prohibited the poor from wearing any cloth except blanket and russet at 1s. a yard, but when it is remembered that 6 or 7 yards went into the making of a gown, the cost, even of this, was enormous.

The nobility themselves used considerable quantities of silk, imported from France, Italy and the East, and much more expensive than English wools. In 1256 King Henry paid Luke de Lucca, the leading Italian merchant in London, £6 for 3 gold-wrought 'baudekins' (a brocade of silk from Baghdad) and £4 for a piece of saffron samite (a Greek silk). Other imported cloths included sendal (a type of taffeta), damask and camlet. Fur was also an important article of medieval dress – often, one imagines, a necessity in draughty castles and courtyards. Nearly all robes were trimmed with it – ermine in the case of royalty, squirrel for the nobility, and deerskin, rabbit or sheepskin for ordinary people.

Medieval clothes were, of course, not bought ready-made, but as cloth to be made up by the tailor and seamstress. Thus, Sir John Howard in 1462 purchases 3 yards of black velvet for 33s., 3 yards of black frieze at 2s., probably for lining, while 'the furring of my lord's gown' costs 8s. 9d. No price is given for the work on this coat, but 'making a jacket of crimson cloth for my lord' cost 2s. 4d., and the lining added another 12d. There is also a bonnet to go with it, costing 16d., and 4s. for a pair of stockings paid to Perse the hosier. The total cost mounts even more when one adds the necessary accoutrements of girdles, brooches and so on, which, especially for women, could be highly ornate and expensive: a gold head-dress in the mid thirteenth century cost £12 10s., and a girdle of gold and gems £37 12s. Henry V had a jewelled collar worth £800, and Henry VI one valued at £2,800. These are not strictly articles of clothing, though the line between jewellery and jewelled cloth becomes difficult to draw by the fifteenth century. Sir John Howard's long cloak of cloth of gold lined with damask would have cost about £30 – four times the yearly earnings of a tailor – and the practice of gilding cloths became sufficiently common for Parliament to forbid anyone under the degree of baron from wearing them in order that the supply of gold should not run short. Even so, a 'gown of goldsmith's work' remained the ambition of most wealthy men at the end of the Middle Ages, and Sir John Fastolf, who was not especially well-off, had two of cloth of gold, a gown and half a gown of velvet, one of blue satin and several of cloth, besides jackets and doublets. Many of these would be regarded as

THE MIDDLE AGES

investments, and willed at death to other members of the family.

Unlike food, housing and clothes, furniture was not a large or recurrent item of expenditure in medieval households. Even amongst the wealthy classes, the interior of a house was simple and sparse: the few pieces of furniture that were purchased were, until Tudor times, strictly utilitarian and, compared with the skill that was lavished on clothes, jewellery, armour and silverware, crude in their workmanship. Even in a great baronial household of the thirteenth century there would be differences only in the quality and number of the pieces, not in their kind. Beds would certainly be elaborate, and were often the most highly prized of all household effects. They consisted of a heavy wooden frame with a back, canopy, valance and curtains, generally all made to match, while on the frame would be a mattress – preferably of feathers – sheets, coverlets and pillows. The Countess of Leicester had a particularly fine set of bedcovers given by her brother the king, with a mattress and quilt of costly baudekin cloth and a coverlet of grey fur lined with scarlet: they cost more than £20. Under the great bed were often small truckle beds which were pulled out at night for ladies-in-waiting – the linen hangings of the bed ensured reasonable privacy for the lord and his lady in an age not unduly modest. During the day the hangings would be pushed back so that the bed could serve as additional seating in a room which probably only contained an uncomfortable bench and a chest or two. A few long poles or 'perches' served both to hang clothes and as resting-places for hawks and falcons.

The furniture of the hall would, if anything, be more simple still. On the raised dais 1 or 2 trestles or, very rarely until the fifteenth century, a 'table-dormant' of refectory type, 2 great chairs for the lord and his lady, and for the rest, benches or stools, almost completed the inventory. Similar tables and benches at right-angles down the length of the hall provided for the servants. There might be a few folding X-chairs for guests, and there would certainly be a number of large standing candlesticks in all rooms. Lighting by candle was a heavy though unavoidable expense. Since medieval cattle were so lean, fat was very dear and the pound weight of wax candle cost 4d. or 5d.

35

George, Duke of Clarence, spent £64 a year on them. The only other source of light or colour in medieval rooms was provided by wall-hangings – tapestries, arras and striped worsted cloths – which were frequently used to cover the rough masonry with biblical or classical scenes. These, together with the bed-coverings and hangings, must have provided the few patches of colour to brighten an otherwise drab interior: one of Sir John Fastolf's tapestries depicted a giant bearing off the leg of a bear in his hand, while his cook slept under a coverlet of roses and bloodhounds' heads. Such things, together with gold and silver plate, constituted the chief wealth of the medieval household, and it was for good reason that when the Duke of Suffolk's men rifled the Pastons' house at Hellesdon they bore off two feather beds and four mattresses among the spoils. The most valuable single item of furniture recorded throughout the Middle Ages was Queen Philippa's bed with hangings of green velvet embroidered with sea sirens, which cost the enormous sum of £203.

Medieval men were more at home in the open air than in their houses, the peasant at work in the field, the lord watching over his estates, hunting, warring and visiting. The extent of immobility of medieval life has probably been exaggerated, for although the serf might rarely, if ever, journey further than the next market town, other orders of society braved the costs and discomforts of travel to a surprising extent. Carriage, whether of people or goods, was slow and expensive, the cost of carrying in the thirteenth century varying from 1d. per ton per mile to 3½d. per ton for a breakable cargo like wine. Because of the poor state of roads, people of all degrees moved on horseback – carriages, chariots and litters being reserved for ceremonial occasions, for ladies and the sick. A single messenger could often manage up to sixty miles a day on horseback, though when a whole household moved with impedimenta ranging from trestle tables to the best bed, the speed of travel was reduced to an average of thirty miles a day in the summer and a mere fifteen through the mud of winter.

Such journeying required the maintenance of a large stable of horses, of which a typical baronial household might possess thirty or forty. Many of these would be fine, costly animals lavishly decked with ornamental saddles, bridles and cloths.

THE MIDDLE AGES

Pride of place went to the war-horse, which could cost as much as £40 to £80: they were required to be immensely strong in order to carry the great weight of a knight's armour, and were greatly sought after as the victor's prize in tournaments. The ordinary saddle-horse of the upper classes was the palfrey, costing anything from 5 marks to £27 for a specially valuable animal given as a royal present. Ordinary fighting men used the rouncey (40s. to 66s. 8d.), while sumpter-horses carried the gear of households on the move. In Bogo de Clare's household one carried the bed, one the wardrobe and one the buttery: in larger establishments, others would be set aside for the kitchen utensils, for the chapel furniture, for the candles, and so on. Edward IV's brother, the Duke of Clarence, had a 'ridings householde' of 188 persons with 8 'coursers for his sadelle', 2 palfreys, 'a maile horse and a botell horse ... four sompters ... seven chariotte horses' and 2 to carry the litter, a total of 25.

Recreation to a medieval lord meant, pre-eminently, hunting, and this required costly equipment and the skill of highly paid servants. A thirteenth-century huntsman received the extraordinarily high wage of 7½d. a day, a fowler the almost equally high 3s. 4d. a week. The large sums paid for good horses have already been noted, but a falcon, at 100s., could cost as much, and was equally indispensable to the keen sportsman. Richard II paid £21 6s. 8d. for a pair which he gave to the King of Navarre, and some of Edward III's falconers received as much as £18 a year. Hounds could also be expensive, and expensive to keep: ¾d. a day was allowed for their maintenance at Windsor, and in Henry IV's reign a payment of £130 was made for one year's keep of a pack.

Many other items in a noble lord's accounts are broadly classifiable as 'recreation'. Sir John Howard's Household Expenses, for instance, covering the years 1462 to 1469, mention 'a dagger, 20d., twelve pounds of gunpowder, 12s., nine sheaf of arrows, 12s., thread for string for crossbows, 6d., a new bow, 2s. 4d., shooting glove, 4d.,' and many more. In wintertime, indoor entertainments to enliven the long evenings had to be paid for, and minstrels and musicians appear to have commanded good fees: 12d. a day in the fifteenth century was not uncommon for a visiting player, and Lord Howard's accounts record a payment in December of 20d. to the waits. Sir John Howard's bailiff gave 4d. 'to a child that sang before my lord', and the fact that children had toys very like those of the present day is attested by the entry in a thirteenth-century account, 'the small cart bought for the young lord as a plaything, 7d.' Probably the 16d. paid for 'four cheynes to tey dogges' was for a child's pets.

Education was an expense which only the rich would normally have to meet. The exceptionally talented poor boy had a recognized route to learning through church and monastic schools, and here the only cost to his father might be the fines payable to his lord in order to secure release from manorial services: thereafter, Mother Church would be expected to provide. For the sons of wealthy parents there were a number of alternatives. At the highest social level, apprenticeship as a page in a royal or noble household was considered the best education for life and, like all apprenticeships, had to be paid for: as much as £1,000 is charged about 1450 for the 'apprenticeship' of a page to the Earl of Warwick for four years. This, of course, was a training in manners, sport and social graces. An academic education cost very much less, and was acquired at schools (typically 4d. per term for fees) and the Universities of Oxford and Cambridge, where the main expense was boarding rather than tuition. At Winchester in the fifteenth century 8d. per week was charged by boarding-houses for scholars' commons, and an estimate of the expenses of a University student for one year gives:

	£	s	d
For lectures		8	0
For rent of room		10	0
For food at 10d. a week, 38 weeks	1	11	8
For payment for servants		1	4
	£2	11	0

This was very much a minimum, allowing little for food and nothing for amusement. A list of University fines at Oxford – 'for threats of personal assault, 12d. ... for drawing of weapons for violence, 4s., for striking with stone or staff, 6s. 8d.' and so on up to 40s. – suggests that undergraduate 'rags' were a frequent occurrence, and many students must have run up bills for clothes, books, ale and other necessities. One of the Pastons at Oxford in the 1470s kept an account of all his expenses from October to April, showing a total of £6 5s. 5¾d. Books and paper were a major expense for any scholar before Caxton's invention of printing. Some 240 leaves of fine parchment in the late thirteenth century cost 10s., and the writing of a breviary 14s. Imported paper in the fifteenth century was certainly cheaper than this – 1s. for 4 quires was paid by Lord Howard – but before Caxton's revolutionary invention of 1477 the laborious work of the scribe had still to be paid for. Printing, it has been estimated, reduced the cost of a book to one-tenth of that of a manuscript.

Taxes of various kinds entered importantly into medieval life and affected all classes to a greater or lesser extent. Some were purely local like the relief or fine payable to the feudal lord on inheritance to an estate – the best animal in the case of a villein – the £100 which earls and holders of baronies owed to the king, or the payment which gilds required of their members for admission. Feudal lords also required payment for manumission, and not uncommonly continued to hold villeins in bondage merely in order to extort large sums: a sixteenth-century payment of the very large amount of £120 has been recorded. Again, it was common for townsmen to be collectively taxed in order to pay the annual 'farm-rent' which guaranteed the city the continuance of its liberties under royal charter: London paid as much as £300 in the thirteenth century, though no other town approached this amount.

In addition to these were numerous national taxes, exacted both by the State and by the Church, which fell with irregular though occasionally heavy incidence. One of the earliest of all was the 'danegeld', a tax levied in order to buy off the Danish invasions, which in 1084 was imposed at the rate of 6s. per hide (120 acres of land). War and the threat of war were the main causes of medieval taxes, and armies were always expensive to keep in the field: at the end of the Middle Ages to maintain 10,000 archers for a year required £100,000, and the largest single tax imposed in any year throughout the period realized only £130,000. The main source of royal revenue was 'tenths and fifteenths', a tax on the personal estates of all householders in boroughs and counties: at least 11 were granted by Parliament in the 16 years of Edward III's reign, and appear to have realized about £40,000 each. They represented a tax of about 5 per cent on a £30 estate. But the great wool tax of 1340, when Parliament voted the king 30,000 sacks of wool or their equivalent, represented about 18 per cent of the annual profits of an estate. More unpopular still, because inequitable in its incidence, was the poll tax of 1380, requiring the payment of three groats (1s.) 'by every person in the kingdom, male or female, of an age of fifteen, of what rank and condition soever, except beggars': it was paid 'with great grudging and many a bitter curse', and was one of the immediate causes of the Peasants' Revolt which broke out in the next year. In addition to these truly national taxes, many estates and individuals were assessed for particular purposes – for foreign service, for the king's gabelle, for 'ward of the sea', for defence of the Scottish border, and so on. When we add to these the sums due to the Pope and his cardinals, the archbishops, bishops and archdeacons – usually in the form of a percentage on receipts, and amounting not uncommonly to 2½ per cent of income – it is evident that taxation was, for many, a significant and resented aspect of the medieval cost of living.

The rich were also expected, though not obliged, to give freely during their lifetime and at their death to the poor and needy. Charity was a duty constantly enjoined by the Church, and a necessity in the absence of public provision, and alms-giving in one form or another seems to have been widely accepted by all of even moderate means. Noble households, like the monasteries, had their almoners, who daily distributed food and money to those who came to the gates: the Countess of Leicester provided 4d. a day for the purpose in the early thirteenth century, though the rich pluralist cleric, Bogo de Clare, brother of the Earl of Gloucester, gave only 1d., even on feast days. Probably no other private individual was as generous as John of Gaunt, who distributed 12s. 6d. every Friday and 10s. every Saturday: in 1372 he sent the poor lazars of Leicester 3 cartloads of wood for winter fuel, and the prisoners at Newgate Gaol a tun of Gascony wine.

5

Already in medieval society there were the beginnings of a middle class. On the land, there were substantial farmers who had rented part of the lord's demesne after the break-up of estates that followed the Black Death: though not 'gentry' or even freeholders, they were often men of some wealth, growing corn or producing wool for the expanding town markets. In the towns, merchants were already acquiring a dominant economic and political status, freeing the inhabitants from feudal authority by gaining incorporation under royal charter, controlling the trade and the government of the borough through their gilds and town councils. Mere craftsmen early became excluded from this inner circle of the 'bourgeoisie', though professional men like lawyers and doctors were acceptable if they owned property within the town boundaries.

A knowledge of the law, and of the property market which that knowledge brought, was perhaps the surest road to wealth in the later Middle Ages, but trade, and especially the cloth trade, could also bring handsome rewards. Whilst looking for 'good' matches for their sons, the Pastons hear of a young widow, the wife of one Bret, a cloth merchant of Worsted, 'and with £1,000 . . . She is called a fair gentlewoman', while in the small town of Rye there were at least five burgesses with £400 a year each.

Payments for professional services varied greatly according to demand, but in general were much less than the profits of trade. Architects employed on royal building operations seem to have been among the best paid. Walter of Hereford, the king's architect at the end of the thirteenth century, received the high salary of 2s. a day for a 7-day week. Though not qualified as an architect or mason, William of Wykeham was the prototype of the capable administrator and organizer. Entering Edward II's service in 1347 as a superintendent of building work, he became in turn clerk of the works at Henley and at the castles of Windsor, Leeds, Dover and Hadleigh, receiving when resident 1s. a day, and 2s. when travelling. He was, ultimately, bountifully provided through the chief means of preferment available in the Middle Ages, the Church, taking Holy Orders in 1361 and being

A HISTORY OF THE COST OF LIVING

appointed Bishop of Winchester in 1367. In later life some of his own considerable fortune was spent on the Cathedral and on Winchester College. In another age Wykeham would have been a distinguished civil servant or leading company director. Geoffrey Chaucer, no doubt, would always have been a poet, yet his income, like that of Wykeham, was derived from building administration: he held the responsible position of clerk of works at Westminster Palace, the Tower of London and seven royal manors, also at a salary of 2s. a day.

Doctors and surgeons were still growing to professional status, emerging slowly out of the craft of barber and bloodletter. Most of them were paid at little more than artisans' wages, though by the fifteenth century a few doctors of skill and reputation were able to command up to £100 a year for their services. Unlike the lawyers, they had no recognized system of education until the foundation of the College of Physicians in 1518. But architecture, law and medicine had all had their origin in the Church, which remained throughout the Middle Ages and for many subsequent centuries the major profession. At its summit, the princes of the Church – cardinals, archbishops and bishops, abbots and priors of monasteries – rivalled and sometimes exceeded the wealth of the lay nobility: at its base, monks, friars and hermits were among the poorest of all the king's subjects. The middle tier of priests and parsons holding livings seems to have generally had a comfortable maintenance, with incomes guaranteed by the endowment of glebe-land or money and the receipts of tithes and fees. The total income of a country parson in the thirteenth century could be anything between £5 and £15 a year, while the living of a town rector might be worth as much as £100; parliamentary rolls of the fifteenth century even contemplate others at £200. The Church's fees for its offices often seem unduly high by modern standards. At the rectory of Bicester in the fourteenth century, for example, weddings were charged at from 2s. to 5s. 3d., churchings at 1s. to 1s. 10d., burials at ¾d. to 9s. 3d.: we also know that the Fellows of Oriel College, Oxford, who obtained the principal church of St Mary in High Street, derived a substantial part of their corporate income from religious offices and from the manufacture and sale of wax candles to devotees. Again, the

THE MIDDLE AGES

fifteenth century chantry-priest, endowed by a wealthy gild with £10 a year and his lodging, was comfortably maintained. Thomas Rotherham, Archbishop of York, provided not illiberally for the school which he founded, a Provost at £13 6s. 8d. a year, a Fellow in Grammar at £10, a Fellow in Singing at £6 13s. 4d., a Fellow in Writing ('because in that same place are young men most quick of mind, not all of whom wish to rise to the dignity of the priesthood – so that these may be better fitted for the mechanic arts and other such business') at £5 6s. 8d., and 6 choirboys at 40s. each. To support the foundation the Archbishop gave to his 'college' 25 manors, farms and tenements, besides the produce – about £40 a year – from 2 parish churches. The scale of values given here is instructive. Mere literacy, it seems, was not very highly regarded, unless it went with administrative or executive skill, for the medieval scribes and scriveners who copied manuscripts, kept manorial accounts, wrote letters and executed wills were the lowest paid of all professional workers. Even in the fifteenth century the usual charge for scrivening was 2d. per leaf (i.e. two pages), and the cost of 'transcribing a little book of physic' is set down at 20d. The scribe who wrote out the long account of the Cuxham bailiff in the thirteenth century, a document filling 13 closely written octavo pages, and balanced the account, received only 2s., though another 2s. was later added as a favour. An advocate, retained to defend a will, received the already traditional 6s. 8d. (half a mark).

Some idea of the expenditure of this lowest stratum of the middle class is afforded by the account book of William Savernak of Bridport, Dorset, covering the years 1453–60. The small household consists of two priests and a servant, and the weekly expenditure averages 40d., or about £9 a year. Food takes 80 per cent of the total budget – meat and fish 35 per cent, drink 23 per cent, bread and other cereals 20 per cent, butter and cheese a mere 2 per cent. Fuel and candles account for another $7\frac{1}{2}$ per cent; there is no adequate record of outlay on clothes, but presumably these, together with other necessities, come out of the remaining $12\frac{1}{2}$ per cent. This is certainly not a 'representative' middle-class household, for the priests have a free house and some land, but the predominant importance of food in the budget, and of meat in particular, is typical enough.

In the towns, houses were by now usually professionally built, and records of their costs have sometimes survived in municipal accounts. Where this is so, they seem modest enough – as late as 1483 a builder of Gloucester contracts to construct a sizeable 2 storeyed house 47 feet by 15 feet and 18 feet high, of 'standard works' and 'all the timber of oak' for £14. Town houses were already growing in size, comfort and elegance. In the fourteenth century they had usually not been more than 2 storeys high, but by the fifteenth century 3 and 4 storeys were common, and shopkeepers often had cellars in addition. Timber was still the usual building material, though stone and brick for the lower parts were common, and roofs were more often covered with tiles than with thatch to reduce the fire hazard. The better houses and shops would be ornamented with mouldings or carvings, and the external walls painted and decorated with gilded signs, figures or armorial bearings. Glass at 4d. to 6d. a foot was increasingly used, and the number and size of windows was growing: fireplaces were now built at the sides or corners of rooms in place of the open hearth in the centre. The more prosperous tradesmen and merchants could now live in moderate comfort, their houses often containing, besides the shop on the ground floor, a hall, parlour, buttery, pantry, kitchen and bedrooms. An agreement made in the reign of Henry IV by a 'tymbermongere' and a carpenter to erect three shops in Friday Street, London, provides for a cellar, ground floor and 2 additional storeys, the height from the ground to the first floor joists to be $10\frac{1}{2}$ feet, and subsequent storeys 9 and 8 feet respectively: on the first floor was to be 'une sale' (hall), 'une spence' (buttery), 'une cusyne' (kitchen); on the second 'une principal chambre, une drawyng chambre et une forein'; each house was to have 'une seyling-piece' and two 'estaires'.

Rents varied extremely widely for houses of different size in different parts of the country. Age of the property, position (in the case of shops), and general standards of comfort and amenity seem to have been the principal determinants, but London was already infinitely more expensive than the provinces, with rents in the fifteenth century up to the very large amount of £13 6s. 8d. a year. This, admittedly, was for a Lombard Street banker's house: an ironmonger paid £6 13s. 4d., a tailor £4 13s. 4d., a

THE MIDDLE AGES

goldsmith £2 13s. 4d. and a 'poyntemaker' £1 6s. 8d. Shop rents were always higher than mere house rents, southern rents higher than northern. Thus, the surveyor who supervised the building undertaken by the Priory and Chapter of Christ Church, Canterbury, paid £1 a year rent, while a prosperous lawyer at Warrington in 1465 paid only 3s. 3d. yearly for 1 fair hall, 2 high chambers and a kitchen, besides stable, cowhouse, barn, apple-yard 'near an acre of fresh land', and 'a fountain of springing water'. At Leicester in 1432 a substantial cottage and garden is let on a repairing lease for 40 years at 2s. a year, while Norwich records of 1397 speak of tenements let at 3d. and even 1½d. a year. Probably these were purely nominal rentals with labour services or other obligations attached.

Fish, salt and a small quantity of the cheaper spices were perhaps the only foods that the poorest people ever bought. Their diet, as indeed their whole standard of life, was of a different order from that of their lords and from that of prosperous townsmen. Here, in the growing urban communities of the fourteenth century, the existence of professional bakers and brewers, pastry-cooks and pie-makers, suggests a considerable degree of specialization which, to the medieval mind, required control and regulation. Most food-prices were fixed, either by nationally set Assizes (as in the case of bread and ale) or by local municipal ordinances: one such, the Ordinance of the Cooks, for 1378, lays down prices for 'the best roast goose 7d., best roast capon 6d., best roast pullet 2½d., best roast partridge 3½d., best roast pheasant 13d., 5 roast larks 1½d., 10 eggs 1d.' and so on. The best roast capon baked in a pasty is 8d., and a chicken pie 5d. The interesting point about such a list is that even the chicken pie represented 2 days' wages for an agricultural labourer, though it also indicates that the more prosperous townspeople fared well, and were abundantly supplied with the produce of the countryside.

Travelling spread with the growing trade of the later Middle Ages, and many who could not afford to own and feed a horse of their own now found it possible to hire one for occasions as needed. Some at least of Chaucer's pilgrims had probably hired their transport to Canterbury at an all-in price of about 24d. The journey was usually reckoned as 2 days, with 1 night on the way at Rochester, but Chaucer's pilgrims were in no hurry and probably took 3 to 4 days, with stops at Dartford, Rochester and Ospringe, to cover the 54½ miles. By contrast, the Vice-Chancellor of Cambridge University rode the 50 miles from London in 2 days, dining the first day at Waltham, sleeping at Ware, and stopping for some refreshment next day at 'Barkway': he was back in his college in time for dinner.

Townsmen appear to have been unusually public-spirited in endowing schools, hospitals, almshouses, bridges, water supplies and a score of other amenities, especially after having risen to high office in municipal government. In 1421 Richard Whittington, mercer and three times Mayor of London, gave £400 towards the Library of the Grey Friars, as well as founding an almshouse for thirteen poor men: John Wells, grocer, 'caused fresh water to be conveyed from Tyborne ... for service of the city': Richard Rawson in 1477 left legacies for highways and hospitals, besides £340 'to poor maids' marriages'. Outside the capital there was less wealth, but the same regard for public good: when, for example, in 1485 repair of the bridge over the Trent at Nottingham became urgently necessary, the largest legacy was 33s. 4d., the smallest only 1d. The significant point is that both donors felt an obligation to contribute within their means to the needs of the community.

6

Until the later Middle Ages money entered much less frequently and importantly into the lives of the working classes. For example, the construction of the houses of all but the wealthy was a simple and inexpensive process, generally requiring only locally available materials and no very high degree of skill. Throughout the countryside, the peasant's cottage was built of whatever was close at hand – usually wood, occasionally stone, the roof thatched with straw, reeds or sedge, or covered with shingles or slates. Generally it was a single-storey building with only 2 rooms, one serving for all purposes of living, eating and cooking, the other reserved as far as possible for sleeping. Animals were equally at home in both. Ventilation was unconsidered: there was usually no chimney, and smoke from the centrally placed fire escaped as best it could through the door and windows. The atmosphere of such cottages must have been like that of Chaucer's poor widow, 'ful sooty', for chimneys were rare in all but the greatest houses until the late fifteenth century. It must also have been excessively draughty, since glass was still too dear for the peasant, and windows were simply small openings covered by a wooden shutter or canvas blinds. The floor was of earth, usually covered with straw or rushes.

Such dwellings had one – and probably only one – advantage in ease of construction. One of the most widespread types, especially in the Midlands, north and west, had for its main timbers curved uprights (crucks), placed opposite to each other, with a ridge-pole running the length of the house and holding the various pairs of uprights together. Such a house gave some, though limited, headroom, and an improved version was for the lower part to be constructed of heavy timbers forming the corners and intermediate posts, upon which were erected the principal rafters and ridge-tree. Once the framework was built, the walls were filled in with either wattle-and-daub, or earth and mud. In the first of these, a number of upright sticks were stuck into the ground, and twigs woven in and out to form a lattice: the 'dab' was then thrown on until it was of the right thickness. An alternative was mud or 'cob' walling, in which successive layers of mud and straw were gradually built up to a thickness of from 5 to 7 inches. Finally the roof was thatched or tiled.

Such cottages were built in a few days, generally by the commonsense knowledge and skill of ordinary country-people, helped by the carpenter and thatcher who were to be found in every sizeable village. Cost was scarcely a measurable quantity where the materials were partly or wholly free and much of the labour performed by the occupier, his friends and relatives.

Similarly, the price of food and drink would have little direct relevance for the peasants who constituted the majority of English society in the Middle Ages. They in general ate what they could grow themselves: their range of food was therefore much more limited than that of their peers, and its quantity would depend critically on the weather and the harvest. Britain, it seems, did not suffer the repeated famines which plagued the continent throughout the Middle Ages, the only very long-continued one occurring between 1315 and 1321, but there must have been few years indeed when the peasant could say that he had eaten enough of the foods he enjoyed. Breakfast was a brief meal – a piece of coarse bread, rarely of wheat, more often of rye or maslin (a mixture of the two), and a draught of ale; for dinner there was pottage, usually made from peas or beans, with cheese and more bread; for supper perhaps eggs, oat-cake, bread, cheese and ale. Meat and poultry were a luxury for the labourer, and his main opportunity of getting them was on his days of forced labour when the lord provided a meal in the harvest- or hayfield; on these occasions bread, ale or cider, a mess of pottage and a dish of flesh or fish seem to have been regarded as a feast. No doubt there was an occasional rabbit, hare or chicken for the pot, occasionally salt beef, bacon or fish, and there would be whatever vegetables and fruit could be grown in the garden or on the baulks of land which divided the strips in the open fields. Thorold Rogers has written of the peasant of the Middle Ages living 'in ordinary times, in coarse plenty'. Perhaps the more prosperous villeins did so, though even for them diet was monotonous and lacking in vitamins if not also in protein. But for the poorer there could scarcely have been 'plenty' of anything. Chaucer's Poor Widow, who lived on a diet of 'milk and brown bread, singed bacon with sometimes an egg or two', was probably all too typical, but even more poignant are the pictures of medieval life drawn by Langland in *Piers Plowman*. 'No chickens, geese, pork or bacon came their way, but two green cheeses, curd and cream, and a cake of oats': this, together with bread of pease or beans, is all the food they can look forward to until harvest. 'Also in winter they suffer much hunger and woe. It would be a charity to help them: bread and penny-ale are a luxury ... on Fridays and feasting days a farthing's-worth of mussels or so many cockles were a feast for such folk.'

Most peasants' wives could spin and weave a coarse household cloth which served for everyday use in tunics and smocks, though the raw wool would probably have to be bought at a price, which in the middle of the fifteenth century varied from £2 10s. to £13 a sack (364 lb.), according to quality. The medieval fleece, weighing on average only 1½ lb., was justly regarded as a scarce and valuable commodity. Apart from what he

THE MIDDLE AGES

could produce himself, the peasant therefore relied on receiving the cast-off garments of others, on clothes belonging to the family group and passed on from one generation to another, and, in the case of servants of many kinds, on clothes provided as part of the wage. The gift of an annual robe (which often included a tunic, super-tunic and cloak), or, at a lower degree of friendship, gloves, stockings or shoes, was a very common Christmas practice and one that must have relieved a substantial section of the population from the necessity ever of purchasing clothes. Their qualities were determined by a rigid scale, the guardian of the king's children in the thirteenth century receiving £30 a year and a robe worth 45s. 6d., the clerk of the household 4½d. a day and a robe costing 30s. 8d., the cook, tailor and usher 2d. a day and a 9s. robe. Two centuries later Sir John Howard gives a pair of hose costing 10d., 'a pair of shoes for little Harry, 3d.', and a pair of shoes and a pair of galoshes ('galaches') for Anne Fuller, 10d.

The everyday clothes of the working classes would be made of a coarse wool or linen, even of canvas in the case of the very poor, with perhaps one better robe reserved for special occasions. The young carpenter's wife in 'The Miller's Tale' has a white smock with embroidered black silk collar, a silk girdle, and a broad silk fillet on her hair, though she, like the haberdasher, carpenter, weaver and dyer who were clothed in the livery of a 'great fraternitee' and had their knives, girdles and pouches ornamented with silver, was more representative of the aristocracy of labour. But, as in the case of food, the gap between the standard of working people and the nobility was huge. For them, the favourite woollen cloth was scarlet, selling, in the thirteenth century, at 7s. an ell (45 inches): russets at 3s. an ell and perse at about 2s. were cheaper cloths for everyday use, and serge, probably the cheapest of all, at 17s. for ten ells. Canvas at 2d. an ell, and linen at 9d., were used for a variety of household purposes and for the garments of servants and retainers, as were also the cheap chalons and blanchets. Twenty-nine archers in the Countess of Leicester's household were attired in a 'rayed' or striped cloth, for which she paid 1s. 7d. an ell.

It is doubtful whether, for the peasant, furniture was an article of expenditure at all, since most of his simple needs would be home-made. A beaten earth floor covered with rushes required no carpet – which, indeed, was rarely seen in any house before the fifteenth century. A trestle table, which could be taken down and stored against a wall when not in use, was the principal item: a few stools and perhaps a bench provided the only seating accommodation, and there might be a chest to hold the best clothes and the few valuables. Apart from these would be found only a bed – occasionally a valuable feather-bed, though more commonly bags of straw or flock resting on rudely constructed frames placed by the walls of the room. The total value of a peasant's goods was minute and usually not worth recording. One who died in 1293 left only a bolster, a rug, 2 sheets, a brass dish and a trivet. A century later a jury assessed a prosperous villein's estate at £5 3s., the household goods amounting to less than £2. They included bedding, kitchen utensils (pans, cresset, tripod, skillet and colanders), a cloth and 5 silver spoons.

Recreation would hardly appear as an item in the cost of living for the great mass of medieval people. 'Merrie England', if it existed at all, had meaning only for a privileged few, and the peasant's life was one of unremitting toil, broken only by brief periods of pleasure-making at the great church festivals, Christmas and Easter, on May Day and Midsummer Day, or when fairs, weddings and wakes provided an opportunity for heavy eating and drinking. From time to time there might also be the free entertainment provided by the 'mystery plays' of a near-by town gild, or touring mummers, jugglers and acrobats.

7

Throughout this long period of time, prices were rising slowly: medieval England was already a land of inflation, though, by contrast with modern times, the upward movement would have been noticeable only between one generation and another, not between one year and the next. The best guides to long-term movements are the series of corn prices which have been compiled for the whole period from 1208, though, because of their incompleteness, and because local variations in weights and measures make strict comparison difficult, it would be wrong to assume that they can bear minute examination or analysis.

THE MIDDLE AGES

Nevertheless, it is clear from these that what really mattered to most people were the violent short-term fluctuations in price from one season to another, dependent on the size of the harvest and the availability of corn in the local markets: wheat, for example, might cost 3s. 4d. a quarter one year (1245), 6s. 5d. the next, while famine conditions could raise the price to 13s. 8d. (1315) compared with 6s. 7d. the previous year. It is also clear that the 4 grains – wheat, rye, barley and oats, in that order of cost – moved in close parallel, so that little substitution would be possible in times of dearth. These gross seasonal variations would be of much more direct concern to contemporaries than the long-term trends which are interesting in retrospect.

It seems that prices rose quite sharply during the first 2 or 3 decades of the thirteenth century, and thereafter more slowly. From 2s. 10½d. a quarter in 1208, wheat moved to 4s. 6d. in 1218 and 4s. 10d. in 1228, but throughout the rest of the century only another 1s. was added. Similarly the fourteenth and fifteenth centuries, apart from the post-Black Death period, show gently upward movements marked by wide seasonal variations. Over the whole period 1316 to 1485, the extreme prices of wheat were 15s. 5d. a quarter in 1316 (a famine year) and 2s. 10d. a quarter in 1357 (a year of exceptionally good harvest), but the average for 5-yearly periods varied only between 8s. 3d. (1364–8) and 4s. (1393–7). The usual price of wheat, over nearly 200 years, was 5s. or 6s. a quarter. Only in the years after the Black Death was there a noticeable and sustained upward movement from 4s. 3d. in 1340–4 to 5s. 10d. in 1345–9, 6s. 10d. in 1350–4, 7s. 5d. in 1355–9, 7s. 9d. in 1360–3 and 8s. 3d. from 1364–73: thereafter, the trend was downwards, and fifteenth-century corn prices were no higher than those of the fourteenth century.

An interesting attempt to construct a 'price index' that will reflect movements in the price of a composite 'basket' of consumers' goods for the whole period from 1264 to the present day has recently been made by Professor E. H. Phelps Brown and Sheila V. Hopkins. Its validity is perhaps best of all for the Middle Ages, when changes in consumption habits were much less marked than they were to become in later centuries. The years 1451–75 are taken to represent 100 points, and all other prices are expressed as a fraction of this. Two distinct periods of price-history emerge from the study. From 1260 to 1380, although there is little difference from end to end, there were regular cycles of rise and fall during which prices fluctuated widely. In 1264 the index stood at 83: by 1272 it had risen to 130, to fall back to 83 again by 1285, and to as little as 69 by 1289. Another rise then takes it up to 131 again in 1295, and, after another fall, to 135 in 1310. Especially bad harvests in 1316 and 1317 raise the index to 216 and 215, the highest points throughout the whole period: the Black Death causes a rise to only 160 points in 1352, considerably less than the 184 of 1370.

From 1380 to 1510 there followed a period of much greater constancy of prices, with peaks and troughs much less marked than in the previous century. There are still occasional 'bad' years due to harvest failure, like 1439 (154) and 1483 (162), but for many years together in the fifteenth century the price-level stayed within 10 points of the 1451–75 average, without the marked cyclical swings that characterized the previous period.

Throughout the later part of the Middle Ages silver, the basis of the coinage, was in short supply. Demand for it grew with growing population and trade, and as country after country changed over from a barter economy to a monetary one. In the earlier part of the Middle Ages, however, the output of the mines more than kept pace with demand, with the result that the general level of prices was rising from the middle of the twelfth century onwards up to about 1380: debasement of the coinage and the great plague encouraged the general trend upwards. But from the beginning of the fifteenth century the tendency was for prices to fall, associated with growing trade and increased demand for silver at a time when supplies were restricted. Wages, as we have seen, remained high and stable.

What part the conscious policies of medieval governments and municipalities played in determining the course of wages and prices is difficult to judge. That there was a strong sense of the 'just price' for goods and of a fair wage for services, that usury was regarded as immoral, and market offences such as 'forestalling' and 'regrating' dealt with, when they could be detected, with great severity, is well known. A code of mercantile ethics, based ultimately on the precepts of the Church, decreed that craftsmen should make their goods honestly and well, that sellers should give good weight and be satisfied with reasonable profits. In such a philosophy the laws of supply and demand took a subordinate place to natural justice and the needs of the community. Many aspects of medieval economic life were therefore subject to regulations – some national, like the Assizes of Bread, Ale and Cloth, which controlled the price and quality of these essential articles; many more local, like the control of wages and prices by gilds, and of markets by municipalities. The greatest single attempt by the state at a 'prices policy' – the Statute of Labourers in 1351 – was, by all accounts, largely ineffectual; it lacked the administrative machinery for enforcement and depended on the cooperation of those whose interest lay in its non-observance. But the local control of prices, wages, weight and quality was much more of an economic reality, having behind it numerous communal organizations for the detection and punishment of offenders. It is likely that in the towns at least – and this, after all, was where trade was mainly carried on – such sanctions had a significant effect in protecting the consumer against the greed and dishonesty which seemed an inevitable concomitant of trading activities.

These considerations led the great historian of prices, Thorold Rogers, to describe the fifteenth century as a 'Golden Age', the most prosperous period of all for the English peasantry.

At no time were wages, relatively speaking, so high, and at no time was food so cheap. All the necessaries of life, in ordinary years when there was no dearth, were abundant and cheap, and even in dear years the margin of wages or profits over the bare wants of life was considerable enough to fill up the void even though the labourer had to subsist for a time on some cheaper food than wheaten bread. Meat was plentiful, poultry found everywhere, eggs cheapest of all. The poorest and meanest man had no absolute and insurmountable impediment put on his career if he would seize his opportunity and make use of it.

Rogers's enthusiasm for the past was not merely romantic nostalgia. Writing in 1884, he was well aware of the impressive advances in agriculture and industry, in building and communications, in science, medicine, learning and the arts, which Victorian England was showering upon the world, but, unlike many of his contemporaries, he was also conscious of what had been lost and of what had been left undone by the progress of civilization.

It may be well the case ... that there is collected a population in our great towns which equals in amount the whole of those who lived in England and Wales six centuries ago, but whose condition is more destitute, whose homes are more squalid, whose means are more uncertain, whose prospects are more hopeless, than those of the poorest serfs of the Middle Ages and the meanest drudges of the medieval cities.

No strict comparison between the standard of life at distant periods of time is possible. The statistics of prices and wages can inform us, at best, only about the quantity of life, not about its quality. That men and women of all ranks had in medieval society an assured place and were, in general, free from such anxieties as unemployment and homelessness is true: in contrast with life in an industrialized, urbanized society like our own, they enjoyed a security of existence and a simple faith in the certainty of immortality which may seem enviable. On the other hand, the comforts and refinements of modern life were almost wholly lacking for the vast majority of medieval people, whose lives were laborious, whose homes uncomfortable, and whose food monotonous and nutritionally inadequate. Human happiness is, after all, immeasurable. Medieval life was of a different order from our own, not necessarily inferior or superior: the standards, values and ideals, the assumptions, beliefs and aspirations of the twentieth century are not relevant criteria to apply to an age which resembles the present only remotely.

CHAPTER 2

Tudor and Stuart England

I

To external appearances, the England of the Tudors and Stuarts was still in many ways medieval. As from time immemorial it was still a nation of farmers, of dwellers in hamlets and villages, not in cities: if some crafts were practised in the countryside, then some agriculture was carried on almost into the hearts of towns. No sharp line divided urban from rural, industrial from agricultural society. And although few Englishmen were now the feudal vassals of a manorial lord, life on the land was much as it had been centuries earlier. Farming on the open fields was still mainly for subsistence rather than profit, its methods traditional and unchanging, its yields poor and uncertain. The lot of the mass of the people was as laborious and precarious, as exposed to the vicissitudes of nature as it had always been.

In some important respects, however, the apparent continuity of medieval life was slowly being eroded. Where the strips of land in the open fields had been thrown together to form compact, enclosed farms – a process that had begun in Kent, in Cornwall and in Devon even before the sixteenth century – parts of the countryside already presented a very different appearance. Although the midlands and south were to remain open-field for two centuries yet, it is in Tudor times that communal farming significantly begins to give way to farming 'in several' – that is, for individual gain. This new attitude towards land-ownership was especially evident where arable strips were enclosed for pasture, and flocks of sheep grazed where once the ploughman and reaper had toiled. In other areas the great medieval forests were shrinking before the demands of agriculture and industry, and even the private parks, estimated by a Venetian visitor in 1500 to number 4,000, where deer were carefully preserved for the chase, were yielding to the incessant demands of house-building, ship-building and the iron furnaces. Before the end of Elizabeth's reign plans to drain the fens, as the Dutch had drained Holland, had been projected, and in 1630 the Earl of Bedford promoted a company with an investment of £100,000, for initiation of work around the Isle of Ely: his son, the first Duke, was to reap handsome returns on the reclaimed lands.

The river Trent still divided two societies, two economies, almost two nations. To the south lay the mass of the people, the fertile lowlands, the three most important towns of the kingdom, the thriving woollen villages, the ports, and, above all, London; to the north was mountain, forest and moorland, a sparsely populated region whose inhabitants struggled to wrest a living from the soil without, as yet, the blessings of industrialization. In Stuart times the growing scarcity of timber was to foster the development of coal-mining in the midlands and the north-east, with some economic gain to the inhabitants, but even at the end of the period three-quarters of the whole population lived in the south, and Excise returns allocated to it four-fifths of the wealth.

All over England, but especially in the south, population was slowly growing and towns were expanding. Although no entirely reliable statistics are available for this period, it is likely that on the eve of the Black Death in 1348 England had numbered some 3¾ millions, which the great plague had reduced by 1400 to a mere 2·1 millions. Thereafter, a slow recovery brought it to 3·2 millions by 1545 (compared with 15 millions in France and 8·8 millions in Italy): by the end of Elizabeth's reign it had passed 4 millions, and by 1688, if Gregory King's evidence is correct, it was 5½ millions. Although this was no population explosion, the steady growth in numbers was to have profound economic and social consequences. The most conspicuous effect was in fact the growth of towns, and, most marked of all, that of London. Already in 1545 she was one of the great cities of the world, with a population of perhaps 80,000: by comparison, Norwich with 17,000, Bristol with 10,000 and Exeter with 8,000 were little more than market towns. But by 1600 London had swollen to 200,000, and during the following century it is likely that it at least doubled again. The existence of this vast and growing market for food, manufactures and products of all kinds intimately affected the economy of the south-east and, to a less extent, that of England as a whole.

It was the size and opulence of London that most impressed contemporary observers. Compared with countries like France, the Netherlands or Italy, Tudor England was thinly populated, poorly developed and with a low standard of living: less than a quarter of her soil produced grain crops, and of her total exports – a mere £1,100,000 in 1565 – wool and cloth accounted for no less than 82 per cent. Yet visitors and travellers were astonished at the wealth of the capital and the evidence of growing luxury – the rows of goldsmiths' and jewellers' shops, the noblemen's palaces springing up along the Strand, the elaborate dress of men and women of all ranks, and the increasing luxury of houses, furniture and food. London only exemplified and magnified a national trend.

Everyone, said a contemporary, 'gaped for gain'. Unlike a later age, Tudor and Stuart England believed that wealth was to be spent, not hoarded. Harrison's contemporary *Description of England* complains that whereas 'of old time' bran bread was good enough for servants, now they have to have a portion of rye meal mixed with it, that his ancestors were content to sleep on pallets of straw with a good, round log under their heads ('if they had anie sheet above them it was well: for seldom had they anie under their bodies to keep them from the pricking straws that ran oft through the canvas and razed their hardened hides') but now even cottagers require bolsters and pillows, mattresses and sacks of chaff. Wooden platters, spoons and candlesticks no longer satisfy the farmer, who must have pewter, a silver salt-cellar, tapestry hangings for his bed and 'naperie' for his table. The complaint is old enough, but it is repeated so frequently in the sixteenth century as to suggest veracity. Another summed up his countrymen as 'desirous of new-fangles, praising things past, condemning things present, and coveting things to come; ambitious, proud, light-hearted, unstable, ready to be carried away by every blast of wind'.

These characteristics were the outward and visible expression of deep-seated economic changes that were profoundly affecting Tudor and Stuart society. Individualism and capitalism were fast replacing medieval ideas of cooperation and public benefit: on the land, in industry and in trade wealth was now deliberately sought and accumulated where, in the past, a comfortable subsistence had satisfied. Materialism and secularism were typical of the age which broke from the Roman Church and dissolved the monastic foundations. Thereby, Henry VIII acquired a vast property worth more than £100,000 a year which, if preserved, might have rendered his successors independent of Parliamentary revenue: instead, most of the estates were sold within a decade for £1½m. to finance the French Wars – a poor enough price considering the rising land-values of the time. It is doubtful, however, whether this gigantic transfer had very much effect on the agricultural changes of the period. A wave of enclosure of common lands and open fields had begun well before the 1530s, and was not significantly speeded up by the dissolution. Until mid-century most were for pasture, since a booming cloth industry was raising the price of wool faster than that of corn: after the trade depression of 1551 enclosures were more often made for arable to feed the growing population and the swelling towns. But there was no 'general movement' towards enclosure in Tudor times, and the contemporary complaints about heartless, racking landlords and the sheep which devoured whole towns and villages were at best gross exaggerations. The significant change was in attitudes towards land-ownership rather than in the adoption of new techniques. That the yield and profit of land were rising is undeniable: in the thirteenth century most arable farms produced only 6–12 bushels to the acre, while the Elizabethans could expect at least 16. But it was the insatiable appetite of London that affected the economy of the south-east, and away from the influence of the capital, in the midlands, the west and the north, it is unlikely that anything approaching an 'agricultural revolution' occurred in the sixteenth – or, for that matter any other – century.

More impressive and significant than agricultural advances were the developments in industry and trade. Here, the pressure of an expanding home demand was supplemented by the exploitation of new overseas markets opened up by the geographical discoveries of the period. The era of chartered trading which culminated in the foundation of the great East India Company in 1600 led on naturally to colonial enterprise in the following century, and the country whose ambit of trade had, a few years since, been limited to France and Flanders, now found herself, almost unwittingly, at the centre of a nexus stretching to Canada and New England, the Spanish Main, Africa, Russia and the Indies. The £72,000 capital that had floated the East India Company was soon to be counted in millions.

In many branches of manufacture the period witnessed the decay of the medieval gilds, ministering to their small, local markets by craft methods of production, and the substitution of capitalist industry catering for a wider demand by the essentially modern methods of centralized control and the employment of wage-labour. Outside the jurisdiction of the old, corporate towns, still gild-dominated, grew the new 'clothing villages' of East Anglia, the West Riding and the West Country, where entrepreneurs like the Springs of Lavenham or the Stumpes of Malmesbury employed hundreds of spinners and weavers on an 'outwork' system in their own cottages or even gathered together in large buildings which lacked only steam-power to merit the designation of 'factory'. In the seventeenth century the invention of new processes in the iron industry, the use of coal for smelting, and the development of new textiles such as hosiery and 'cottons' continued the advance, while at the very end of the period the motive power of steam came to be employed in the pumping-engine of Thomas Savery. 'This industrial development', Professor Nef has written, 'leads us to suggest very tentatively that the late sixteenth and seventeenth centuries may have been marked by an industrial revolution only less important than that which began towards the end of the eighteenth century.'

2

The description of 'revolution' has been given so often to political, economic and social changes that little real meaning is left. It can, however, more aptly be applied to a sudden yet sustained rise in prices which to contemporaries certainly appeared revolutionary and often disastrous in its effects. Throughout the whole of the fifteenth century prices had remained remarkably stable while wages had maintained the higher levels they had achieved after the Black Death: during this long period buyers and sellers, rent-payers and receivers, wage-payers and wage-earners, had come to expect a comfortable constancy in the cost and standard of living. But from the beginning of the new century onwards Europe as a whole was hit by a long wave of inflation, the consequences of which on national life were profound and enduring. Its time-sequence differed in different countries, Spain being the first affected, then France, then England. In Andalusia a 5-fold increase in prices had been recorded by 1600, in France only half as much. In England the rise was both longer, lasting until at least the mid-seventeenth century, and more irregular.

The best cost-of-living index for the period is that constructed by Professor E. H. Phelps Brown and Sheila V. Hopkins, which is based on a supposed 'basket' of goods typically consumed by a family living in southern England: it relates to basic necessities of life – bread, meat, fish, butter, cheese, beer, fuel, light and clothing – and is therefore a better guide to the expenditure of the less prosperous than to that of the rich. The former, in any case, greatly outnumbered the latter. An index figure of 100 represents the period 1451–75, nearly at the end of the long period of stable prices. Until 1510 there is little change, but by 1521 the figure has already soared to 167, to be followed by a period of 20 years when it hovers around 150. A particularly rapid rise then recurs in the late 1540s and 1550s – to 214 in 1549, 270 in 1555, 370 in 1556 and 409 in 1557. The 300 point is not reached again until 1570, and in the 1580s the median is about 340. The last few years of the sixteenth century saw very violent fluctuations associated with exceptionally bad harvests – 381 in 1594, 505 in 1596 and 685 in 1597. The level was never again below 400, between 1610 and 1630 it was normally over 500, and its highest point of the century, 839, was reached in 1650: the usual level thereafter was between 600 and 700, with some low 500s in the 1680s.

These figures suggest a 4-fold increase in the cost of living during the sixteenth century, a 6- or 7-fold increase for the whole period 1500–1700. By comparison with our own times, when a 4-fold price rise has occurred within the last 40 years, this may not seem very 'revolutionary', and perhaps the term is best reserved for the particularly sharp rises of the first half of the sixteenth century, which must have been even more disturbing after the generations of stability. Not all prices rose by the same amount, and one or two, together with interest rates, actually fell. J. D. Gould has calculated that in the 100 years before the Civil War the geometric price rise was no more than 1·1 per cent per annum, compared with 7 per cent between 1935 and 1955: 'moderate inflation', he suggests, is perhaps the best description of the period. But Tudor society was less familiar with inflation, less adaptable than our own, and one in which custom and law hindered adjustment to sudden change.

The Phelps Brown index was based upon material collected by Lord Beveridge which related principally to the prices paid by public and private institutions – schools, hospitals, the Navy Victualling Department and so on: these have the outstanding advantage of referring to specifically described articles over long periods of years, thus enabling valid comparisons to be made. On the other hand, they are contract rather than retail prices, and their occasional stability over many years suggests that they do not adequately represent the monthly and daily fluctuations that affected ordinary purchasers. Another index, constructed by Professor Douglas Knoop and G. P. Jones on the material of Thorold Rogers and Giffen, refers only to a 'basket' of twelve food items, but draws more heavily on actual retail prices. The base is 100 for the decade 1501–10, so that a direct comparison with the Phelps Brown index can be made.

1501–10	100	1603–12	470
1511–20	101	1613–22	506
1521–30	132	1623–32	520
1531–40	131	1633–42	519
1541–50	180	1643–52	557
1551–60	290	1653–62	541
1561–70	260	1663–72	554
1571–82	298	1673–82	596
1583–92	318	1683–92	585
1593–1602	437	1693–1702	682

These calculations differ in detail and are, on the whole, lower than the Phelps Brown index, although they exhibit the same trends and indicate the same critical periods – the 1540s and 1550s, the 1590s and 1600s and the period of comparative stability after about 1650, broken only by a further sharp rise at the end of the seventeenth century.

The contemporary comments on the price revolution are confused, uninformative, often contradictory. Some writers speak of England as still a land of plenty. 'Thanks be to God', said Bishop Jewel in 1570, 'never was it better in worldly peace, in health of body and in abundance of victuals', and about the same time the poet, Thomas Churchyard, wrote

> Here things are cheap and easily had,
> No soil the like can show,
> No state nor kingdom at this day,
> Doth in such plenty flow.

But many recognized that there was a 'dearth' in the midst of plenty, that, as the perceptive John Stow put it, 'there was no want of anything to him that wanted not money'. Scapegoats were easy to find – the encloser of lands for sheep farming who thereby forced up the price of corn, the rack-renting landlord, the merchant, the monopolist, the foreigner all came in for their share of abuse. That the country was experiencing anything more than a temporary and local, though unusually acute, scarcity, did not occur.

The prices of different commodities rose at varying rates, though in the same order of proportion. Contemporaries believed that food and rent saw the largest increases, probably because these were of most immediate concern to ordinary people. Wheat prices rose from 5s. 6d. a quarter in 1501–10, a price which had been typical throughout the latter half of the previous century, to 10s. 8d. in 1541–50, 34s. 10d. in 1593–1602 and 48s. 11d., the highest point in the period, in 1643–52: by 1700 it had eased a little to 43s. 3d. Bread prices moved in close parallel, rising from 1½d. for the 4-lb. loaf in the 1540s to 6½d. in 1700. Wool prices, on the other hand, showed much less regular increments. An index recently constructed by P. J. Bowden shows rapid increases in the 1540s and 1550s, by which time they had doubled since the beginning of the century, followed by stable or even falling prices in the period 1570–90: although the 1590s were again a time of sharp inflation the increase was not nearly so great as in the case of food. At the end of the sixteenth century the tod (28 lb.) of wool typically cost 25s. compared with 8s. at the beginning. Such considerations undoubtedly influenced Tudor farmers in deciding on land use. Up to mid-century it probably paid to convert arable to pasture, since the market for wool was booming and sheep-farming was more economical of labour costs; after 1570 it was often more profitable to convert back to arable, which would explain the fewer number of complaints about enclosure for pasture towards the end of the century.

Cloth prices are no very sure guide because of innumerable variations in size and quality. The broadcloth, traditionally 24 feet in length, was made in a score of grades, the finest being the 'russets' of Kent and East Anglia, which cost between £5 and £7 the piece in the 1530s: West Country 'whites' averaged about £3, while Yorkshire 'kerseys' and 'dozens' were among the coarsest and cheapest. The evidence suggests that the fine cloths rose in price very much more rapidly than the coarse, the Thorold Rogers statistics indicating an 8-fold increase for the former and a mere doubling for the latter. Although it is likely that skill was increasingly at a premium during the period, such a wide disproportion seems improbable; so too the cloth supplied to Winchester College, which remained unchanged in price over eighty years, can hardly have reflected normal retail trends. According to the Beveridge figures, Holland cloth supplied to the Lord Steward's Department doubled between 1556 and 1639, that of the cheaper maundy cloth rose by only 10 per cent.

A Prayer for Landlords issued in the reign of Edward VI began, 'O Lord, we pray thee that the landlords may not rack and stretch out the rents.' The most constant complaint in Tudor England was the inflation of rents and the heavy 'fine' or 'gressom' imposed on an incoming tenant for entry into a copyhold or renewal of a lease for a term of years. The gressom was by custom, though not by law, generally limited to 2 years' rent, but to raise this, or the rent itself, was the most obvious way for landowners to protect themselves against rising costs and prices. Nor was it necessarily unjust that a tenant-farmer who was receiving substantially higher profits from the sale of corn and meat should be expected to pay more for his holding. Despite the complaints, it does not seem that rents were generally raised unduly, though doubtless there were individuals who could not meet the increases demanded and were therefore, in effect, evicted from their holdings. The difficulty was that copyholds, as hereditary tenancies, were, for all practical purposes, freeholds, and could not normally have their rents raised: landlords not unnaturally tried to compensate for rising costs by imposing heavy 'fines' – as on the manor of Thingden, where the lord extorted a fine of 30s. on copyhold, of which the yearly rent was only 5s. Such drastic expedients were, in fact, caused by the failure of landlords to intercept the surplus value of land in the shape of enhanced rents, and there was probably some justice in their excuse for having failed to raise money for the recapture of Calais, 'The noblemen and gentlemen for the most part receiving no more rent than they were wont to receive, and paying thrice as much for everything they provide ... are not able to do as they have done in times past.' On the other hand, where leases had been granted for short terms and could be raised at frequent intervals, the landlord was more able to adjust to price changes. An analysis of rents on Suffolk manors during the period 1530–1660 indicates a rise, in general, of from 6 to 9 times. By contrast, in Wiltshire the prevalence of long leases prevented a comparable rise in rents in that county. On the whole, it seems more likely that agricultural prices, rather than rents, led the inflation, and that landlords were more or less able to keep up with or exceed it according to the particular tenurial patterns of their estates.

Coal, though not yet in universal use, was increasingly employed in the sixteenth and seventeenth centuries as supplies of wood diminished. For the domestic hearth the 'sea-coal' of Newcastle had long been known: now it was being used for industrial purposes such as brewing, soap-boiling, glass manufacture and, experimentally, for iron-smelting. Little is known of its early price, but Westminster School was buying it in the 1580s for 15s. the chaldron (26–27 cwt.), which by 1700 had doubled to 30s. Here, no very large increase occurred until after the Restoration in 1660, probably reflecting increasing demand as the timber famine became ever more acute.

Although it is not difficult to chart the course of the great pricerise, its causes are still a subject for speculation and dispute among economic historians. One striking, though inexplicable, fact is that there appears to be a cyclical regularity about price movements in general, each period lasting for rather more than a hundred years before it is replaced by another of different character. Thus, as we have seen, the period of stable prices from about 1380 to 1510 was followed by one of inflation from 1510 to 1640, to be succeeded in its turn by comparative stability again from 1640 to 1760.

The most usual explanation of Tudor inflation has been the bullion or, in economic language, the quantity theory – that it was the influx of new supplies of gold and silver from the New World, first into Spain and later to Europe as a whole, that put more money into circulation without a corresponding increase in goods, and, hence, forced up prices. Because of the development of a monetary economy and the expansion of trade, fifteenth-century Europe had experienced a growing scarcity of precious metals, the first result of which was to stimulate the more intensive exploitation of mines in the Tyrol and Germany. From the early sixteenth century gold and silver had begun to flow from the New World, and in much greater quantities after 1545 with the discovery of the Potosi mines in Peru and others in Mexico. Between 1520 and 1660 some 18,000 tons of silver and 200 tons of gold were despatched in royal ships to Spain. The argument is that this vast hoard of treasure did not remain in Spain, despite the government's efforts to keep it there, but gradually found its way throughout Europe: England, it is assumed, acquired its share mainly by trade with her great export market, the Spanish Netherlands, and partly by way of capture of Spanish treasure ships during the cold – and later, hot – war with Spain. The difficulty about this theory is that it does not explain the early part of the price-rise, from 1510 until mid-century, nor the precise mechanism by which Spanish silver is supposed to have penetrated to Britain. Much of Elizabeth's reign saw a trade recession during which it is improbable that great quantities of specie would have been involved in the balance of payments. Spanish bullion may have been a contributory cause, but it cannot have been the mainspring of Tudor inflation.

Another contributory reason was undoubtedly the debasement of the coinage carried out by Henry VIII and Protector Somerset as a device to increase royal revenues. Although the weight of the silver penny had, as we have seen, been gradually reduced over the centuries, there had been no serious tampering with the quality of 'sterling' which, up to Tudor times, had still been 92½ per cent fine. Between 1542 and 1547 Henry reduced the fineness of silver by one half. About £400,000 worth of the old coin was reminted into £526,000 worth of the new, the metal thus extracted, valued at £227,000, representing the king's gross profit on the transaction. In the following reign Somerset further debased the coinage, issuing some at only one-quarter fine.

The immediate effect of increasing the value of currency in circulation without a corresponding increase in the volume of goods was inevitably to send up the price-level still further. Another was to lower the value of sterling abroad. In 1542 the pound had been worth 27 Flemish shillings: by 1547 it was worth only 21. At first, the relative cheapness of English money had a favourable effect on exports, and the cloth trade in particular experienced a period of boom under this monetary stimulus: at his death Henry could point to the fact that London was exporting twice as many shortcloths as at his accession. By 1551 the pound was worth no more than 15 Flemish shillings, but this year marked the end of the brief economic boom. By now the Netherlands market was saturated, and merchants were complaining of over-production and bursting warehouses. When Somerset's successor, Warwick, carried out the necessary act of devaluation by calling the coinage down to half its face-value, the exchanges took a sharp upward turn and high prices now completed the work which over-production had begun. At home, meanwhile, the bad money continued to drive out the good, until at the beginning of the new Queen's reign, in 1560 and 1561, Cecil called in the old currency and issued a new one of the former 'sterling' quality of fineness and at a face-value corresponding to its intrinsic worth. The new penny was of 8 grains troy, compared with the 22 grains of 1300. Although it was a salutary measure, greatly increasing public confidence at home and abroad, it did not end inflation or further currency frauds by individual clippers and counterfeiters. Their activities were eventually curtailed by the introduction of milling in 1663, while three years later the Crown gave up its ancient privilege of making money out of coining by permitting anyone to have bullion assayed and coined at the Mint without charge. Finally, between 1696 and

1699 a full-scale recoinage was carried out, new coins of full weight replacing many worn and clipped ones.

As an explanation of the great price-rise the debasement theory suffers from the same disadvantage as the bullion theory – that it does not account for the early decades of inflation, nor for its long continuation into the middle of the seventeenth century. Both must have played some part, as did other inflationary tendencies of the period. The vast acreage of monastic land put up for sale in the 1540s enormously enriched the real-estate market and enhanced prices. So, too, the unprecedented volume of government expenditure on the war against Spain at the end of the century inflated the price of supplies of many kinds: between 1588 (the Armada year) and 1603 the record total of £4 million was spent on the army and navy, approximately half of it raised by taxation, by increased customs duties and the profits of royal monopolies. Again, generally easy credit terms and the development of banking during the period facilitated borrowing and encouraged spending in an age that was addicted to luxury.

But if one looks for a 'prime mover' of the price-revolution it is probably to be found in the ever-mounting pressure of population on resources as yet insufficiently developed. Not only had more people in total to be fed, clothed, housed and provisioned, but, as towns expanded, more ceased to be able to supply themselves and became dependent on purchases from professional producers. It is doubtful whether the small advances of Tudor agriculture were able to keep pace with increasing demand, and it fits the population explanation well that it was corn prices, for which demand is highly inelastic, that rose most, manufactures least. One of the characteristics of the period was the way in which prices outstripped wages, so lowering relatively the cost of articles in which labour was a major factor. It seems most reasonable to accept a multiple causation for the great price-rise – to believe that individual commodities such as wheat and timber increased owing to the pressure of growing population on scarce resources, and that this pressure was superimposed on a background of general inflation associated with enlarged credit facilities, debased coinage and heavy, unproductive, wartime expenditure.

Lastly, the population theory also helps to explain one

mysterious pause in the long price-rise which has puzzled historians. It is noticeable that for some twenty years, between the mid 1550s and the early 1570s, the upswing of grain prices was slowed, and that for this period they remained almost stable while wages continued to rise: for this short space, the general deterioration in the economic position of labour stopped, and some recovery was made. We know from contemporary accounts that a serious epidemic of 'sweating sickness' broke out between 1556 and 1558, now believed to be the first major attack of influenza in this country. Commentators complained that rich and poor were equally affected, that crops lay ungathered in the fields, and that those who survived 'took twelve pence for that which was wont to be done for three pence.' No precise statistics of the mortality can be assembled, but a study of the number of wills proved during the years concerned suggests that these doubled, tripled and even quadrupled in some areas: a reduction of the whole population by one-fifth might be no great exaggeration. This could easily explain the temporary buoyancy of wage-rates in the 1550s and 1560s. But shortly afterwards the effect had worn off, and by the 1590s Lambard was in no doubt that the population was again growing strongly: 'That the number of our people is multiplied it is both demonstrable to the eye and evident in reason ... we have not, God be thanked, been touched with any extreme mortality, either by sword or sickness, that might abate the overgrown number of us.' If the Malthusian check had, for a couple of decades, relieved inflation, it seems logical to suppose that, over the longer period, the absence of restraint was a major cause of its incidence.

If the causes of the great price-rise are complex, its consequences are still more difficult to assess. That it had a profound influence on the economy, on social structure and on government policy is certain, but on the precise nature of each of these historians are still in dispute. It is tempting to suppose that the rise in prices was in some way related to the undoubted industrial advances of the period, and the attractively simple explanation was advanced by Professor Hamilton that as prices rose more rapidly than wages entrepreneurs were presented with an unexpected increase in profit margins which facilitated capital accumulation and the development of capitalist structures in industry. Lord Keynes followed this theory in the *Treatise on Money*, where he wrote, 'Never in the annals of the modern world has there existed so prolonged and so rich an opportunity for the businessman, the speculator and the profiteer.' But industrial development requires a rising level of investment, not merely a widening gap between prices and costs, and it remains to be demonstrated that in an age of conspicuous expenditure one invariably led to the other. In any case, it was, as we have seen, the prices of foodstuffs which rose most rapidly, those of manufactures least. An alternative and more viable explanation of the industrial progress of the period has been offered by Professor J. U. Nef – that the chief factor was a fall in costs due to technological advances, increases in the scale of production, and the discovery and use of new supplies of raw material such as coal, alum and calamine. It was, according to this view, the fall in 'real costs' which was the major factor in industrial development: increasing disparity between wages and prices alone would have checked consumption, and, ultimately, production.

In the sphere of economic and social policy, inflation had more directly traceable consequences. The Tudors inherited from the Middle Ages the concept of a 'just price' for labour as for goods, and the view that profit which did not derive from work was unfair if not positively immoral: such ideas had hardened into accepted practice during the preceding century of price-stability. Under the Tudors food supplies were carefully watched and the prices of a number of articles, particularly in times of dearth, controlled through national or local assizes. Laws against forestalling, regrating and engrossing were tightened and market frauds suppressed. The export of corn was restricted and, at times, totally disallowed, while acts from 1545 onwards regulated usury by providing a legal maximum of 10 per cent interest on loans. But, most significant of all, the government of Elizabeth embarked on the first major 'prices and incomes' policy when it passed the Statute of Artificers in 1563. From the time of the Black Death there had been sporadic and largely ineffective attempts to peg wages by fixing maximum rates, but there had been no coherent policy of relating wages to prices. The principle of the new act was, 'to yield to the hired person, both in time of scarcity and in time of plenty, a convenient proportion of wages';

this was to be achieved by the local magistrates making an annual assessment of wages according to skill and with reference to the prevailing prices of provisions. It became a punishable offence to offer or accept higher wages than the legal maxima.

The act was enforced with some thoroughness during the first hundred years of its life, with a good deal less during the succeeding century and a half before its final repeal in 1813. Much depended on the energy of the local magistrates, and the degree of prompting from the Privy Council, but in some areas, both urban and rural, wage-assessments were regularly made during the Tudor and Stuart period, and with elaborate detail in respect of skill. In Hertfordshire in 1592, for instance, masons alone were assessed on three scales – 12d., 10d. and 8d. a day – corresponding to skilled workers, roughmasons and masons' servants: similarly, agricultural workers were assessed differently for different occupations – for ploughing, reaping, threshing and so on. But how far the Statute of Artificers can be regarded as a genuine attempt to maintain standards of living during a period of price-inflation is open to doubt. The act provided for the fixing of maximum, not minimum, rates, and its enforcement was in the hands of those who, as employers, had an interest in keeping wages down. At times the official scales certainly lagged behind the wages actually paid, indicating that they did not correspond very closely to economic reality. Thorold Rogers concluded that the act was the first hypocritical step in a conspiracy to keep wages low and pauperize the English worker, and although one need not necessarily accept the extreme view it is difficult to avoid the conclusion that, in general, it favoured the wage-payer rather than the receiver.

It is a commonplace that inflation affects adversely those whose incomes are fixed and inflexible, while those who can adjust to the new economic opportunities may benefit from it. The effects of the Tudor price-rise varied from class to class, and from individual to individual, some gaining, some losing, others remaining almost unaffected. Much depended on personal effort and adaptability to change, and it would be quite misleading to generalize that, for example, those whose incomes were drawn from the land suffered a deterioration while manufacturers and merchants were invariably favoured. Landowners who themselves farmed could, by more intensive methods and more efficient administration, profit from the rapid increase in food-prices, whereas their landlord cousins, living on unalterable rents, might be faced with a seriously declining standard of life.

If lawyers and speculators benefiting from an active land market, innovative manufacturers and adventurous merchants were the main legatees of inflation, the chief victims were wage-earners whose incomes lagged seriously behind prices and who, in any case, had least to lose. The urban worker, with little or no land on which to grow food for himself, was probably the worst hit of all. The Phelps Brown index of wage-rates for building craftsmen, measured against the prices of consumables, indicates that these declined from 100 in 1500 to 48 in 1552 and a mere 29 in the worst year of inflation, 1597. They remained at around 40 during the first three decades of the seventeenth century and had slightly recovered to about 50 by the end of the century. According to this view, the standard of living of the craftsman fell disastrously during the Tudor period, so that at its end his wage purchased a mere two-fifths of the goods it had done at the beginning. Another way of illustrating the trend is by setting actual wages against the price of corn at different periods:

	1541–82		*1583–1642*		*1643–1702*	
	s	d	s	d	s	d
Wheat (quarter)	13	10½	36	9	41	11¼
Barley „	8	5¾	19	9¾	22	2¼
Oatmeal „	20	4¾	37	9¼	52	11
Agricultural labourers (weekly)	3	3	4	10	6	4¾
Masons „	4	9	6	5¾	9	10½
Carpenters „	5	0	6	2¾	10	2¾

On this shorter span of years, which omits the period of rapid inflation before 1540, wages had doubled, but the cost of grain almost tripled. That many wage-earners were impoverished by inflation, and some pauperized, seems certain. Inflation was by no means the sole reason for the poverty of the age, though it widened the gap between plenty and want and created a new category of the poor – those who had employment but whose wages were inadequate to support life at a reasonable level. And if economic forces had increased the incidence of poverty, it seems that they had also hardened the public attitude towards it. 'They live in the streets,' wrote the contemporary Stubbes, 'in the dirt as commonly is seen ... and are permitted to die like dogs or beasts, without any mercy or compassion showed them at all.'

3

The social structure of Tudor and Stuart England, the income and expenditure of different classes and their position relative to others, was undoubtedly influenced by the price-revolution, though any generalization which does not take account of the degree of success or failure with which individuals were able to adjust to the new circumstances is likely to be wide of the mark. At the head of the social system, though no longer automatically wielding the political and military power of their predecessors, stood the aristocracy, the hereditarily titled peers and baronets whose wealth depended on the ownership of landed estates. They still enjoyed great prestige, were expected to maintain lavish establishments and to act, when required, as ornaments of the Court and servants of the Crown. But since the Wars of the Roses both their numbers and influence had shrunk: the Tudors had dissolved the private armies that had been the basis of their military power, made few new creations to the peerage, and had deliberately elevated men of humble birth like Wolsey and Thomas Cromwell to be their chief ministers. Some recovery was made under the Stuarts, but the English aristocracy never enjoyed the power and privileges of an exclusive caste such as the French 'noblesse'.

The composition of the class constantly changed as families died out – from natural as well as unnatural causes – and new creations were made, but the total number of peers remained remarkably stable throughout the sixteenth century, 55 in 1485 and precisely the same number a century later. Between 1485 and 1547 43 noble families passed out of the peerage, and 39 new ones were raised, the majority of them for political or administrative services or on account of wealth acquired in law, trade or, less frequently, farming. More new creations followed under the Stuart kings and in 1688, at the end of our period, Gregory King calculated that there were 160 'temporal lords', together with 26 spiritual lords and a further 800 baronets. Although possession of land was the characteristic of the class, and although some estates were undoubtedly vast, the share of the nobility's land-owning was not, in fact, impressive and became less so as time went on. Peers owned only 1·3 per cent of the value of lay property in Rutland in the early sixteenth century, 6·3 per cent of that in Buckinghamshire, and everywhere they were easily outstripped in property-ownership by their social inferiors, the gentry. Nor was wealth, in itself, a determinant of membership, for although a few peers were immensely rich, others would have been considered poor by a prosperous merchant or lawyer. The highest assessment for tax purposes in the early Tudor period was £3,000, and it is likely that the average income of peers was in the region of £1,000 a year. By the end of the Queen's reign £2,000–£3,000 a year was probably the average, and in 1688 Gregory King gives £3,200 for peers, £1,300 for spiritual lords and £880 for baronets. But returns of income for tax assessment are notoriously unreliable, and there were always individuals who rose, at least briefly, much above these figures. In the 1520s Thomas Wolsey, as Archbishop of York, Bishop of Winchester and Abbot of St Albans, the richest monastery in the land, had £10,000 a year, enough to make him the richest man in the kingdom: his fees from Chancery, profits from legatine jurisdiction, pensions and presents may have brought this to £50,000 by the end of his life. Hampton Court was only one of the four palaces he built for himself. His successor, Thomas Cromwell, never achieved such phenomenal wealth, though his income for only 8 months in 1535–6 is estimated at £8,000: Burghley, Queen Elizabeth's chief minister, was treated less generously still with a mere £4,000 a year from lands. Next to the Queen, the richest woman in Elizabethan England was the Countess of Shrewsbury, Bess of Hardwick, one estimate giving her the immense income of £60,000 a year. But the average value of the estates of 41 peers in the middle of the seventeenth century was £30,000, the wealthiest the Earl of Thanet (£150,000), the Earl of Westmorland (£90,000), and the Duke of Richmond and Lennox (£73,500), the poorest the Earl of Norwich (£3,300), Viscount Ogle of Catherlough (£1,800) and the Earl of Marlborough

(£340). Of the estates of 93 baronets the average value was £11,000, the extremes £60,000 (Sir William Portman) and £200 (Sir Henry Moody).

The precise expenditure of the peerage is no more easy to determine than their income. In an age of extravagance, many were extravagant builders, devoting a high proportion of income to the erection and maintenance of houses – Burghley with his palaces of Burghley, Theobalds and Waltham, Suffolk with Audley End, Northumberland with Syon House, the Countess of Shrewsbury who believed, rightly in the event, that if her builders ever stopped work her life would be at an end. But the biggest recurrent expenditure was on the provisioning and servicing of the household – the purchase of food, drink, clothing, furniture, fuel and light, and the salaries of a host of officials, servants, cooks, grooms and outdoor workers. The Berkeley estate required 150 servants, the Derby 140 to maintain a family of 5, and King in 1688 gives 40 as the average size of peers' households. The Derby household expenses totalled £3,000 in 1561, the Earl of Bedford's £4,400 in the 1640s. A significant part of these vast sums went in entertaining guests and their retinues since, at least until Tudor times, the medieval practice of hospitality and open house to travellers still survived. To give only one instance, Edward Stafford the Duke of Buckingham entertained for dinner on Christmas Day 1507 at Thornbury Castle, Gloucestershire, 95 gentry, 107 yeomen or valets and 97 garçons or grooms – a total of nearly 300: as on every other day in the year, a detailed account was kept of all food and drink consumed – 491 loaves (13s. 8½d.), 11 pottles and 3 quarts of Gascony wine, 1½ pitchers of Rhenish wine and ½ pitcher of Malvoisey (14s. 9d.), 171 flagons of ale (13s. 7¼d.), meat and game totalling 90s., candles 4s. 3d., 6 loads of fuel 6s. and 6 quarters of charcoal 2s. The total cost of one meal on one day was, therefore, about £7, rather more than a labourer's earnings for a whole year. Clothing was a much more variable expense, depending on the individual's taste and love of finery, though it is known that the Earl of Arundel ran up debts of £1,000 to tailors and mercers, and that the Earl of Leicester spent £543 on seven doublets and two cloaks. Even to leave the world in appropriate style could involve an enormous cost in mourning clothes and other expenses – £750 for the Earl of Bedford's funeral, £1,600 for that of Sussex and £3,000 for that of Leicester.

The pattern of a wealthy peer's expenditure in Tudor times was probably not unlike that of Matthew Parker, Archbishop of Canterbury 1558–75, who had an annual income during that time of £3,428. Of this, £2,400 was consumed annually in basic expenses – £1,300 on household items, £300 on wages and liveries, £400 in annuities and fees, and £400 in pensions and contributions to hospitals. Of the remaining £1,028 a year over the seventeen years of office, £2,270 went in entertaining the Queen, £2,400 in benefactions at Cambridge, £2,600 in building, £1,100 in marriage portions for three nieces and a few hundred pounds to authors: the remainder went on such things as furnishing, plate, books, travel and litigation. A temporal lord would be unlikely to have so high an outlay on pensions and charities, but would probably spend much more than Parker on land and building. Parker's contemporary Bacon, the Lord Keeper, was devoting £1,150 a year to the purchase of land alone.

That individual peers were closely affected by the price-rise and the economic changes of the sixteenth and seventeenth centuries is obvious, but whether any generalization about their fortunes as a class is tenable is far from clear. The traditional view, derived ultimately from the economic interpretation of history of Marx and Engels, modernized and quantified by R. H. Tawney and Lawrence Stone, suggests that in the century between 1540 and 1640 the aristocracy steadily lost ground as a result of rising prices, a failure to adjust their incomes to the new conditions, and a continued habit of extravagant expenditure. Weakened by the Wars of the Roses, shut out of the royal councils and deprived of their armies of retainers, they now found that their ownership of copyholds and long leases made it impossible for them to raise their incomes in proportion to the rise in their expenses. This explains many apparently arbitrary and grasping acts which, for some, only staved off the eventual sale of lands to prosperous gentry, merchants and professionals. According to Tawney,

The facts were plain enough. The ruin of famous families by personal extravagance and political ineptitude ... the mounting fortunes of the residuary legatee, a gentry whose aggregate income was put even in 1600 at some three times that of peers, bishops, deans and chapters and richer yeomen together ...

But the facts are not plain enough. While some peers were undoubtedly extravagant and inept, like the third Earl of Cumberland who squandered £100,000 on privateering ventures, others like the Spencers of Althorp steadily enriched their inheritance by efficient farming, restraint in expenditure and well-planned marriages. The Bedfords invested wisely in the Covent Garden development and the reclamation of the Fens, others in the industrial developments of the period such as coal, lead and glass production: it has been estimated, for instance, that no less than 22 per cent of the Elizabethan aristocracy owned ironworks. Tawney's main statistical evidence for a decline of the aristocracy consists of showing that a fall occurred in the number of manors owned by them at the expense of the gentry, but his sample covered only 7 counties and since manors varied enormously in size and wealth it is quite conceivable that some peers were exchanging small properties for fewer, larger ones.

The maintenance of an appropriate household for himself, his children and dependants was the first responsibility of any nobleman, and in an age of ambition and social imitation, it was doubly important that the establishment should reflect – if not magnify – the status of its patron. Quite apart from the fabric of the house, its furnishing and provisioning, a noble household required to be serviced on a lavish scale, to be heated, lighted, cleaned and managed by a staff of domestic workers whose roles and remunerations were themselves carefully graded. The cost of the household was often the principal item of recurrent expenditure, growing rather than diminishing throughout the period. A great household like that of the Earl of Northumberland absorbed £938 in the year 1521, providing for 166 persons of the family, household servants and guests: meat alone took £254, fish £36, wheat (59 tons) £79, drink £102, salt (3¾ tons) £3, seasoning £33, light £17, fuel £28, household equipment £14, horses £30, wages £234 and extras £106. A hundred years later, in 1612, Lord William Howard's expenses for the year totalled £1,015, of which services and raw materials took 67 per cent, food and cooking utensils 20 per cent, manufactured goods a mere 8 per cent and miscellaneous expenses 5 per cent: wages and tips alone took 17 per cent of all expenditure.

Sir William Petre, one of Queen Elizabeth's principal secretaries and the owner of Ingatestone Hall, is representative only of a middle-rank household, certainly not of a noble one. Even so, in 1550 there was a staff of 21 – a house-steward and an acater who received no wages but held neighbouring farms at low rents, a law-steward (13s. 4d. a quarter), gardener (10s. 6d.), cook (10s.), butler (10s.), part-time brewer (5s.), 2 horse-keepers, a stable-boy, 2 carters and 8 other men-servants, a housekeeper (10s.), a nurse for the children (10s.), and 4 maids, the youngest of whom received 5s.: the highest stipend, 33s. 4d., was paid to the household chaplain. These quarterly payments all included board and liveries, so that the wages, though small enough, were clear of all living expenses. The annual wage-payments in 1550 were £51 for Ingatestone, but there was also a London house at Aldersgate with another dozen servants and attendants at Court, and a smaller country house at East Hondon. Altogether, Petre was spending around £250 a year in the 1550s on the staffs of his modest households.

Inside the house there were other regular and unavoidable expenses. The heating of large rooms in winter was a difficult problem, especially as timber in the form of faggots and billets was becoming scarce and dear: Petre bought them at the rate of 18s. for 1,500 faggots, and charcoal at about 6d. the sack, but had to supplement them with the newer coal: '9 chalder of sea coals' cost him £3 6s. 8d., with 3s. 6d. for unloading, 2d. to the 'ship-lads', 8s. for measuring and 14s. for carriage from the quay to Aldersgate. In 1519 it had cost only 3s. the chaldron, but by 1590 the Lord Mayor of London was explaining that the monopoly exercised by the town of Newcastle had enhanced the price to 9s., and to this had to be added delivery charges and duty – generally 1s. the chaldron up to the 1670s when it was raised to 3s. for rebuilding the London churches after the Great Fire: Westminster School paid, for delivered coal, about 14s. the chaldron at the end of the century, rising to 30s. by 1700.

Illumination of the baronial hall and chambers was still by candle and rush-light, not yet by oil-lamp. The Lestranges of Hunstanton bought wax candles at the beginning of the sixteenth century at 3d. the pound, a price which had been typical throughout the later Middle Ages. Unlike coal, candles appear to have held their price or actually cheapened during the earlier part of the period, for Petre paid only 2d. The Office of Works, established by Henry VIII to purchase supplies for the royal palaces at Greenwich, Richmond and Hampton Court, bought them at 2s. 9d. per dozen lb. in 1563, rising to 8s. by 1700. But many public institutions supplied their own tallow and paid a chandler for making them up, Winchester College using 1,600 lb. a year in 1600. Many households, large and small, also supplied themselves with soap, sometimes perfuming it with oil of almonds or musk, though it could be bought, as the Bertie family purchased it at Stourbridge Fair in 1562, for 50s. the barrel. It must have come in many qualities, for prices per pound ranged from 1d. to 4d.

The modest Petre household of the mid-sixteenth century may be compared with the far grander one of William Earl of Bedford a hundred years later, at Woburn Abbey and Bedford House. The late Earl had left some £1,500 of ready cash in his trunk in London, but his funeral had cost £255, mourning another £500, and there were annuities of £1,000 a year for his widow and £500 a year for his younger son to be found: in addition, William inherited his father's debt of £20,000 incurred over the Covent Garden rebuilding and the Fen drainage schemes, and was charged to provide a dowry of £7,000 for the marriage of his sister, Diana. In his early years the new Earl necessarily exercised economy in household expenses, some £260 a year going to salaries and wages in the 1640s, plus £130 for coal and £230 for the upkeep of the stables, kennels and mews: he also required £260 a year for his personal expenses on visits, recreation, tips to servants and so on. Total expenditure at this period, when his income was around £8,000 a year, was £4,400, with a further £150 for taxes in addition to those paid directly by the estate. But by the time of the Restoration in 1660 the Earl's fortunes and style of living had improved considerably. For the coronation of Charles II his wardrobe cost £538 and the liveries of his servants £245: a new carriage, specially ordered from Paris and costing £170, arrived too late for the event. His household was now headed by a receiver-general, earning £50 a year, later increased to £100, plus 2s. a day for board when travelling: there was a steward, responsible for all the household staff, at £40 a year, a Gentleman of the Chamber, the Earl's personal attendant, at £20, and so on down to the 12 footmen whose wages were from £2 to £6 a year. Pages received no salary, only board and liveries, scullions had from 10s. to £2 a year, watchmen £1–2 and porters £3–4. The cost of maintaining a servant was reckoned at 10s. a week, and the total expenses of £600 or £700 a year in the latter part of the century suggest a household staff of around 30. But although all were technically servants, a world of difference separated the scullion from the head falconer, the most highly paid of all at £120 a year, or the head gardener of Woburn, John Field, at £80. The Gentleman of the Horse also had his own separate departmental responsibility for stables and mews, with an annual expenditure of between £1,000 and £1,500, and a staff of 14. For all these the Earl provided food, lodging and clothes, medical care, pensions, at least to the more senior (£20 per annum for the Clerk of the Kitchen) and, where necessary, the cost of burial.

Within the household, the provision of food was the principal item of recurrent expenditure. The cost of this varied greatly with the degree of self-sufficiency of the estate, some establishments still managing to provide themselves with basic necessities like bread, meat and beer. But as the range of luxuries grew to include such things as sugar, coffee and tea, foreign wines and spirits in addition to the well-known spices, the food expenditure of all noble households steadily mounted. Tudor England already had a reputation for good food in profusion, and was renowned among foreign visitors for meat-eating and hospitality. Harrison comments that 'white meats' – that is milk, butter and cheese – 'are now reputed as food appertinent onelie to the inferiour sort', and that the wealthy dine on flesh of all kinds, all sorts of fish from the coasts and rivers 'and such diversitie of wild and tame fowls as are either bred in our iland or brought over unto us from other countries of the maine'. Some contemporaries thought the English gluttonous, and Stubbes in his *Anatomie of Abuses* (1585) wrote

And nowe a dayes if the table be not covered from the one ende to the other, as thicke as one dish can stand by an other, with delicate meate

A HISTORY OF THE COST OF LIVING

of sundrie sorts, one cleane different from an other, and to everie dishe a severall sauce appropriate to hys kinde, it is thought ... unworthy the name of a dinner.

And all this, he complained, was only the first of three courses, each of similar size, and rounded off with 'swete condiments and delicate confections of spiceries'. One of the difficulties is to distinguish the ordinary fare of a noble household from the banquets given to visiting royalty – like that which Leicester gave to Elizabeth at Kenilworth in 1575 when 1,000 dishes were served in bowls of silver and glass by 200 gentlemen. The queen was fond of food, especially of sweet things, a fact which may well account for the blackness of her teeth, but her £50,000 a year expenditure at Court was doubled by the more lavish Stuarts until Puritanism enforced a return to simpler tastes. Oliver Cromwell's favourite dish was roast veal with oranges.

The accounts of Edward Stafford, Duke of Buckingham, provide a good picture of the fare of a noble household at the beginning of the sixteenth century. Most of the food here was home-grown or produced by the estate's own baker and brewer, but it is all costed for each meal for each day of the year. On 6 January 1508 special meals were served for the feast of the Epiphany for 459 guests and household: bread, 678 loaves (18s. 11¼d.), – 'the bear 2' – 33 pottles of Gascony wine (66s.) and 12 pitchers of other wines (10s. 2d.), 259 flagons of ale (21s. 7d.), 36 rounds of beef (21s.), 12 carcasses of mutton (14s.), 2 calves (5s.), 4 pigs (8s.), 1 dry ling (6d.), 2 salt cods (5d.), 1 salt sturgeon (18d.), 3 swans (10s.), 6 geese (2s. 6d.), 6 sucking pigs (3s.), 10 capons (6s. 6d.), 1 lamb (16d.), 2 peacocks (2s.), 2 herons (8d.), 22 rabbits (4s. 7½d.), 18 chickens (18d.), 9 mallards (22½d.), 23 widgeons (2s. 10½d.), 18 teals (18d.), 16 woodcocks (16d.), 20 snipes (8d.), 9 dozen great birds (3s.), 6 dozen little birds (6d.), 3 dozen larks (9d.), 9 quails (4½d.), half a fresh salmon (18d.), 4 dog fish (3s. 8d.), 2 tench (14d.), half a fresh conger (8d.), 21 little roaches (8d.), 6 large fresh eels (3s. 4d.), 17 flounders (6d.), 100 lampreys (10d.), 3 plaice (9d.), 400 eggs (3s. 4d.), 24 dishes of butter (2s.), 15 flagons of milk (15d.), 200 oysters (4d.), herbs (6d.). These were divided between the two main meals, though on this special day a breakfast of bread and wine was allowed: on a fast day, such as Friday 10 December, no breakfast or supper was permitted, and only fish, eggs and white meats were eaten at dinner.

The quantities given above are somewhat difficult to translate into modern terms, but the Lestrange household accounts of the same period are in more recognizable form. For Rhenish wine they paid 1s. the gallon, for beer 2s. the barrel, for almonds 3d. the pound, and for raisins the same, for 3 oz. of ginger 4d., for sugar 6d. a pound, for a bottle of vinegar 3d., a fresh turbot 2s. 4d. and a salmon-trout 10d., for 200 white herrings 3s. and for 300 red ones 4s.: sack was 2d. a pint, claret 5d. a quart, cherries were 1d. a pound and prunes 12 lb. for 22d. Clearly, transport was a major item in cost, the imported foods being vastly more expensive than the home-grown ones. Chickens were 1d. each when raisins were 3d. the pound, a goose 4d. – the same as three ounces of ginger. England was rightly supposed by the foreigner to be well endowed with flesh, fish and fowl in abundance, although there could be temporary shortages when prices rose rapidly: in 1549, for instance, the Court of Aldermen of the City of London ordained that the best beef should not be sold above 3½d. the lb. and the best mutton not above 1½d., 'that the people may have reasonable peniworthes for their money'. Oysters at 4d. the bushel were scarcely a luxury, nor milk at 3 pints for a halfpenny in the towns. But a lemon at 6d. represented a day's wage for a workman, and, as we have seen, foodstuffs were hit most sharply of all by Tudor inflation. Sugar, which could be had at 4d. the lb. at the beginning of the century, fetched 14d. at the end, and records from Wollaton Hall in Nottingham show that chickens rose from 1d. in 1515 to 3d. in 1603 and a goose from 4d. to 1s. 4d. A 2-lb. jar of marmalade at the later date cost the enormous sum of 5s. 3d. By the middle of the seventeenth century poultry, once so cheap as to be almost despised, were becoming something of a delicacy – chickens now 1s. 4d., geese 3s., and the expenses of the Privy Council's Star Chamber in the reign of James I show some startling increases – 1½ fresh salmon cost 38s., a great conger 14s. 4d., six plaice 9s., 1½ lambs 15s., 2 pheasants 20s., a dozen quails 16s. and 18 rabbits 16s. There is also one of the earliest mentions of 'potatoes, 3s.', though no quantity is given. Fruit was also dear in the seventeenth century – not only imported oranges at 1s. each, but English cherries at 5s. 4d. for 8 lb. and 6d. for 2 quarts of gooseberries. Probably the only commodity which became cheaper in this period was sugar which, because of the development of sea routes to the East, fell from 1s. 6d. a lb. to 4d – 6d. by the end of the century: this largely accounts for its growing use in cooking, particularly in such things as pies, puddings and fruit tarts. Wine prices and consumption were hit badly by Cromwell's Navigation Act of 1651 and the imposition of a duty at £4 a tun in 1688: beer-drinking increased correspondingly towards the end of the century, as did the consumption of the new drinks, tea, coffee and chocolate, among the middle and upper classes. These all appeared in London for the first time in the 1650s, tea at the fantastic price of £3 10s. a pound, coffee considerably cheaper at 1d. the dish in the coffee-houses: by 1700 tea was being imported by the East India Company and its price had fallen to £1 a lb., but it was still a luxury reserved for the wealthy and the invalid.

The rising cost of living is clearly reflected in the household accounts of the Earl of Bedford for the latter half of the seventeenth century, and it is noticeable that the household is much less self-sufficient, even in basic foods, than those of Tudor times. At the time of the Civil War, the Bedfords were spending approximately £300 a year on food for a household of between 30 and 40, in addition to the supplies, principally of meat, that came from the Woburn estate. Meat, in fact, accounted for some £50 a year, the weekly purchases varying enormously according to the number of carcases in stock and the supplementary provisions of venison, game and rabbits from the estate: one week there might be a heavy purchase of 27 stone of beef at 1s. 8d. a stone, besides mutton, a pork weighing 12 stone, 2 gammons of bacon, tripe and a neat's tongue (10d.), another there might be merely a quarter of mutton (4s. 6d.), a pig (2s. 10d.) and 2 calves' heads (1s. 10d.). Butter was bought at prices between 6d. and 9d. a pound, according to quality, some 30 lb. being consumed each week: cream cost between 3d. and 5d. the pint, artichokes were 3d. each, quinces 7 for a penny and a peck of apples 1s. But by 1660 the household was spending £540 on food, partly because of the continued rise in prices, partly because of the rather grander scale of life which the Earl had adopted; meat and poultry had risen sharply in recent years, and the cheapest butter available was now 7½d. instead of 6d. the pound. The Earl was also developing a taste for delicacies – lobsters at 1s. each, salmon at up to 18s., oysters at 1s. 6d. a quart and asparagus, usually at about 2s. the hundred heads. By 1664 he was devoting £750 a year to food, by 1668 £870, and in 1671, the heaviest year, £1,400, though married sons and daughters visiting, with their servants, for extended stays contributed, as was the custom, some £300 for their keep. But the family was now eating very well indeed, with quails at 19 for 15s., ruffs at £1 a dozen, and 16 pike at £9 7s. with another £7 7s. for their transport by river to Woburn. Wheat now cost about £35 the year, groceries between £25 and £35 (currants 6½d. a lb., rice 4d. a lb., prunes 2½d. a lb., Jordan almonds 1s. 6d. a lb.), a list constantly extending as new items appeared. In 1685 coffee powder was purchased for the first time at 3s. a lb., and tea, from a separate account, at prices from 25s. to 3 guineas the pound. Finally, there was the drink bill, again rising steadily to a maximum of £254 in 1684. The Abbey brewer did not supply nearly enough beer for household requirements, and several hundred barrels were bought annually, at around 10s. the barrel according to strength: cider came by the hogshead (£5) and, by the 1690s, by bottle (6s. a dozen). The Earl kept a good cellar, and most of the expense went on wine, both of traditional type like sack (1s. a pint), white wine (8d. a pint) and canary (8s. a gallon) and the newer types like Chablis (62 bottles for £4 12s. 6d.) and Lesbos (£10 the hogshead). Two entirely new wines appear – champagne for the first time in 1665 (£6 for 4 dozen bottles) and port in 1684 (£5 the hogshead). Brandy also makes its first appearance at this time at 1s. the bottle.

Many noble families faced, at some point in the sixteenth or seventeenth centuries, the construction of a new house or major rebuilding of an existing one. In the past, the finest craftsmanship in stone and wood had gone into ecclesiastical building, but with the Reformation came an almost complete cessation of church-building until the late seventeenth century, and Italian and German artists as well as English workmen were now employed to embellish the town mansions and country seats of secular patrons. At first, manor-houses like Penshurst and

Haddon Hall were converted, still in Gothic style, into more comfortable and splendid homes; later in the century new ones were deliberately designed in the Italianate or Renaissance style, like Longleat, Audley End, Kenilworth and Montacute. By the early seventeenth century a distinct profession of architect had separated from the mason-builder, with Inigo Jones as the art's first great exponent.

Materials as well as styles underwent a transformation. Smaller houses might still be made of the traditional material, wood, patterned and embellished into the Tudor 'black-and-white' half-timber style, but the finer mansions demanded brick at least and stone for preference. The internal construction was also changing. Properly made flues and chimneys replaced the open hearth, at least in principal rooms; plain, clear glass (not yet plate glass) filled the lattice windows which occupied a far greater proportion of wall-space than formerly: walls were panelled and wainscoted in oak or hung with costly tapestries or arras, ceilings embellished with moulded and painted stucco. The insanitary rushes that had once covered floors were now replaced by polished wood, carpets or, at least, rush-matting (4d. the foot in 1603), and the 'houses of office' to which contemporaries referred sometimes even included a water-closet, the first of which had been constructed by Harington at a cost of 33s.

Building materials were still cheap at the beginning of the period, though, like all commodities, they suffered at the hands of inflation. Winchester College was paying a mere 6s. per thousand for roofing tiles in 1500, a price which had risen to 20s. by 1700: Eton purchased bricks at 7s. per thousand in 1550 and 13s. in 1690, and lead for pipes and gutters cost about 15s. the hundredweight at the latter date. Transport charges have to be added to the basic prices, and these tended, as in the Middle Ages, to be heavy: the bricks used by Eton College, for example, were brought only from near-by Slough, yet this added from 6d. to 1s. 8d. per thousand in 1560, rising to 4s. to 6s. in 1690. Even so, building materials and the cost of labour were, especially in the sixteenth century, sufficiently low to permit construction on a magnificent scale at relatively small cost and rapid speed. The Crown was itself a large builder, particularly in the reign of Henry VIII; work on the fortress of Calais was costing £2,800 per month in 1541, while at the same period the entire castle of Sandgate was erected in the extraordinarily short time of 18 months. The construction of magnificent royal palaces at Nonsuch, St James's and Whitehall was also begun, while on Wolsey's Hampton Court Henry was spending £400 a month, a considerable sum when set against the fact that the massive chimney-shafts were built for a mere 45s. each and an elaborately carved chimney-piece for £15.

After Henry's reign the nobility increasingly took the place of the Crown and Church as builders. Municipalities might erect an occasional public building, like Exeter which rebuilt its Guildhall between 1593 and 1596 at a cost of £789, and a good deal of the stone from former monastic foundations went into the rapidly expanding colleges at Oxford and Cambridge: the second court of St John's College, Cambridge, was built for £3,400 (1598–1602), the Perse building at Caius College for £500, and the pavement of Trinity College Library for 2s. 3d. a foot in 1688. But under Elizabeth and the first two Stuarts most large-scale building was private, not public, until the Great Fire of 1666 compelled a massive redevelopment of London, to which the coal tax alone contributed £32,000 a year. In the meantime the nobility had endowed themselves – and posterity – with town and country mansions of splendour and, often, great beauty. The Protector spent £10,000 in less than 3½ years on Somerset House: Sir William More £1,600 between 1561 and 1569 on the modest Loseley Hall, near Guildford: Audley End cost the enormous sum of £190,000 between 1603 and 1616. But this was quite exceptional, only approached by Kenilworth, Leicester's country seat, which cost £60,000, and was described as 'all of hard stone, every room so spacious, so well lighted and so high-roofed within: so seemly to sight, so glittering of glass a-nights by continual brightness of candle-fire and torchlight, transparent through the lightsome winds'. By comparison, Syon House at £5,000, Redgrave Hall at £6,000 and Verulam House, Lord Chancellor Bacon's splendid mansion, at £10,000, were not unduly expensive, nor was Fountains Abbey, sold at the Dissolution for £11,000.

The furnishing and interior decoration of a noble household, though much more elaborate in the Tudor and Stuart periods than in earlier centuries, does not appear to have been a major item of expenditure for most families. No doubt it was preferred to put money into the fabric of the building and into readily saleable assets like silver plate, of which some noble households accumulated at least £2,000 worth, whereas furniture was regarded as primarily utilitarian and, until the emergence of skilled cabinet-makers in the eighteenth century, fit work for the local carpenter or joiner. Nevertheless, the multiplying rooms of the mansion – Ingatestone Hall had 60 including perhaps the first (1530) 'long gallery', Woburn Abbey, reconstructed by Inigo Jones, 90, including 11 sitting-rooms – required furnishing and decorating in a style more ostentatious and more comfortable than had satisfied previous generations. Contemporaries noted particularly the walls panelled in oak or covered with rich hangings, the plastered ceilings, 'the abundance of arras, rich hangings of tapistrie, silver vessels and so much other plate as may furnish sundrie cupboards'. Tapestry, as opposed to painted cloth, could be very costly indeed, especially when bought from France or the Netherlands, but even for five pieces from the royal factory at Mortlake, which depicted the Acts of the Apostles after the cartoons of Raphael, the Earl of Bedford paid £229 14s. in 1664. By comparison, the work of skilled masons was miserably paid, even when it amounted, in effect, to sculptured figures. For instance, the Earl of Cork recorded in his diary his negotiations for the interior decoration of a new house,

I have agreed with Christopher Watts, freemason and carver ... to make me a very fair chimney, also for my parlour, which is to reach up close to the ceiling, with my coat of arms complete with crest, helmet, coronet, supporters, mantling and font-pace, which he is to set up and finish all at his own charges, fair and graceful in all respects, and for that chimney I am to pay £10, and I am to find carriage also. He is also to make twelve figures each three foot high, to set upon my staircase, for which he demands 20s. apiece and I offer him 13s. 4d.

In the sixteenth century furniture was still practical and unsophisticated and based on earlier, traditional forms – the refectory table, perhaps now with extending draw-leaves, the joint stool, the high-backed arm-chair which, with the back folded down, also did duty as a table, the panelled coffer or chest and its near-relation, the buffet. The most expensive single item was still the 4-poster bed, with carved or inlaid pillars, ornate head, tester, curtains, vallances and fringes, which could easily add up to several hundred pounds: next in cost was probably the court-cupboard or cabinet, increasingly made of fine woods such as rosewood or walnut, or of oak inlaid with marquetry: in the next century, a fine tortoiseshell specimen was valued at over £100. Chairs, too, were becoming more elaborately turned and carved, and more often covered and upholstered for comfort, particularly after the fashion for wide, padded breeches went out towards the end of the century. The Duke of Rutland bought for his house at Belvoir in the 1550s a stool covered with red cloth at 14s. 7d., 2 black and 1 red leather-covered chairs costing 44s. The inventory of Sir Henry Unton of Wodley in Berkshire records 2 chairs of green cloth, 1 in black wrought velvet laid with silver and gold lace, a velvet chair and 6 stools in tuft taffeta, and in a bedroom, 1 yellow velvet chair, 2 yellow velvet stools and a yellow velvet cushion for the window seat. At about the same time Sir William Petre bought for his long gallery a musical instrument which, at £50, must have been either a large organ or a fine, decorated virginal with cover: a small, portable organ cost him only 40s.

During the seventeenth century furniture-making first began to develop into a specialized craft with styles distinguishable as Jacobean, William and Mary and so on. Noblemen's houses were required to reflect changes in fashion, and some families spent a good deal in re-equipping themselves in the current style. Bedford House in the Strand, the Earl's London residence, was refurbished just before the Civil War, the Terrace Room with tapestries, a couch, elbow-chairs and stools covered in figured satin or velvet decorated with silver lace, the Long Gallery with red velvet, and the writing room in green silk and silver: £25 was spent on a billiard-table for Woburn. A little later in the century Randle Holme, Server of the Chamber in Extraordinary to Charles II, specified the necessary furnishings for a dining-room and bedroom: the dining-room should be 'well wainscotted about . . . hung with pictures of all sorts', should have a large table in the middle, square with leaves to draw out or round or oval with folding leaves, side-tables or court cupboards for cups and glasses, sugar-box, mustard-pots etc., a cistern of brass or pewter for bottles of wine and beer, chairs of leather or Turkey-work, flower-pots and alabaster figures to adorn the windows and a large looking-glass at the high end of the room. The bedroom required a large poster bed with curtains, a dressing-box with drawers, a large mirror, a couch, chair, stools, a close-stool, window curtains, flower-pots, grate and implements, 'pictures of Friends and Relations to adorne the roome' and the usual hangings of arras, tapestry, damask, silk or cloth. Pictures feature importantly in most seventeenth-century accounts, not only for the gallery but for all principal rooms, and the prices demanded even by fashionable artists seem not excessive. Abraham Staphorst in 1660 charged the Earl of Bedford a mere £3 apiece for portraits of his sons, Lely £25 for a portrait of Lady Diana and, for a three-quarter length painting of the Earl himself, £31: a suitable frame cost another £3. Godfrey Kneller painted six portraits of the Earl, at prices rising as his reputation grew, from £8 to £40, and one of his grandson, Wriothesley, for £25 plus £2 10s. for a gold frame.

All contemporary observers of the social scene speak, usually in strongly critical terms, of the extravagance and expensiveness of the clothes worn by wealthy Englishmen and their women. The example was, indeed, set from above, Queen Elizabeth being reputed to possess no less than 3,000 gowns, and the royal court continued to lead the way in sumptuous attire until, in 1665, Charles II resolved to spend nothing on dress that was not 'of the growth of England'. But high fashion and expensive clothes were no longer restricted to the nobility, for, according to Stubbes, 'it is very hard to know who is noble, who is worshipfull, who is a gentleman, who is not, for you shall have those . . . go daiely in silkes, velvettes, satins, damaskes, taffaties and suche like, notwithstanding that they be bothe base by birthe, meane by estate and servile by callyng'. Sarcastic comments follow, especially about men's dress and their extravagant hats, ruffs, embroidered shirts, doublets 'slashed, jagged, cut, carved, pinched and laced' and 'stuffed with four, five or six pound of bombast at the least'. Women are similarly condemned for their extravagant gowns, their ruffs 'smeared and starched in the devil's liquor', their head-dresses and false hair sometimes, it appears, snipped from the head of a fair-haired child for the present of a penny. 'How much cost', complained Harrison in 1587, 'is bestowed nowadays upon our bodies, and how little upon our souls'.

It is not easy to estimate the average expenditure of a noble household on clothing. Large sums were spent on special occasions such as a wedding or funeral, but otherwise the family still purchased cloth and had it made up as needed. The cost of the material and its trimming was always much greater than the tailor's charge, and fine materials could be very costly. For instance, the Lestrange family at Christmas 1519 bought various materials for their servants' liveries at prices ranging from 4d. a yard (for canvas) to 4s. 8d., but 3 yards of black satin, enough for a coat or tunic, cost 21s. and $1\frac{1}{4}$ yards of cloth of gold 58s. 8d.: a black bonnet was 5s., 'six pairs of gloves for my master 2s. 4d.', and 2 lady's velvet hats 28s. It is the range of prices that is most striking – a day's wage for a labourer would buy a yard of the cheapest cloth, his wages for half a year would scarcely buy a yard of the dearest, and a fine cloak at £20 would require 3 years' labour. A single gift to Queen Elizabeth on one occasion was of £700 worth of clothes. Cambric cost around 20s. the ell, Granado silk, used for shirts, 2s. 8d. the ounce, satin 10s. a yard and green taffeta sarcenet, used for lining bed hangings, 7s. the ell. When Dorothy, Sir William Petre's eldest daughter, was married in 1555 to Nicholas Wadham (the founder of the Oxford college) the whole affair cost Petre £73, mostly in clothes, £11 of which went on the wedding-gown. The same year another daughter, Thomasine, aged 10, was fitted up to be educated in the duties of a lady by entering the house of the 'Marquess' of Exeter, and her wardrobe of a black damask gown, a French hood, an expensive hat and one of the new farthingales cost £10.

The seventeenth century saw even greater variety in the number and quality of materials, both home-produced and imported as trade with the East developed. The list now included baize, bewpers, buffins, busyarns, bombazines, blankets, callamancoes, carrells, chamblettes, dormicks, durance, damask, Ypres frisadoes, fustians, felts, flannels, grograines, linsey-woolseys and wrekadoes, to name only a few of what some described as 'outlandish garments'. The best indication of regular dress expenditure at this time is given by the Earl of Bedford's household accounts. At the funeral of the old Earl in 1641 over £100 was spent on black cloth for the mourning, which lasted the servants through the following year: nearly as much again, however, was spent by the family, principally in children's clothes, and another £60 was added for replacements of household linen at Woburn. For the coronation of Charles II in 1661 the Earl and his son William were dressed in satin and brocade suits costing £120, with a similar sum paid to gold and silver workers for the embroidery, fringes and other trimmings: the Countess had a new set of jewellery, rubies and diamonds, at £255, while new liveries for the servants cost a further £245. Altogether it was an expensive year, for two younger sons had to start school at Westminster and their school outfits cost another £35: £6 4s. went on 2 stuff suits and coats, £1 4s. on 2 frieze coats and £1 12s. on shoes. At all times the household staff seem to have been well clothed, with a new suit each year of hard-wearing material: porters, for instance, were bought 6 yards of broadcloth at 10s. the yard and orange baize to line it at 2s. the yard, the making-up costing £1 18s. Footmen had frieze coats at 15s. and cloaks at £1 13s., while frocks and trousers for the postillion cost 12s. and falconers' hats bound with orange galloon 10s. each. On his personal attire the Earl spent between £120 and £280 a year, the variation representing the fluctuating state of his wardrobe as old clothes wore out and replacements became necessary. Materials were bought from drapers and mercers and made up by a London tailor or, for plain suits, a local man in Woburn, but it was always the gold and silver trimmings – buttons, thread, fringes and so on, that accounted for the greater part of the bill. A knotted fringe belt could cost £5, a silver embroidered hat £5 10s., broad gold wire £3 13s. the yard and a fine, large muslin cravat 7s.: in 1689 the Earl purchased a pair of the first umbrellas to appear in England at a cost of £4 2s.

The education of children was a growing expense of noble

households as greater importance came to be attached to culture and intellectual pursuits. In the past noble children had been 'educated' in what was then considered most important – courtly manners, the arts of war and the hunt – by a kind of apprenticeship as page in a leading courtier's household, and this continued to be the practice of most of the greatest families up to the reign of Elizabeth. But from this time onwards the claims of formal learning, either at school or under a private tutor, were being increasingly urged and accepted, while by the seventeenth century the continuation of this at university and, sometimes, even in foreign travel, had come to be recognized as requirements for a gentleman. Thus, Sir Thomas More had been brought up in the household of Cardinal Morton, but his own children were given a private tutor: later in the century, in 1564, it was characteristic that two such noble youths as Sir Philip Sidney and Fulke Greville should be sent to the recently refounded Shrewsbury School.

Formal education most often now began at home with a tutor for the children of the family and the numerous wards who were often in care: John Thornton, tutor to the Bedford children, received £30 a year, though this seems to have been unusually generous. There would be writing-paper to be bought, usually at about 4d. the quire, ink – a large jar for 2d. – and school-books, which were certainly cheaper since the development of printing, but still relatively costly. At the age of 9, Sir William Petre's son John was bought a copy of Terence, and during the next 2 years Aesop's *Fables* in Greek and Latin, Lucian's *Dialogues*, Ovid, Livy and a Greek dictionary: the price of books ranged from 8d. for a little Phraseologia to 11s. for a dictionary, with a Bible at 6s. and a Latin Testament at 2s. These would probably be children's editions, for much higher prices were often paid for original works, like the first edition of Froissart's *Chronicles* at 18s., Thomas Ogilby's *Book of the Coronation* at £2 and the 7 volumes of Sanford's *Genealogical History of the Kings and Queens of England* at £5 each volume. Noble patrons often helped struggling authors on a subscription basis, a typical contribution being £5. But there was also lighter reading in the later seventeenth century, including murder and witchcraft pamphlets at from 1d. to 6d.

each, and weekly newsletters of political intelligence, the annual subscription for which was about £4 or £5.

After a few years of tutoring, a boy (though not a girl) might go to a preparatory or 'petty' school like the one at Twickenham to which Bedford's sons went from Woburn, or the one at Dinton where the total fees, in 1633, were £4 a quarter: here, besides the headmaster, was a single usher and the headmaster's wife, who did duty as matron. At a London day-school £2 a year was a typical charge. From here boys went on to a public school, which, in this period, still merited the title by having a substantial proportion of free places for local children and a scale of fees for others according to income. At Winchester in the sixteenth century fees, including boarding, were £20 the year, at Westminster in 1660 £40; Shrewsbury gave free education to all on payment of an admission fee (10s. for a nobleman's son, 6s. 8d. for a knight's son and so on down to 4d. for the son of a local burgess). Harrow had 40 free scholars, and at Merchant Taylors 100 places were reserved for the poor, 50 for those who could afford 2s. 6d. a quarter and a further 100 for others at 5s. a quarter. The fact that there were so many new foundations about this time – Repton 1559, Rugby 1567, Uppingham 1584 and Harrow 1590 – indicates the growing interest and importance attached to education and the conscious efforts made by headmasters like Dr Busby to enrol the sons of the wealthy.

At university, entered now commonly at 16–18 rather than the 13–15 of medieval times, necessary costs appear to have been rather less than at boarding school. One of Petre's wards spent a year at Cambridge in the 1550s for a total cost of £9 which included tuition, food, books, clothes, laundry and fuel. This was probably a somewhat spartan existence, and by the seventeenth century life at Oxford or Cambridge was becoming, for some at least, a more enjoyable and expensive experience: tuition now cost from 13s. 4d. to £1 a term, a room from 5s. to 7s. 6d., but this required furnishing and Mathew Hutton had to pay for a chest (8s.), a desk, the hiring of a chair and table, the putting up of shelves, and 'my part for sealinge of my chamber' (£2 5s.). He also paid 5s. for the Freshman's feast, 2s. to the laundress, 1s. to the porter and £2 'to the tennis court': he went down owing his tutor £9 16s. 1d. Most undergraduates were still poor men's sons, though the infiltration of the wealthy like the Earl of Essex who had glass put in his chamber windows and paid 16s. for hangings of painted cloth for the walls, was beginning to change the character of university life. In most college halls there were three tables – the Fellows' Table which admitted earls, barons, gentlemen and doctors, a second for MAs, BAs, and eminent citizens, a third for 'people of low condition' – with a different standard of diet for each. Fellows received an allowance of 3d. for each dinner (11 a.m.) and supper (5 p.m.), but the scholars' table, according to Thomas Cogan, received 'boiled beef with pottage, bread and beer and no more', and lack of means compelled many to do without breakfast and to 'fag' for the better-off. Similarly, at Eton, the college caterer received a set weekly allowance for the feeding of each member according to rank — 3s. 4d. for the Provost and Fellows, 1s. 6d. for chaplains and 1s. for scholars and choristers. University statutes imposed strict penalties for attending the playhouse, frequenting inns or shops where tobacco was sold, the wearing of extravagant dress such as silks, satins and 'excessive ruffs' and for 'inordinate growth of hair'.

For the sons of the very rich, university education was, increasingly from the seventeenth century onwards, followed by a further two or three years' travel and study abroad, partly to acquire a degree of fluency in modern languages, partly to develop social graces such as fencing and dancing, partly merely for sight-seeing and pleasure. Such travels could be by far the most expensive part of a nobleman's education. When two of the Earl of Bedford's sons undertook a grand tour in the 1660s they required a travelling tutor at the high salary of £100 a year plus expenses, as well as stays of several months in numerous French and Italian cities and a period of study at the Protestant University of Saumur: altogether, the young men were abroad for six years at a total cost of over £5,000.

Recreation was also becoming, for the wealthy at least, a more organized and expensive activity than it had been in the past. Pride of place still went to the sports of the chase, which perhaps took on an even greater importance as warfare became a less frequent and more professional occupation: the country life of the nobility assumed horses and hunting as a normal part of existence. Fashions in sport changed somewhat over the period, hawking beginning to give place in the seventeenth century to the shooting of birds and the hunting of deer to fox and hare as a result of the break-up of deer-parks during the Civil War. The subsequent Cavalier Parliament, however, saw to it that the Game Laws were strengthened by an act which prevented all freeholders of less than £100 a year – by far the great majority – from killing game on their own property: a more blatant example of class legislation could hardly be found in the annals of English law. A great noble was prepared to devote an astonishingly high proportion of income to blood-sports, for not only had horses, hounds and hawks to be bought and kept but a large staff had to be maintained to feed and equip them. In 1550, for instance, Sir William Petre was buying hawks' hoods at 2s. 11d. each, two pairs of sparrow-hawks' bells 12d., and three pairs of couples 12d., besides which the 12d. for a pound of gunpowder 'to shoot at crows about the house' seems modest. The Earl of Bedford spent, in the first year of his inheritance in the 1640s, a mere £230 on the Woburn stables, kennels and mews, but as his fortunes advanced after the Restoration far greater sums were spent – from £1,000 to £1,700 a year, and an average of about £1,200. This, of course, included everything new that was bought, whether horse, hawk or dog, coach or chair, as well as the liveries of the Gentleman of the Horse and his 15 stablemen. Up to £50 was paid for geldings, coach horses were usually about £30, a falcon could cost £11 5s., a goshawk £8, a tercel-gentle £2 2s. 6d. The hawks, fed on pigeons, cost between £40 to £50 a year in food, the less delicate spaniels and beagles about £30.

So much was traditional and unchanging: it was the indoor and the urban pastimes that altered most noticeably during Tudor and Stuart times. At the beginning of the period one still finds payments to itinerant entertainers, the direct descendants of the medieval mummers and jugglers: Sir William Petre in the 1550s was still paying three minstrels who played at the door 6d., morris dancers 3s. 4d., 'the waits of St Edmund's Bury' 2s. and 'Gylder the tumbler at two several times' 3s. 4d. He was also employing more renowned performers for special occasions, like the boy choristers of St Paul's who sang a this town house, when he was convalescing, for 6s. 8d., and the 5 London musicians who played on the Ingatestone viols at Christmas for £3. But increasingly people of any rank were expected to make their own music, by singing and by playing on the lute, the viol or the virginals. A small viol in Tudor times cost 13s. 4d., a canvas bag to put it in 4d., and strings another 12d.: a gittin could be had for 6s., a lute from 8s. to 50s. and strings 2s. 10d. Petre paid 40s. for an organ, probably of the 'regal' type which stood on a table. A fine pair of virginals could cost up to £50, with as much as 14s. for 'mending and trimming'. Additionally, of course, were payments for music and for instruction, which were occasionally high, as Pepys discovered when he was required to pay Mr Berkenshaw £5 for a month's instruction in composition.

Less improving activities also cost some a good deal. Card-playing was an increasingly popular pastime, and always for money: Princess Mary's personal records for 1536–44 show that she drew from 12s. 6d. to 40s. each month from the Privy Purse for gaming, and Sir William Petre's steward was frequently lending him 5s. for play at cards, dice and backgammon, although Sir William saw to it that his tenants and labourers were fined (4d. or 8d.) for the offence. The theatre was, of course, another new recreation for the Elizabethan townsmen, who paid from 1d. to 3d. admission, and sometimes more for a seat in the galleries and rooms: the 'groundlings' stood in the open yard for their penny. The same amount also enabled one to climb to the top of St Paul's steeple, the best vantage point for the visitor to London to see the sights. The Elizabethan visitor to the capital might also have been surprised to see so much smoking of tobacco 'by an instrument formed like a little ladell' which 'is greatlie taken-up and used in England'. Barnaby Rich in 1614 estimated that tobacco was sold in 7,000 shops with an annual trade of £399,375. Some men were already heavy smokers. In the late seventeenth century the Earl of Bedford consumed between 20 and 30 lb. a year, approximately an ounce a day: Virginian was about 2s. 6d. a pound, Spanish 10s., while clay pipes, bought from Gauntlett's, cost £1 16s. for a dozen gross.

Much leisure time in the Tudor and Stuart period was taken up merely by visiting friends and relations. Even a medium-sized household like that of Sir William Petre regularly had some 40 guests in winter and 80 in summer, while the Lestranges entertained a couple of hundred at festive seasons. Perhaps the cost of such lavish entertaining, apart from the travel involved, tended to cancel out since similar hospitality would be expected in return. The one exception to this was a royal visit, a practice extensively employed by Elizabeth as a way, it was claimed, of reducing her expenses as well as seeing and being seen throughout the country. A 2- or 3-day visit by the Queen and her travelling retinue to a noble household was a dreaded event, always involving considerable expenditure. A 3-day visitation in 1561 cost Petre £136, with expenses ranging from the purchase of 3 oxen (£4 each), 6 cygnets (10s. each) and 18 herons (22d. each) to 3 dozen extra trenchers (18d.), 13 ells of taffeta sarcenet to line the curtains of the royal suite (£4 11s.), and '¼ lb. of fusses for perfuming of chambers' (20d.). This was a visit early in the reign, before Elizabeth's more extravagant tastes had developed, and in fact Petre escaped lightly. A 4-day visit to Sir Nicholas Bacon in 1577 cost him £577, each of a dozen to Cecil at his palace of Theobald's about £1,000, and a mere three days at Lord Keeper Egerton's in 1602 £2,000. The cost of 3 weeks' princely entertainment by Leicester at Kenilworth Castle in 1575 is unrecorded, although one contemporary put it at £1,000 a day.

Travel was a growing expense at a time when personal movement was easier and more pleasurable than in previous centuries. The main roads at least were generally serviceable, so that coaches and waggons were slowly beginning to replace horseback and sumpter-horse for the carriage of people and goods respectively. Establishments of any size kept their own animals and vehicles – the largest of all naturally being that of Elizabeth, whose travelling retinue consisted of 400 carriages and carts, each drawn by 5 or 6 horses – but there was also increasing use of public provision as facilities improved. Coaches without springs were not especially comfortable on the uneven surfaces of the day, and for fast travel of up to 70 miles a day a man could hire post-horses at fixed stages for 3d. a mile (2½d. if on government business) with a further 6d. to the post-boy who returned with the mount. In London the horse-litter was still much used by ladies until the sedan chair became popular in the reign of Charles I. In 1607 Fynes Morison reported that it was possible to hire a coach for journeys near London at the rate of 10s. the day, and by this time most provincial towns had an organized carrier service for goods at fixed prices: the Oxford carrier, for instance, charged 2s. 4d. for each hundredweight on the 2-day journey to London. From this kind of service developed in the seventeenth century the passenger stage-coach, not cheap, but offering a generally reliable service: a single day's journey, like London to Tunbridge, cost 8s., a 4-day journey such as London to York, Exeter or Chester 40s. in summer and 45s. in winter, and to Durham 55s. (no time of arrival guaranteed), plus at least 3s. from each passenger for the coachman's drink. The connexions thus established in the late seventeenth century between towns and large villages throughout the length of the country were an important economic and social advance, initiating the process of unification which the railways completed two centuries later: letters, news and goods, as well as people themselves, acquired a new mobility probably unequalled in Europe.

From the accounts of the Bedford family it is possible to glimpse some of the problems and costs of transport for a noble household in the late seventeenth century. In addition to the heavy expenses of his own horses and stables, to which previous reference has been made, the Earl and his servants spent about £100 a year on public transport around London and between his London house and Woburn. The Flying Coach charged 11s. for this journey, the slower Dunstable coach 6s. For journeys in London the Earl often hired a hackney coach, the first regular stand for which had been established on the Strand by one Captain Bailey in 1633: this could be had for 8s. 6d. the day, and had the advantage of being exactly opposite his London house. When the Countess was seized with smallpox at Woburn and the famous Dr John Clarke sent to effect her cure, as much as £2 4s. was charged by the coachman. The Thames was still a great highway, and river travel probably offered the most comfortable journeys of the day: the Earl

A HISTORY OF THE COST OF LIVING

kept his own barge (stored in Rayner's Yard for £1 a quarter) but occasionally hired a river boat from the Strand to Westminster (6d.) or to Chiswick (2s. 6d. return). A chair to St Clement Danes at 2s. 6d. seems expensive, and in coronation year the Earl decided to buy one for his wife's use at £6: a new 'chariot' in 1682 cost him £130, the 'extras' such as velvet upholstery, glass for the windows and japanning amounting to more than the basic cost.

Movement about the country was also growing in comfort as a result of the extensive provision of inns offering meals and lodging of a generally high standard. 'Ordinaries' – that is, set meals – were available at 6d. and sometimes 4d., but a gentleman and his guests usually dined in a private room and commanded what food they pleased: in this case the bill, with appropriate tips to the cook and waiters, could be considerable. In the reign of Charles I Lord Conway's supper at Jeronymo's in London cost 11s. 6d. and a dinner at The Bear with a party of friends £3 9s.: when the Earl of Bedford made a ceremonial visit to Cambridge, accompanied by harps, trumpets and bells, splendid dinners were given at The Red Lion to leading citizens and dignitaries of the University, one of which alone cost £18 11s. – it consisted of 28 dishes ranging from 'a brace of carp stewed with some perches ranged about them' (£1 9s.) to 'a dish of tongues, udders and marrowbones, with cauliflowers and spinach' (11s. 6d.).

Finally, sickness and its cure also involved noble households in growing expense. Advances in medical knowledge were slowly raising the status of the profession to a point where fashionable doctors who attended the Court could command up to £100 for a cure, while the growing concern for the health of one's family and servants required more frequent resort to doctors, surgeons, barbers and apothecaries. In the sixteenth century a single attendance usually cost 5s. or 6s. 8d., apparently with little distinction between surgeons' and physicians' fees, but a serious illness would involve many visits and innumerable prescriptions. When Sir William Petre was gravely ill with the stone, an ulcerated leg and a rupture his bill totalled £20, of which £17 went in professional fees and the remainder in pharmaceutical stuff. The prevailing belief in polypharmacy –

the mixing of many ingredients in one prescription in the hope that at least one would cure or relieve – often resulted in heavy drug bills and a plethora of herbs, oils, liquids and potions. In a period of 2 months Petre was prescribed 38 distinct remedies ranging from 'maidenhair 2d.' and 'a box of unguentum album 8d.' to 'allocium to gargle with 12d.' and 'a plaster for the stomach 5s.'. Seventeenth-century medical expenses were higher still. The Earl of Bedford paid £20 for the cure of his wife from the dreaded smallpox in 1641, with another 5s. to the porter for fumigating the house with pitch and frankincense, and in addition to bills for serious illnesses of this kind paid out around £30 a year to apothecaries for medicines and the treatment of minor ailments. Barbers regularly came to Woburn to treat the toothache, for which service 5s. was the usual fee: a corn-cutter paid regular visits to the Earl at 2s. 6d. a time. Spectacles, by contrast, seem cheap at 5s. the pair, and the extraction of a tooth was generally done for 1s. The whole household, from the Earl down to the chamber-maids, was bled several times a year, not in connexion with particular illnesses, but merely as a precaution against 'hysteria': 1s. 6d. to 2s. 6d. was the normal charge for 'opening a vein'. Next to this, the most frequent expenses were for purging potions (1s. 6d.), and for anti-scorbutic juices and tinctures (2s. 6d.) necessitated by the prevalence of scurvy.

4

If no easy generalization about the fate of the aristocracy under the impact of the economic changes of the sixteenth and seventeenth centuries can be made, the same is true of their social inferiors, the gentry. One of the liveliest historical debates of recent years has centred round the undoubted shift in the balance of power between these two classes, and whether this shift was due fundamentally to their differing abilities to adapt to the new economic pressures of the period. R. H. Tawney and Lawrence Stone have suggested that the aristocracy in general failed to adjust to rising prices owing to their traditional methods of farming and land-holding and their unwillingness to reduce expenses, while the more go-ahead gentry were able to apply the capitalist techniques derived from trade and the law to make their estate-management much more profitable: political as well as economic power, it is argued, therefore gradually swung to them during the century that preceded the Civil War.

One of the difficulties of the discussion is to know precisely who the gentry were. The nobility were at least a homogeneous class distinguished by the possession of a title, but the equivalent grant of arms does not serve to differentiate a class in which there were so many false claims to gentility. The gentry were those who were so regarded in their localities, largely on the basis of wealth and hospitality, but a gentleman in a poor county might be richer than a noble, and in a rich one poorer than a mere yeoman. Frequently they were distinguished by the possession of a knighthood or by appointment to the magistracy: they were the men of middling wealth, sharply divided from their superiors though imperceptibly from their inferiors.

The members of a class which is, by definition, 'middling', are unlikely to be standing still, more likely to be moving either upwards or downwards in the social hierarchy. Undoubtedly, some of the gentry increased their fortunes at this time by efficient estate-management, by watching market-trends and enclosing lands for whatever was most profitable – sheep or corn – at different times. In areas not populated by freeholders or protected copyholders, rack-renting of tenants could also be lucrative. But in general it seems that mere landowning rarely conferred great wealth, and that those gentry prospered most who combined the possession of estates with the holding of office under the Crown – the grant of wardship, monopolies, export licences or posts in the customs service – or with practice in the law, business or trade. Professor Trevor-Roper has therefore stressed the division between the court gentry and the country gentry, only the former of whom participated in the alleged 'rise'. Five per cent per year was considered a fair profit from land in the sixteenth century, but Sir Richard Gresham, the great Tudor merchant and financier, made 15 per cent a year and could afford to pay £11,000 for Fountains Abbey. It does not, of course, follow from this that the 'mere landlord' who had no such supplements to income necessarily suffered a reduction in wealth. It has been calculated that sheep-farming, which brought a profit of from £3 12s. to £5 per 'long hundred' (120) in the 1540s, was yielding about £14 in the 1620s; from this it does not seem that the sheep-farmer had much to fear from inflation. Similarly, rents in general moved upwards, in fairly close conformity with the cost of living. If mere agriculture brought no vast profits, it gave a dependable livelihood and it seems likely that 'the declining gentry' were not a product of the agrarian changes *per se* but of idiosyncratic characteristics and circumstances.

Of the 'new men' who forced their way into the ranks of the gentry through public service Nicholas Bacon, the Lord Keeper, is an outstanding example. The son of a sheep-reeve of the monastery of Bury St Edmunds, Nicholas had the advantage of birth in the prosperous farming country of East Anglia: other examples of social mobility from the same area include Wolsey and Gardiner, the children respectively of a butcher and a cloth-maker. In each case the key to success was education. After studies at Cambridge and Gray's Inn Bacon received his first appointment as solicitor to the Court of Augmentations in 1537 at a salary rising from £10 to £70 a year: 9 years later he was promoted to attorney to the Court of Wards at £90 a year, and after 12 years more to the altogether different status of Lord Keeper at £1,200 a year. Gratuities from litigants may have added another £1,600 a year, and by the end of his life his total income from offices and lands was not less than £5,500 a year. Throughout his career Bacon consistently bought land as and when he could, and during the 20 years of his Keepership his annual expenditure on it amounted to £1,380. By the end he had bought £40,000 worth of property, including 30 manors and 3 country houses, Redgrave Hall, Gorhambury Hall and Stiffkey Hall. At his death in 1579 he left, besides his vast estates, £2,450 in cash and another £2,000 in plate.

Even in the early sixteenth century the gentry constituted by far the largest landowners in the country, easily outstripping in total the possessions of the nobility. In Rutland in the 1520s they owned 54·6 per cent of all lay-owned land, in Buckinghamshire 57·6 per cent. The annual value of gentry property, based on the subsidy assessments, averaged about £140 for knights (with only one at £1,000), £60 for esquires and £15 for gentlemen: it is clear that the ownership of a £10 freehold just conferred the status of gentility. As in the nobility, there was an enormous range of wealth between the top and bottom, between a knight like Sir William Waldegrave of Suffolk with a household staff of 2 esquires, 2 gentlemen and 24 manservants, and a plain 'gentleman' almost indistinguishable from a yeoman farmer. Assuming the class to have been fairly equally distributed through the country, estimates would give a total size for the gentry in the early sixteenth century of some 5,000. In 1688 Gregory King estimated knights at 600 (average income £650 per family), esquires at 3,000 (average income £450) and gentlemen – the loosest of all categories – at 12,000 (average income £280): a rise of 300 per cent may not be unlikely in view of the total growth of population and the undoubted ease of mobility into the class.

Although predominant in land-holding, the gentry owned a much smaller proportion of movable goods – a mere 15·8 per cent of those in Buckinghamshire, 16·3 per cent of those in Rutland. The total possessions of knights and squires accorded quite closely with the annual values of their estates, those of the former amounting to some £150 on average and of the latter to about £75. By contrast, the wealth of gentlemen was often measured in chattels rather than in real estate. As a class their average possessions perhaps totalled £30–£40, but individuals having a connexion with trade or a profession could be as rich in personal property as a knight. Thus William Lane of Hogshaw, Bucks, who was also a Merchant of the Staple, had his goods assessed at £300 in 1522, and Robert Ashbrooke, mercer of Chipping Wycombe, was one of the richest men in the county with £240.

A collection of household inventories of Oxfordshire, covering the years 1550–90, records the possessions of the wealthiest member of the gentry, Mrs Katherine Doylye, as totalling £590 18s. 1d. She occupied a house of 5 main rooms – a hall, parlour, great chamber and 2 other chambers – besides 7 service rooms such as kitchen, dairy, buttery, cheese chamber and so on. The house must have been furnished comfortably, though not luxuriously: items included a draw-leaf table (£2), 8 feather beds and linen (£19 16s. 8d.), 5 iron-bound chests (£3 10s.), painted hangings, cupboards, chairs, stools, a looking-glass, 12 cushions (£3), a lute (£1 10s.), pewter (£2 13s. 4d.), silver plate (£3 6s. 8d.) and gold jewellery (£37 12s. 8d.). There were 109 sheep (£13 12s. 6d.) and 3 old horses (£6). At the other end of the gentry scale, Anthony Hall of South Newington had goods totalling £48 10s. and lived in a house containing only a hall, some chambers and a dairy. There was a single table surrounded by 2 forms and 5 stools, but no chairs or settles, painted cloths or carpets. His most valuable property was his cattle – 7 cows, 1 heifer and 3 yearlings – worth £11.

It is, in fact, the contrasts within the gentry class that are most significant. Many so-called 'gentlemen', and even some properly styled knights, existed at a standard of comfort no higher than that of the husbandman, occupying a scantily furnished cottage and deriving their living from their own toil in the fields. Thus a knight, Sir Harry Firebrace of Driffield, Staffs., died in 1543 with goods totalling a mere £5 15s. 10d. He owned 2 bedsteads, 3 pairs of sheets, 2 blankets and 4 coverlets, 1 chest, 1 meat board, 2 forms, 2 shelves, 2 stools and 1 chair: it seems that he occupied a 2-roomed cottage, perhaps with a loft above. A somewhat better-off knight, Sir William Bee Clarke, died in 1551 possessed of goods worth £7 2s. 10d. He seems to have been reasonably well-supplied with clothes, since he left 2 gowns, a lined russet frock, 1 short gown, 1 cloak, 1 short worsted jacket and 1 cloth jacket among other items: the contents of his house, however, were much the same as a husbandman's, embellished only by 2 little hangings, a candlestick, 5 pewter dishes and 3 saucers. The standard of living of mere countrymen, unassisted by the profits of office, trade or law, had a broad similarity, varied perhaps by the possession of a few 'luxury' items – a feather bed instead of a flock one, a few pewter vessels, a cushion or two and a candlestick in place of rush-lights.

At the other end of the scale, the rich gentry could easily outstrip the wealth of some of the nobility. Sir Thomas Gresham, merchant, royal financier and banker, accumulated furniture and effects valued at £7,550, and left his widow an annuity of £2,000, twice as much as a peer might have done. Even a 'mere landlord' like Sir Henry Slingsby, without trading connexions, could live on his country estate in Yorkshire in the 1630s in a patriarchal, self-sufficing style comparable with that of a feudal lord. At the Red House he maintained an establishment of 16 men and 8 women servants to minister to a family of 6: he had no London house until he entered Parliament as MP for Knaresborough, when he rented one in Lincoln's Inn Fields at 22s. a week. Sir Henry, though the heir to a Jacobean baronetcy, had before going up to Cambridge been educated for 9 years, like many a yeoman's son, at the local free school kept by the parson.

When land-owning was combined with high office under the Crown, as in the case of Sir William Petre, the pattern of life was indistinguishable from that of the aristocracy. On an estate purchased at the Dissolution for £849 12s. 6d., Petre built a 60-room mansion with one of the first ceilinged halls and long galleries in the country (1540–44). Here he maintained an almost self-sufficient existence, his purchases of food amounting, on average, to a mere 12s. a week, yet he entertained lavishly besides supporting the family and 60 servants. Enormous quantities of food and drink were prepared and consumed – 20,000 loaves of bread a year, up to 168 lb. of cheese each week, pigeons by the thousand and eggs by the long hundred (120): home-brewed ale was produced at the cost of 200 gallons for 20s. and drunk at the rate of a gallon per head per day; wine cost on average 1s. the gallon. The 60 staff for his 3 houses took £250 a year, in addition to which there were innumerable expenses for services of special kinds – messengers and carriers, carpenters and furniture-makers, blacksmiths, tailors, musicians and jugglers. In winter the house was lit with candles at 2d. a pound and heated with coal at about 10s. the chaldron, while the estate itself constantly demanded tools and materials ranging from bricks at 4s. the thousand to a farm-cart 57s., a plough 3s. 8d., horse-shoes (2d. to 4d., according to size) and 'a trap of wire to take mice' requested by the butler and costing 10d.

In return for all this expenditure Petre, and others like him, undoubtedly lived handsomely. In particular, there was always an abundance and wide variety of food – no French chef, but dishes highly spiced and sauced and no doubt attractive to an Elizabethan palate. A typical day's meals consisted of

Dinner: six pieces of boiled beef, a neat's tongue, a leg of pork, three humble pies, two loins of pork, a shoulder, breast and rack of veal, two pigs, two joints of mutton, two capons, a coney, half a lamb, three teals and two woodcocks; Supper: nine joints of mutton, three capons, a hen, half a lamb, a pheasant, a venison pasty, a coney, two woodcocks and a partridge.

Bread, wine and ale were always available, and could be had on rising, though no formal breakfast was served. A century and a half later the pattern of meals had hardly changed. 'A Bill of Fare for Gentlemen's Houses of Lesser Quality' published in 'The Queen-like Closet' of 1684, suggests a dinner menu of 13 separate dishes. 'After these are taken away, then serve in your cheese and fruit. Note, that this Bill of Fare is for Familiar Times.'

Below the gentry in status, though not necessarily in wealth, stood the class of whom Tudor sovereigns always expressed the greatest pride – the yeomen. They would have been hard put to it to offer a definition. Yeomen – the earlier term 'franklin' had dropped out of use by the sixteenth century - were those substantial farmers who came between gentlemen and mere husbandmen: legally, the term suggested the ownership of a freehold of 40s. a year, but yeomen frequently rented former demesne land in addition, and in some areas they were exclusively copyholders. It was, in fact, an economic and social status, not a legal one, and a tenant-farmer could qualify as well as an owner 'in fee simple'. If a line between them and the husbandmen can be drawn, it may be at about 100 acres: dietetically, they were distinguished by the composition of their bread, the yeoman having good 'yeoman bread' of wheat, the husbandman usually eating a mixture of whatever grains were available.

The characteristics of the class were supposed to be their industry, frugality, patriotism and solid worth. Although some aspired to, and achieved, gentility, most were content to farm their lands quietly, to invest wisely, to educate their sons and pass on a better inheritance than they had acquired: they were not expected to maintain lavish establishments for hospitality, nor were they liable to onerous burdens of office. Robert Loder's farm accounts for the decade 1610–20 indicate a yearly income of from £200 to £300, and this was probably not untypical of a wealthier yeoman. They were certainly large accumulators of land, Tawney's analysis of some 4,000 transactions between 1570 and 1640 showing purchases of up to £2,100, and although more than half were of properties under £100, 14 per cent ranged from £200 to £500 and 8 per cent over £500. Some of these richer yeomen were also taking advantage of the booming industry of the period to invest in coal and iron, alum and calamine, or to use their capital as entrepreneurs in the wool and cloth trades. But there were great variations of wealth within the class. In 1600 Thomas Wilson estimated that there were 10,000 wealthy yeomen with incomes from £300 to £500, a further 60,000 less wealthy, from £40 to £100 a year. Nearly a century later Gregory King put 'freeholders of the better sort' at 40,000 and 'freeholders of the lesser sort' at 120,000. If the two sets of figures are accurate and comparable, the Stuart period had witnessed a remarkable growth in the size of the yeomanry.

It seems likely that the great price-rise favoured rather than injured the class. The general increase in food prices and rents, running ahead of wages, would be an advantage to farmers who produced for the market and who held their land in freehold, in copyhold or on long leases. For the efficient, industrious man such times were likely to produce, if not sudden wealth, at least wider opportunities and rising standards of comfort. Many yeomen were in the forefront of the enclosure movement, exchanging uneconomic strips of land for compact farms, adding to their holdings by 'intakes' from the waste or fen: they farmed, not for subsistence, but to sell corn, meat and cheese to the near-by towns, wool and skins to markets farther afield. 'Yeomen', wrote Harrison, 'are farmers to gentlemen; and with grazing, frequenting of markets and keeping of servants (not idle servants such as gentlemen do, but such as get their own and part of their master's living) so come to great wealth.'

This was no doubt an idealized picture, and not all men were able to survive the competitive pressures of an inflationary economy. Latimer, in a famous sermon delivered before Edward

VI in 1549, complained that whereas his father had been able to rent a farm for £3 or £4 the year which had provided work for 6 men, pasture for 100 sheep and 30 cows, and had enabled him to educate his sons and portion his daughters, now his successor paid £16 'and is not able to do any thing for his Prince, for himself, nor for his children, or give a cup of drink to the poor'. Although Latimer describes his father as a yeoman, he sounds more like a husbandman, for whom the price-rise did not necessarily bring benefits. The evidence of wills and inventories suggests substantially rising standards of comfort for the yeoman proper throughout the Tudor and Stuart periods. A large number of inventories from Lincolnshire and Nottinghamshire between 1575 and 1639 give a median value of possessions (household goods, furniture, clothes, livestock and cash) of £111 for yeomen and £61 for husbandmen, and comparing the value of possessions with the rise in prices it appears that the former had considerably outstripped the latter by the closing years of the seventeenth century.

It was the accumulation of goods that marked the yeomanry from the classes below them. Their houses might be indistinguishable from those of husbandmen's; those who had no connexion with Court or pretensions to gentility dressed simply, even rudely, but one and all bought property to pass on to their descendants – land if they could, and personal property of a durable kind. Thus Robert Child of Peddington, Bedfordshire, who died in 1582, left goods worth the substantial but typical sum of £107: he lived in a cottage with hall, parlour, kitchen and buttery, with 2 rooms above furnished as bedrooms, but like other richer yeomen he had started to build himself a half-timbered 2-storey house of a size and style previously unknown in the village. Inside the house were goods of a luxury that would also be rare – 2 carpets, 3 window cloths, 4 cushions, besides tables and cupboards, forms and stools, bedsteads, feather beds and bolsters, blankets, coverlets and table-cloths. Probably the wealthiest yeoman's inventory recorded was that of Thomas Taylor of Witney, who died in 1583 with goods valued at £408. He lived in a large courtyarded house of 25 rooms, many of them service rooms like the buttery, the milk-house, the brewery and the wool-house, and it is clear that apart from selling agricul-

A HISTORY OF THE COST OF LIVING

tural produce such as barley, hops, cheese and wool, he dealt in many commodities used in industry and building. The mention of a warping-house suggests that he may have supplied the Witney blanket weavers with yarn, and he also traded in leather, hides and skins, timber and laths. From the contents of the house this was clearly a man of substance and probably education: there were a number of books, a Venetian carpet, many cushions of silk and velvet, glass in the windows (all separately valued) and curtains of red and green says besides the more common court cupboards and settles, joint chairs and stools. Taylor's wearing apparel was valued at £9 7s., his wife's at £8 16s. 10d., so they must have been well dressed by the standards of the day. The sum of 11s. 2d. was paid to the physician and the apothecary who attended him at the end, and he was buried simply in the village churchyard, £2 being distributed among the poor in bread and 2 graves for Thomas and his wife costing a mere 3s. 4d.

The food of the yeoman had no distinctive features beyond the generally high quality of his bread. Much depended on his personal wealth and the degree of self-sufficiency of his household, but most seem to have fared simply yet plentifully from traditional dishes on which the growing sophistication of the town had as yet had little influence. Thomas Tusser writes of 'roast meat on Sundays and Thursdays at night', but for the rest of the week pease and bacon, fish and 'white meats' washed down with home-brewed ale or cider: there would be pies of meat or fruit, brawn, pudding and souse, and for more special occasions a goose or turkey, capons and chickens. But winter fare must have been sparse and monotonous enough, with few vegetables or fruits, and only preserved meat and dried fish. Many inventories of the period mention the sides of beef or bacon hanging in the chimney which had to serve the family until the following spring, for even at the end of the seventeenth century the winter-feeding of cattle by turnips was still sufficiently rare to make fresh meat prohibitively expensive: at this time of year pigeons and small birds of all sorts were a welcome addition to the table.

5

The yeoman – the basis of the rural middle class – had his urban counterpart in the merchant and the professional man. It has been said with some justice that there has never been a century in recent history that did not witness 'the Rise of the Middle Class', yet there can hardly be any doubt that the rapid growth of towns, especially of London, the development of new industries, and the exploitation of new markets that characterized Tudor and Stuart England favoured those whose occupation lay in buying and selling, in lending or in providing skilled services. Inflation no doubt benefited the merchant, selling the product of other men's labour, more than the professional man with only his own skill to sell, but with the possible exception of the clergy it seems that the times brought, in varying measure, prosperity to all members of the class.

The great merchant was a new phenomenon of Tudor times. It may be that England still had none to compare with a Continental business firm like the Fuggers of Augsburg, reputed to be worth £875,000 in the middle of the century, for the Venetian ambassador in 1557 estimated the wealth of the richest London merchants at between £50,000 and £60,000. Yet this was vast wealth in a relatively poor country, placing its possessors on an economic equality with the greatest aristocrats in the land. 'They have sought out the East and West Indies', wrote Harrison, 'and made voyages not only into the Canaries and New Spain, but likewise into Cathay, Muscovy, Tartary and regions thereabout, from whence (as they say) they bring home great commodities'. By the end of the century these same men were venturing into the Pacific, and the East India Company was soon paying 20 per cent and, later, 40 per cent profit on its original stock. One of its Stuart directors, Sir Josiah Child, was reputed to be worth £200,000.

As with the classes previously discussed, the extreme range of income between top and bottom makes any generalization about the wealth of the merchants impossible: they were distinguishable as a class by their identity of interests, not by equality of income. John Winchcombe, the prototype of the capitalist merchant clothier with his hundreds of employees, William

Stumpe, who bought Malmesbury Abbey for conversion into a cloth factory, and Thomas Spring of Lavenham, whose widow was the wealthiest person in the county after the Duke of Norfolk, were the exceptional magnates, quite untypical of the class as a whole. Similarly, the substantial and often beautiful merchants' houses of brick, stone and half-timbering that have survived in some old boroughs have survived precisely because they were larger or more solidly built than the majority that perished. The merchant oligarchies that controlled civic life were small, exclusive and largely hereditary, inter-marrying mainly within their own circle and passing on their wealth and power to their own children: an almost impassable gulf separated such men from the petty shopkeepers, chandlers, mercers and general dealers who constituted the bulk of the trading class in any Tudor or Stuart town. But, in trade pre-eminently, little men always had a chance, by outstanding merit or great good fortune, of entering the ranks of the merchant princes. London, which probably grew in population 5 times during the period, required a massive influx of new recruits, and it is highly significant that of 172 Lord Mayors between 1480 and 1660 only 14 were London-born, and of the 403 wealthiest merchants (ascertained by the value of their wills) only 10 per cent. About half probably had some previous connexion with trade in the provinces, the rest being merely the sons of yeomen and smaller farmers: their only entrance requirements were aptitude, ambition and the premium demanded by a gild for its apprentices – at least £10 by a great company like the Goldsmiths, £1 or £2 by a lesser one.

Even in the mid-sixteenth century some merchants' wills indicate personal estates of £6,000 and more, in addition to land. Most successful men bought country estates, partly for a safe investment, partly for social prestige. Rowland Heyward died owning 18 manors, besides numerous properties in London; Richard Gresham owned lands of an annual value of £800. But these were the successful few, alongside whom were others who went bankrupt, had to be relieved by the charity of their gild, or died in poverty. Which were the more numerous cannot be known.

The extent of charity nevertheless indicates something important about the wealth and the social conscience of the class.

Professor W. K. Jordan has calculated that the 438 'greater merchants' donated, in the period 1480–1660, charitable bequests amounting to £907,000, almost half the total for the capital. This represents an average of more than £2,000 each. They gave to charities throughout the country – no doubt in remembrance of their own provincial origins – and in almost all cases gave, not indiscriminately, but in the form of well-organized trusts. £178,000 was left by these greater merchants for the foundation of grammar schools: Gresham founded a college in London, Thomas White St John's College, Oxford. Relief of the poor was, of course, the major concern but, equally significant, religion was now the lowest in order of priority. The figures suggest that the wealthy burgesses of Tudor and Stuart England were no less public-spirited than their medieval predecessors, though the direction of their philanthropy had changed noticeably.

A particularly well-documented account of the career of a successful Stuart merchant has survived for Sir Thomas Cullum. His father was a substantial yeoman, able to afford the £50 demanded by the Draper's Company for his son's apprenticeship: this lasted for eight years, and Thomas began his professional life in 1615 with £92. Another £200 was paid to him by his brother John under the terms of their father's will. For the next 5 years Thomas worked for his old master as a journeyman, at a wage rising from £20 to £40 a year, and by frugal living, wise investment and money-lending he was able to raise his capital to £1,000 and to buy a one-eighth share in his employer's business. His profits from the sale of cloth and from dyeing at the end of the first year's trading were £205 on an investment of £1,250. On his marriage to Mary Crisp, a wealthy merchant's daughter with relatives in the booming African trade, he received a dowry of £600 and a promise of a further £100 for every child born of the union. By 1623 he had made his second thousand pounds, and next year started his own business, becoming one of the privileged 80 or so liverymen of his Company in 1627. During the next 20 years profits averaged around £1,000 each year, so that by 1641 he had amassed the very substantial fortune of £20,000. His household expenses at this period averaged about £550 a year, made up of food (£294 average), company entertainment (£67), rent (£73), apparel for family and servants (£77), household goods (£33), fuel and light (£20), doctor's bills and medicines (£17) and wages (£50): though he clearly ate well and gave considerable hospitality, he still lived in a rented house, and the value of his silver plate, which was £80 at his marriage, was only £150 20 years later. But after the Civil War his years of hard work and careful husbandry of resources bore rich fruit. By the 1650s profits were £2,000–£3,000 a year: he was buying property in London, East India Company shares and a country estate, Hawstead Place, costing £18,000. A baronetcy was conferred in 1660. He had now been a sheriff, an honour which cost him £3,400 for a year's service, and was able to portion his daughter with £2,000 and to bury his wife at a cost of £257. At the end of his patient career Sir Thomas Cullum had built his original £92 to a fortune of £40,000.

Cullum's phenomenal success was, of course, quite untypical of the merchant class as a whole, the great majority of whom measured their wealth in hundreds, not in thousands of pounds. Again, much is revealed of their standard of life by wills and inventories of personal goods. A tailor of Marlborough, Wiltshire, died in 1679 with personal property valued at £150, placing him in the same category as a substantial husbandman or small yeoman. Ten years later, a Cornish miller died possessed of the same value of live and dead stock, his simple furniture consisting of a press, a chest, a box, 3 tableboards, 2 great stools, 2 chairs, 3 pans, a salt cellar, 8 pewter dishes and 3 beds: it seems that he inhabited a cottage consisting of a hall, kitchen, parlour and chambers above. Both these men were merchants with a thriving trade, and it is likely that the miller owned land as well. A mere shopkeeper, even in the capital, often had to be content with an existence no higher, yet more precarious, than that of a wage-earner. An estimate made in 1614 of an average shopkeeper's turnover puts it at only 5s. a day, and the comment is made that if it were to fall to as little as 2s. 6d., 'he would be ill able to pay his rent or to keep open his shop-windowe'. All the evidence of retail trade at this period points, in fact, to a very slow turnover coupled with necessarily high profit margins. A Quaker shopkeeper of 1680 is described as buying prunes for 8s. or 9s. the hundredweight and selling them at 3 lb. for 4d., tobacco at 2d. the lb. (which must have escaped customs duty) for sale at 6d, 'which caused a great consumption'. Turnover was equally small, and profit margins equally high, in most inns and taverns of the period. The cheapest wine, claret, cost 8d. a quart up to 1639, 12d. at the Restoration and 2s. by the end of the century, the increases being mainly due to taxation: in 1639 the cost price was 2½d. the quart plus 1d. for tax and another 1d. for the importer's profit, leaving 3½d. as the retailer's profit. But it has been calculated that the average sale of a London tavern was only 212 quarts a day, to achieve which an inn-keeper had to provide premises furnished, warmed and lighted, servants, and hospitality at any hour of the day or night.

The houses of town merchants were usually now of three storeys, rather than the one or two of most farmhouses and cottages. Besides a shop on the ground floor there would be a hall used as the living-room and still, quite often, for cooking, a buttery or spence where barrels of beer and 'powdering troughs' for salting meat were stored, possibly a kitchen, a parlour for sleeping and, increasingly, for sitting, and a number of chambers on the upper floors used as bedrooms and storerooms. Thomas Heath, a blacksmith of Oxford, slept in such a room together with 46 cheeses. In many houses the late Tudor and Stuart period saw considerable improvement and refinement. Staircases were beginning to replace movable ladders to give access to upper chambers; glass was increasingly common in town houses instead of lattice-work and shutters, and was usually valued separately in inventories to indicate that it was not regarded as a fixture; wainscoting was also found in more opulent households, not generally covering a whole room, but in the form of panel draught-excluders behind settles or forms.

Yet although the houses themselves might be growing in size, privacy and comfort, their contents were still surprisingly small. An alderman of Banbury, who inhabited one of the finest houses in the town, died with personal possessions worth £58, of which, as usual, the most valuable single object was a bedstead, mattress and feather bed, priced at £2: he seems to have been a general trader selling anything from haberdashery and stone pots to spades and tallow candles, the whole value of the contents of his shop being less than £4. But another shopkeeper, probably more typical, had possessions of only £11 13s. 1d., of which £3 12s.

was a debt owed by a Mr Anthony Ollings and a further £3 16s. 1d. 'debtes oyinge desperetly by dyvers men'; his stock consisted of a few chests and boxes, leather girdles, buttons, a dog-chain and a mouse-trap, and was valued at 16s. 1d. His wearing apparel is described as a jerkin and a pair of hose, valued at 3s. 4d. Even lower in the scale was Robert Bridges, mercer of Kidlington, who died in 1581 possessed of only £3 6s. 8d., of which his 'mercery ware' was put at £2: 2 bedsteads and a flock bed with coverlets were valued at 6s. 8d. Whether such men could ever have existed by trade alone seems doubtful. Most of them kept a few pigs and chickens in the back yard, they may have tilled a few acres of land outside the town and grown much of their food, or hired themselves out by the day to a farmer. Outside London and the provincial capitals trade was not yet a full-time occupation for many men, and even in 1688 Gregory King's estimates do not suggest a large trading class – 2,000 eminent merchants and traders by sea, 8,000 lesser merchants and 50,000 shopkeepers and tradesmen out of a population of 5½ million.

Most professional men – the class was still effectively limited to law, medicine and the Church – fell somewhere in between the two extremes of the great merchant and the little shopkeeper. Church livings were generally not as lucrative after the Reformation as they had previously been, and there are constant complaints that only men of little ability were now attracted, but the stipends and the houses that went with them were usually sufficient to give a reasonable standard of life. This, at least, was true of the larger town livings, though in small, country parishes a benefice might be worth as little as from £10 to £30 a year, and even this might be burdened with taxes and other charges, and no longer endowed, as in the past, with Church lands. The vicar of Hampton in Middlesex, however, had an income of £65 in 1650, amply sufficient to pay his curate £20 a year, while the Mastership of the Charterhouse, a clerical appointment, brought £100 a year and a living. The parsonage terriers that have survived indicate that the houses of the country clergy were often the largest and most substantial in the village, a typical vicarage of Lackington, Leicestershire, in 1638 consisting of a hall with plastered walls, 2 parlours, a study, a kitchen with an oven, a buttery and 3 chambers. Much improvement in the construction of parsonages took place during the seventeenth century. In the 1605 terriers walls of mud, earth and clay were still the commonest and the house itself was usually of 2 bays: by 1665 the most typical size was 3 bays, comparable with the largest farmers' houses, and most parsonages were chambered over – often, it is true, not with fixed boards, but with earth floors laid on straw or rushes. By the time of the 1707 terrier stone and brick were increasingly used as the building material, halls were paved or cobbled and some parlours boarded.

But as the major profession the Church was now rivalled, probably exceeded by, the law. Contemporaries were astonished and somewhat perturbed by the hundreds of young men who thronged the Inns of Court, some of them merely pursuing a legal education as a kind of finishing-school, others destined for an attorney's practice or, if fortune and friends were kind, for public service. Admissions at the four Inns, which had averaged about 40 a year at the beginning of the sixteenth century, reached 200 by the end and continued to increase up to the Civil War. In an intensely litigious age with an unprecedented volume of land-transfers there was no shortage of business, but the really lucrative opportunities were confined to those who achieved a Judgeship or became one of the Serjeants who had the monopoly of pleading civil cases in the Court of Common Pleas. Most attorneys depended on their quite modest fees and achieved no more than a reasonably comfortable livelihood. Again, outside the four large towns, the law probably did not provide a full-time occupation for very many. A Mr Barrell, a lawyer of Cuckfield in Sussex in the 1680s, farmed a small estate with a staff of 6, and records in his diary many payments to him for professional work in kind – haunches of venison, 24 'china' oranges, 18 woodcocks, and so on. By contrast, the eminent lawyers who attended the Earl of Bedford received £2 to £3 per visit, and charged, together with Court expenses, £100 for the proving of his father's will.

Doctors and surgeons occupied a lower position in the social scale. A few men of outstanding reputation might command as much as £100 for a cure, say, from smallpox, and the famous Court physician, Dr King, was once promised by the Privy

Council – though never received – £1,000 for saving the life of Charles II when the King was in a fit. Most medical men of the period could expect nothing like this. Visits by a tooth-drawer to Woburn Abbey in the late seventeenth century cost as little as 1s., by a doctor to bleed the servants 2s. 6d. each, although the cure of William Russell from smallpox in 1661, requiring several attendances by the eminent Dr Micklethwait, was charged at £45. An apothecary who successfully treated one of the Earl's servants for the same illness received only £2 7s. for visits and medicines. The profession was still very far from developing any accepted standards of competence or remuneration, and a man might describe himself as a surgeon without the smallest qualification other than the experience of cutting hair: such a one was John Wyllyby, who died at Banbury in 1574 where he had lived in a 2-roomed cottage with personal estate valued at £1 9s. 10d. Where standards of competence were required as, for instance, in the appointment of a naval surgeon, the salary seems to have been not unreasonable – 5s. a day, 2s. 6d. a day for each mate and 3d. a day for medicines for each man – which must have totalled at least £100 a year. Some apothecaries also lived very comfortably. In Bury St Edmunds in 1685 Celia Fiennes described the house of one who 'is esteemed a very rich man': it had a pleasing prospect of the town, with four rooms to each floor 'pretty sizeable and high, well furnished, a drawing room and chamber full of China and a damask bed embroidered, 2 other rooms, camlet and mohair beds, a pretty deal of plate in his wife's chamber, parlours below and a large shop . . .'

The Tudor and Stuart teacher was on a scale still lower than that of the doctor. The travelling tutor in a noble household might be quite handsomely rewarded, since he was required to instruct in the gentlemanly graces as well as polite learning, but the ordinary schoolmaster often worked for a pittance less than that of a wage-earner. A master at Hampton Grammar School at the end of Henry VIII's reign had £10 a year, less than the carpenter's 1s. a day, while the Master of Oundle School's £30 a year in 1686 had done little more than keep up with the rise in prices. Masters in a boarding school like Eton College were perhaps somewhat better off since they had food and liveries provided: here the Provost received £50 a year up to 1674, plus

£25 as Rector of Eton, plus £5 for clothes, the Fellows having £10 a year and 50s. for liveries.

Townsmen differed from the classes previously discussed in being necessarily more dependent on professional producers for their daily needs. Not only did they have fewer opportunities of growing their own food, making their own clothes or household goods, but their specialized occupations demanded more of their time and precluded the degree of self-sufficiency that was still achieved by many country people. On the other hand, their command of the market gave them a wider variety and choice of products, and habituated the town-dweller to a degree of sophistication unfamiliar in rural England. Dependence on the 'ready-made' was noticeable in all spheres, particularly, perhaps, in respect to food, dress and furniture. Whereas country households, great and small, spun and wove wool and linen, boiled soap, brewed, baked, dipped candles and cured meat and fish, the middle-class townsman spent a much higher proportion of income on manufactured goods and was thus able to economize on domestic service, the lavish employment of which was demanded by the self-sufficiency system. Thus when the Reverend Giles Moore needed a new bed in 1656, he did not buy feathers by the stone and cloth by the yard, but simply bought a ready-made article, 'of Mr Hely in London, a bed with purple rug, curtains etc. which cost me altogether £20 16s. 7d and a pair of fine middle blankets 15s, two flock beds and bolster ticks £1 1s ...': the list continued with sheets, coverlets, striped curtains, valances and so on. Similarly, a wide variety of food could be bought from town butchers and fishmongers, bakers, grocers and even ready-for-the-table, at cookshops. The townsman paid more for his food because he was also buying services, and even 1s. 'ordinary' at a tavern represented a day's wage for a skilled workman. But those who could afford it seem to have eaten very well – 3 meals a day rather than the 2 of the country, and ample quantities of meat. Nutritionally, the diet was deficient in vegetables, fruit and milk, though it probably had an excess of protein and carbohydrate. Another dietary characteristic of the towns was the use of white, wholemeal bread in place of the darker rye and brown flours still used in the countryside: some captured Dutch seamen in 1665 complained that it was too fine for their taste, and that they would prefer coarser bread. Amongst the more well-to-do by the later seventeenth century, variety and refinement of food were taking the place of mere volume: Pepys, for instance, gives his guests a breakfast on New Year's Day of 'a barrel of oysters, a dish of neat's tongues, and a dish of anchovies, wine of all sorts and Northdowne ale', while for a dinner-party he had oysters, a hash of rabbits and lamb, a 'rare chine of beef', a 'great dish of roasted fowls', a tart, fruit and cheese. On other occasions there were carps, lobsters, pigeons, fricassee of rabbits and lamprey pies.

6

There can be little doubt that the class which suffered most from the great price-rise was the wage-earner, and, probably most of all, the town worker. Even in modern times we are familiar enough with the effects of inflation, and at a time when the wage-earner lacked any powerful bargaining associations he was peculiarly exposed to an upward movement of prices that constantly outstripped his earnings. The independent craftsman and small master could raise the price of their products, the husbandman needed to buy little and in any case received more for whatever surplus he had to sell, but mere labour – especially at a time of increasing population – was the one commodity whose value did not grow in parallel with the general advance.

Wage-rates at the beginning of the price revolution were much as they had been for a century and more past. Labourers working on Hampton Court in the 1540s had 6d. a day, and the highest-paid master mason, responsible for the execution of whatever plans existed, 12d.: the chief clerical officer, the Clerk of the Check, received the same. Skilled bricklayers, plumbers and joiners were earning 10d., painters 8d., while some workers on particularly unpleasant jobs – 'standing in the water, lading of the same out of ye foundation' – had double rates. The lowest rate for unskilled labour was 4d. a day, with the exception of 'Weeders in the King's Garden' – probably juveniles and women – who received 3d. Up to 1550 the general average of masons' wages was 6d. – 7d., with 1d. or 2d. more for work in London or for especially important projects such as royal building or fortifications. The highly skilled masons employed on King's College, Cambridge in 1509 had 6¾d. a day. A municipal regulation by the Common Council of the City of London in 1538 attempted to specify the wages of carpenters, masons, joiners, tylers, plasterers and bricklayers as 8d. per day in summer and 7d. in winter. Their hours during summer were to be from 5 a.m. to 7 p.m., with 1½ hours allowed for meals and drinking, and during the winter months 2 hours less. It seems that the once considerable gap between London and provincial rates was narrowing, as also was the difference between skilled and unskilled: in the fourteenth century the building craftsman had often received double the labourer's wage, whereas by Tudor times skill was rewarded by increases of not more than 25 to 33 per cent. Thus 5 days' work by a joiner making cupboards at Ingatestone Hall in the 1540s brought him 3s. 4d., but his boy assistant got 20d., precisely half. What may reasonably be supposed to be the lowest town wage, for it was paid to 'sturdy beggars' rounded up to clean out the filthy City ditches, was 4d. a day.

In the countryside the situation was different, for labourers hired by the day often received meals as part of the wage, a practice which survived until late in the nineteenth century and one which easily lent itself to abuse by the employer. In the mid-sixteenth century field-workers generally had 2d. to 3d. a day with food, threshers from 3d. to 7d. according to the grain, and the skilled hedger 6d. Other categories of agricultural labour were hired by the year, sometimes with board and lodging, sometimes with various emoluments in kind such as land, fuel and livery, all of which make their money wage unrealistic. Thus a Norfolk shepherd received a mere £3 a year in wages, but had an acre of land, the right to keep 80 sheep in his master's flock, and other, smaller benefits.

Already by the end of the sixteenth century prices, as we have seen, had increased some 5 times compared with 1500, and some 3 times compared with 1550. Wages, on the other hand, had continued to slump, resulting in many cases in what must have been a catastrophic fall in the standard of living. At Wadham College, Oxford, masons were now earning 10d. to 16d. a day, carpenters 12d. to 16d., labourers 8d. to 12d. A shilling a day appears to have become the standard rate for masons and similar skilled men, with London rates of 14d. to 16d: with meat and drink 8d. was the common wage. Field labourers were now receiving 8d., or 3d. with food – a clear indication of how rapidly food prices had risen and of what a large proportion of income they now absorbed. But worse was to follow in the Stuart period, until prices finally stabilized around 1660. By the middle of the seventeenth century the mason's wage stood at 16d. to 18d. a day, with the labourer's rate at 10d. to 12d: by the last decade of the century the figures were 18d. to 20d. and 12d. to 14d. respectively. By this time prices had risen 6 or 7 times since 1500, and the average wage bought almost precisely half what it had then: the single consolation was that real wages had been slowly moving upwards since the 1620s, when their purchasing power had been a mere third of 1500.

Knoop and Jones, the historians of the mason, have commented that 'to judge solely by the statistics . . . the decline in the masons' standard of life during the second half of the sixteenth and the first half of the seventeenth centuries must have been little less than calamitous'. It was not, they point out, a case of a temporary reduction which could be met by postponing urgent needs for a time, but a period of a hundred years in which earnings were cut by half and, occasionally, considerably more than half. Thorold Rogers long ago calculated how much food the average wage would buy at different periods – in 1495 the artisan's wage would provision his family for a year with 3 quarters of wheat, 3 of malt and 2 of oatmeal in 10 weeks' work, in 1533 in 15 weeks, in 1564 in 32 weeks, in 1593 40 weeks, in 1610 43 weeks and in 1651 the same. The unskilled labourer could supply his family in 1495 with the result of 15 weeks' work, but in 1651 a whole year's labour would scarcely bring the same.

It is of course true that the labourer did not generally subsist on wheat flour, but on bread made from coarser grains and mixtures of grain with peas and beans. In many areas he still had the opportunity of producing some of his own food, of keeping pigs and a cow, and of increasing his earnings by engaging his wife and children in domestic industries such as spinning, weaving, hosiery and straw-plaiting. It is difficult to see how he could have survived simply on his own earnings without a drastic reduction in his standard of life. Similarly, it is likely that the town artisan was able to make some adjustments by increased overtime working during his lunch-break, in the evening and on Sundays. In Norwich there are complaints that building operatives have deserted the city in order to find work in the country, an indication that, however low agricultural wages were, the opportunities of supplementation were greater than in the town. Above all, it seems likely that the intensity of work was increased substantially compared with the relative ease of the later Middle Ages, that men worked longer and harder, and that women and children were much more frequently employed than in the past with the increasing opportunities offered by the development of the domestic system in industry. A substantial change in the pattern of life and work was the inevitable and enduring response of many wage-earners to the great price-rise.

Not all workers, of course, were so vulnerable to price-movements. 'Servants' – a category which included farm-workers hired by the year as well as domestic staff – had the advantage of board and, often, lodging and livery, which at least provided for their basic needs and so maintained a fairly constant, if low, standard of living. At Ingatestone Hall in 1550 quarterly wages ranged from 5s. for maids to 10s. for the cook and 13s. 4d. for the household chaplain, but small as these seem they are to be regarded as payments clear of all living expenses, more like pocket money than a wage. Similarly, the Earl of Rutland in 1537 was paying his top-grade kitchen staff only 33s. 4d. per year, and Katheryne, who helped to strew rushes and clean the chambers, got only 4d. for 11 days' work. At Winchester College the baker received 26s. 8d. a year up to 1558, 40s. in 1559 and 53s. 4d. after 1560. Inflation, it seems, was having its effect even in a protected employment such as this, and by the seventeenth century it is evident that board wages had moved up considerably. By 1650 an ordinary maid living-in was receiving about £2 a year, a cook maid about £3 and a personal servant £3 10s. to £4: they might also expect to receive, besides food, shelter and liveries, the cast-off clothing which, in wealthy households, could have considerable re-sale value, and, in addition, substantial tips or 'vails'. These were given from Tudor times onwards, not only for extra services such as errands and message-taking, but whenever the head of the family received guests or when some happy event such as a birth occurred. Early in the eighteenth century Defoe observed that a maid in a gentleman's or merchant's family 'often doubles her Wages by her Vails'. In a noble household, however, most of such perquisites of office would go to the principal servants – the steward, butler, housekeeper and so on – and probably little came down to the level of the scullions and stable-boys. In the middle of the seventeenth century some children worked in the kitchens at Woburn without any wages, but simply in return for food and clothing, but casual labour employed by the day without board or lodging received 1s. to 1s. 6d. for washing and cleaning, and from 10d. to 1s. 6d. for work in the garden, according to the degree of skill.

Small as board wages were, their recipients were at least assured of the next meal and a roof over their heads. Many Tudor and Stuart working-people had no such certainty. Some of the wages paid seem impossibly small to support a family, and although the man himself might be given food at his work this was small consolation to a hungry wife and children at home. Under the Chester wage-assessments of the 1590s, for instance, a linen weaver receives only 1d. a day with food, a joiner and a shoemaker 2d., a bricklayer 2½d. Textiles, leather and building were the principal occupations of the town, probably employing between them some 40 per cent of the labour force. It seems unbelievable that such meagre earnings could have supported family life, even at the lowest level, without the possibility of home-production of a substantial amount of food. Many of the assessments must have been based upon the assumption that the artisan and journeyman still had access to land, an assumption that was rapidly ceasing to be true, at least in the larger towns. The alternative and more justified assumption was that wife and children were also engaged in gainful employment and contributing their share towards a total family income. In some areas this was possible: in others, where capitalist industry was still unknown, it was not. Increasingly as the period went on, and prices constantly outstripped earnings, more and more wage-earners must have lived on the margin of existence and have passed beyond it into penury and destitution.

With a rising population pressing on underdeveloped agricultural and industrial resources, unemployment was an intractable problem for Tudor and Stuart England, yet behind this lay a larger problem of under-employment – of men who had work, but whose labour did not bring a remotely adequate standard of life. By all contemporary records the numbers of the poor increased steadily. In London alone there were perhaps 100,000 existing on the edge of destitution by the end of Elizabeth's reign, and this was paralleled in Norwich and York, Coventry and Exeter. It is significant that in 1688 Gregory King calculated artisans and handicraftsmen at 60,000 (yearly income per family £38), labouring people and out-servants at 364,000 (income per family £15) and cottagers and paupers at 400,000 – the largest class of all – with a yearly family income of £6 10s: with their families this category numbered 1,300,000, or one-quarter of the total population of the country.

The fact that population continued to grow argues, of course, that low as standards were they were at least capable of supporting life. But for many people, life was supported by charity, not by earnings. The development of the Tudor Poor Law from 1536 onwards was a recognition of the existence of a new problem and of a new responsibility: it was rendered necessary not by the breakdown of earlier forms of relief, but by the emergence of new causes of destitution for which those remedies would, in any case, have been inappropriate. The Poor Law was, however, more significant as an expression of attitude than as a substantial contribution to the solution of the problem, at any rate during Tudor times. The evidence suggests that compulsory levies of poor-rate were only made in times of dire emergency, and that the total sum disbursed between 1560 and 1600 was a mere £12,000, a sum that can hardly have been more than a drop in the ocean of Tudor poverty. Private charity bore almost the entire burden of relief down to 1660, some £174,000 being given by individual donors during the same period that public charity subscribed less than one-tenth as much.

Labouring people and out-servants, cottagers and paupers, in King's terms, made up half the population of Tudor and Stuart England. Their standard of comfort – if such it can be called – was almost indescribably low by comparison with that of the merchant, the professional man or the yeoman. According to a contemporary observer, they 'lived in houses such as a man may build within three or four hours'. It was usually single-roomed, of the one-bay cruck construction, with an earth floor, mud walls and thatched roof, a hole in the wall for window and another for smoke to escape from the open hearth. There might be one or two 'outshots' for kitchen and buttery, perhaps a small chamber or loft above, though more likely merely a single room divided by partitions for living and sleeping: there might be a draught-screen beside the front door, or in some parts of the country a Welsh dresser served the same purpose. In some areas stone made a more substantial construction than mud: brick was increasingly used by the seventeenth century for patching and paving, though rarely yet for the walls. Life in such cottages must have been uncomfortable, dirty and often verminous, lacking in privacy or any of the amenities of civilized life. It was a shelter from the rain and the cold that the labourer frequently shared with his animals, no more.

Contents were similarly frugal – a table-board, stools, cooking utensils, a bed or sometimes merely a flock mattress or bags of straw. Inventories and wills are not a safe guide to the personal property of such people, since only those who possessed something of value were worth recording, and there must have been many, perhaps a majority, who owned too little to merit the trouble of writing down. Even allowing for the fact that the labourers' inventories that have survived are not typical, they indicate a pitifully low level of comfort. In a group of villages in Lincolnshire and Nottinghamshire between 1575 and 1640 the median value of 94 labourers' inventories was £13, compared with £18 for craftsmen and £61 for husbandmen. Of 10 Oxfordshire labourers between 1550 and 1596, 7 had less than £5 worth of goods, the other 3 from £5 to £10 worth, and these totals included some farm livestock – a cow or two, a few sheep and pigs, which were grazed on the common or on small closes behind the cottages. This implies that the house contents were often worth only a few shillings, and at most a pound or two. Thus Robert Holland, day labourer of Hampton Poyle, Oxfordshire, who died in 1568, had, besides a cow, a heifer and a sheep, only 3 kettles, 1 little pot of brass, 1 bedstead, 1 coffer, a sack, 4 platters and a saucer, 2 pairs of sheets, 1 bolster, and one twill cloth: his clothes must have been too poor to record, and the whole value of his personal estate was only 19s. Where clothes are specified, they generally range in value from a couple of shillings to about a pound. For a man they typically consisted of a pair of leather breeches, a coat, waistcoat, a couple of shirts, stockings, shoes and hat: in a much higher income bracket Dorothy Titcombe, the wife of a Marlborough husbandman, possessed 2 petticoats, 2 waistcoats, 1 new pair of bodices, 2 pairs of stockings, shoes and a riding hood, valued at £3.

Some idea of what it was considered the working man ought to eat can be gathered from the records of diets provided by public institutions and the armed forces. A Tudor soldier's daily ration was 24 oz. of wheat bread (1d.), two-thirds of a gallon of beer (1d.), 2 pounds of beef or mutton (3d.), half a pound of butter and a pound of cheese: on fish days a quarter of a cod or ling, or 7 or 8 red or white herrings replaced the meat. The interesting point is that such a diet cost about 6d. a day for a single person, closely comparable with the 5d. a day which the Navy Victualling Department allowed for the feeding of sailors. Representing what was no doubt considered the lowest level of existence, the dietary at the Bury House of Correction in the year of the Armada provided for 2 meals a day, each consisting of 8 oz. of rye bread, a pint of porridge, a quarter of a pound of meat and a pint of beer. Many of the labouring poor did not fare so well as this, and would have thought the soldiers' rations a feast. Bread was their staple, though not usually wheat bread such as the yeomen and wealthier classes ate. 'As for wheaten bread', wrote Harrison in 1577, 'they eat it when they can reach unto the price of it. Contenting themselves in the meane time with bread made of otes or barlaie: a poore estate God wot!' He goes on to say that in times of scarcity mixtures of rye, beans, peas, tares, lentils and even acorns are all pressed into use. It may be, as Harrison believed, that the English labourer had a preference for rye and barley bread 'as abiding longer in the stomach' than wheat, but this must have been a Hobson's choice for many. Farm servants living-in probably enjoyed much the same fare as their masters – meat or fish every day, vegetables and fruit, porridge, pies, puddings and so on, but the day-labourer rarely saw much of these, and existed on a diet no more varied though smaller in quantity than that of the Middle Ages. According to the Reverend Richard Baxter in 1691 poor tenants were glad of a piece of hanged bacon once a week, 'enough to trie the stomach of an ostrige', and 'he is a rich man that can afford to eate a jointe of fresh meate once in a month or fortnight'. If their sow pigs they must sell the litter, and any fruit, eggs, butter or cheese they may produce must go to market, keeping for themselves only skimmed milk and whey curds. The labourer's diet was at best coarse and monotonous – brown or black bread, soups and porridge 'messes', a few cabbages, lettuces, parsnips and onions, some eggs, butter and fruit in season and occasionally a little meat or fish, more often salted than fresh. No significant innovation in food production or use occurred during the period. At the very end, potatoes were being introduced as a garden-crop, though not yet in the field, and it was the unavailability of root vegetables for winter feeding of cattle that made meat so scarce and dear. The cottager substituted whatever he could – barley or rye for wheat, oats in place of malt for brewing – but in seasons of dearth which, according to Thorold Rogers, occupied as many as 24 years of the seventeenth century, hunger and starvation became the only real alternatives.

The worst conditions of all were experienced by the urban worker, practically the whole of whose food had to be purchased with a wage that only went half as far as it had a century earlier. Beef at 5d. a pound in the middle of the seventeenth century was for the rich only, and when meat was eaten by the town worker it was usually the cheapest cuts of bacon, a sheep's head or pluck. Even bread could become prohibitively expensive in bad seasons like the 1690s, when wheat at 56s. the quarter was double the price of the previous decade. In normal times, however, the bread of London was made of white wholemeal flour, no longer of rye, oats or barley as in the country districts and, again in contrast to the countryside, it seems likely that the consumption of butter and cheese was increasing in the towns. Vegetables and fruit were scarce, however, and the diet of the poorer townsman must have been monotonous indeed: it is noticeable, for example, that the regime provided by St Bartholomew's Hospital in 1687 included only 10 different items in the week's menu – wheaten bread, boiled beef, boiled mutton, broth, milk pottage, sugar sops, water gruel, butter, cheese and beer – and this, with the exclusion of the meat, must have fairly represented the diet of many townspeople at this period.

The sixteenth and seventeenth centuries therefore marked a turning-point in the standard of living of the English worker. In the fourteenth and fifteenth centuries he had benefited from the labour shortage created by the Black Death and the deflationary trend in prices: now, the effect of the first prolonged period of inflation was to lower his standards of comfort, to intensify his labour and that of his dependants, and to expose him to the vicissitudes of price and seasonal fluctuations whose course he was powerless to change. In the 'glorious' age of the first Elizabeth, when a few enjoyed unprecedented wealth and luxury, almost half the population was hovering perilously close to hunger and destitution.

CHAPTER 3

The Eighteenth Century

I

It is a truism that history never stands still, and that any period through which a man lives is, for him, a period of change. Chaucer's England was a very different one from that of William the Conqueror, and as different again from that of Shakespeare. Yet it remains true that England in the eighteenth century was, in many respects, a society in transition from the old to the new, that the changes which occurred were of a scale and character different from those of the past, and that it was in this century that those revolutions were initiated, the full consequences of which are still to be realized.

The most evident change was of greatly increased numbers. After long centuries during which growth had been almost imperceptible, constantly being set back by mass outbreaks of plague and disease, a sudden spurt began in the 1740s which carried the population of England and Wales up from an estimated 6 million to as many as 9 million by the end of the century. The precise causes of this growth are still a subject for debate among historians, though it seems certain that a decline in the death-rate, and particularly of the infant death-rate, was more important than increases in births. And although England in the eighteenth century was still a land of farms and villages – only 20 per cent of the population being classified as urban when the first census was taken in 1801 – it was the gathering influx into towns and cities, and the extremes of wealth and poverty, luxury and want, elegance and filth which these displayed, that captured the interest of contemporaries and bequeathed such problems to posterity.

It was also clear that, however unequal its distribution might be, the wealth of England was increasing faster than at any previous time, and faster than in any other country. Contemporary estimates of the national income indicate a figure of £8–9 per head per year at the end of the seventeenth century, rising to

£12–13 in 1750 and almost doubling to £22 by 1800. If these figures are multiplied by 6 to put them into something like modern values they suggest an average income per head for 1750 of about £75, compared with an estimated £30 for Nigeria and £25 for India at the present time. The English people on the eve of the Industrial Revolution were substantially better-off than those in the underdeveloped countries of today, and better-off than their near neighbours and rivals, the Dutch and the French. Arthur Young, travelling in France in the 1780s, thought that the French labouring classes 'are 76 per cent less at their ease; worse fed, worse clothed, and worse supported than the same classes in England', a view which French visitors to these shores readily endorsed. The British economy in the eighteenth century was already well above subsistence level and was producing substantial surpluses of agricultural and industrial products for sale in the markets of the world. Over the hundred years exports and re-exports expanded nearly 7 times – from £6·5 million in 1700 to £40·8 million in 1800. Down to the 1770s we regularly shipped large consignments of wheat and flour to the Continent, while in 1751 more than 7 million gallons of British spirits were charged to duty besides vast but incalculable quantities that were illegally distilled.

All this argues a generally rising standard of life, which found expression in the formation of new habits and tastes ranging from food to furniture, from drink to dress. During the century white, wheaten bread gradually replaced the rye, barley and mixtures of grains which earlier generations had used: by 1795, it has been estimated, wheat constituted 94 per cent of the bread-corn of England. A period of remarkable building activity lay between the Queen Anne house, the Georgian country mansion and the Regency villa, activity that can be quantified in the output of bricks (from 359 million in 1785 to 675 million in 1801) or the newly introduced wallpaper (from 197,000 yards in 1713 to 2,100,000 yards in 1785). Mahogany wood from the West Indies transformed the craft of the furniture-maker; tea and coffee ultimately overcame the gin epidemic that was threatening to destroy the populations of London and other cities; mass-produced cotton clothes and pottery dishes were cheaper and cleaner than wool and pewter. And if the snuff habit was no less injurious to the user than tobacco, it was perhaps less offensive to the rest of society.

Change was evident, too, even in the traditional countryside. The need of a rapidly mounting population to be fed, and the growth of urban areas necessarily dependent on outside supplies, imposed new demands on English agriculture that were met only by a radical transformation of existing practices. Essentially, more land came to be cultivated more efficiently. With gathering momentum after the middle of the century Enclosure Acts threw together the long, narrow strips of the medieval open fields into compact farms and brought derelict commons and wastes under the plough: in many cases their effect was to increase the demand for agricultural labour, and the disinheritance of the peasantry was more a consequence of the post-Napoleonic depression than of enclosures themselves. Undoubtedly, however, the enclosure movement fostered the concentration of English landownership into fewer, larger units, and it is noticeable that it was on these large, model estates of 'improving' landlords that experiment and innovation in agricultural techniques were mostly practised. The seed-drill and the horse-hoe, the field cultivation of turnips and rotational grasses, the scientific breeding of cattle and sheep and the other innovations associated with the 'agrarian revolution' were limited in their immediate application, and became only widely adopted in the following century. Nevertheless, the combination of enclosure and improvement had profound effects on agricultural prosperity and land-values. The average weight of oxen sold at Smithfield increased from 370 lb. in 1710 to 800 lb. in 1795, of sheep from 38 lb. to 80 lb. Coke of Holkham, perhaps the most successful of the eighteenth-century improvers, raised the rentals on his Norfolk estates from £2,200 to £20,000 a year within 40 years. The productiveness of English land as a whole, it has been estimated, was at least 4 times greater than it had been in the fourteenth century: the average rent in Arthur Young's time was 10s. an acre, compared with 6d. in the Middle Ages, and the average cost of land $33\frac{1}{2}$ years' rent instead of 20. Profits ranged from 14–20 per cent a year, amply sufficient to account for the prosperity that the farmer now enjoyed.

But the English landowner, unlike his French counterpart, was prepared to channel some of his surplus capital not only into en-

THE EIGHTEENTH CENTURY

larging and adorning his estates, but also into industrial development. Aristocratic landlords not infrequently mined the coal and iron beneath their broad acres, speculated in overseas trade and invested their savings in cotton-mills and iron-foundries. In an intimate way the population growth, agrarian change and industrial development of the eighteenth century were linked together, one constantly feeding the other to produce that decisive and sustained increase in national output which characterizes a modern economy. The origins of this Industrial Revolution went back to well before the eighteenth century, and its completion is not yet; but from some point in the second half of the century, perhaps in the decade 1770–80, a 'take-off' occurred which launched Britain, before any other country, into the first stages of a modern, industrialized, urbanized society. Demand was the spur, invention the response to that demand, and the cluster of technical innovations in spinning and weaving, iron manufacture and steam power that came in the closing decades of the century was the reaction of a small but creative people to a great and growing demand for their products. The Industrial Revolution was the most important agent of economic and social change in modern times, ultimately affecting every aspect of life, material and intellectual, religious and philosophical. In the eighteenth century its influence was only just beginning, but already it was changing the face of the Midlands and the North, raising the sparsely populated Lancashire to the second most populous county in the kingdom, compelling the improvement of roads and the construction of canals, docks and harbours to move its personnel and its goods. In 1700 change and growth had been unusual: by 1800 they were normal. The English people had come to believe in progress, both for their country and for themselves, to expect that this year they would be better off than last, though not so well off as they would be next. The extent to which their expectations were realized is the subject of this chapter.

2

Strangely in a century of violent, even revolutionary, change, prices remained remarkably stable until almost the end of the

A HISTORY OF THE COST OF LIVING

period. After the rapid inflation of the Tudor and Stuart era, prices had levelled out in the 1660s and for the next hundred years exhibited no long-term movement in either direction. Again, it seems, some law of equilibrium was operating – that just as the stable price-levels of the fifteenth century were overturned in the sixteenth and early seventeenth centuries, so the balance was now restored in the eighteenth.

This is, of course, not to suggest that the cost of living remained stable throughout a century which witnessed an unparalleled increase in the range of things to be bought. Wedgwood vases, Sheffield steel, Sheraton furniture and a thousand other products were unknown before the eighteenth century, tea and coffee so rare as to be beyond the wildest hopes of most. Even in a period of relatively stable prices the cost of living may rise drastically if the pattern of expenditure changes, if people increase their consumption of luxuries, and if former luxuries come to be regarded as necessaries. Richardson's comment in *The Rambler* (1751) on the extravagance of women – 'Two thousand pounds, in the last age, with a domestic wife, would go farther than ten thousand in this' – is a perennial complaint, never more true than in the age of elegance.

But estimates of comparative price-changes can only be made on the basis of precisely similar 'baskets' of commodities, usually of essential articles rather than luxuries. In 1700 the cost of the Phelps Brown 'basket' stood at 671 points compared with 100 in 1500, before the beginning of the great price-rise. In the decade 1700–1709 it averaged 591, from 1710 to 1719 663, from 1720 to 1729 608, 1730 to 1739 553, from 1740 to 1749 599, from 1750 to 1759 628, from 1760 to 1769 704, from 1770 to 1779 805 and from 1780 to 1789 824. (The decade of the 1790s is the beginning of another period of quite different character and is reserved for later treatment.) It will be seen that the Phelps Brown index suggests stability – even falling prices – during the first half of the century, followed by relatively small increases after the 1750s.

The other price-index for the century is one estimated by Mrs E. B. Schumpeter and Dr Gilboy, using the material collected by Sir William Beveridge: this is admittedly a crude index, drawn almost entirely from the contract prices paid by institutions such as schools, hospitals and government departments, and therefore not necessarily representative of actual, retail prices. Even so, it is likely that it indicates accurately enough the broad, secular trends of prices, particularly since it accords well with the Phelps Brown estimates. Apart from single years of high prices, due generally to harvest failure, the trend is slightly downwards till the 1760s: from a base-point of 100 in 1700, consumers' goods generally remain in the 80s or 90s until after 1763, after which they climb gradually to 124 by 1790. It is also noticeable that producers' goods – bricks, coal, lead, copper, tallow and so on – follow a slightly lower level than consumers' goods, reflecting to some extent the economies of more intensive exploitation of resources.

On this evidence the first half of the eighteenth century might be regarded as something of a 'Golden Age' for labour, only slightly less gilded than that of the fifteenth century. An especially favourable period was from 1730 to 1750, when wheat averaged only 31s. 9d. a quarter, less than it had been for 150 years past, and all the staple foods, in normal years, were cheap and plentiful. Meat, which had been 5d. and 6d. a lb., could now be had for 2d. or 3d., and a rabbit for 4d. The quickening pace of industrialization was lowering the cost of many manufactured articles such as cotton and soap necessary to the working classes. Meat is again on the labourer's table 2 or 3 times a week, 'white meats' more common, and varieties of vegetables unknown to earlier generations. After a long period of deterioration, it seems likely that standards of living were moving upwards during the first half of the century, and that England was again, as a contemporary observed, an 'opulent' land. But no more lost ground was recovered after about 1760 – rather, some of the gains could no longer be held. Price-rises, catastrophic harvests and, at the end of the period, war and monetary inflation, ended the century for many with poverty and famine.

The precise effects which these price-changes had on the economic developments of the period is still a matter for debate. It is not too difficult to explain the fact that population growth coincided with the low food-prices of the 1730s and 1740s, which, it is reasonable to suppose, would have contributed to the better care and feeding of children as well as their parents. But the relationship between low prices and the Industrial Revolution is more obscure. One view suggests that 'a working population with a high, or more important, a rising standard of living, is necessary for industrial expansion', since it both provides a market for the sale of the products of mass production and encourages desires for more commodities which induces workers to accept the unpalatable consequences of factory labour: it is no coincidence, it has been said, that the home of the factory system was in the North of England, where real earnings were at their highest. On the other hand, a diametrically opposed view holds that rising prices are a requisite for capital accumulation and industrial development: that the low prices of the first half of the century caused a deceleration of growth, which only recovered after 1750 due to the rising levels of both prices and population.

The effects on agriculture seem more direct and uncomplicated. The low grain-prices of the first half of the century demonstrated the advantages of convertible husbandry, by which the farmer could spread his risk and recoup his losses on one crop from gains on others: fattening and dairying were often more profitable than corn at this time, partly because their prices were more stable, partly because a rising standard of living meant that people had more to spend on meat and dairy produce. But after 1760 the rise in price of wheat benefited arable rather than pasture farms, and caused some conversion to the plough: in particular, there is a direct connexion between the rising grain-prices and the spurt of enclosure in the second half of the century. In fact, both low and high prices resulted in a search for greater efficiency and more intensive methods of farming which characterized an important sector of English landed society in the period.

The price-series for particular commodities follow the same pattern as the indices, though with much more yearly variation. Wheat fluctuated most of all, because it was acutely subject to the state of the harvest and because the demand for it was highly inelastic. Thus the price of the bushel of wheat at Windsor could jump from 6s. 6d. in 1708 to 11s. 6d. the next year, and could fall back to 2s. 11d., the lowest point in the century, in 1743. In general, however, 30s. to 40s. the quarter was the prevailing price up to the 1760s, with some particularly low prices from 20s. to 30s. in the 1730s and 1740s, followed by rises up to 50s.

and 60s. in the later decades: our present period ends with the famine year, 1795, when it exceeded 80s. (For comparison, prices in the middle of the seventeenth century had generally been 40s.–50s., and in the middle of the sixteenth 10s.–20s.) These prices meant that the 4-lb. loaf of bread generally sold in London at 4d.–5d. in the first half of the eighteenth century, rising to 6d.–7d. towards the end (6d.–7d. in mid-seventeenth century, 2d. in mid-sixteenth).

In most towns, and in some country areas, people now heated their houses with coal, much of it still the 'sea-coal' from Tyneside, though the Midland and other coal-fields were now being exploited. The price per chaldron (26–27 cwt.) moved up from about 30s.–32s. at the beginning of the century to 36s.–38s. at the end: seasonal fluctuations were less than in the case of wheat. Already 15s. the chaldron when Westminster School began its records in 1585, the price was being held down by the enormous expansion of the industry that was now taking place. Again, despite a rapidly growing demand, wool prices remained remarkably stable until the end of the century due to the expansion of flocks and the increased weight of the fleece brought by scientific stock-breeding: in 1700 the tod (28 lb.) of Lincoln long wool sold for 17s. 6d., in 1780 for 20s. At the latter date, when wool cost about 9d. a pound, West India cotton was much more expensive at from 1s. 8d.–3s. 6d. the pound.

Contemporary reports in the first half of the century all stress the abundance and variety of food that working people could afford. Deering, the reporter of Nottingham in 1751, observed that even in this provincial town carrots, turnips, parsnips, cabbages, savoys and potatoes were regarded as 'immediate necessaries', while the list of 'less necessaries' included poultry, rabbits, freshwater and sea fish, broccoli, asparagus, wines, tea, coffee, chocolate and spices, and 'all sorts of Grocers Goods almost as cheap as in London'. Small beer cost 1½d. a gallon, 'middling' 2d., and strong ale 4d. a quart, but tea was beginning to compete, and 'almost every Seamer, Sizer and Winder in the hosiery trade will have her Tea and will enjoy herself over it in a Morning, not forgetting their Snuff . . . and even a common Washerwoman thinks she has not had a proper Breakfast without tea and hot, buttered white Bread.' Meat was also cheap at this time, with beef, veal, mutton and pork at about 2½d. the pound: eggs were 3 or 4 a penny, rabbits 3d., fowls 1s. 4d. a pair and a pig about 2s. 6d. Clothing and furniture were the dear commodities at this period, and continued to be until mass-production cut their costs. But after the middle of the century, the picture of life in Nottingham, as elsewhere, worsens markedly. Bread which had been 4d. the quartern (4-lb.) loaf in 1754 rose to 10d. in 1757, causing angry miners and their wives to riot against millers and corn dealers: a few years later, in 1766, occurred the famous cheese riots, in which cheeses were rolled and flung about the streets and the Mayor, reading the Riot Act, was struck with one.

The great London markets were, of course, the cheapest and best-supplied of all. Not only were imported fruits like oranges and lemons, limes and bananas now commonplace, but the market-gardens of Kent and Middlesex poured their produce into the metropolis at astonishingly low prices. 'The Price of Garden Stuff', remarked Tucker in 1748, 'is prodigiously sunk to what it was in former Times.' Potatoes could be had at as little as 4d. the peck, a cabbage for ½d., milk 1d. a quart, Cheshire cheese 2d.–2½d. a lb. But here, as everywhere else, prices rose after mid-century, and by the 1770s meat was fetching 4d.–5d. a pound, butter 8d. and bread 1s. 6d. the quartern loaf.

Some years ago [wrote Arthur Young at this time] they [the poor] could buy bread and beer and cheese etc. etc. much cheaper than they can at present, while their earnings were the same. What was the effect of such cheapness? . . . Whatever was gained by such cheapness was constantly expended by the husband in a proportionable quantity of idleness and ale, and by the wife in that of tea.

There were many similarly unsympathetic comments by contemporaries. Not all, in fact, even admitted the rise in prices. Writing in *The Wealth of Nations* (1776) of the effect of the taxes on soap, salt, candles, leather and spirits, Adam Smith observed that 'The quantity of these, however, which the labouring poor are under a necessity of consuming, is so very small that the increase in their price does not compensate the diminution in that of so many other things.' In precisely which articles there had been a diminution is not clear. In fact, it was the cost of provisions that was the decisive element in the standard of living of most people, and there can be no doubt that these were already rising rapidly at the time Smith wrote, and continued to do so for the rest of the century. The Reverend David Davies made a careful estimate of the changes in prices in his own parish of Barkham, Berkshire, which showed the following:

	About 1750		About 1794	
	s d s d	£	s d £	s d
Flour: per bushel	3 4 to 4 0		6 8 to	8 4
Bread: half peck	7 to 8		11 to	1 2
Bacon: per lb.	5 to 6		8 to	9
Beef and Mutton: per lb.	3 to 3½		4½ to	5
Pork: per lb.	3½ to 4		4½ to	5
Cheese: best quality, per lb.	3 to 3½		5½ to	6
Cheese: second quality, per lb.	2½ to 3		4½ to	5
Malt: per bushel	3 0 to 3 6		5 3 to	6 6
Fresh butter	5 to 6		10 to	1 0
Salt Butter	4 to 5		7 to	8
Soap and Candles	5 to 6		8½ to	9
Pair of Men's Shoes	4 6 to 5 0		6 6 to	7 6
Pair of Women's Shoes	2 6 to 3 0		4 0 to	4 6
Wool: per 28 lb.	14 0 to 15 0	1	5 0 to 1	10 0

Similar reports from Norfolk and other counties confirm that many prices rose from 50 to 100 per cent between the middle of the century and the early 1790s, and that the economic position of the labourer had fallen drastically during this time.

Long-term price movements extending over several generations are of interest to the historian, less so to men and women of the time concerned with the daily cares of existence. For them the important price-changes were the short-term fluctuations which made bread or coal twice as dear this week as last or, when fortune smiled, only half as much. Throughout the eighteenth century it was these short-term fluctuations that most affected the standard of life of ordinary people, bringing plenty in one year, want in another. In a period which saw an unparalleled growth of income and capital, the upward slope was not continuous but broken by declivities, and it was especially at these points that most of the instances of misery were concentrated.

In a society still predominantly agricultural the major cause of fluctuation was the elements themselves and, consequently, the state of the harvests. Other influences played a part in an economy developing towards industrialization – inaccurate estimations of the market for particular goods, the underdeveloped state of the banking system and, not least in a century of colonial expansion, investment in war. But the vagaries of the English climate were the prime determinants of prices, as they had been in the Middle Ages and continued to be until we came to import the bulk of our food from more predictable latitudes late in the nineteenth century. Thus in the particularly good seasons of the 1730s beef and pork were sometimes selling at 1d.–2d. the lb. which, in the previous decade had cost 5d. In a season of flood and disease in 1735 sheep were offered at 6d. apiece, though after a long frost in the winter of 1710 lambs had fetched as much as 10s. 6d. In the severe winter of 1740 butter rose from 2½d. to 7d. a pound, potatoes from 2s. 6d. to 10s. the load: many cornmills froze up, and the Assize price of the peck loaf in London increased from 23d. to 39d. Examples might be indefinitely multiplied, nor was food the only commodity affected by the elements. The movement of coal by sea from Newcastle was sometimes impossible during the North Sea storms of January and February, or inland when the rivers froze or the roads were reduced to mud – hence, in January 1740 coal was selling at 70s. the chaldron in London when a few months before it had been 25s. Timber, bricks and many other commodities were similarly affected by transport difficulties.

Throughout the century, then, there was a succession of depressions, crises, recoveries and booms which could render the same people comfortable at one season, distressed the next. The century of change ended in conditions verging on famine, when even nettles and docks were sold at 2d. the pound, but there had been altogether no less than twelve periods (1704, 1709–10,

THE EIGHTEENTH CENTURY

1714, 1728–9, 1740–41, 1752–3, 1757–8, 1765–8, 1772–5, 1782–5, 1795–6, 1800–1801) when the prices of grain and other foods were abnormally high. These periods of dearth were longer, and more concentrated, in the second half of the century than in the first, yet the standard of living for a section of the working classes must have been rising even during the inflation of the last decades. Between 1785 and 1800 the population of England and Wales increased by about 14 per cent: the percentage increase in consumption of strong beer was 11·4, of small beer 14·5, tallow candles 33·8, soap 41·7, tobacco 58·9, British and foreign spirits 73·9, tea 97·7, printed fabrics 141·9. Many of these items were still luxuries, or near-luxuries, and the fact was that bread and potatoes increased in price very much more than soap or candles: the further removed the commodity was from being a sheer necessity, the smaller the rate of increase. This meant that it was the poorest workers, the agricultural labourers, the unemployed and casually employed, who were hardest hit, but it also meant that the growing number of artisans and factory operatives whose earnings commanded something more than a bare subsistence were beginning to enjoy a range of comforts and luxuries hitherto unattainable.

3

It is still appropriate to begin an account of the social structure of eighteenth-century England with the land-owning aristocracy, economically the wealthiest of all classes, at the pinnacle of social prestige, the monopolists of political power, local and national. They were, on the whole, gainers from the price-rise of the later decades. Costs of production climbed less slowly than prices after 1750, and there were no substantial wage-increases until late in the period: on the other hand a rapidly mounting population, increasingly concentrated in towns, provided a ready market for agricultural produce. Given an efficient administration of their estates – and many large land-owners now employed professional stewards – and not too extravagant personal tastes, the English nobleman at this period could live more luxuriously and with more real power than many a European Prince.

For a hundred years past English land had been concentrated into fewer and fewer hands: the enclosure movement and the more intensive techniques of farming developed in the eighteenth century encouraged the process still further. This implied that those 400 families who constituted the territorial aristocracy now enjoyed vast wealth and possessions. At their pinnacle were the Dukes like Newcastle, with £40,000 a year and lands scattered throughout the kingdom, or Bedford, who owned vast estates in four counties. Below these were the temporal lords, whom Gregory King numbered at the end of the seventeenth century at 160, together with 26 spiritual lords, some at least of whom would qualify for admission on grounds of wealth. Although some minor bishoprics, like Oxford and Bristol, were worth a mere £300 a year, Winchester, Durham and London brought 10 times as much, and supported a style and habit of life almost indistinguishable from that of a lay peer. The hereditary class was, too, constantly enriched by new creations, often for political, legal or military services, and the fruits of office could then be converted into broad acres and country mansions: thus, the Lord Chancellor Lord Eldon's income from fees was reported to have reached £22,730 in 1801. Many of the successful merchant princes and industrialists also sought to cement their fortunes in real property, and some, at least, were ennobled.

People bought land [Professor Habbakkuk has written] who were peculiarly susceptible to considerations of social prestige and political power. . . . They were not so much investing their money in land as buying up the perquisites of a social class, the undisturbed control of the life of a neighbourhood.

But by the later eighteenth century it is likely that there were fewer new entrants into the ranks of the great landlords than for 200 years past, partly because the size of the necessary investment was now so vast – £100,000 would be needed to buy 10,000 acres and a large house to go with them – partly because investment in government Funds was now safer and more advantageous than it had once been. So, although it was still possible to start, like Chandos, from a minor government post, or from a legal career, as Hardwicke did, or even as the son of an apothecary, like Bubb Doddington, it required exceptional ability and enterprise. Frequently, too, success depended on an advantageous match and settlement from the bride's parents: the Bedfords, the Pelhams and many other families only arrived at their greatness as a result of gradual, patient progress through accumulation and marriage.

Throughout most of the century the number of English peers remained fairly static at between 160 and 170, though towards the end Pitt's liberal grant of new titles raised the number to nearly 300. They were socially and politically, though not always economically, distinct from the much larger class of gentry below them, for the peers monopolized the House of Lords, frequently took the leading roles in government, and provided the Lords-Lieutenant of the counties. But membership of the peerage did not necessarily confer economic predominance, for although none were richer than the richest dukes, some of the gentry enjoyed incomes considerably greater than the £3,000–£4,000 a year of the poorest peers. It seems best, therefore, to first categorize 'the great landlords' – a wealthy élite of about 400 families consisting mostly of English peers, but also containing some baronets and others – whose estates produced at least £5,000–£6,000 a year at the end of the century. This wealth and style of life distinguished them from other classes: above all, they possessed great houses which served as centres of social and political influence, and engaged in the ritual of the London season, equally essential for match-making as for the transaction of legal and government affairs. If income was derived exclusively from the rents of land, this would imply an estate of at least 10–20,000 acres, but the wealthiest owned 50,000 and more. The average income of the 400 was probably about £10,000 a year, and their combined estates totalled some 6 million acres, or one-fifth of the cultivated area of England. Over the century 1690–1790 it is likely that rents almost doubled, leaving the great landlords, whose estates, but for a small 'home farm', were almost invariably let out to tenants, the chief beneficiaries. Thus the predominance of the peers was unchallenged throughout the period. It is significant that, even in 1801, Colquhoan estimated their average income at £8,000, while that of the 2,000 'eminent merchants and bankers' was put at only £2,000.

The accumulation of the estate, the building or rebuilding of the country house and, thereafter, the maintenance of its fabric and household staff were the major items in the budget of any great landlord. If the estate had to be purchased *ab initio*, the sums required were enormous, sometimes crippling. Daniel Finch, second Earl of Nottingham, had succeeded his father, the former Lord Chancellor, in 1682. The first Earl had had no country seat, only a house in Kensington, but his son's second wife had brought a portion of £10,000 from an ancient aristocratic family, and he wished to live in the country. He eventually found what he sought at Burley-on-the-Hill, near Oakham in Rutland, for which he paid £50,000, calculated at 20 years' purchase. Even so there was no house, only stables on the property. It seems that Daniel Finch designed the new house himself, for there is no mention of an architect: he certainly supervised the supplies of materials – stone, bricks made on the site, and so on. The house, of second rank, probably cost about £30,000, double what Finch had estimated, but far less than Bubb Doddington's Eastbury, which is said to have totalled £140,000. Thereafter, his biggest single expense was for the portioning of his daughters, the eldest of whom had £20,000 and the four younger girls £5,000 each: a Grand Tour for his eldest son cost £3,000 and the education of two younger boys at Eton £2,000 a year. Against this, the Earl's income from his estates rose from £5,000 to £8,400 a year during his lifetime, though taxes took £1,100 of the latter sum: he had his wife's portion of £10,000, and £19,000 from the sale of the Kensington house. But above all, he depended like many other peers on his profits of office as Secretary of State, which brought some £45,000 during his lifetime, £37,000 of it within four years. Half the cost of Burley was, in fact, met out of the profits of office, the rest being invested in mortgages and government stocks. Even so, by 1710 Finch had no surplus out of current income, and the later portions for his daughters had to be borrowed: he died £22,000 in debt.

No nobleman gained more from office than Robert Walpole, and many regard the palace he built for himself at Houghton in Norfolk as the finest in England. Thirteen years' work went into the house itself, while Bridgeman changed the landscape for miles around and moved a whole village which detracted from the vista: Kent designed the furniture and decoration, Rysbrach the chimney-pieces and statuary, but Europe had to be scoured to find pictures good enough to adorn the walls. The whole cost is unknown, but must have been some tens of thousands, for the house was comparable with Audley End, which itself has been reckoned at £100,000. And Houghton was only one of several houses. There was also the Old Lodge in Richmond Park, altered at a cost of £14,000, and a London house in Arlington Street rented for £300 a year. The upkeep of these establishments was on an equally colossal scale – a wine bill of £1,000 a year, 77 weeders employed in the gardens at Houghton, £90,000 personal expenditure within a period of 4 years from 1714 to 1718. Like Finch, Walpole died in debt, to the tune of £40,000.

Such establishments required an immense number of servants – ranging from stewards and bailiffs to cooks, valets, kitchen-maids and stable staff – for their provisioning and maintenance. A staff of from 50 to 70 was common for the great landlords, in addition to outside gardeners and gamekeepers and a host of occasional servants. The Duke of Dorset's 45 servants at Knole cost him £474 a year in wages: at Audley End in 1773 the bill for indoor staff was £500. Alteration and improvement to the fabric often went on almost continuously, with scores of masons and carpenters to be paid, lodged and fed: at Syon the remodelling of the Jacobean gallery of Robert Adam alone cost £5,000, while the stables and kennels at Thoresby added another £4,000 to the house's £30,000. The total annual running expenses of a great landlord for housekeeping, repairs, stables, park, gardens, home farm and taxes were frequently in the region of £5,000–£6,000 a year. Of this, food was usually the largest single item, for in addition to the feeding of the household and staff, lavish hospitality to relatives and acquaintances was still expected and given. Some idea of the cost of this may be gathered from the growing practice of making yearly contracts with a provision merchant for food at a fixed price: thus, the Marquis of Anspach contracted in the 1790s at 10s. per head per day, the contractor retaining all broken meats. The Duke of Bedford's kitchen accounts were already costing £1,465 in 1671, but when the Duke of Kingston spent a mere 3 months at Thoresby in 1736 the household expenses were £1,477, £307 of which went on meat. The wages bill, in particular, tended to rise more rapidly than most other items in the later part of the century, as household staffs increased and the specialized functions of such key men as the gentleman of the horse, clerk of the kitchen, butler and cook became more highly valued. A total bill of £1,000 a year was not uncommon by the end of the century, with a hierarchy of earnings from £100 a year for the house steward, £60 for the clerk of the kitchen, £43 for the head keeper, £40 for the head cook, £28 for the housekeeper, down to £8 for footmen and £4 for maids: board, lodging and livery were, of course, supplied, and in some kitchens a supply of cold meat, tea and punch was always on the table.

In return for all this outlay a great household could expect a life of comfort and luxury, relieved of all petty, domestic cares and with time to devote to the important affairs of state, culture and recreation. Eating was more civilized than it had been in the past, or was to become in the future, more care devoted to quality and appearance, to flavour and variety, less sheer gorging than formerly. The usual pattern was of a very light breakfast – tea and rolls, bread and butter, perhaps toast – followed by the chief meal of the day, dinner, the hour of which advanced during the century from about 2 p.m. to 4 or 5 p.m. in polite society: supper was the last meal of the day, served any time between 9 p.m. and 1 or 2 a.m. at, say, a ball or late party. Both were substantial meals with large quantities of meat, fish and game. Foreign visitors complained, perhaps enviously, that 'English people prefer meat to bread, some people scarcely touching the latter', that 'No vegetables are eaten except with meat, and then always put under the roast or boiled meat', and, with more justice, that 'Desserts are only little used in England; a good butler is more esteemed here than a confectioner would be. . . .' But in fact the great household still baked and brewed, supplied itself with a variety of fruits and vegetables, fattened its own stock, shot its own game and frequently caught its own fish from its streams and ponds. And despite the foreigners' strictures, the increasing availability of sugar encouraged the use of cooked fruits and of the art of confectionery generally: Mrs Glasse, a forerunner of Mrs Beeton, whose recipes included quarts of the best cream and dozens of egg-yolks, was also responsible for introducing 'The Compleat Confectioner' in 1770. Great households could now more easily supplement their own produce with fresh (not salted) sea-fish, oysters (2s. the hundred), Scotch beef or Wiltshire ham, oranges and lemons (2s. 6d. the dozen) and other imported fruits, the prices of which had been lowered by improved communications. Some were undoubtedly tempted to over-eat, more to over-drink. Large quantities of claret, burgundy or Rhenish were taken with the meal, port or madeira with the dessert and after the ladies had withdrawn to their tea: in particular, the Methuen Treaty of 1703 greatly encouraged the use of the sweet Portuguese wines by placing a heavy duty of £55 a tun on French, so that it now became almost a patriotic duty to drink oneself insensible on port.

For other household needs which had formerly been supplied domestically or, at any rate, locally, there was also increasing dependence on specialized, professional producers. This was especially true of clothes and furniture, both of which increased in elegance and in frequency of change of style during the century. Dress materials, for men as well as women, included many imported fabrics such as Dutch linen, Flanders lace, Italian silks and Indian cottons, and they required to be made up to a standard of fashion and elegance that was usually beyond the skill of the local tailor and seamstress. Men's fashions reached their most absurd in the styles adopted by the 'macaroni', one of whom appeared in the Assembly Rooms at Bath in a shot-silk coat, pink satin waistcoat, breeches covered in silver net, white stockings with pink clocks and pink satin shoes with large pearl buckles: his hair was dressed very high, and stuck full of pearl pins. Though few of the great landlords went to such excesses, they, their wives and families had at least to dress in a fit style, and to do so usually cost several hundreds a year. Even the inelegant Dr Johnson spent £30 on a new suit and wig for his visit to Paris: a three-cornered beaver hat cost at least 2 guineas, a wig anything from £5 to £20. Oliver Goldsmith paid his tailor from £50 to £100 a year in the 1760s for such items as a blue velvet suit £21 10s. 9d., a Queen's blue dress suit £11 17s., a half-dress suit of rattan lined with satin £12 12s., a pair of silk breeks £2 3s. and a velvet waistcoat £1 1s. Women's clothes could, of course, cost infinitely more than this, a really wealthy noblewoman's wardrobe being reckoned in thousands of pounds. In addition to the clothes themselves were accessories ranging from an additional head of hair (£50–60) to the jewels worn on the hair or dress which were sometimes reckoned at £50,000.

Furnishing the country house was also an increasing, though less frequently recurring, expense, as the simple, locally made tables and chairs of Tudor and Stuart times were replaced by the elegant designs of Chippendale, Sheraton and Hepplewhite. The great number and size of rooms – of 11 Suffolk peers, 8 had houses with an average of 34 rooms – required many pieces to fill them, and the principal apartments, such as the dining-room, drawing-rooms, gallery, library and bed-chambers, needed to be refurbished from time to time in the current style. Chippendale's *Gentleman and Cabinet-Maker's Director*, published with the avowed intention 'to improve and refine the present taste', was especially influential in introducing new items of furniture such as side-tables, Pembroke tables, gilt console tables with mirrors, library and writing tables, besides many new designs for chairs and sofas. Although the price of individual pieces was still modest – typically £10 to £40 – the cost of furnishing a new house in contemporary style was very considerable. Thus James Best, the wealthy parvenu brewer who had an income of £5–6,000 a year, spent £1,000 furnishing his mansion at Chatham 'in the most fashionable and Genteelest Tast as can be (Sparing no Cost)'. In one respect, however – wall-coverings – costs were less than in the past, as plaster and wallpaper replaced panelling and tapestries. The vogue for the classical might tempt English lords to pay up to £1,000 for a (reconstituted) Roman statue, but paintings could still be had at reasonable prices, like the Guido for £20 discovered by Sir Richard Grosvenor's agent, or the sale of Dr Mead's collection in 1754 when works by Holbein, Rubens and Claude sold for about £100 each. Hogarth's unappreciated set of six pictures 'Marriage à la Mode' was sold in 1750 for 120 guineas, from which 24 guineas must be deducted as the cost of the frames. Reynolds and Gainsborough, through fashionable connexions, could command hundreds of guineas for a portrait, and there were, of course, the undiscerning like Lord Darnley, who simply bought 'all the small pictures in the collection of the Duke of Orleans' for £20,000 to cover the walls of Cobham Hall.

The education of children was also an increasing expense to the eighteenth-century household, as polite society demanded higher standards of learning and culture, and the maintenance of political power a superior and separate system of instruction. The sons of the gentry might go to one of the four hundred or so grammar schools, but a peer's son required to be educated either at home by a private tutor or at public school, before proceeding to university or one of the Inns of Court. A private tutor would typically cost £50 a year and his board and lodging, still comparable with the earlier period, but at Oxford or Cambridge costs had risen greatly as the style of life of wealthy undergraduates came to include gambling, horse-racing and heavy drinking. Chandos's son spent over £400 a year at Oxford, including 100 guineas for his own tutor there. The premier boarding schools like Eton were of a similar cost. But these sums were negligible compared with the expenses of foreign travel which now usually followed the years of formal education. The Grand Tour – an opportunity to visit the great monuments and galleries of Europe, to acquire some fluency in a foreign language, and to be instructed in the arts of fencing and dancing – had now become *de rigueur* for the sons of the wealthy, Gibbon being told in 1785 that as many as 40,000 Englishmen and their servants were travelling or resident on the Continent. Few spent as long or as much abroad as the Duke of Kingston, whose 10 years' Tour cost in excess of £40,000: 2 or 3 years at a cost of £3-5,000 was more usual, but the large families of the period implied that this would probably have to be repeated, on a more modest scale, for 2 or 3 younger sons. Girls were, of course, a far lighter liability until their marriage settlements had to be found: even so, it was becoming more common to send them to a boarding-school, where some education in reading, writing, arithmetic (for household accounts), foreign languages and deportment was given: they varied in cost from those like Mrs Whitney's Boarding School for Young Ladies at Buckingham (12 guineas a year, plus a further guinea if tea and sugar were required) to 60 guineas a year for a fashionable school at Hayes where there were many 'extras'.

The last principal head of expenditure of a great landlord could broadly be described as leisure or recreation. For some peers, of course, this consisted of political activity in the House of Lords, to which their rank entitled them, but sons and relatives who desired a seat in the Commons might require considerable financial support. The costs of an election campaign rose substantially after the Septennial Act (1716) lengthened Parliament's life from 3 to 7 years and the possibilities of fruits of office were proportionately increased. A seat at Harwich in 1727 cost the Earl of Egmont £900: in 1754 Bubb Doddington lost an election on which he had spent £2,500, and had been obliged to waste much time 'in the infamous and disreputable compliance with the low habits of venal wretches' (he polled 105 out of 338 votes). A surer way of entering Parliament was by the purchase of an uncontested 'pocket borough', where the few enfranchised dutifully cast their votes for the owner's nominee, but a pocket borough could cost £5,000–£6,000 for a term of 7 years which might be all too short a time to establish a political reputation. Most great landlords and their families, however, found their real recreation on their country estates, in the London season, and on holiday at a spa or watering-place. Some noble families were impoverished by gambling at hazard, brag, loo or commerce, where hundreds and thousands of pounds were sometimes lost in an evening. In 1770, for instance, Lord Stavordale lost £11,000 at one sitting at Almack's, but was lucky enough to recover it all by one hand at hazard: according to Walpole, 'he swore a great oath – "Now, if I had been playing deep, I might have won millions!"' Rural recreations were still chiefly those of the chase, though fox-hunting was now more common as the forests and deer-parks dwindled, and the shooting of birds was taking the place of hawking. Several hundreds a year on horses, hounds and their keepers was common for a sporting lord, but far larger sums were needed by the great patrons of the turf as horse-racing became a fashionable pursuit. To keep racing stables, a string of horses, jockeys and stable-boys could run away with thousands, and at least one noble lord was practically ruined by the addiction: Lord Grosvenor, with an annual income of £20,000, was spending £7,000 a year on his activities at Newmarket, and at one point had accumulated debts of £151,500. After such extravagances, the costs of a few weeks' stay at Bath or one of the dozen or more other spas were quite modest. The distinguished visitor to Beau Brummel's city was always welcomed by the bell-ringers (10s. 6d.) and was required to subscribe 2 guineas towards the balls. Concert tickets cost 5s. each, a subscription to the booksellers 10s. 6d., and a similar sum to the coffee-houses for pen, ink and the conveyance of letters. At Harrogate's less fashionable spa a dinner could be had for 1s. and a modest breakfast for as little as 2d. The development of Brighton and other seaside resorts begins only in the 1770s, and properly belongs to the next period.

4

The gentry were far larger, and much less homogeneous in origin and in wealth than the great landlords. Their distinguishing characteristic was the possession of an unearned income from land – rents, mortgages or investments – perhaps supplemented by some farming for profit on their own account, or by the profits of office or a profession. They lived the life of leisured gentlemen, though on a more modest scale than the peerage. Their size must be less certain than that of the aristocracy, since there was no precise definition of membership, but Gregory King in the late seventeenth century placed the wealthy gentry – that is, baronets and knights – at 1,400 families, and the lesser gentry, the esquires and gentlemen, at 15,000. Socially and politically they belonged with the great landowners in the ruling class, but found their functions in the Commons rather than the Lords, county magistrates rather than Lords-Lieutenant. Economically there was a wide spread of income from decayed squires with £200 or £300 a year to the wealthy gentry with rent-rolls of up to £5,000, hardly distinguishable from the great, landed families with whom they often had familial connexions. In 1790 there were probably about 800 families of these wealthy gentry, with incomes of £3,000–£4,000 a year, sufficient to maintain a large house, servants, carriages, and at least an occasional London season. Below them were 3–4,000 squires, with incomes of £1,000–£3,000 a year, and below these again a much larger group of perhaps 15,000 gentlemen, living modestly on incomes from £200 or £300 up to £1,000 a year. Altogether the gentry held about half the total cultivated land of England, with the 4,000 or so wealthier members themselves owning between a quarter and a third in estates ranging from 1,000 to 7,000 acres. To purchase such a property, yielding say £1,000 a year, would have cost in the middle of the century around £30,000.

The great landowners were, as we have seen, substantial gainers from the economic and price changes of the period. It seems likely that the wealthy gentry, at least, shared in the gain, their incomes rising perhaps by about a third over the century: gentry property was, on the whole, already more enclosed and more fully exploited at an earlier date than the really great estates had been, and the proportional increase was consequently less. But there is little doubt that numbers of the small gentry had suffered from the growing concentration of landownership into great estates, and had been hard hit by the heavy war taxation of William III and Anne at the beginning of the century.

Those who had once been courted were now ignored [Professor Plumb has written].... So men whose fathers had voted for Shaftesbury or welcomed William III as a deliverer turned Tory. What strength and vigour the Tory party possessed in the early part of the century sprang from the social animosity of the country gentlemen of modest means....

Some put their younger sons to the Church, where the income of livings was rising and pluralism encouraged: others found opportunities in commerce, in law or medicine. Above all, many of the gentry sought to arrest their dwindling wealth and power through public office. A judgeship and the fees that went with it could bring thousands a year, but political office was the greatest prize, which could elevate a family from obscurity to an earldom in a generation. James Brydges, fourth son of an impoverished Herefordshire gentleman, built Cannons out of his tenure of the Paymastership, and as Duke of Chandos had a quarter of a million pounds in South Sea, India and other stock, £80,000 in mortgages and an income of £10,000 a year from estates. Similarly Henry Fox, first Lord Holland, had risen from the mere gentry by court favour and government office, and at his death was able to pay off his sons' debts of £200,000 and still leave them well endowed.

The Purefoy household of Shalstone Manor, near Brackley in north Buckinghamshire, is a not untypical gentry family of the middle rank. The widowed Mrs Purefoy ran the estate with great efficiency and meticulous detail: her son, Henry, was a local justice, for some time Sheriff of the county, a scholar rather than a sportsman. The family and its six servants were largely self-supporting for their basic foods – there were milking cows, sheep, goats, poultry, a dovecote and 3 fish-ponds – and did their own baking and brewing. But almost everything else was obtained from London rather than the poorly stocked market towns of Brackley and Buckingham. The Purefoys seldom had the time to spend two days travelling to the capital: instead, like many similar families, they had London agents who were commissioned to buy anything from Canary wine (8s. a gallon) to an iron chest 'that will secure papers from fire in case a house be fired'. The agent's task must have been unenviable, for the Purefoys set high standards. One consignment of Canary was 'on the fret', and was 'like bottled Cyder and flew all about ye Cellar and broke ye Bottles': chocolate was 'so bitter and high dried she [Mrs Purefoy] can't drink it'. Groceries were bought in large quantities – raisins by the hundredweight, sugar by the half-hundredweight ($10\frac{1}{2}$d. the lb.), rice by the stone, and so on, every few months: fish and oysters were also bought in London, though many consignments suffered during the heat of summer, and some were uneatable. Henry's clothes were naturally made there, and he often addressed letters to his tailor to inquire 'whether they button their Cloaths with silver or gold buttons' and 'what Cloaths are most fashionable'. A suit, which turned out to be too long in the coat and too short in the breaches, cost £13 15s. Much less was paid for furniture, a 4-ft round mahogany folding table costing only £2 7s., and a 4-ft by 2-ft mirror in a gold frame £3 16s. The difference lay in the relative cost of materials – velvet at 24s. the yard, serge at 5s. the yard and gold wire buttons at 9s. the dozen ($4\frac{1}{2}$ dozen were used in the coat) made a fashionable suit a very expensive commodity.

The same fashion dictated that such a coat was now a necessity even for an unpretentious country squire.

A similar pattern of expenditure is suggested by the Diary and Letter-Book of Nicholas Blundell, Squire of Crosby and Ditton near Liverpool, which covers the years 1702-28. When courting his future wife at Oxford, Nicholas paid £4 9s. 9d. for a new black coat and, somewhat inappropriately, £1 10s. for a pair of pistols: he must have impressed, for the lady consented and brought a dowry of £2,000. A new 'Campaign Perry-Wig' for his wedding cost £10, his wife's ring only 25s. Like many of his class Blundell was a careful man. When he stayed in London with a servant for 12 days his bill was 4d. less than the charge for keeping their 2 horses: for wine he paid 28s. a dozen, for 5 pairs of shoes for his wife 13s. 9d., a copy of Aesop's *Fables* 3s. 6d. and toys, bought at the fair, 3d. each. For drawing a tooth he paid 1s., and bleeding was performed by the local butcher at the same price. But 2 liveries for his servants cost £13 6s. 2d. – far more than their annual wages – and when his two little girls grew old enough to enter society their complete wardrobes cost £177. There were few pure luxuries, either of food or anything else, in this careful household. London pewter plates at 18s. a dozen were for everyday use, a silver coffee-pot at £9 12s. a rare extravagance, for the coffee-cups cost only 6d. each. Furniture was purchased at local auctions – a chest of drawers for 30s. and a 5s. chair – and working suits and alterations were made by a visiting tailor whose board was carefully costed at 4d. a day.

There were others, of course, who squandered their estates on gambling, racing, drink or all three, who were uncultured, boorish survivals from a less civilized age. Fielding's Squire Western, who spent all the morning in field exercises and all the evening with bottle companions, retiring to bed 'so drunk that he could not see', was, if contemporary observers are to be credited, not grossly overdrawn. Drunkenness was the national vice of all Englishmen, though 'four bottle men' were especially a product of the hunting-field. The worst vulgarities of speech and manners were now subject to public criticism, and a new ideal of the sober, kindly, polite gentleman was emerging, though as late as 1784 François de la Rochefoucauld could still notice that after the ladies withdraw from dinner 'the sideboard is furnished with a number of chamber-pots, and it is a common practice to relieve oneself whilst the rest are drinking: one has no kind of concealment. . . .' But standards of behaviour, as well as of accommodation and comfort, generally improved throughout the century as aristocratic fashions percolated downwards. Much attention was given to the improvement and modernization of manor-houses and farmhouses to convert them into desirable gentlemen's residences: some of the wealthy gentry's houses were given classical façades and ornamental lakes and gardens, with the stables and domestic offices well removed from the principal rooms. Even the careful Nicholas Blundell converted a dairy into an additional parlour at a cost of £58, and a house with twenty or more bedrooms – some comfortably furnished with 4-poster beds, down mattresses and quilts for the family, others with truckle beds for the servants – was not uncommon for the class. The number of servants naturally depended on the position of the family and size of house: 6 was probably the minimum, 12 to 20 more usual for the prosperous gentry. Dudley North at Glenham Hall had 8 men, 4 boys, a housekeeper and 3 maids; the Bests at Boxley had a total of 13 – butler, groom, coachman, postilion, gardener, housekeeper, cook, nurse and 5 maids, at total yearly wages of £106 14s. A country estate would need steward, huntsman and gamekeepers besides.

Country squires were traditionally fond of good living, of heavy eating and deep drinking, though here too it is likely that there was some reformation of manners as the century progressed. Few could afford a French chef, but many English cooks had absorbed something of French practice, could make a sauce and dress vegetables better than their mothers had done. The meal-pattern was like that of the aristocracy – a small breakfast at 9 or 10 a.m., followed by sherry and biscuits at midmorning, dinner at 2 or 3 p.m. and a cold supper at 9 or 10 p.m.: increasingly tea was becoming interposed between the last two. A 'polite' dinner was served in 2 courses, several dishes to each:

The first course was part of a large Cod, a Chine of Mutton, some Soup, a Chicken Pye, Puddings and Roots etc. Second course,

A HISTORY OF THE COST OF LIVING

Pidgeons and Asparagus, a Fillet of Veal with Mushrooms and high Sauce with it, Roasted Sweetbreads, hot Lobster, Apricot Tart, and in the middle a Pyramid of Syllabubs and Jellies. We had Dessert of Fruit after Dinner, and Madeira. White Port and red to drink as Wine.

Everyday fare is more typically represented by the dinner described by Catherine Hutton:

Three boiled chickens at top, a very fine haunch of venison at bottom; ham on one side, a flour pudding on the other, and beans in the middle. After the cloth was removed we had gooseberries, and a remarkably fine dish of apricots.

Food and servants were the biggest recurrent items in gentry accounts, but from time to time there might be a major expense for refurnishing and redecorating a room, especially if it were to be done in a fashionable style. An upholsterer's bill for a fine new bedroom totals £66 9s. 6d., the main items being 60 yards of green silk damask for the bed-hangings (£34 15s.), a large feather bed, bolster and fustian pillows (£8 10s.) and a 4-post bedstead, sacking, bottom and casters (£3 10s. 6d.): blankets cost 24s. each, and 65 yards of red and white sprigged wallpaper £2 8s. 9d. Nor were Josiah Wedgwood's vases cheap at 2 and 3 guineas the set of 3. Education was not nearly so expensive an item for the gentry as for the aristocracy, especially if they were content with a local grammar school for their sons where they would mix with the children of yeomen and even shopkeepers: alternatively, there might be tutoring at home by the local parson, or, for older children, a few years away at a school like Westminster, where £20 a year for boarding and another 5 or 6 guineas for schooling was a modest outlay from an income of £1,000 a year. There was usually no Grand Tour for the sons of the gentry, though they might continue to be a burden of some hundreds a year if they took an Army commission rather than entering trade or a profession. Again a London season, with its round of entertainments and lavish hospitality, was not usually possible for the gentry. Wealthy men like Sir Thomas Chester of Knole Park might manage it occasionally – a 4-months' stay at lodgings in Golden Square (4 guineas a week) cost £755 (£371 for housekeeping, £51 for wine, £31 for meat, £4 14s. for candles), but this was modest indeed compared with the Duke of Kingston's £2,000 for a fortnight's stay or the Duke of Devonshire's £1,000 on a single masked ball and supper. The gentry stayed with friends and relatives, perhaps managed a month at Bath or one of the less fashionable spas now and again, visited London singly and for business rather than pleasure, though, like all visitors, they would take the opportunity of making some purchases for their womenfolk, visiting the famous Vauxhall Gardens (1s. entrance fee) and perhaps sampling a Sunday 'ordinary' there at prices from 9d. to 8s. But generally the squires lived quietly in the country, busying themselves about their estates, legislating and politicking, reading, riding and enjoying themselves at table: their standard of living had, perhaps, more ingredients of the good life than any other in the period.

5

The rural middle class, far more numerous though generally far less prosperous than the gentry, consisted of the freeholders, or yeomen, and the tenant-farmers. They were distinguished from the classes above them by being occupiers who actually cultivated their lands and derived the bulk of their income from them, rather than rent-receivers who had let out their estates to others. The yeomen were freeholders, and as such entitled to vote in the county elections: farmers were tenants, not necessarily less prosperous, though generally unenfranchised. King assessed the freeholders at 180,000 families, 11 times as numerous as the gentry, and the farmers at 150,000, but it is likely that the freeholders declined subsequently, with the growing concentration of landownership, to perhaps 100,000 by the end of the century. They held between them some 6 or 7 million acres, or one quarter of the total cultivated area, in properties averaging about 50 acres each, but with a range from 20 to 150 acres. There was a similar range of incomes, from perhaps £30 to £300 a year (average about £100) for the smaller freeholders and farmers to £150–£700 (average £300) for the large farmers at the end of the century. On the large estates farm incomes rose considerably in the latter half of the century as the market for food expanded, bringing to some a standard of living quite comparable with that of the lesser gentry: this was especially true of the good farming country of the Home Counties and East Anglia which was easily accessible to the great market of London. In such areas the farmer could expect to make a profit of the traditional 'three rents' – one for the landlord, one for himself and a third for his working expenses.

Contemporary comment is full of admiration – or complaint – at the progress of the farmer towards prosperity and gentility – his fashionable clothes, well-furnished house, his wine and his silver plate, the education and accomplishments of his daughter who is indistinguishable 'from the daughter of a Duke by her dress, both equally wishing to imitate something, but they know not what'. Arthur Young's ideal of the farmer who lived in his 'large, roomy, clean kitchen' with smoked bacon and hams hanging from the ceiling, went in for no show of any kind, shot but did not ride to hounds and had a single good nag in his stable, was fast disappearing as rising incomes brought luxury and social imitation. The reformation of manners had beneficial effects on the farmers as it did on the gentry and nobility. Coarseness and drunkenness were ceasing to be socially acceptable by the end of the century, literacy and an interest in affairs outside the parish necessary acquisitions.

The poorer sort of farmers ... who before that period spent their evenings in relating stories of witches, ghosts, hobgoblins etc. now shorten the winter nights by hearing their sons and daughters read tales, romances etc., and on entering their houses you may see Tom Jones, Roderick Random and other entertaining books stuck up on their bacon racks. If John goes to market with a load of hay he is charged to be sure not to forget to bring home Peregrine Pickle's Adventures. ...

The circulation of newspapers doubled between 1753 and 1792, and some at least of the 15 million of the latter date penetrated into the countryside, helping to break down the ignorance and isolation of centuries: the folio of 4 pages was still dear at 2d. or 3d., but Cowper could now have it delivered every evening to his country retreat, and farmers could, after the right to report Parliamentary proceedings was conceded in 1771, follow the debates on the Corn Laws and take an intelligent interest in affairs of state. Most recreations were still local – visits to markets and fairs, hunts and race-meetings – with occasional journeys to the county town for a new suit or set of chairs, even occasionally to the capital. For the womenfolk there were balls and dinner-parties at the great house, for the men the monthly meetings of the local Lunar Society (or Lunatick Club) where friends assembled when the moon was full enough to light the country ways.

Above all, the eighteenth century farmer and his family travelled far more than their ancestors had ever done. This was partly a consequence of an improved economic position, partly a result of better roads and public conveyances. Horse or gig took him to the market town, but longer journeys to relatives and friends, to London, spas and beauty-spots (even the once-despised Lake District had come to be regarded as 'picturesque' well before Wordsworth), depended on the efficient system of stage and mail-coaches developed in the latter half of the century, and on the improvements in road surfacing made by Telford, Macadam and other civil engineers. The mid-century 50–60 miles a day was doubled by the end of the period: the 4-day journey from London to Exeter was halved in 1764 by turnpikes and faster coaches, while by 1784 Palmer's improved mail-coaches were covering London to Bristol in 16 hours at a cost of 28s. Stage-coaches generally charged 2½d. a mile, plus another ½d. in winter: posthorses for the single rider in a hurry cost 7d. to 9d. the mile. These charges still made long distances expensive, especially when the costs of food and lodging at coaching-inns were added in – thus, the fare from Edinburgh to London was £4 10s., but with meals, tips and over-night stops Sir Walter Scott paid nearly £50 for the journey. Coaching-inns varied greatly in price and quality. There were good ones, like 'The Lion' at Liverpool, where 'a very good supper, consisting of veal cutlets, pigeons, asparagus, lamb and salad, apple-pie and tarts' cost only 6d. a head, and bad ones like the hotel in Windsor where Moritz was offered a room which 'much resembled a prison for malefactors': on his departure, the chamber-maid stood at the door and asked to be remembered: ' "Yes, yes," said I, "I shall long remember your most ill-mannered behaviour and shameful incivility," and so I gave her nothing.' By the end of the century hundreds of coaches were leaving the great London terminal inns daily – as many as 5 a day to Dover and Bath and at least 2 or 3 a day to most principal towns. The traveller without a coach of his own had acquired a new mobility unknown to earlier generations, as had the despatch of letters, parcels and small packages. The movement of heavy goods was affected much more by the development of canals after 1760, reducing freight charges to between a quarter and a half those of the coach companies.

For education, freeholders and farmers depended largely on the grammar schools, where endowments generally kept the fees down to a few guineas a year, or on private schools and academies of various kinds. The curriculum of the grammar school was still narrowly classical, and ill-adapted for anything except entrance to one of the learned professions. In consequence middle-class parents in particular had turned increasingly to private schools where mathematics, modern languages and even science gave a more practical and relevant training. A boarding-school of this kind might cost £30–£40 a year, compared with the 20s.–30s. of a country day-school, and would be patronized only by the 'better' freeholders with social aspirations. Increasing numbers chose one of the nonconformist academies, where perhaps the most progressive education and best teachers of the eighteenth century were to be found. As a typical example, Warrington Academy in 1777 charged £17 a year for commons, £3 3s. for an apartment, and offered courses of lectures ranging from theology, ethics, classics, mathematics and natural philosophy, theoretical and experimental, at 3 guineas each, to chemistry, anatomy, book-keeping and surveying at 2 guineas and arithmetic, writing and drawing at 1 guinea; boys were entered at 13 and normally completed the courses in 5 years.

Though Thomas Turner was himself a village shopkeeper at East Hoathly, Sussex, his Diary gives a fair picture of the standard of life of the smaller farmer in the middle of the century. He is literate and religious, yet frequently drinks too much and enjoys himself at roisterous parties where the parson, Mr Porter, presides over the festivities. He will read Tillotson's *Sermons* or Sherlock *'On Death'* before supping with friends and being carried home early next morning, 'not thoroughly sober'. At the beginning of the New Year he draws up 'rules of diet' for himself – not more than 4 glasses of strong beer or 8 of wine a day – which are as regularly broken a few days later. He enjoys food, and when trade is good eats amply, though not luxuriously – for Sunday dinner a piece of boiled beef and carrots, followed by currant suet pudding, or a saddle of lamb with onion sauce, or a roast goose with apple sauce. Herrings are bought in quantity (1,100 for 33s.), some for sale in the shop, but some for a dinner of 'salt-fish, egg sauce, parsnips and potatoes', and when he gives a party to 18 of his friends there are 4 boiled chickens, 4 boiled ducks, minced veal, sausages, cold roast goose, chicken pasty and ham. He pays 10s.–14s. a lb. for tea, £1 15s. for a new wig and 4s. for renovating an old one, and complains at having to pay 10s. 6d. for Dr Poole's visit to his sick wife – 'What a fine thing to be a physician, and charge as they please.'

One of the most visible signs of prosperity was the improvement of farmhouses that went on particularly in the second half of the century. Though some farmers continued to live in the simple, traditional style that delighted Arthur Young, others enlarged and modernized, furnished and adorned parlours and dining-rooms to a standard quite comparable with that of the gentry: in so doing they inevitably separated themselves from the domestic staff and from servants living-in with whom they had previously shared meals and leisure hours. Thus Crabbe described the house of his great-uncle who farmed his own estate of about £600 a year:

On entering the house, there was nothing at first sight to remind one of the farm: a spacious hall, paved with black and white marble, at one extremity a very handsome drawing-room, and the other a fine old staircase of black oak, polished until it was as slippery as ice, and having a chime clock and a barrel organ on its landing place.

But he went on to say that these apartments were only used 'on great and solemn occasions', and that at other times the family lived in the old-fashioned kitchen along with the servants. At the other extreme was the Yorkshire farmhouse described by Southey, the home of Dr Daniel Dove, which had only 7 rooms including cellar and dairy: the kitchen had a huge open fire-place, and the furniture consisted of a pair of 'beehive' chairs, some oak settles and chests, a great oak table and a corner-cupboard in which were displayed as treasures a silver saucepan, a silver goblet and 4 apostle spoons. But the Tudor or Stuart farmhouse was already almost a curiosity, for in many parts of the country it had either been remodelled out of recognition or entirely replaced by new buildings in the simple Georgian style. Brick was replacing stone and timber, even in the stone counties, and even though, in some areas at least, it was more expensive: William Halfpenny's *Useful Architecture in Twenty-One New Designs for Country Parsonages, Farm Houses and Inns* (1752) estimated that a house costing £208 in stone would cost £50 more in brick. Ware's *Complete Body of Architecture* (1756) describes the requirements of a country parsonage which was to set the pattern for the next 200 years – a central door, hall and staircase, parlour on one side, dining-room on the other, behind these a study and a kitchen with out-buildings for wash-house and stable, bedrooms above – until it was disturbed by the 'open plan'. Especially after about 1760, a phase of major rebuilding greatly improved the construction, comfort and cleanliness of the English farmhouse, raising its general standard to probably the best in Europe.

Inside, the improved farmhouse typically had 6 to 8 rooms – a living-room, 1 or 2 parlours, kitchen, brewery, dairy and bedchambers above: there might also be a third, garret floor of servants' rooms. The contents of such houses varied enormously with income. Thomas Furber, a Cheshire farmer, set up house in 1767 with £25 worth of furniture and household goods, but a number of yeomen died with inventories valued at £400 to £700, about half of which usually represented farm stock and implements. Besides beds and bedding, tables, chairs and cupboards, some of these inventories contain evidence of a new degree of wealth and refinement – books and musical instruments, rugs, clocks, desks, mirrors, tablecloths, napkins and silver plate – which distinguish the eighteenth-century farmer from his seventeenth-century ancestors. Pottery and china were rare until late in the century, the usual cooking and eating utensils being of pewter, brass and tin. It was still common, at any rate in the North of England, for farmers' daughters

THE EIGHTEENTH CENTURY

to spin and for clothes to be home-made: many households bought an annual web of linen and woollen cloth and either made it up themselves or hired a local or travelling tailor to do so for them. Bought clothes, like bought bread and beer, were common only in the decadent South.

Life in the mid-eighteenth-century farmhouse was perhaps more pleasant than it had ever been before. Parson Woodforde, on £400 a year, was able to keep 5 or 6 servants, to travel freely, entertain friends, above all to eat heartily and with some discrimination. To the traditional staples of meat, fish, home-baked bread and home-brewed beer and ale, the eighteenth century added tea and coffee, port and brandy, and reduced the cost of imported foods such as sugar and fruit: it also greatly increased the supply and variety of home-grown vegetables. Hams were home-cured in the smoke of the open fire, some pork and fish still salted down for winter use, though fresh meat was more available than in the past. Offal was not despised, and in less wealthy households meat was eked out with pies, puddings and dumplings, and, of course, with bread. But Woodforde's bill for flour in 1790 was £5 7s. 6d., compared with £46 5s. for meat and £22 18s. 6d. for malt. His was essentially a carnivorous diet, a typical ordinary dinner consisting of 'a leg of mutton boiled, a batter pudding, and a couple of ducks' or 'a couple of rabbits smothered with onions, a neck of mutton boiled and a goose roasted, with a currant pudding and a plain one, followed by the drinking of tea'. 'Plumb pudding' was a great favourite, and numerous fruits, vegetables and salads are mentioned, though rather as afterthoughts. Woodforde's food bill was something over £100 a year, or about £2 a week for a household of 6. In 1808, when prices had climbed considerably from the late-eighteenth-century level, Batchelor estimated the average cost of feeding a farmer's family at 7s. 3½d. per person per week, which corresponds quite closely; the basic diet for this calculation included 2 lb. of meat, 1 lb. of cheese, ½ lb. of butter and sugar, 2½ gallons of skimmed milk, 10½ pints of beer and 7 of ale each week, besides vegetables, bread, tea and other items. But 7s. a week was also a typical wage on which the agricultural labourer had to feed, house, clothe and otherwise support a family: it is to this much more numerous class, whose lot in the period was, by contrast, often one of increasing poverty, that we must now turn.

6

Numerically, agricultural labourers must have made up almost half the total population of England in the eighteenth century. The contemporary calculations are not easy to disentangle, but Gregory King in 1688 placed 'labouring people and outservants' at 1,275,000, cottagers and paupers at 1,300,000: some, at least, of his 30,000 vagrants also belong, by origin, to the category, and the poorest of the 750,000 farmers must have been little removed in standard of life from wage-earners. This would give a figure for the rural poor of about 2¾ millions out of a total population of 5½ millions. But the more interesting part still of King's statistics is his estimates of the average annual income of the categories. Farmers' families earn £44 a year (£8 15s. per head) and spend £42 10s.; labouring people's families earn a mere £6 10s. a year (£2 a head) but spend £7 6s. 3d. According to these calculations half the population was 'decreasing the wealth of the kingdom', and was maintained only by the generosity of the other half in the form of poor relief. The cost of this, in fact, rose steadily throughout the century, from a mere £400,000 in 1700 to more than £2 million in the 1780s.

Eighteenth-century writers were much given to 'political arithmetic' – to calculations of what the poor earned and what they needed to spend, usually with the object of showing that their wages, if wisely laid out, were amply sufficient for a comfortable subsistence: they were representative of the mercantilist interest in cheap labour and the belief that higher earnings would both demoralize the recipient and price the nation out of her overseas markets. Such estimates were usually mere mental diversions, having little basis in observed facts. Ten years after Gregory King's calculations, Richard Dunning estimated that a labourer's wage of 2s. 6d. a week would support himself and 2 children in food, drink and clothes, while his wife's earnings would maintain her and one further child: it was left unclear as to what would happen if the wife were unable to work, or if the family were improvident enough to have more than 3 children. In 1756 Joseph Massie calculated the average wage of the labourer at 5s. a week, or £13 a year, while in 1768 Arthur Young estimated an average labouring family of husband, wife and 3 children as earning £37 15s. a year and spending £21 17s.: he then, unsuccessfully, tried to discover poor families who would confirm his statistics. The variety of these estimates indicates the great uncertainty that existed about the labourer's real earnings and standard of life. Much depended on the size and age of his family, on the part of the country in which he lived, perhaps above all, on the state of the harvest in a particular year. But on one basic fact – that throughout the century about half the total population was so poor as to be very close to the margin of existence – there seems to have been wide agreement, for almost a hundred years after King's gloomy conclusions, *The Universal Dictionary of Trade and Commerce* of 1775 reached almost precisely the same conclusion – that, of a population of 6 million, 2,950,000 still constituted the 'decreasing' class.

Until about the end of the century, when the investigations of the Reverend David Davies and Sir Frederic Eden introduced a more realistic and compassionate element into the discussion, contemporaries were usually content to explain the poverty of the poor in terms of extravagance and self-indulgence, idleness, improvidence and drunkenness. According to Daniel Defoe,

Where an English labouring man, with his 9s. per week, lives wretchedly and poor, a Dutchman with that wages will live very tolerably well, keep the wolf from the door, and have everything handsome about him. . . . There is nothing more frequent than for an Englishman to work till he has got his pocket full of money, and then go and be idle, or perhaps drunk, till 'tis all gone, and perhaps himself in debt. . . .

What Defoe ascribed to the ale-house, Jonas Hanway blamed on tea.

Look into all the cellars in London, you will find men or women sipping their tea, in the morning or afternoon, and very often both morning and afternoon: those will have their tea who have not bread. . . . You may see labourers who are mending the roads drinking their tea; it is even drunk in cinder-carts; and what is not less absurd, sold out in cups to Hay-makers. . . . Were they the sons of tea-sippers who won the fields of Cressy and Agincourt . . . ?

In fact, Eden's careful estimate was that an average of £2 a year was spent by labourers on tea out of a family income approaching £40 (1797). Tea, wheat bread, sugar, butter, luxurious clothing all had their critics, partly because many of these things had to be imported and therefore took wealth out of the country, partly because they encouraged desire and greed and made the labourer demand higher wages. The view that found general acceptance was that expressed by William Temple: 'The only way to make them [the labourers] temperate and industrious, is to lay them under the necessity of labouring all the time they can spare from meals and sleep, in order to procure the common necessaries of life.'

Some of the difficulties of assessing the labourer's real earnings have already been mentioned. However, it may be said that up to the middle of the eighteenth century 6s. a week would be a typical wage for an adult male agricultural labourer, finding his own accommodation and keep, that 7s. was a more common wage in the 1770s, and that there were further increases during the price-rise of the 1780s and 1790s. Many wage-trends appear to have begun to move upwards in the 1740s during the period of exceptionally good seasons, to fall back, relative to prices, in the later years of the century. But there were many variations around these figures, particularly with respect to locality. Thorold Rogers places the labourer's wage up to 1750 at from 1s. to 1s. 6d. a day (for a 6-day week). Arthur Young, who carefully noted agricultural wages in his series of tours which began in 1767, estimated the wage in Hertfordshire at £18 a year (7s. a week), in Northamptonshire and Derbyshire £17, in East Anglia £20, claiming that there had often been increases of 20 or 30 per cent within the last 20 years. The best-paid labourers were those of Kent and Middlesex, with 11s. 4d. a week, the worst-paid those of Wiltshire and Gloucestershire with 5s. 2½d. These findings led Young to the general theory that wages declined as the distance from London increased: in the southern counties they fell from 10s. 9d. a week in districts up to 20 miles from the capital to

6s. 3d. in areas from 110 to 170 miles distant, while in a northerly direction they moved from 7s. 1d. at a distance of 50 miles to 5s. 8d. over 300 miles from London. Finally, the careful calculations of Reverend David Davies for Berkshire in 1795 give:

	£	s	d
35 weeks at 7s.	12	5	0
17 weeks at 10s. (piece-work)	8	10	0
Per annum	20	15	0
The wife at 6d. a week	1	6	0
Total	22	1	0

Extra harvest earnings were reserved to cover the cottage rent, typically about £2 a year.

Clearly, the standard of comfort of the labourer varied greatly, and no general trend throughout the country as a whole is discernible. In her study of wages in 3 distinct regions – London and the metropolitan area, the north of England and the west of England – Mrs Gilboy discovered differences so wide as to make any general statement about the labourer's standards almost meaningless. Thus, in Kent rates moved up from 1s. a day (1s. 2d. in summer, 10d. in winter) in the 1720s to 1s. 6d. to 1s. 8d. in 1793; in the west they were generally lower, though comparable around Oxford and Bristol which constituted minor metropolitan areas, and there was almost no tendency for wages to rise throughout the whole century; in the North Riding of Yorkshire wages were low in the western moorlands and high in the south-east, while in the industrialized areas of the West Riding and Lancashire agricultural wages of up to 2s. and even 2s. 6d. a day were being paid by the 1770s. In fact, northern wages showed a continuous rise, doubling over the century: in the metropolitan area the rise was much less, and chiefly occurred during the first third of the century, while in the west it was less still and confined to the years after 1770. It is clear that there was already developing that contrast, well-known to nineteenth-century observers, between the high-wage north of England, where the growth of mining and manufacturing industry forced up agricultural rates to a competitive level, and the low-wage areas of the south and west, where there was often no alternative to an already over-supplied agricultural industry.

The wages that have been quoted do not, of course, represent the real earnings of the labourer. His wife was expected to work, either on the land or at domestic 'out-work' trades such as spinning, and his children, at 7 or 8 years old, would pick stones, scare birds or take part in simple farming tasks. Their contributions to the total family budget were often vital. Children could earn 3d. or 4d. a day, a wife 6d. to 10d. and more in the harvest: in a family of husband, wife and 4 children, the wages of the wife and 2 children might double the man's earnings. Again, however, the opportunities for additional earnings varied in the different regions, being greatest in the north, where women traditionally took part in heavy agricultural work like haying and manure-spreading, and also had the advantage of domestic or factory textile employment; in the west, on the other hand, the early decline of the woollen industry reduced such possibilities. In some areas, too, there were important supplementary benefits to the man's wage – a midday meal or drink in the fields, an allotment or potato-patch, the opportunity of buying grain, meat or milk from his employer at cost price, a cottage at nominal rent (for example, 2s. a year) or an annual suit of clothes. Again, such perquisites were most valuable in the north, less so in the south-east where land was heavily enclosed and there were few spare acres for a cow-pasture or potato-ground, least of all in the west, where 'perquisites' were often deductions from, rather than additions to, the wage. Enclosure may well have increased the demand for labour in some areas, but the price to the cottager in loss of common and pasture-rights and the virtual disappearance of free fuel was a heavy one, and the transition which it implied from a degree of self-sufficiency to total dependence on a money wage profoundly affected his standard of life. Arthur Young correctly observed that 'the labouring poor is a term that none but the most superficial of reasoners can use; it is a term that means nothing'. If the historian is forced to generalizations, he would probably conclude that the standard of living of the northern labourer improved steadily and substantially throughout the century, that of the southern labourer remained largely unchanged, while that of the western labourer deteriorated. There was no 'general trend' and no transition from a 'Golden Age' in the first half of the century to a 'great depression' in the latter.

From the actual household budgets collected by Davies, Eden and other observers towards the end of the century, as opposed to the fictional ones invented by earlier writers, it is possible to see how the labourer's scanty earnings were laid out. Writing of Stevenage in 1767, Jonas Hanway had said

> The food of the poor is good bread, cheese, pease and turnips in winter, with a little pork or other meat when they can afford it; but from the high price of meat, it has not lately been within their reach. As to milk, they have hardly sufficient for their use.

In the south of England, the labourer's family practically lived on wheat bread, with some vegetables (though not generally potatoes), typically about 1 lb. of bacon and 1 lb. of cheese a week, and small quantities of butter, sugar and tea (2 oz. a week). A typical Davies budget from Berkshire, for a family of husband, wife and five children, is:

	s	d
Bread or meal	6	3
Yeast and salt		4
Bacon or other meat (1 lb.)		8
Tea, sugar and butter	1	0
Soap and starch		2¼
Candles		3
Cotton and wool		3
Rent, clothing, firing, etc.	2	2¾
Total	11	2

This man's wage was 8s. a week, and his wife added another 6d.; each week there was a budget deficit of nearly 3s., covered partly by parish relief but also by increasing debt. In fact, from a study of scores of budgets Davies came to the general conclusion that no labourer in the south of England could cover his expenses who had more than 2 children not employed. Eden found, for instance, a family from Diss, in Norfolk, which had a surplus in 1792 of £4 3s. 5d., but there were only 4 in the family, and they consumed no meat, sugar or beer. But in the north of England, cheaper food and a different dietary pattern enabled many families to live comfortably. Thus, a family in Kendal, Westmorland of man, wife and 3 children, with an income of £30 a year, bought per year:

	£	s	d
75 stone of oatmeal, 2s. 4d. stone	8	15	0
Butcher's meat at 5d. a lb.		5	0
Milk at 1½d. quart	5	0	0
Tea and sugar	1	12	0
Potatoes (3d. for 4 quarters)	2	12	0
Butter at 9d. a lb.	1	10	0
Treacle		8	0
Total	20	2	0

The availability of milk in the north, the existence of potato-grounds and cow-pastures, above all, the preference for oatmeal and barley, which could be used in broths and stews, undoubtedly gave a more varied and nutritious diet than the white bread, cheese and tea of the south. Not least important was the existence of free or cheap fuel, which encouraged home cooking and baking, whereas in the south the dependence on bought bread, and uncooked meals was, quite largely, a consequence of the disappearance of wastes and the dearness of coal. To blame the southern labourer for extravagance, as most contemporaries did, was to ignore the changed pattern of life which intensive agriculture had imposed on him. To keep alive a family of 5 or more children on wages of 6s. or 7s. a week was, in itself, no mean achievement. At the Bristol Workhouse, as early as 1714, the cost merely of feeding 100 girl inmates worked out at 16d. each a week, and there is general agreement throughout the eighteenth-century reports that the diet given in such institutions was usually better than the employed labourer could get for himself.

Most agricultural labourers owned so few possessions that it was not worth-while anyone recording them at their death. The few inventories that have survived indicate goods worth a few pounds at most, often only a few shillings, and it must have been the case that many labourers passed their lives, and died, in debt. Where there are records of goods stolen from labourers' cottages, they were almost always clothes – a great coat (valued at 12s.), waistcoats, breeches, handkerchiefs, hats and stockings, or gowns, petticoats, stays and shifts. Andrew Clarke, a labourer of Brentford in Middlesex, who ran away leaving 3 children chargeable to the parish, must have been quite untypical with goods valued at £11 15s. 9d. and including, besides the usual utensils and bedding, such luxuries as 'a four post Bedstead with Green Harrateen Furniture', a 'leather covered Elbow Chair', a 'Mahogany Tea Chest', 8 prints, 8 old books and 2 small looking-glasses. Much more usual were the possessions of Ann Whitiker of Cowling, who had 2 tables, a chest, a coffer, 3 chairs, 2 stools, a spinning wheel, an iron pan, a bread pan, a bedstead with chaff mattress, 2 blankets, a quilt and 2 bolsters. In Cornwall and Devon household furniture was often more primitive still, sometimes consisting merely of a rough table, benches and 3-legged stools and blocks of wood for the children to sit on. What the labourer spent on dress is difficult to assess – partly because it was still customary in the north to make clothes at home, whereas in the Midlands and south nearly all were purchased new or second-hand; partly because a good deal must have been given, passed down the family and altered for children's use. Eden estimated that a man's 'foul-weather coat' lasted him 2 years, breeches only 1 year, and that he needed 2 shirts, 2 pairs of stockings and 1 pair of shoes a year: his wife needed a stuff gown, a cloak, a petticoat, 2 shifts, 2 pairs of shoes and stockings and 2 aprons a year, but her stays should last 6. A Lincolnshire budget compiled by Young gives a man a coat, waistcoat and breeches (£1 2s.), 3 shirts (10s.), 3 pairs of stockings (3s.), and 2 pairs of shoes (8s.) a year, totalling £2 3s., while the clothes for his wife and 2 children are double this amount: this would be an exceptionally fortunate family. Foreign visitors to the Home Counties often remarked that the peasants were well-dressed and shod, but here again there were important regional contrasts, for in the south-west women often went barefoot, and wore a dress only on Sundays, appearing for the rest of the week in their stays.

It is likely that the housing of the labourer was no better than it had been in the past, and that it tended to deteriorate later in the century with increasing pressure on accommodation from a growing population and from squatters dispossessed from the commons by enclosure. In this respect, however, standards were probably best in the south, and declined towards the north as well as the west. John Wood, the architect of Bath, wrote that 'The greater part of the cottages that fell within my observation, I found to be shattered, dirty, inconvenient, miserable hovels, scarcely affording a shelter for the beasts of the forest, much less were they proper habitations for the human species'. The best were of brick, timber or stone, but many still had walls of mud or even road scrapings, no floor and no flued chimney: usually they had one living-room with, perhaps, a kitchen 'out-shot', and one chamber above in which the whole family slept, no privy, drainage or water supply. Most were damp and dark, many were insanitary and verminous; only from the outside, and then only occasionally, was the eighteenth-century cottage attractive. Their value ranged from £15 to £20, the price which a carpenter would charge to run up a simple shack on the waste, to perhaps £40 to £50 for a more substantially built cottage with 2 bedrooms. In the latter part of the century some 'improving' landlords began to erect 'model' cottages for their regular farm-servants, often in the current 'romantic' or even 'Gothic' idiom: most of these were well-constructed, though convenience was sometimes sacrificed to the picturesque. Nathaniel Kent's specifications for model cottages included a living room (12½ ft square), a small pantry and cellar, and 2 bedrooms (12½ by 11 ft and 12½ by 7½ ft), and cost £66 in brick, £58 in wood: Thomas Davis's smallest cottage was to cost £50. These were by no means extravagant, but a model cottage was as remote from the expectations of most eighteenth-century labourers as a yearly suit of clothes or a daily joint of meat. Their hope was to live from one season to the next, and to 'live' often meant, as Canon Girdlestone said of a later age, that they 'merely didn't die'.

7

Town life in the eighteenth century was still untypical, though its economic and social significance was far greater than mere numbers suggested. Outside London, which contemporaries already placed at some 700,000 inhabitants by the middle of the century, there was only a handful of towns that really merited the description – Bristol, the other great port, with flourishing glass and china industries, perhaps reaching 100,000, Norwich, the great market centre for the East Anglian cloth trade, with 50–60,000, and the 'new' towns of Manchester–Salford (50,000), Liverpool (35,000) and Birmingham (30,000). After these, there was little above the rank of a large market town. Hull and Sheffield had about 21,000, Nottingham and Leeds 17,000; Bolton and Northampton contained a mere 5,000, while Newbury at 4,000 was as large as Bradford. In such places, where the countryside was no more than a few streets away, rural crafts still predominated, and the great new mills and factories, coalmines and iron-works, that were to transform the landscape of the Midlands and north in the next century, were still isolated curiosities. Even at the census of 1801 only 20 per cent of the people of England and Wales were classified as urban dwellers.

Yet the towns represented, in many respects, the dynamic, innovative elements in society which were ultimately responsible for Britain's economic preponderance in the next century. When Gregory King classified the population in 1688 he itemized 10,000 'persons in the law', 16,000 'persons in sciences and liberal arts' and 40,000 'shopkeepers and tradesmen'; additionally, there were 9,000 naval and military officers, and 10,000 clergymen, some at least of whom would be town-dwellers. These categories broadly composed the urban 'middling ranks' (not yet 'classes'). Significantly absent in 1688 was any mention of manufacturers 'employing capital in all its branches' as the early nineteenth-century censuses were to say, though even by 1730 Thomas Lombe, the silk-yarn manufacturer of Derby, had become one of the wealthiest men in the kingdom with a fortune of £120,000, and before the century was over Arkwright, Dale, Boulton, Wilkinson and a hundred more were to join the ranks of the newly rich. In King's time the wealthiest of the middle classes were the larger merchants and traders, whose incomes in 1688 averaged £400 a year: holders of greater offices had £240, lawyers £140, shopkeepers £45, comparable with farmers at £44. But within each of these groups there was a wide range of earnings from top to bottom. Amongst the richest men in the kingdom were a few of the great merchant princes – directors of the Bank of England and of the chartered trading companies like the East India and the Hudson's Bay – whose thousands a year enabled them to purchase country estates and to marry into the ranks of the gentry, if not the peerage. Fees and gratuities of office, though not official salaries, might raise a few leading judges and civil servants to a similar eminence. A successful London shopkeeper in one of the new, fashionable trades might expect £1,000 a year; a few did more, though most much less, and in the provinces £50–£100 a year represented a fair trade. Similarly, in the slowly emerging medical profession there were many gradations from the educated and sometimes titled physicians who treated the nobility and better-off classes for handsome fees, through the licensed surgeons and barber-surgeons down to the apothecaries and unqualified practitioners who served the poor and the country districts: the physician's fee was usually one guinea per visit, or two-thirds of a guinea a mile if he had to make a journey, while the apothecary charged a few shillings for his medicines and was not, in the eighteenth century, lawfully entitled to charge separately for advice. In general, the rewards of medicine grew steadily during the century, as did those of the Church. Mainly, it seems, because of the agricultural improvements of the period, with consequent effects on the value of tithes and glebe farms, a country parsonage sometimes became a very acceptable living for the younger son of a squire, while appointment to one of the major sees could bring a truly aristocratic income. At the opening of the century 5,500 of the 10,000 Church livings had been worth £50 a year or less, while at the end only 4,000 were below £150. Many curates, even at the later date, were still drawing a mere £30–40 a year from a vicar who, all too often, was himself an absentee pluralist, and such men were on a level with the other great poorly paid profession, that of the schoolmaster. As little as £20 a year was not uncommon here, though there might be a cottage to go with the job. A headmaster of a grammar school received up to £100, a workhouse chaplain about £25. The compensation for such small salaries was that duties were generally not very onerous, and often allowed a second employment to be carried on at the same time – it was not uncommon, for instance, for a country schoolmaster to combine the offices of clerk and shopkeeper.

THE EIGHTEENTH CENTURY

It was, in fact, the growth of shops, large and small, that most impressed contemporary observers of the social scene. To many, it was a condemnation of the growing luxury of the times, to some, the evidence of Britain's increasing wealth and comfort, to all, a source of wonder that so small a population could support so many retailers. To the chandler's shop – the universal provider of the poor man's food, soap, candles and coal – the eighteenth century added a range of specialist retailers in the new luxury trades. Tea, at first sold by the coffee-houses and the apothecaries, soon came to constitute a separate retail business, probably the first being Twining's shop, opened in 1713 as an off-shoot from Tom's Coffee-House. Furniture-makers were also well-established in retail trade by mid-century, some specializing in cabinet-making and chair-carving in the new styles, others offering a complete furnishing service of carpets, hangings, mirrors and interior decoration; most work was still to customers' orders, though it was becoming common to hold stocks of chairs, chests and other everyday pieces. Another new development, though at an inferior social level, was the appearance of 'ready-made' tailors and shoemakers with stocks of standard patterns and sizes: it was at first a much-despised business, though one of the very few instances of a retail trade developed especially with the interests of the poorer classes in mind. They were in sharp contrast to the new china shops selling exquisite Chelsea, Worcester and Derby ware, and to Wedgwood's London showroom, 'Elegant, Extensive and Convenient', which was already taking £100 a week in 1769. 'My present sort of Customers', he wrote, 'will not mix with the rest of the World', and on them he successfully tried original sales techniques, setting out for display whole dinner and tea services, moving articles round every few days 'so as to render the whole a new scene, even to the same Company every time they shall bring their friends to visit us'.

The capital required to set up shop varied, according to the trade, from a few pounds to several hundreds. Even in 1732 Defoe could complain that ''Tis a small matter to lay out two or three hundred pounds,' not in stock, but in 'painting and gilding, fine shelves, shutters, boxes, glass doors, sashes and the like', and that, 'Two thousand pounds is reckoned a small stock

A HISTORY OF THE COST OF LIVING

in copper pots and lacquered kettles'. The tea trade was, of course, the particular object of his vituperation. It was a prosperous tradesman of this kind, who had set up shop with a capital of £1,000 and made about £350 a year profit, who was in mind in a household budget drawn up in 1744. For a family of husband, wife, 4 children and 1 maid, food took £112 10s. a year (meat and fish 10s. 2d., a week, bread 3s., butter 3s., tea and sugar 4s. 1d., 11¼ gallons of small beer 3s. 1½d., ale 2s. 6d., milk 5¼d., soap 6½d., candles 1s. 3d.), clothes £60 a year (£16 each for husband and wife, £7 for each child), rent and taxes £50 a year, 'extraordinary expense attending every lying-in £10, supposed to be about every two years', schooling £8 (10s. per quarter per child), 'pocket expenses for the Master of the family' £10 8s., maid's wages £4 10s., shaving £1. 10s., and 'a Country lodging sometimes, for the Health and Recreation of the family' £8: this left £75 a year to be invested for 20 years in order to leave each child and the widow £500.

Trade, like manufacture, was one of the main avenues of social mobility, of progress from poverty and obscurity to wealth and fame. Not a few men of humble origin and little formal education made this transition – perhaps more in the later eighteenth century than at any time until the present. One such was James Lackington, one of 11 children of a poor journeyman shoemaker of Wellington, Somersetshire, who drank himself to death 20 years before his time. James, born in 1742, had 3 years of schooling at 2d. a week until poverty obliged him to be withdrawn: at this time his mother existed on oatmeal broth, turnips, carrots and potatoes, the children on much the same. At 10 James started work for his father, and at 14 was bound apprentice to another shoemaker at Taunton, where he worked from 6 a.m. until 10 p.m., but paid the master's son 1½d. an hour to teach him to spell. In his early twenties he lived exclusively on bread and tea in order to buy books, and on his marriage in 1770 had exactly ½d. As a journeyman shoemaker he was now earning 9s. a week on the fine, stuff shoes, and decided to move to London where prospects and wages were better. In 1774 he set up shop as combined shoemaker and bookseller with a capital of £5 in books and leather: he often dined on potatoes or water-gruel in order to plough back every penny into the business. But Lackington was a brilliant and inspired businessman, who originated sale without bargaining or credit in the book trade as well as the sale of 'remainders' at half or even quarter the list price. Trade prospered to the extent that within a few years he could buy £5,000 worth of books at one afternoon's auction; by the 1790s he was the largest bookseller in London, selling 100,000 volumes a year and averaging £4,000 a year profit. By now he had a country house at Merton, Surrey, and a carriage on which he had inscribed appropriately, 'Small profits do great things'.

Lackington's success story is paralleled by that of William Hutton, the son of a Derbyshire wool-comber born in 1723. When 7 years old he started work at Lombe's new silk-mill, rising at 5 a.m. each day. The family experienced great poverty after his mother's early death, and one day William had no food from breakfast until dinner the next – a meal of flour and water boiled into hasty pudding. After 7 years in the mill he was apprenticed at 14 to his uncle, a stocking-weaver of Nottingham, where another 7 years of servitude earned him £5 10s. At 21 he walked to London and back looking for work, a distance of 125 miles on which he took 3 days each way. Like Lackington, he had a passion for books, and somehow acquired a knowledge of book-binding. First he rented a small shop in Southwell, Nottinghamshire, then a half-shop in Birmingham for 1s. a week. By his marriage in 1755 he had £200, to which his wife's dowry added another £100. From bookselling he went into the retailing of paper, then into its manufacture, then into land-dealing, buying, letting and re-selling as values increased. By 1768 he had accumulated £2,000 worth of property, and was now acquiring public office, first as Overseer of the Poor, then as a Commissioner of the Court of Requests. By 1790 he could buy a coach-house, carriage and horses costing £639, was a local dignitary and antiquarian of some repute, and author of *The History of Birmingham*.

Housing was already becoming a more expensive item for the urban middle classes, especially in London. Shopkeepers still lived over their shops, as they had for centuries, unless, like Lackington, they were prosperous enough to have a house in the suburbs and the necessary coach and horses for commuting. £1 a week was a common rent in London for a shop with living quarters, half or less in the provinces. The freehold of new houses was generally reckoned as 14 years' purchase, giving about £700 as the price of a substantial new house in London. One of these as described by the architect Ware, has a basement ('ground rent is so dear in London that every method is to be used to make the most of the ground plan') for kitchen and servants, a ground-floor comprising hall or foreparlour with a back parlour, the best room, behind and a passage to the garden, a first floor of dining-room and drawing-room, 3 bedrooms on the second floor and smaller, servants' bedrooms in the attic: the 'needful edifice' is to be situated at the bottom of the garden, but this is best laid 'with a good, sound, stone pavement' since 'plants require a purer air than animals, and however we breathe in London, they cannot live where there is so much smoak and confinement'. This was evidently the Georgian terraced house of which many examples survive. Dr Johnson inhabited a larger, double-fronted house in Gough Square, off Fleet Street. This had a central front door, approached by a short flight of steps with iron railings on each side: this opened to a central hall with well staircase, on the left of which was a dining-room and on the right a parlour. All the ground floor rooms were panelled in pine, the windows having interior shutters and window-seats. There was a small powdering-closet leading off the parlour, with a niche where the wig-stand stood. Stairs at the rear of the hall led down to the kitchen with its 2 open fireplaces, one for cooking joints from a jack, the other for boiling kettles and other purposes. On the first floor were 2 drawing-rooms, convertible into 1 large salon by folding doors: on the second floor bedrooms, and above these the garret, used by Johnson as a library, though originally the servants' bedrooms.

Such rooms were decorated and furnished as finances would allow. Walls might be wainscoted, with plastered ceilings, though increasingly in the latter part of the century wallpaper, especially flock paper, was taking the place of panelling. Doors and banisters might be of mahogany or pine, fireplaces of marble or wood, with steel grates and slate interiors. Tables and chairs, chests of drawers, bookcases and corner washstands were the commonest articles of furniture, clothes being kept in closets and presses rather than wardrobes. Turkey carpets might cover the boarded floors and stairs. Foreign visitors, like M.

Grosley, seem to have been surprised by the carpets and by the number of 'large chairs, the seats of which are in part stuffed up very full and covered with Morocco leather, and mahogany tables' (1772).

The urban middle classes, like their rural counterparts, enjoyed good appetites and generally ate heartily. The growth of towns created some problems of food supply, alleviated somewhat after the middle of the century by improvements in roads and the development of canals, but even so cattle still came on the hoof to London's meat markets from as far afield as Yorkshire and North Wales, and poultry were brought on foot from Norfolk and Suffolk. Defoe and other writers complain of the 'stinking fish' which had been too long on the road from the East Coast. But on the whole, ample quantities of good food seem to have been available, at least in London, for those whose purses were sufficiently long. English towns were remarkable for their fine, wheaten bread and their refusal to eat the mixtures of grains that were still common in the countryside: at times of scarcity, when the government authorized the sale of 'Standard' bread containing a high proportion of bran, and 1d. cheaper than the wheaten loaf, little could be sold in London and the other large cities. In any case townsmen preferred meat, and it has been calculated that by the end of the century some 100,000 head of cattle were annually being supplied to the London markets alone. Bread was now increasingly reserved for tea-time when, according to a foreign observer, 'it is cut so thin that it does as much honour to the address of the person that cut it, as to the sharpness of the knife'. Another noticed that 'there is another kind of bread and butter usually eaten with tea, which is toasted by the fire and is incomparably good. This is called toast.' The popularity of toast in England has been ascribed by another Continental writer to the staleness of much English bread. But vegetables and fruit were also playing an increasing part in the townsman's diet, and French cooking was already coming to be accepted in polite society. 'We have of late years refined ourselves out of that simple taste, and conformed our palates to meats and drinks dressed after the French Fashion', complains a writer of 1747. ... 'Poor and Rich live as if they were of a different Species of Beings from their Ancestors ....' This was, of course, a gross exaggeration, for meat was still the mainstay of middle-class diet, and vegetables were still regarded as an optional extra, not as a separate dish, as in France. Dr Johnson, who was in this respect at least typical of his age and class, liked best, according to Mrs Thrale, 'A leg of pork, boiled till it dropped from the bone, a veal pie with plums and sugar, or the outside cut of a salt buttock of beef', though he was also passionately fond of fruit, and would eat 'seven or eight large peaches of a morning before breakfast began, and treated them with a proportionate attention after dinner again'.

Town-dwellers had the advantage of a variety of inns, coffee-shops and chop-houses, at some of which very good meals could be had at remarkably modest prices. At a Bedford inn in 1789 Torrington had 'roasted fillet of mutton (a joint not very common) with cabbage, cucumbers and salad' followed by cheese, for 10d., with an additional 6d. for brandy ('très bonne marché'): at the Saracen's Head, Southwell, there was cold beef, cold veal and gooseberry tart 'to my great contentment'. But a Swiss observer, Moritz, considered that the ordinary Englishman's midday meal consisted of 'a piece of half-boiled or half-roasted meat, and a few cabbage-leaves boiled in plain water, on which they pour a sauce made of flour and butter, the usual method of dressing vegetables in England', though 'the fine wheaten bread which I find here, besides excellent butter and Cheshire cheese, makes up for my scanty dinners'.

8

Few generalizations can be made about the cost or standard of living of the urban working classes in the eighteenth century. In the rapidly growing towns there was a greater variety of conditions, more extremes of wealth and poverty, than in any other area of English social life. The developing industries of the Midlands and North were already creating vast new sources of wealth, were lightening human labour and, not least important as a necessary condition for the improvement of domestic comfort, were removing the place of work from home to factory. But the extent to which the working man was sharing in the profits of industrialization is still as hotly disputed by historians as it was by contemporaries. Whatever blessings the Industrial Revolution has brought in the longer term, it is fair to say that it did not necessarily improve the standards of the worker in its early, formative stages. It may be that most of the wealth derived from more intensive exploitation of resources was monopolized by capitalists and entrepreneurs; that development at this period was concentrated on capital goods rather than on usable consumer goods; that despite the expansion of production in both industry and agriculture, the rapid growth of population at the same time meant that there was little or nothing more available per head of the population than in pre-industrial days. The available statistics are an inadequate criterion on which to base any firm conclusions.

The eighteenth-century town presented a strange contrast of squalor and vice alongside culture and riches. Most of the social evils associated with the nineteenth century – desperate overcrowding, sometimes of 10 persons to a single room, back-to-back houses, a complete absence of sanitation, paving or water supplies – were already commonplace, nor had the towns yet developed the administrative machinery and social equipment by which such evils were eventually checked. Children from the age of 4 or 5 were commonly employed in noisome 'sweated' trades which used the home as a miniature workshop and totally prevented the creation of decent domestic life: only half of them could expect to survive the first few precarious years of existence in their disease-ridden hovels. Yet an optimist could point to facts that indicate a large, and perhaps rising, expenditure on things that can by no means be regarded as necessaries – especially to the extent of drinking and gambling. During the 'gin mania' of the 1730s and 1740s there were no less than 6,000 places in London (excluding the City and the Surrey side) where gin was publicly sold, besides innumerable barrows and stalls, chandlers' and tobacconists' shops. A penny a quartern was the usual price. Fielding, the magistrate, commented in 1751 that 'Gin is the principal Sustenance (if it may be so called) of more than a hundred thousand People in this Metropolis. Many of these Wretches there are who swallow Pints of this Poison within the Twenty-Four Hours....' Gin-production increased rapidly even during periods of dearth in the first half of the century, from 2 million to 9 million gallons a year, before heavy taxation in the 1750s finally reversed the trend. Thereafter, as spirit consumption fell, that of beer increased, the new drink 'porter' (so-called because it was considered nourishing and especially suited to heavy workers) becoming particularly popular at the controlled price of 3d. a quart to 1761 and 3½d. thereafter. In the latter half of the century the consumption of beer – almost exclusively by the working classes – stood at around 35 gallons per head per year. Similarly, the growth in the use of wheaten bread in place of barley and rye, which had become all but universal by 1795, can be interpreted as an indication of rising living standards for the poor: it was almost twice as dear as barley bread, but widely regarded as more palatable and nutritious. Tea and sugar may not be such good indicators of working-class standards, though contemporaries make it clear that even the poor were using both by the later decades: tea imports rose from 1,494,000 lb. in 1740 to 14,765,000 lb. in 1788, sugar consumption from 4 lb. a head to 13 lb. At least some working men – the skilled artisans and the factory operatives whom the Industrial Revolution had called into existence – must have shared in these benefits, while poverty became increasingly concentrated in the unskilled, the casual and underemployed workers, whose distress and discontent were all too visible. Francis Place, a true friend of the working man, was convinced that standards had improved remarkably in the later years of the century, not merely through increased wages but because of a more rational use of resources: that because less was spent on drink and gambling, more was available for the satisfaction of everyday needs. It may well be that the Wesleyan revival, and the movement for 'the reformation of manners' later in the century, had important effects on the standard of living.

The range of earnings, and the social and cultural 'gap' between different categories of labour, were immense, and probably greater in the eighteenth century than at any period before or since. A skilled artisan might earn as much as a small master or shopkeeper – indeed, many workers in domestic industry were still independent craftsmen owning their own tools and materials. In the new luxury trades like cabinet-making a skilled man could earn immensely high wages – a chair-carver up to £4 a week, for instance. London compositors were earning about 24s. a week in the later decades of the century, journeymen tailors 21s. 9d. At the time of Arthur Young's tours in the 1770s, Newcastle colliers made 15s. a week, Sheffield cutlery workers 13s. 6d., porcelain workers at Worcester and Burslem 9s., weavers and spinners in Lancashire and Yorkshire 8s. 7d.: the average wage of women in the textile industries was 4s. 2½d., and of boys 2s. 11½d. But, as usual, averages conceal the individuals. Wool-combers were the best-paid group of textile workers, earning 12s. to 14s. a week: the steel-polishers of Woodstock could earn anything from 15s. to 42s., depending on skill and overtime; Wilton carpet-weavers had from 10s. to 12s. and Gloucester pin-makers from 10s. to 15s. A London saddler in 1775 earned 15s. a week, yet his budget (for husband, wife and 3 children) worked out at £1 0s. 6½d.: it included 12 lb. of coarse beef at 3½d. a lb., 4s. 11d. for bread, 2s. for 3 lb. of salt butter and 2½ oz. of tea at 4½d. the oz.; he paid more for coals (2½ bushels, costing 3s. 1d.) than for the rent of his lodging (2s. 6d.), more for 3 lb. of sugar (1s. 5d.) than for 2 pounds of cheese (1s.). Probably the deficit in the budget was made up by the work of wife and children, though there is no mention of this. The saddler's earnings were comparable with those of a building craftsman – a mason, bricklayer or joiner – whose average daily wage-rate moved up gradually through the century from 20–22d. a day from 1700 to 1730, to 22–24d. 1730–70 and 24–29d. up to 1790; assuming a full 6 day week, which would be rare in this industry, he would be earning about 15s. a week by the end of the century.

But these skilled men were all, in some degree, aristocrats of labour. The majority of town-dwellers were semi-skilled and unskilled, casual workers, frequently unemployed. About their actual earnings we know next to nothing. The daily wage-rates of builders' labourers in southern England rose from 14d. at the beginning of the century to 22d. in the 1790s, indicating a maximum of about 11s. a week at the latter date: there must have been many weeks in which not half so much was earned. The head joiner who worked on Blundell's house in the 1720s had only 1s. a day, and his unskilled assistants a mere 6d. Highway labourers at Bath were getting 8s. a week in the 1780s, moving up to 9s. during the inflation of the 1790s, and these seem to have been quite representative of non-agricultural wages in the area. For domestic workers in the textile trades wages fluctuated violently with changes in fashion, booms and slumps in the market, and, after about 1770, the effects of factory competition. Thus when Arthur Young toured the north of England in 1769 Manchester cotton weavers were earning 7s. to 10s. a week on their handlooms. Within a few years Hargreaves's invention of the spinning jenny was producing so much yarn that weavers were now in great demand and could earn 15 to 20s., even up to 30s. a week in the early 1790s. But so many weavers now flooded into the trade that, already by 1800, it was reported that 'a good workman working fourteen hours a day was hardly able to earn 5s. or 6s. between one Sunday and the next'. Other textile workers were not, as yet, so disastrously affected by the onset of industrialization. William Felkin, a Nottingham stockinger, was still able to earn on average 12s. a week, and found food relatively cheap, though clothing and furniture were dear. Wiltshire weavers in 1725 could make from 8s. to 17s. a week, less deductions for loom rent, and there was at that time a fair degree of mobility into the ranks of small, independent masters: here again, however, the period of good times was quite brief, for the West Country cloth industry went into a state of decay from the middle of the century onwards due to the growing predominance of the West Riding.

The worker's standard of life therefore depended on a multitude of factors – the fortunes of his chosen craft, his degree of skill, the size of his family, the opportunities for food production and alternative employment – which could result in a range of earnings from 4s. or 5s. a week to £3 or £4. It was also affected, in the same critical way as that of the agricultural labourer, by the state of the seasons: bad harvests brought high prices and, with increasing frequency after the middle of the century, mob violence, riots and the sacking of bread-shops and corn-mills. Not least important, it depended to a large extent on geography. The outstanding characteristic of eighteenth-century wage history is the wide regional variation in both levels and trends, amply demonstrated by Dr Gilboy in her study of three areas – London, the west of England and the north. In London the wage-rates of common building labourers moved up slowly during the first 3 decades of the century from about 1s. 8d. to 2s. a day, remaining at this level until the 1790s. The skilled journeyman's rate rose from about 2s. 6d. to 3s. a day in the 1730s, again remaining practically stationary until some small increases in the 1780s. How many weeks – or months – in the year such open-air workers were obliged to be idle is quite incalculable. In London it seems that the worker may have held his slightly improved position of the early decades, at least until the 1790s. In the metropolitan districts of Middlesex and Surrey, however, he had to meet London prices with somewhat lower wages, and it seems possible that here the worker suffered some deterioration towards the end of the century. In the west of England wage-rates were both lower and more constant, that for labourers averaging 1s. 2d. a day from the beginning of the century until the 1770s, with an increase of 2d. thereafter, that for craftsmen 1s. 8d., rising to about 2s. in the 1750s; the standard of life of the Western labourer was an extremely low one, showing no improvement and, when measured against rising prices, probably some worsening in the latter half of the century. But in the north of England the position was quite different. Here, the growing opportunities for industrial and mining employment forced up the levels for all workers, so that between 1700 and 1781 the wages of building labourers more than doubled, from 8d.–10d. a day to 1s. 8d. For skilled men the rise was not so spectacular – from 1s. 6d. to 2s. to 2s. 6d. a day. By the end of the century northern wages had reached, and even exceeded, London rates, and with lower prices to pay there can be no doubt that the standard of life had improved appreciably. This narrowing of the formerly wide regional wage differentials was a further characteristic of the century, marking an important stage in the development of an integrated, national economy.

The growing prosperity of the middle and upper classes, and the increasing size of their establishments, required a lavish provision of domestic servants, and many workers in the eighteenth century, both male and female, found at least an assured existence in a lifetime of service. How well-off they were depended on their place in a rigid hierarchy, and on the size of the establishment they served. A maid-of-all-work, in the house of a tradesman, would typically start at £2 a year, rising slowly to a maximum of about £4: wages of course, included board and lodging – usually in a cellar for the men and a garret for the women. Blundell in 1707 employed a dairymaid and a housemaid at 10s. a quarter, a coachman and a groom at 15s. and a butler and gardener at 18s. 9d: maids did not wear uniform in the period, though the coachman, groom and butler were supplied with liveries which could cost as much as a year's wage. But if contemporary comment is to be believed, good servants were in very short supply. There are constant complaints that they are idle and dissolute, always changing their places, deceiving and robbing their employers. The men are rude and insolent, take endless time to deliver messages and even attend the theatre when supposed to be about their masters' business; the maids insist on having tea morning and afternoon, dress up like their mistresses, and all too easily fall victim to dishonourable advances. Both sexes are relentless in their demands for 'vails' (tips) which every visitor to the house is expected to give: to dine at one of the best houses could cost from 10s. to a couple of guineas, and even in middle-class households it was usual to give the maid 1s. after a visit. The difficulty of getting, and keeping, good servants led some to employ Negroes, like Johnson's faithful Francis, while others competed by offering higher wages. Sarah Kemble (later Mrs Siddons) began work in 1771 as a lady's maid to Lady Mary Bertie, daughter of the Duke of Ancaster, at the unusually high salary of £10 a year for an untrained, 16-year-old girl. But by the latter part of the century women's wages had typically moved up to £5–£8 a year and a good butler's to as much as £20. With uniform, tips, board and lodging, this could represent a very good living, amply sufficient to provide for a family and old age. The general impression is that the eighteenth century was a favourable period for the servant, with rising wages and a social status considerably higher than it was to become in Victorian times.

Servants at least had the advantage of regular meals, often consisting of the ample leavings from the master's table. The food of the ordinary urban worker was neither so varied nor so assured. In general it seems that standards of diet were improving up to the mid-century, with rising earnings, and that they deteriorated during the period 1760-92 when food prices rose by 40 per cent and most wages lagged behind. But even in the 'good' period there were individual 'bad' years, and throughout the century the towns had a high proportion of unskilled, casual and unemployed workers whose standard of life was always very near to the margin of existence. Poverty and hunger were as characteristic of the eighteenth-century town as the growing display of wealth and luxury; deaths regularly exceeded births, and if few of these could directly be attributable to starvation, there were many in which the disease had been encouraged by inadequate diet.

The better-off town worker breakfasted on bread and butter, cheese, sometimes meat, with beer or tea to drink: for dinner, meat and vegetables, and for supper cold meat or bread and cheese and beer. Smollett describes a London cook shop, full of hackney coachmen, chairmen, draymen and footmen out of place or on board wages, 'who sat eating shin of beef, tripe, cowheel and sausages at separate tables, covered with cloths which almost turned my stomach'. But there were many who could not afford meat, at 3d.-6d. a pound, more than once a week and some who scarcely tasted it from one month to another. At a time when 2s. 6d. a week was reckoned as the cost of boarding a pauper child, James Lackington and his wife were existing on 4s. 6d: the little meat they could afford was made into broth, they took no beer, but made substitute tea from toasted bread and coffee from fried wheat. When tramping the country in search of work William Hutton made a meal of a pound of cherries ($\frac{1}{2}$d. in Birmingham Market), or a halfpenny bowl of soup from a London street-stall. A good deal of substitution must have become necessary during the rising prices after 1760, as meat, butter and cheese became increasingly out of reach: it is in this period that white bread, potatoes and small quantities of tea became the staples of the poor, and attempts by philanthropists like Hanway to encourage the use of vegetables, or by the government to introduce maize and Carolina rice, met with little response. The poor were more conservative in their food habits than the rich. In good times there would be a Sunday joint of cheap meat and a pudding, probably cooked at the baker's since many rooms had no adequate cooking arrangements; in poorer times there was bread, a little butter, an occasional herring or bowl of broth. But, as always, there were wide regional variations. In the north of England, although wheat bread became more common as the century progressed, oats were still an important part of the diet, eaten both as porridge, and as bread or puddings flavoured with milk, butter, beer or treacle: milk, potatoes and broth all had a more important place than in the diets of the south, and meat was economically boiled to make soup rather than roasted. A typical Preston budget for 7 persons, recorded by Davies in 1789, gives oatmeal bread 3s., potatoes 9d., salt 3d., bacon or other meat 4d., beer and milk 5d., tea, sugar, treacle and butter 11½d.

Other items of expenditure of the urban working classes are difficult to quantify. Rent was probably, after food, the largest, for in the towns there were no free cottages and no possibility of running up a shack on the common: most workers rented 1 or 2 rooms, typically at about 30s. or £2 a year in the north, and rather more in London. A whole house, rented at about £6 10s. a year, was beyond the reach of most workers, except perhaps highly paid artisans. Fuel was put down in Davies's Yorkshire budget at £1 a year, and must have been much more in the south, away from the coal-fields: in one Surrey budget rent and fuel combined to as much as £7 6s. a year, though this was unusually high. Clothing for a large family could also be a very heavy item, and here, too, the town-worker was at the disadvantage of not being able to spin and weave his own, as many rural workers did, especially in the north. Nearly all clothes were bought second-hand at a 'slop-shop', but even so a great-coat could cost 10s. 6d. (up to 25s. new), a pair of shoes 4s. 6d. or, in the north, of clogs 3s. A family of 7 or 8 might easily spend £5 a year on dress, though about half this seems to have been the more usual amount. As cotton came to replace wool late in the century, the cost of clothes fell considerably and their number and variety increased, but the change to cotton was a slow one, the first indication of which was Sunday dresses for women. The fashion had clearly not extended to women prisoners in 1784, who were attired in six yards each of 'stout woolsey' and 'Home made Cloth' at a cost of 11s. 4d. Always included in the Davies and Eden budgets is a small sum – usually 3d. a week – for thread and worsted for mending, which extended the life of many clothes until they finally fell to pieces. Soap, starch and blue for washing typically added another 4d. a week, and a halfpenny candle a night another 3½d.

In most of the budgets collected in the late eighteenth century there is little or no margin, in many an unexplained deficit which must have been made good by other earnings, by poor relief or by the accumulation of debt. Better-off families allowed for some contingencies, the most common being 'lying-in' which was put down at about 30s. a year. But sickness could be calamitous to the precarious standard of life of many families, especially when it happened to the chief breadwinner. Medical charges at 10s. 6d. a visit, or 2s. 6d. for four doses of 'Dr James's Fever Powder', precluded many from calling in the doctor until the patient was dying, and despite the considerable building of new hospitals after the middle of the century, there was still very inadequate provision for the treatment of the poor. If an applicant for admission failed to get a letter of recommendation from a governor or subscriber – no easy matter for the very poor – he was required to deposit the sum of 19s. 6d. for burial fees, returnable if he was fortunate enough to recover.

Yet, despite all their obvious defects of dirt, disease and maladministration, the towns offered amenities and opportunities not available to the country labourer. Here there were fortunes to be made by the inventive, the industrious and the quick-witted, a vast and growing market for goods and services of all kinds. In short, the towns afforded a degree of social mobility that was unknown in the countryside. And, with improving communications between the main centres, travel became more available, at least to a section of the working classes: from London or Bristol one could even emigrate to the American plantations for a cost of £5. By the later decades of the century urban improvement was occurring on a considerable scale, and the country visitor to London, Birmingham or Liverpool was struck with the beauty of the buildings, the width and cleanliness of the main streets, the energy and sense of purpose of the inhabitants. 'There is good reason to believe that Manchester is more healthy now than formerly' wrote Thomas Percival, a Manchester doctor, in 1773: 'The new streets are wide and spacious, the poor have larger and more commodious dwellings, and the increase of trade affords them better clothing and diet than they before enjoyed.' Soame Jenyns wrote in similar vein in 1767. 'The consumption of everything is also amazingly increased from the increase in wealth in our metropolis, and indeed in every corner of this Kingdom, and the manner of living, throughout all ranks and conditions of men, is no less amazingly altered.' Contemporaries in the late eighteenth century were in no doubt that England was on the threshold of a new age of unparalleled expansion and opportunity: few observed that this new wealth was being built upon a sub-structure of poverty more extensive than it had been for centuries past.

CHAPTER 4

The Nineteenth Century

I

ONE of the liveliest debates which has divided economic historians in recent years has centred around the effects of industrialization on the standard of life of the worker. One school, deriving its inspiration ultimately from the teachings of Marx, has argued that Britain's early Industrial Revolution came as a calamity to the working classes, condemning small farmers and skilled artisans to the impersonal routine of mill and mine, destroying the unity of family life, and shutting up the new urban populations in insanitary slums and tenements where traditional standards of culture, morality and learning could only wither and die. Another, more optimistic school has, by contrast, viewed industrialization as the saviour of the working classes, rescuing millions from the toil and poverty of rural life, raising them to new plateaux of prosperity and opportunity which were the necessary conditions of democratic enlightenment and emancipation.

The standard of living is a concept that amalgamates many elements, material and non-material, and one that varies for different individuals and social classes. To all, however, a central element is the movement of prices, and their relation to earnings and incomes, since it is this that determines purchasing power and the ability to command the necessaries and luxuries of life. It is not in dispute that the Industrial Revolution vastly enlarged the productive capacity and output of a small island, and raised it, in the course of a hundred years, to the wealthiest and most influential nation on earth, the largest exporter of manufactured goods and commercial services, the owner of the greatest fleets, civil and military, and the centre of the most extensive empire the world had ever known. Britain's Victorian pre-eminence rested upon the foundations of iron, coal and railways, and although her Industrial Revolution was, in origin, a phenomenon unique to this country, it became a process through which many other nations passed – or are now passing – on their way towards wealth and power in the modern world.

The Industrial Revolution was, in fact, not so much an event as a series of events, not a violent overthrow of an old order, but a process of evolutionary change the origins of which were certainly earlier than the eighteenth century and the completion of which is not yet. Nevertheless, to compare 1800 with 1900 is to compare two different worlds. During the course of the century Britain passed from a mainly agricultural society to a mainly industrial one, from a country in which four-fifths of the people lived on farms and in villages to one in which four-fifths inhabited towns, from a nation that could support itself with basic foodstuffs to one that had to rely heavily on overseas producers. A great and growing demand for British manufactures, both at home and, more especially, abroad, was the spur to industrialization: the series of inventions, which came in ever-quickening numbers from the 1770s onwards, the response to that demand. One industry after another became transformed by mechanization from handicraft to factory production – first cotton, the newest of the textile trades, next wool, the oldest, then iron and chemicals, steel and engineering, and only towards the end of the century clothing, boots and shoes, and furniture. Some industries obstinately opposed change, others passionately embraced it: some multiplied and grew rich by it, others contracted and declined.

Accompanying, and inseparable from, the revolution in production, were revolutions in communications, in commerce and in fiscal policy. The keynote of all these was to achieve greater mobility, to remove obstacles that impeded the free flow of goods, services, men and ideas, in accord with Adam Smith's axiom that the greatest wealth (and hence, happiness) of nations was to be realized by specialization and free exchange, at a national and an international level. Thus the isolation of centuries was broken down first by improved roads and canals towards the end of the eighteenth century, by railways after 1825 and by steamships after the middle of the century. At the same time vast new areas of the world came to be opened up as British markets, sometimes by peaceful negotiation, at others by colonial acquisition. New techniques of banking and credit, of industrial organization and finance were made necessary by the growing scale of operations: new methods of distribution and marketing were required as consumers multiplied and became ever further removed from the ultimate producer. Equally important, a policy of Free Trade, permitting the free import of food and raw materials and the free export of manufactured products, came to be considered a vital requirement of the 'workshop of the world' in place of a protectionist policy that in fact restricted trade.

The statistics of the achievement were staggering to contemporaries, impressive even by comparison with the more rapid rates of growth realized by recently developed economies. In 1800 Britain's domestic exports, at current prices, valued less than £40 million, in 1900 nearly £300 million. Coal production expanded from a mere 30 million tons a year to 225 million tons, while the consumption of raw cotton soared from 50 million lb. to 1,700 million lb. a year. From the length of railway lines to the tonnage of merchant shipping, from the output of steel bars to that of steam engines, the examples might be endlessly multiplied. In sum, the achievement amounted to a substantial and continuous growth in the total national product of around 2 per cent per annum in the first half of the century and 3 per cent per annum in the latter half, sufficient, that is, to double the average standard of living within 50 years.

Intimately associated with the Industrial Revolution, though in a way still not entirely clear to historians, was a rapid expansion in the size of the population that was, in itself, not far short of revolutionary. After long centuries of slow growth, population had first started to mount rapidly after 1740. In 1801, when the official census was taken, England and Wales numbered 9 million inhabitants, by 1851 the figure had doubled and within another sixty years, by 1911, had doubled again to 36 million. This was increase of a quite phenomenal magnitude, averaging between 11 per cent and 14 per cent during each decade of the century, though increasing less rapidly towards the end than it had at the beginning. It seems certain that the main cause of increase was a sharp fall in mortality, particularly of infant mortality, rather than a rise in births, and that from the 1870s onwards the deliberate limitation of conceptions was beginning to slow down the rate of increase. But whether the growth in numbers preceded the Industrial Revolution and, in fact, provided the wider market which stimulated it, or whether industrialization began first and created the growing wealth on which a larger population could be supported, is still a matter for conjecture. In any case, the effects were mutually advantageous: a growing population provided both a market and a labour force without which an Industrial Revolution would have been impossible, while the great increase in national wealth which industrialization brought enabled an expanding population to be maintained, ultimately at higher levels than it had ever previously enjoyed.

It is unlikely that our own agriculture, even with the encouragement and protection which other countries gave to theirs, could have expanded sufficiently to meet a 4-fold increase in population whose standards of consumption were, in any case, rising. Between 1750 and 1850 there were far-reaching changes on the land which some writers have designated an 'agrarian revolution' – the completion of the enclosure of open fields which had begun in the sixteenth century, the introduction of root-crops and new rotational systems which made more efficient use of resources, the adoption, on a limited scale, of agricultural machinery, land drainage and artificial fertilizers. Up to the middle of the nineteenth century Britain largely succeeded in supplying herself with her basic foodstuffs, and the estates of the more progressive landowners continued to be the model of farming practice for the world. But in repealing the Corn Laws in 1846 Britain was making a conscious decision against self-sufficiency. She, as the apostle of Free Trade, would specialize in those things that she was best fitted to do – the manufacture of cotton, iron and engineering products, the supply of shipping and financial services – and would buy her food from the vast wheatlands and pastures of America and Australia, where Nature smiled more predictably than in the Old World. From the 1870s the flood of imports began, and by the eve of the first world war British farmers supplied only half our meat and a mere one-fifth of our wheat requirements; the nation, on the other hand, ate more cheaply than it could ever have done under a protected agriculture.

The Industrial Revolution was also responsible for revolutionary social changes that profoundly affected the lives of all people in all strata of society. Probably the most immediate was the change in occupational structure that followed from the new needs of industry, commerce and trade, and the declining importance of agriculture in the economy. The general effect of industrialization was to require a higher level of economic specialization, of men and women who were skilled in performing a limited range of functions, whether mechanical, clerical or administrative. Whereas in the past many men had divided their time between, say, farming and weaving, or between the making and selling of goods, increasingly now they found themselves performing only one function, perhaps even only one operation, continuously and repetitively. In 1770 probably half the total working population had been engaged in agriculture: in 1800 it was about 35 per cent, in 1851 16 per cent and by 1911 only 8 per cent. The proportion engaged in manufacturing industry grew correspondingly, to reach one-third of the total labour force by 1851. Not all of these – not, indeed, a majority of them – were yet employed in factories revolutionized by mechanization, and the 10 largest occupational groups of 1851 still included members of important hand-trades such as tailors, shoemakers, milliners and seamstresses, besides the domestic servants, the second largest occupation of all. There were more cobblers in 1851 than coalminers, more blacksmiths than workers in iron foundries and furnaces, more concerned with horses than with railways. But, as it developed, industrialization needed fewer of these old skills and more of the new ones – at the professional level, those of the engineer, the chemist and metallurgist, and at the operative level, those of the draughtsman, the pattern-maker and the machinist. It was also noticeable that, as it grew to maturity in the latter half of the century, the industrial system ceased to recruit any larger fraction of the working population directly to manufacturing occupations, but required more and more in clerical, supervisory and managerial functions, and in financial, distributive and transport services. Thus, the numbers of clerks doubled in the 1860s, and doubled again in the 1870s. Those engaged in commerce increased from 8 per cent of the working population in 1871 to 12 per cent in 1911, those in transport from 5 to 8 per cent, and those in public administration from

2·3 to 4·4 per cent. And although for women domestic service continued to be easily the largest occupation, growing to its peak of 1½ million in 1911, technology, in the shape of typewriters and telephones, was beginning to open up important new careers. In 1851 the census classified precisely 19 female clerks and bookkeepers, in 1881 7,000 and in 1911 146,000.

Changes in the sources and distribution of wealth, in occupations and employment, also induced important changes in the class-structure of English society. To say that in pre-industrial times England had consisted of a 2-tier society of landowners and peasants would be a gross over-simplification, for ever since the Middle Ages there had been a small but increasingly influential third element of farmers, traders and professionals which was the envy of less-endowed European nations. Yet it is true that it was the Industrial Revolution that called to power – economic, political and, ultimately, social – an essentially new middle-class of manufacturers, industrialists, merchants and a host of ancillary professions ranging from banking and insurance to civil engineering and surveying. It was the Victorian middle classes who constituted the new, dynamic element in society, whose standards and values became the accepted norms, and whose opinions and actions shaped public policy at home and in the Empire. Numerically they were still small – in 1851 perhaps not more than about 10 per cent of the total population, or, if the minor categories of clerks and shopkeepers are included, at most 20 per cent: about half were engaged in commercial operations, a quarter were farmers and a quarter professional, administrative and employing classes in industry and commerce. It was this last group, numbering not more than 300,000 persons, who constituted the risk-takers and innovators and who made the major economic decisions on which Victorian prosperity rested.

But industrialization affected the other classes of society hardly less importantly. For the worker it ultimately created more new skills than it destroyed, it offered greater opportunities of advancement to the quick and diligent who had imbibed the gospel of Samuel Smiles, expounded in his best-selling book *Self Help*, though it also introduced a new dimension of precariousness into working life. In the past, labour had been of

2 kinds, skilled and unskilled, and there had rarely been sharp differences of earnings or conditions between different occupations within each category: now, there were infinite gradations of skill and an infinite range of earnings, which gave some workers unprecedented standards of comfort while plunging others into unparalleled poverty. Probably the only class which consistently suffered from the effects of industrialization was that of the large landowner, for whom the decay of agriculture in the closing decades of the century brought a serious loss of economic power as well as of political and social influence. Nevertheless, throughout the period territorial magnates continued to be numbered amongst the wealthiest men in the kingdom, and the concentration of English landownership was such that, even in 1873, half the total area of the country was owned by only 4,200 persons; the 'decline of the aristocracy' was a decline in relation to the rise of the middle classes rather than in absolute terms.

Structural changes of this kind took place slowly, below the surface of society, and were not always obvious to contemporary observers. To them the most evident and startling effect of industrialization was the rapid growth of towns which, within a century, completely changed the face of the country and the habits of its people. The factories, mines and iron works exerted a magnetic effect on population, drawing ever more people into the new cities of the Midlands and north. Within a half-century, between 1801 and 1851, Manchester, Birmingham, Leeds and Sheffield increased 3 times, Glasgow and Aberdeen 4 times, Bradford 8 times. Such growth was unparalleled and unplanned: it raised a host of problems – of accommodation, administration, public health and leisure – to which our own century has not yet offered complete answers. To the Victorians, many of whom were first-generation town-dwellers, the problems of life in the new environment must often have seemed overwhelming, and the relative advantage of factory-work against farm-work, of accommodation in a back-to-back house or tenement compared with an over-crowded and insanitary country cottage, must have been among the most important, though quite incalculable, aspects of the cost of living. But to all town-dwellers one inescapable consequence of the new way of life was that, compared with their rural ancestors, they had little opportunity of supplying their own everyday needs. When food and clothing, fuel and accommodation, had to be paid for in cash, the level and movement of prices became of primary importance in determining the standard of living.

2

Throughout much of the eighteenth century, and reaching back into the late seventeenth, prices, as we have seen, had retained a remarkable stability, beginning to turn upwards only after about 1760 as the mounting population exerted a growing pressure on resources. The price history of the nineteenth century is again different in character. From end to end of the period – from 1790, that is, to 1914 – there was almost no alteration in the general level of prices, but within this span of time there were both important periodic changes, known to economists as secondary, secular movements, and equally significant changes in the prices of particular commodities. In other words, although the cost of a defined 'basket of goods' was much the same in the early twentieth century as it had been in the late eighteenth, it had varied greatly over the intervening years, and the cost of the constituents of the 'basket' had also changed significantly.

Throughout the century the economy was subject to periodic fluctuations, some short, some long-term, which profoundly affected the level of prices. In the past the state of the harvest had often caused violent changes, forcing up the cost of food in bad seasons, depressing it in good, making the roads impassable in winter and drying up the mill-streams in summer. But as industrialization developed the tyranny of natural forces came more under control: new sources of power replaced water, improved communications made it possible to move supplies from one part of the country to another, and, ultimately, from other parts of the world to Britain.

The more important fluctuations now were those of the trade cycle, those rhythmical sequences of revival, boom, recession and slump in economic activity which characterized Britain throughout the nineteenth century. Although the distance between boom and boom, or between trough and trough, was variable, the average length of each cycle was about 5 years, with a range from 3 to 10 years: as the economy became more industrialized the cycles became more pronounced, both in the distance from top to bottom and in the area of the economy that was affected. Economic historians are still uncertain about the precise nature and causes of the trade cycle. An early theory suggested that they were related to sunspot cycles, which affected climatic – and, hence, economic – conditions on earth, but since the recent researches of Gayer, Rostow and Schwartz the more likely explanation seems to have been the fluctuations in demand for British exports, particularly for textiles, and the effect which these had on the level of domestic investment.

The trade cycle brought a new degree of insecurity into working life, directly influencing the demand for labour, the price of goods and the rate of earnings. There were also longer-term fluctuations in the nineteenth-century economy which had even more important social consequences. So far as the history of prices is concerned there was a regular succession of periods, each of some 20 to 30 years, when prices moved in a consistent direction, upwards or downwards: thus, they rose rapidly between 1790 and 1820, fell from 1820 to 1850, rose from 1850 to 1873, fell from 1873 to 1893, and rose again after 1893. A more detailed account of these movements and their causes will be given shortly. But clearly, if these periods are paired together they produce a regular pattern of upswing and downswing, each of some 50 to 60 years. The Russian economist Kondratieff developed a theory of 'long waves' in economic life which he believed were, in developed Western societies, superimposed on the shorter trade cycles. Schumpeter suggested a theoretical explanation for 2 of these waves, from 1787 to 1842 and from 1842 to 1897, on the basis of the economic effect of technical innovations. In the first period, coinciding with the Industrial Revolution, developments in the textile industries and the iron industry, and the use of steam-power, at first produced a spectacular up-phase until retarded by the depression and falling prices after the Napoleonic Wars: in the 1840s and 1850s another group of innovations, based on the new railways and steel-making processes, gave rise to another upswing which again faded during the depression of the 1870s. According to these

A HISTORY OF THE COST OF LIVING

theories, a capitalist industrial economy is inherently subject to such swings as inventions at first stimulate activity but ultimately lose their effect.

Numerous price-indices have been constructed for the period under discussion – more, in fact, than for earlier periods, since price-material now becomes more abundant. One of the most recent and interesting is that of Professor E. H. Phelps Brown and Sheila V. Hopkins, which takes the base as 100 for the period 1451–75. In 1790 the cost of this same unit stood at 871, having risen from 643 in 1760. Thereafter, its course through the nineteenth century was as shown in the table on p. 199.

The peak year, according to this index, was 1813, when prices were more than twice the 1790 level, the lowest point 1893, when they had almost returned to their position of a century before.

A much more detailed index for the years 1790 to 1850 was constructed by Gayer, Rostow and Schwartz (p. 200). Though still based on wholesale and import rather than retail prices, it covers nearly 80 commodities and is carefully 'weighted' to represent the relative importance of the different items in a typical budget – thus, wheat is weighted at 745 in the composite index, tea at 111, turpentine at 4, quinine at 1 and so on. Whether these can claim any absolute accuracy is debatable, but the index represents the most elaborate attempt that has yet been made to chart the movement of prices over this period. The base of 100 refers to 1821–5, and on this scale the figure for 1790 is 89. As in the Phelps Brown index, the peak year is again 1813, though this index shows a rise of just under, rather than just over, 2 times. In both 1850 is the lowest point in the first half-century, and although there are individual differences the patterns agree closely enough to command considerable confidence.

It will be noticed that the most violent price-changes of the whole period come at the beginning and end – in the 1790s and early 1800s, and again after the 1890s, separated by almost a hundred years of less marked fluctuations. Much the most dramatic of all occurred during the wars with France from 1793–1815, when rapid inflation forced up the level from 89 in 1790 to peaks of 156 in 1801 and 169 in 1813 (Gayer, Rostow and Schwartz). Thereafter prices began a steady fall, though in

Price of Composite Unit of Consumables, 1790–1914*

Year	Price	Year	Price	Year	Price	Year	Price
1790	871	1820	1353	1850	969	1880	1174
1791	870	1821	1190	1851	961	1881	1213
1792	883	1822	1029	1852	978	1882	1140
1793	908	1823	1099	1853	1135	1883	1182
1794	978	1824	1193	1854	1265	1884	1071
1795	1091	1825	1400	1855	1274	1885	1026
1796	1161	1826	1323	1856	1264	1886	931
1797	1045	1827	1237	1857	1287	1887	955
1798	1022	1828	1201	1858	1190	1888	950
1799	1148	1829	1189	1859	1214	1889	948
1800	1567	1830	1146	1860	1314	1890	947
1801	1751	1831	1260	1861	1302	1891	998
1802	1348	1832	1167	1862	1290	1892	996
1803	1268	1833	1096	1863	1144	1893	914
1804	1309	1834	1011	1864	1200	1894	982
1805	1521	1835	1028	1865	1238	1895	968
1806	1454	1836	1141	1866	1296	1896	947
1807	1427	1837	1169	1867	1346	1897	963
1808	1476	1838	1177	1868	1291	1898	982
1809	1619	1839	1263	1869	1244	1899	950
1810	1670	1840	1286	1870	1241	1900	994
1811	1622	1841	1256	1871	1320	1901	986
1812	1836	1842	1161	1872	1378	1902	963
1813	1881	1843	1030	1873	1437	1903	1004
1814	1642	1844	1029	1874	1423	1904	985
1815	1467	1845	1079	1875	1310	1905	989
1816	1344	1846	1122	1876	1370	1906	1016
1817	1526	1847	1257	1877	1330	1907	1031
1818	1530	1848	1105	1878	1281	1908	1043
1819	1492	1849	1035	1879	1210	1909	1058
						1910	994
						1911	984
						1912	999
						1913	1021
						1914	1147

* From 'Seven Centuries of the Prices of Consumables, Compared with Builders' Wage-Rates', *Economica*, Vol. XXIII; No. 92, 1956.

A HISTORY OF THE COST OF LIVING

Indices of British Commodity Prices, 1790–1850*
(Monthly Average of 1821–5 = 100)

	Domestic and Imported Commodities	Domestic Commodities	Imported Commodities
1790	89·3	87·1	87·5
1791	89·7	84·5	94·6
1792	88·1	80·6	99·0
1793	96·6	91·6	100·6
1794	98·5	96·3	95·9
1795	114·9	113·6	109·5
1796	116·1	115·8	108·6
1797	106·2	100·8	114·2
1798	107·9	100·2	123·4
1799	124·6	119·9	129·8
1800	151·0	156·6	122·5
1801	155·7	161·7	127·3
1802	122·2	122·3	113·2
1803	123·6	120·4	125·9
1804	124·3	119·7	132·8
1805	136·2	133·5	138·6
1806	134·5	131·9	137·5
1807	131·2	128·3	137·0
1808	144·5	141·3	152·1
1809	155·0	153·8	157·1
1810	153·4	153·5	151·4
1811	145·4	149·2	133·4
1812	163·7	172·2	141·1
1813	168·9	173·1	155·8
1814	153·7	148·5	167·0
1815	129·9	124·6	144·3
1816	118·6	155·0	128·3
1817	131·9	131·8	130·7
1818	138·7	139·8	133·9
1819	128·1	130·4	120·3
1820	115·4	117·4	108·7
1821	99·7	98·4	101·8
1822	87·9	83·9	100·2
1823	97·6	97·0	99·3
1824	101·9	104·2	95·3

200

Indices of British Commodity Prices, 1790–1850 – cont.

(Monthly Average of 1821–5 = 100)

	Domestic and Imported Commodities	Domestic Commodities	Imported Commodities
1825	113·0	116·5	103·4
1825	100·0	106·7	83·1
1827	99·3	106·2	82·1
1828	96·4	102·9	80·0
1829	95·8	102·8	78·2
1830	94·5	101·7	76·5
1831	95·3	103·0	76·3
1832	91·5	97·9	75·2
1833	88·6	92·2	79·1
1834	86·5	88·4	85·2
1835	84·5	84·3	85·2
1836	95·2	98·4	87·1
1837	94·3	101·6	76·1
1838	97·8	106·0	78·0
1839	104·3	113·4	82·2
1840	102·5	110·4	83·1
1841	97·7	105·9	77·9
1842	88·8	95·3	72·5
1843	79·7	84·5	67·6
1844	81·1	86·7	67·2
1845	83·3	92·0	62·9
1846	86·0	97·2	60·8
1847	96·8	114·0	61·3
1848	81·8	94·8	54·1
1849	73·9	81·4	56·1
1850	73·5	77·4	63·3

* Based on the Gayer, Rostow and Schwartz Monthly Indices, Abstract of Statistics, p. 470.

1820 they were still 29 per cent above their starting-point. The special economic conditions created by the long war were largely responsible, coupled with a series of particularly bad harvests at a time when imports had been rendered perilous by enemy blockade. A rapidly mounting population was, in the words of Malthus, pressing on the means of subsistence. Thousands of acres, formerly in wastes and heaths, were brought under the plough in a desperate attempt to meet the demand, though the use of land which was unsuitable for crops under normal conditions only forced up prices further. Government demands for munitions, ships, army clothing and supplies of all kinds again inflated the economy, as did heavy government borrowing: increased duties and taxes, many of them on necessities of life, seriously hit the purchasing power of the worker. Throughout most of the war years cash payments by the Bank of England were suspended, and the exchange of notes for gold prohibited: this departure from the gold standard caused some loss of confidence in the currency and hoarding of gold, particularly at times of threatened invasion. All these factors contributed to soaring prices until the war finally turned in Britain's favour.

From 1820 to 1850, however, the general trend of prices was downwards – from 1353 to 969 on the Phelps Brown index (a fall of 29 per cent) and from 115 to 74 (fall of 36 per cent) on the Gayer, Rostow and Schwartz index. This downward movement was interrupted by peaks in 1825, 1840 and 1847, corresponding with boom years in the trade cycle, but closely followed in each case by down-swings to depression. In 1819 Britain had returned to the gold standard, and henceforward for the rest of the century the price-level was largely determined by the volume of gold in circulation and the total quantity of things – goods and services – to be bought: if the volume of currency and credit increased without a corresponding increase in goods, prices rose, while if currency was restricted and credit in short supply, prices fell. This was, in fact, the situation during these years. World supplies of gold were restricted by the civil wars in South America which had followed the breakaway of the former Spanish colonies, while the increased output from Russian mines did not take effect until the late 1840s: nor could the currency be expanded to any great extent by other kinds of credit instruments, since English banking was still under-developed and note-issue tightly controlled. On the other hand, industry and trade were now expanding rapidly under the influence of revived demand from the Continent, lower tariffs and the development of railway systems both at home and abroad. The fall in prices was therefore mainly due to the inability of the currency to expand in proportion to the work it had to do. Prices did not, however, fall equally, and one of the reasons for social distress in this period was the fact that it was raw materials, especially cotton, iron and timber, that fell most while wheat and corn hardly changed: the advantage of lower prices thus went to the manufacturers rather than directly to consumers.

The period from 1850 to 1873 was again one of quite different character, a period which saw the height of Britain's Victorian power and prestige and which has often been designated the 'Golden Age'. Prices now rose from 969 in 1850 to 1437 in 1873 (Phelps Brown), an increase of 48 per cent, most of the rise being concentrated in 2 periods of boom at the beginning and end – 1854–5 and 1871–3. The reason is that during these years currency and credit both greatly expanded, even outstripping the very considerable growth in industry and trade. New gold discoveries in California and Australia vastly increased world stocks and the value of currency in circulation, while the development of banking and of joint-stock companies after the Companies Act of 1861 both greatly facilitated credit. The result was that the increased value of currency, general economic optimism and, at the end, over-speculation, drove up the level of prices in 1873 and 1874 to a 50-year peak. But, unlike the previous period, the prices that rose most were generally those of raw materials (tin, cotton, pig-iron, leather, wool, coal) while some important foods, notably wheat, flour, potatoes, rice, sugar and pork, either rose considerably less than the average or fell absolutely. During this period, therefore, the movement of prices, irrespective of earnings, was on the whole more favourable to consumers than to producers.

The boom of the early 1870s was broken in 1874, and was followed by a period of falling prices and recession in a number of industries which contemporaries designated the 'Great Depression'. Whether this was a merited description, compared with what was to happen between 1929 and 1932, is debatable, but those alive at the time rightly saw it as the first setback to Britain's industrial predominance in the world, and the time when this position was coming to be challenged by the rising power of Germany and the United States. Except in agriculture, where the depression was caused by the mass import of cheap foods from overseas, there was, perhaps, no irreparable damage to Britain's economy; in iron and steel, in the coal and shipbuilding industries, there were falling prices and falling profit-margins, though by the 1890s recovery was taking place. The permanent legacy of the period was that Britain never again enjoyed the near-monopolistic position in world trade that she had formerly had, and that although production was still expanding it was doing so at a slower rate than that of more recently industrialized countries. Over the period from 1874 to 1896 prices on the Phelps Brown index fell by 33 per cent. In the opinion of Giffen, the contemporary economist, it was 'more like a revolution in prices than anything which usually happens in an ordinary cycle of prosperity and depression in trade'. Many and various reasons were assigned for the fall, but the main influence again seems to have been that demand for gold temporarily outstripped the supply of it. Germany adopted the gold standard in 1873, in 1879 the United States made her bank-notes convertible to gold, and the country which had formerly been a large gold-exporter now began to take supplies from Europe: at the same time, gold output from the mines began to dwindle just as the demand for it increased. As in the last period, many of the price-falls were favourable to the consumer – the price of sugar fell most of all (by 58 per cent), tea by 54 per cent and wheat by 51 per cent, though most meats and meat products fell less than the average (beef 29 per cent, mutton 25 per cent, butter 25 per cent).

In the last period, from 1896 to 1914, prices again turned upward, and by contrast with the 'Great Depression' Britain now experienced moderate inflation: on the Phelps Brown index the rise is of 21 per cent. There were particularly sharp rises during the periods of boom in 1900, 1907 and 1913. The explanation is again to be found in a large increase in world gold production due to the development of the South African goldfields and of more efficient processes of mining generally. On the eve of the first world war gold was being produced at a rate sufficient to double world stocks within 25 years, and the output in these 20 years, £1,400 millions, was more than four times that of the period 1800–1850. The effect of this increase on price-trends might well have been revolutionary had not industrial output also been expanding, not only in Britain but even more in the newly industrialized countries. Even so the rise was steep enough to cause considerable unrest at a time of generally stationary wages – an increase of 20 per cent in the price of mutton, 25 per cent in wheat, 29 per cent in bacon and 30 per cent in coal.

One of the principal causes of the social and industrial unrest that characterized Britain in the early years of the twentieth century was this serious setback to the real value of earnings. The movement of prices throughout the century was of intimate concern to the working classes, raising or depressing standards of life from one year to another, often from one month to the next. The precise significance of such changes must, of course, be measured against changes in earnings – a point that will be taken up in later sections – but it is worth remarking here the coincidence between times of high prices and periods of acute working-class discontent and agitation. The wave of strikes for higher wages in 1825, the peak years of the Chartist movement in 1839–42 and 1847–8, the rioting which accompanied the passing of the second Reform Act in 1867, and the strikes, demonstrations and unrest of the immediate pre-war years are all, in part at least, a consequence of price-changes disadvantageous to the working classes.

3

Price-indices are, as we have seen, constructed from the prices of supposedly typical 'baskets' of goods. What people actually consume of course are the constituents of the 'basket' – the bread, the meat, the clothing and so on – and probably few, if any, consume them in the precise proportions calculated by the statisticians. It is therefore important to review the directions in which particular commodities moved during the period, together with some of the reasons for the changes.

For the majority of the population of the nineteenth century the most important single price was that of wheat, since for all but the wealthier classes bread was the largest item in the weekly budget. Wheat was also more subject than any other commodity to seasonal fluctuation, and since the demand for it was so constant a relatively small failure of the crop could push up prices quite disproportionately. It was no new experience, therefore, to have to pay twice as much this year as last, and for prices to vary widely from one month, even from one week, to another. Even so, the exceptionally high prices at the beginning of the century were quite unprecedented. From 56s. a quarter in 1790 wheat rose to an average of 83s. over the decade 1801–10, and to 106s. in 1810–13: at its highest yearly average, in 1812, it was 126s. 6d., and during one month it reached 176s. a quarter. From these heights, which were twice and 3 times the late-eighteenth-century average, they fell to 70–80s. a quarter after the end of the war in 1815, to about 60s. in the 1820s and about 50s. in the 1830s. The accompanying table illustrates, however, the great yearly variation:

*Annual Average Gazette Price of British Wheat per Quarter**

	s	d	Per cent of 1900		s	d	Per cent of 1900		s	d	Per cent of 1900
1801	119	6	444	1815	65	7	244	1829	66	3	246
1802	69	10	258	1816	78	6	288	1830	64	3	239
1803	58	10	218	1817	96	11	360	1831	66	4	246
1804	62	3	232	1818	86	3	320	1832	58	8	218
1805	89	9	334	1819	74	6	277	1833	52	11	197
1806	79	1	294	1820	67	10	252	1834	46	2	172
1807	75	4	280	1821	56	1	205	1835	39	4	146
1808	81	4	303	1822	44	7	166	1836	48	6	180
1809	97	4	361	1823	53	4	298	1837	55	10	204
1810	106	5	386	1824	63	11	238	1838	64	7	240
1811	95	3	354	1825	68	6	255	1839	70	8	262
1812	126	6	470	1826	58	8	218	1840	66	4	247
1813	109	9	409	1827	58	6	217	1841	64	4	239
1814	74	4	276	1828	60	5	225	1842	57	3	216

Average Gazette Price of British Wheat per Quarter – cont.

	s	d	Per cent of 1900		s	d	Per cent of 1900		s	d	Per cent of 1900
1843	50	1	186	1867	64	5	239	1891	37	0	138
1844	51	3	191	1868	63	9	237	1892	30	3	112
1845	50	10	189	1869	48	2	179	1893	26	4	98
1846	54	8	203	1870	46	11	172	1894	22	10	84
1847	69	9	259	1871	56	8	211	1895	23	1	85
1848	50	6	188	1872	57	0	222	1896	26	2	97
1849	44	3	165	1873	58	8	218	1897	30	2	112
1850	40	3	150	1874	55	9	207	1898	34	0	126
1851	38	6	143	1875	45	2	168	1899	25	8	95
1852	40	9	152	1876	46	2	172	1900	26	11	100
1853	53	3	198	1877	56	9	211	1901	26	9	99
1854	72	5	270	1878	46	5	173	1902	28	1	104
1855	74	8	277	1879	43	10	163	1903	26	9	99
1856	69	2	257	1880	44	4	165	1904	28	4	105
1857	56	4	209	1881	45	4	168	1905	29	8	110
1858	44	2	164	1882	45	1	168	1906	28	3	105
1859	43	9	162	1883	41	7	154	1907	30	7	113
1860	53	3	198	1884	35	8	133	1908	32	0	119
1861	55	4	202	1885	32	10	122	1909	36	10	137
1862	55	5	202	1886	31	0	115	1910	31	8	118
1863	44	9	167	1887	32	6	121	1911	31	8	118
1864	40	2	150	1888	31	10	118	1912	34	9	129
1865	41	10	155	1889	29	9	110	1913	31	8	118
1866	49	11	186	1890	31	11	118	1914	34	11	130

* Layton and Crowther, *The Study of Prices*, p. 234.

After some very low levels in the mid-1830s (39s. 4d. in 1835) there is a doubling by 1839, the depression year and the year of the first Chartist petition. In the year of the repeal of the Corn Laws prices are already somewhat lower than they had been earlier (1846 54s. 8d. a quarter) and it has been argued that the restrictions on import were removed precisely at the point when, for the first time, they might have had any serious effect on prices. However, it is fair to point out that, in general, the price of wheat in the 20 years before the repeal had remained fairly steady in a period of falling prices, so that wheat at this time had been relatively dearer. In the 20 years following the repeal it was again fairly steady from end to end in a period of rising prices, so that it was now relatively cheaper. To have held its price in check at a time of increased purchasing power and rapidly growing demand (the likelihood is that wheat-consumption reached its peak in the 1870s) was, then, an important consequence of the repeal of the Corn Laws. The main effect of repeal, however, came in the 1870s and 1880s, when North America and, later, India, began mass exports to Britain. From 1873 onwards the price-trend is downwards, though it is not until 1884 that it falls to below 40s. for the first time and 1889 before it touched 30s.; thereafter, there were some particularly low levels in the mid-1890s, followed by slight rises from 1907–14 during the period of general inflation. The really decisive price-change in the case of wheat therefore occurred in the late 1880s, by which time it was down to half the price of the earlier part of the century: it seems likely that it was the impact of India in European markets which finally hammered prices down after the initial effect of the United States in the 1870s. Their ability to supply so cheaply a market thousands of miles away was directly the result of the development of new international transport systems by rail and steamship. While in 1860 the rate for carrying bulk grain from New York to Liverpool had varied from 6d. to 1s. 1½d. a bushel, by 1886 it averaged a mere 2½d.

In the great majority of families wheat now made its appearance on the table in the form of professionally baked white bread. The urban environment was not favourable to home baking, which rapidly died out as the century progressed, surviving only in a few pockets of the north and the Midlands where fuel for the oven was still plentiful and cheap: usually in the towns it was convenient, and almost as cheap, to go to the chandler's shop on the corner where the availability of credit was often an added inducement. The baker's trade had been one of the earliest of all English crafts, but in one important respect the nineteenth century witnessed a fundamental change. From 1266 onwards the price – or rather, weight – of bread had been nationally regulated under the Assize system. The penny loaf was to vary in size according to the varying price of wheat: the baker was required to produce a fixed quantity of bread from every quarter, the residue being his profit margin. This early instance of price-fixing by the State was designed both to protect the public and to remove the baker from profiteering and from speculative loss. It was finally repealed in 1815, partly because of difficulties of administration in the growing towns, but principally because the climate of opinion was by now running strongly in favour of Free Trade, and against any interference in the free workings of the economy. Thereafter, bakers were free to sell at whatever price they could get, though loaves were still supposed to be of standard weights and, in law at least, to be marked with a capital M if made from mixtures of grains. The standard loaf throughout the century was the quartern (4 lb. 5¼ oz.), the price of which naturally varied directly with the prevailing price of wheat; thus in the scarcities of 1801 and 1812 it reached 15½d. and 17d. respectively, compared with the usual 6d. or 7d. in the latter half of the eighteenth century: in the 1820s and 1830s it averaged 9d. or 10d. and stood at 8½d. in the year of repeal. Again, the really significant falls came in the closing decades of the century – to 7d. by 1875, 6d. by 1887 and 5d. by 1895. In only one year subsequently (1909) did it return to 6d. The prices quoted have been average figures for London, and bread prices were, in fact, subject to considerable local variation. The nineteenth-century baking trade was characterized, after the repeal of the Assize of Bread, by intense competition between thousands of small producers: high-class areas of towns were supplied by respectable 'full-priced' bakers, while the poorer quarters had their 'cutting bakers' or 'undersellers' who would charge 2d. or 3d. less, usually by extensive adulteration. Growth in the scale of the industry and the gradual suppression of fraudulent practices eventually narrowed the gap, though even in 1903 the price of the quartern loaf still varied between 4d. and 5½d. in different parts of London.

For meat there was, of course, never anything like a standard price, since so much depended on cut and quality. For many of the working classes in town and country meat usually meant bacon, which had moved up in the latter half of the eighteenth century from 5d. to 8d. a lb., and remained at around this figure throughout most of the nineteenth. Below this there were very cheap cuts of coarse meat, described by Mayhew as 'block ornaments', costing 2d. the ½ lb. in mid-century, and cheaper still offal, trotters, cowheels and so on which could be bought by the pennyworth. Fresh 'butcher's meat' was a luxury for most people at 8d. or 9d. the pound, since it could not be sliced up thin and eked out like bacon: a small joint once a week, often bought cheap at the Saturday night market, was all that many working people with wages at around £1 a week could afford. Before the railways, one of the main factors in cost had been distance from the market. Cattle had been brought hundreds of miles on the hoof from the north of England, Wales and Scotland, to supply the vast demand of London, at an addition to the wholesale price, it has been estimated, of 2d. on every lb. for 100 miles. Once the railway system became established in the 1840s distance had a comparatively negligible effect. The other restrictive factor on price was that until Peel's Free Trade measures of 1842 there were prohibitions on the import of foreign meat and fish, designed to protect the English producer in the same way that the Corn Laws supposedly helped the arable farmer. Little importation in fact took place until outbreaks of cattle plague in the 1860s forced up prices to 10d. a lb. for beef and as much as 1s. for rump steak. The main difficulty was to preserve meat in good condition during a journey of thousands of miles, possibly through the tropics, from those countries which had surpluses – chiefly the United States, South America and, later, Australia and New Zealand. The first imports of sizeable scale were from South America in the 1860s – of beef dried in the sun and known as 'chaqui'; it was hoped that it would enable 'our poorer classes' to 'indulge in animal food' at the very low price of 3d. a lb., but was apparently accepted only by 'the poorest classes' of Northern Ireland. Somewhat greater success attended the introduction of tinned corned beef in the 1870s, selling at 4d. the (boneless) lb. and by smaller quantities as the slicing-out practice developed: by the end of the century 39 million pounds of the total United States exports of 61 million pounds were being sent to Britain. The import of live cattle also grew rapidly from the 1870s onwards, reaching an average of 500,000 head a year by the 1890s, and was considered to have reduced the market price for best beef by 2d. or 3d. a pound. But the decisive change came with the import of frozen meat from the 1880s onwards. Experiments in refrigeration had gone on for many years, but it was not until 1880 that the first really successful cargo of frozen beef and mutton was brought from Melbourne to London in the *S.S. Strathleven*. Meat which had sold for 1½d. a lb. in Australia now fetched 5½d. at Smithfield, a price which put fresh meat within the reach of many for the first time. Within a few years frozen pork from the United States, beef from the Argentine and lamb from New Zealand were flooding the English market, and by 1902 had reached a value of £50 million a year, equivalent to 56 lb. a year per head of the population, and approximately half of total consumption. With meat prices at the end of the century ranging from 5d. to 10d. a lb. there were now qualities that all but the very poorest could afford.

Unlike bread and meat, beer prices in the nineteenth century maintained a remarkable stability. This was not the result of national control – the ancient Assize of Ale had been discontinued as early as the seventeenth century – but of the deliberate efforts of the brewers to stabilize prices in the face of a declining demand for their product. At the beginning of the century consumption stood at around 33 gallons per head of the population per year, to be followed by a continuous decline to 19 gallons a year by the 1840s: from this point there was a slow recovery to 34 gallons a year by 1876, followed by a further decline to 27 gallons by 1914. In addition to this basic problem, caused by the growing competition of tea and other drinks, the spread of temperance and of alternative leisure pursuits, brewers had to face constant changes in the levels of duty on malt, hops and on beer itself, which constituted one of the major sources of national revenue in the period. They were able to respond to these difficulties partly by reductions in alcoholic strength and partly, later in the century, by more efficient techniques and by the use of legitimate substitutes such as brewing sugar. There was also a proportion of small brewers and of publicans who economized by adulteration with substances ranging from quassia and coriander seed to the highly dangerous *cocculus Indicus* and *nux vomica*. Intense competition was a characteristic of beer-retailing, as it was of baking, especially after the Beerhouse Act of 1830 threw open the trade to anyone who cared to take out a 2-guinea Excise licence, and many publicans were prepared to cut the price of a quart by ½d. or 1d. by diluting 3 barrels into 4 and making up the appearance of 'strength' with extraneous ingredients. Thus Whitbread's, one of the best of the London porter-brewers, charged 5d. a quart for drinking on the premises of their houses in mid-century, 4½d. for taking it out. Most publicans charged 4d. a quart, the standard price, and some 3½d. and even 3d.; this was achieved either by illicit practices or because some publicans with 'full' licences reckoned to make their profit mainly on spirits and could sell beer at little above the wholesale price. It remained possible up to the first world war to drink at 1½d. the pint, though in London and some other towns the better qualities usually sold at 2d.

During the course of the century beer changed from an everyday to a recreation drink. The alternative that increasingly commended itself, particularly after the Temperance Movement sponsored 'the cup that cheers but does not inebriate', was tea, which in the nineteenth century became the usual drink of all social classes. From its first appearance in England in the middle of the seventeenth century at £10 the lb., progress had been slow, though by the close of the eighteenth century Eden had noted that small quantities, usually 2 oz. per week, were finding their way into labourers' budgets in the south of England. The limiting factors on consumption were price and duty. Down to 1833 the East India Company held a complete monopoly of the import of tea, and charged prices considerably in excess of those in Europe: moreover, governments of the early nineteenth century used tea as an important source of revenue, charging 100 per cent *ad valorem* duty from 1815 to 1836, subsequently a flat rate of 2s. 1d. and, later, 2s. 2½d. per pound. This meant that the rate of duty was at its most severe in mid-century, when in other respects we were moving towards freer trade. The ending of the Company's monopoly in 1833 had brought down the prime cost of Bohea, the cheapest China tea, to 10d.

a lb. by the 1840s, but the duty raised it to 3s. a lb., taxing it at the rate of 350 per cent. Congou, the quality usually drunk by the working classes, cost 1s. 2d. a lb., or 3s. 4d. with duty: it is not surprising that at this period consumption was only 1½ lb. per head per year and had actually fallen slightly since the mid-1830s. Tea was ultimately made a cheap drink by a combination of lower tariffs and new sources of supply. Gladstone began the process in 1853 by cutting the duty to 1s. 10d. a lb.; by 1863 it was down to 1s. and by 1890 to as little as 4d. Equally important, vast new sources of supply were developed by British planters in India and Ceylon, and their strong, cheap tea quickly ousted the popularity of China varieties. Up till 1871–5 China still supplied 85 per cent of Britain's imports, but thereafter her decline was rapid: by 1886–90 we received only half our supplies from her and the other half from India and Ceylon, while by the first decade of the twentieth century China supplied a mere 5 per cent. A fierce price-war forced down world tea prices by 46 per cent between 1878 and 1887, almost ruining the China industry and even cutting the wholesale profit on Indian tea from 4½d. to 2½d. a pound. At first, Indian tea was used mainly to blend with the weaker China, but by the late 1880s the public was generally drinking pure Indian or Ceylon – often, it seems, unawares. The former practice of selling tea by description – Congou, Hyson, Gunpowder and so on – gradually became restricted to high-priced grocers, and most tea was now sold in packets already blended by the grocer or, increasingly, by large wholesale tea companies. This had been the idea of John Horniman as early as 1826, who had used sealed, lead-lined packets as a means of preventing adulteration and deterioration: by the 1870s he was selling 5 million packets a year, though shortly Lipton's, Lyons', the Mazawattee Tea Company and others were challenging his lead. By the 1880s most family grocers were able to offer a tea at 2s. 6d. a lb., usually by blending a strong 'soupy' Assam tea with weak – and now cheap – China varieties. The price-revolution was completed by the multiple stores, usually by grafting on a tea business to an existing trade in provisions and centralizing buying and control. The prototype was Lipton, who in 1889 offered a tea at the phenomenally low price of 1s. 7d. a lb. – 'The Finest the World

Can Produce'. By 1914 he had an immense trade carried on in 500 shops, but also a score of imitators whose multiple stores now dominated the retail trade.

In total the reductions in price of flour, bread, meat and tea, together with lower prices of sugar, coffee and other foods, amounted to a very substantial saving in the cost of living. Most of this improvement was concentrated towards the end of the century, one estimate drawn from a wide range of items showing that the retail price of food in a 'typical' workman's budget fell by 30 per cent in the decade 1877–87 – by far the most important price-change in the century.

Other items of expenditure which were important to all classes, in varying degrees, were clothing, rent, fuel and transport. About the cost of clothes it is particularly difficult to quantify, since materials and fashions changed radically during the century and since many people rarely bought new anyway. In general there can be little doubt that prices did fall substantially, partly because raw material costs fell and partly because Britain's textile factories were able to produce much more cheaply than the former hand-methods of spinning and weaving. Upland and Middling American cotton, the types generally used in the century, fell from 18d. a lb. in 1801 to an average of 8d.–10d. in the 1820s and 5d.–7d. throughout the rest of the century: there were some particularly low prices of 3d. and 4d. a lb. in the 1890s. Wool prices moved less dramatically. Until the 1840s almost all was still home-produced, and the supply was limited, but after this time Australian imports gradually brought levels down. In 1800 Southdown, one of the best English staples, was 17d. a lb., and with a good deal of yearly variation was still in the range 12d.–16d. in the 1840s. Thereafter, as imports grew, the price fell, from an average of 14d. a lb. in the 1870s to 10d. in the 1880s and 8d. or 9d. in the early years of the twentieth century. Cotton was, therefore, far cheaper than wool, and had the good sanitary effect that it was bought and discarded more frequently than woollen clothes had been. It has been estimated that the price of cotton cloth fell by one-third between 1830 and 1850 as mechanical weaving took over from the hand-loom weavers, and the prices paid by institutions for the same goods over a series of years illustrate this downward trend, both for cotton and wool. Thus the cotton sheets bought by Bethlehem Hospital in 1818 cost 2s. 7d. a yard, in 1835 only 1s. 4d.: cotton prints fell from 1s. 1d. a yard to 6¼d., and a pair of six-fourth Witney blankets from 13s. 6d. to 11s. 4d. At Chelsea Hospital privates' coats in 1815 were £1 7s. 1d. and in 1835 £1 0s. 9d., while their shoes fell from 7s. to 4s. 6d. a pair. But many people took advantage of cheap, mass-produced cotton cloth as a substitute for the dearer woollen, both for underclothes and, less desirably, for outer garments. Engels complained in the 1840s that the Manchester working man was dressed almost entirely in cotton:

Shirts are made of bleached or coloured cotton goods; the dresses of the women are chiefly of cotton print goods, and woollen petticoats are rarely to be seen on the washline. The men wear chiefly trousers of fustian or other heavy cotton goods, and jackets or coats of the same.

But the indications are that standards improved considerably in the second half of the century as prices continued to fall under the influence of mechanization and competitive retailing. By the 1870s the sewing-machine, and its adaptation to boot and shoe manufacture, was revolutionizing the trade in ready-made clothes and footwear, while the development of department stores and drapery chains, working on large turnovers and small-profit margins, was bringing a wide range of cheaply yet fashionably made goods before the public. By mid-century black bombazine for mourning cost 1s. a yard, black velvet 18s.: cotton stockings ranged in price from 4½d. to 4s. 11½d. a pair, while a ready-made lady's serge suit cost £1. By the end of the century the Irish Linen Company was offering blouses at 49s. 6d. a dozen, while Selfridges offered silk stockings, still a luxury item, in 5 sizes and 300 shades at 5s. a pair. Prices of this order were infinitely lower than they had been in any earlier century, and brought fashionable clothes within the reach of at least that growing 'comfortable' section of the working classes.

Substantial reductions in transport costs were also made during the century as new means of communication were continually developed. At the beginning of the period the construction of canals had already lowered the cost of moving goods to half and even a quarter that of road transport, and from 1830 onwards the railway was to have a similar effect on the movement of passengers. Early rates were generally about 2½d. per passenger per mile, but after 1844 every railway company was obliged to run a 'parliamentary train' in each direction each day at a maximum of 1d. a mile. Excursion trains followed in the 1850s, when it became possible to travel from London to Brighton and back for 3s. 6d. or to Hampton Court for 1s.: by the 1870s almost all companies carried third-class passengers on all trains. The penny post of 1840 and the telegraph system constructed in the 1850s were also important side-effects of the railways: before this, it had cost several shillings to send a letter from London to Edinburgh. In 1870 a postcard service was added and in 1883 a general parcel post. In 1913 the Post Office carried no less than 3,478 million letters, 926 million postcards and 138 million parcels. On urban transport of course the railways had less effect, although they had a decisive influence on the development of surburban areas around London and other large cities. In the words of Samuel Smiles 'Clapham and Bayswater have become, as it were, parts of the great metropolis, and Brighton and Hastings are but the marine suburbs of London': according to this writer 300 stations were 'in actual use' within 5 miles of Charing Cross. It was not only people whom the railways poured into the cities, but meat and fish, vegetables, fruit and flowers, anything in fact for which speed was important. In 1854 the Eastern Counties Railway alone brought 3 million quarts of milk into London, and St Thomas's Hospital, who for many years had bought their supplies from a near-by town dairyman at 1s. a gallon, now found that they could get fresher milk from a Romford farmer a dozen miles away at 9d. But for internal movement about the cities there were no revolutionary changes until late in the century. By mid-century horse omnibus companies had developed frequent scheduled services at an average cost of 3d. per mile, and there were also suburban services like Brentford to St Paul's (1s.) and Hampton Court to St Paul's (1s. 6d.): in 1862 it was estimated that London omnibuses travelled 15 million miles a year and carried 50 million passengers. For those in a hurry there were cabriolets ('cabs') at 6d. a mile for 1 or

2 persons, day or night: hired by the day they were 18s. to £1, while the larger barouche, or coach, could be hired for 25s. 'with a gratuity (always expected) of 5s. to the driver'. Prices of this order were quite beyond the reach of working men, who lived as near as possible to their work and walked to it: for them the big improvements came with the London Underground, begun in 1863, and the electric trams in the 1880s and 1890s, both with fares going down to 1d. even for journeys of several miles. At a slightly higher social level the bicycle, obtainable in the 1880s for £4 or £5, gave a new mobility about town and country, and was an important emancipatory influence for women as well as men. Farther still up the scale, motor-cars had appeared on English roads by the end of the century, and although the high-powered limousines were still almost in the millionaire class, small one- and two-cylinder cars could be bought for between £100 and £200: a contemporary estimate put the cost of running one of these at 4d. a mile, compared with 6d. for a pony-trap, the least pretentious horse-drawn vehicle. By 1913 there were already about 120,000 cars and 110,000 motor-cycles on the roads.

Improved communications also had an important effect on the cost of coal, now the almost universal domestic and industrial fuel since the timber 'famine' of the eighteenth century. Indeed the immediate cause of the construction of the Bridgewater Canal had been to reduce the cost of transporting coal from the Duke's collieries at Worsley to his customers at Manchester, which it did by half. A few years later the first section of the Birmingham Canal did the same for that town. But practically no coal came to London by canal, where the long association with Newcastle continued to ensure the supremacy of the sea-route. The high prices that London, and the south of England generally, had to pay in the early part of the century were due partly to the length of the journey and partly to the duties which were levied on sea-borne coal down to 1835. Thus in 1815 the price of best coal at Newcastle and Sunderland was 13s. a ton, of the same coal in London 39s.: the duty at this time was 7s. 6d. a ton. By 1845 the Newcastle price was 8s. a ton, and the London price 17s. 3d., the duties having been finally abolished in 1835. Thereafter there was no continued downward movement in prices, although there were enormous variations according to distance from the coal-field. Coal was, in fact, one of the few commodities which, despite greatly increased production, did not fall in price during most of the century, due to the increasing demand for a limited resource, and to the fact that by the closing decades of the century, productivity per man was declining as mines became deeper and seams thinner. At a time when open fires burned in living-rooms, kitchens and bedrooms, fuel was a major item of expenditure in many households, some idea of the size of which is indicated by the fact that one of the claims of the new 'kitchener', a closed kitchen range introduced in the 1840s, was that it consumed only 1½ tons of coal a month, considerably less than an open range. The price of best coal in London in mid-century was usually about 17s. the ton: thereafter there was a gradual rise to around 21s. the ton just before the first world war, with occasional very dear years (1873, 32s.) in between.

Contemporaries were also in no doubt that another important item, house-rent, rose continuously throughout the century. This was one clear case of supply never satisfying demand, for ever since the immensely rapid growth of industrial towns in the early part of the century there had been a housing shortage which private builders and, later, local authorities, never succeeded in satisfying. House-building was not a particularly attractive investment compared with the quick profits to be made from trade or industry; for instance, a back-to-back cottage built in mid-century at a cost of £150–200 was expected to repay its capital cost after about 20 years' rent of 4s. a week. Moreover, much of the demand for house-accommodation in the nineteenth century was not, in the economist's language, 'effective', in that it could not be backed up with sufficient purchasing power. There was always a substantial proportion of people too poor to pay an economic rent, who remained untouched even by philanthropic efforts like the Waterlow and Peabody building trusts later in the century which attempted to provide cheap yet sanitary accommodation in large tenement blocks: at an average weekly rental of 2s. 1¼d. a room these were still too dear for the slum-dwellers who inhabited the 'rookeries' of London or the cellars of Manchester. Nor did the later development of council houses, which accounted for only 5 per cent of all those built between 1890 and 1914, make a significant contribution to the problem except in a few areas where local initiative was particularly strong. The result was that for nearly all families house-rent absorbed an increasing proportion of expenditure as the century went on. In 1801 rents of dwellings probably accounted for £12 million out of a total gross national income of £232 million, or 5 per cent: in 1851 they contributed 8 per cent and in 1901 9 per cent. Statistics of consumers' expenditure indicate that in 1900 rents took £177 million out of a total of £1,626 million, or 11 per cent: they were the fourth largest item of expenditure, after food (33 per cent), goods and services (20 per cent) and alcoholic drink (12 per cent). This accords closely with the estimates given in Victorian manuals of domestic economy that a middle-class household should devote 10 per cent of income to rent – typically £25 a year out of earnings of £250. But lower down the social scale the proportion increased substantially. A highly skilled worker in one of the 'elite' trades might devote something like this fraction, say 5s. a week out of a wage of 40 to 45s., but in labourers' households 2s. 6d. a week out of 15s. was more common, and in some very poor areas of East London it was reported in the 1880s that half the earnings of some families went on rent. At this point it is clearly necessary to turn to the differing expenditure patterns of different social classes.

4

Ultimately, Britain's early industrialization was to shatter the traditional framework of society, to create vast new sources of wealth and a new social and political structure. Yet throughout most of the nineteenth century the landowning aristocracy – the most traditional and unchanging element in English society – retained its hereditary position at the pinnacle of power and prestige, seemingly unaffected by the violent changes taking place around it. Almost precisely half-way through Queen Victoria's reign, in 1867, Dudley Baxter estimated the national income of the United Kingdom at £814 million: as a simple average, this gave an annual income of £27 per head of the population. In fact half the total national income went to one-tenth of the income-receivers and a quarter of it to one two-hundredth. Forty years later, in 1908, the economist L. C. Money put the national income at £1,844 million, half of which still went to one-twelfth of income-receivers. What had happened in the meantime was mainly a growth of 'moderate incomes' rather than any great reduction in the wealth of the very few, so that on the eve of the first world war English society still presented the appearance of a pyramid with vast wealth at the top resting upon a broad base of poverty.

The 'landed aristocracy' in its narrowest sense consisted of the peers of the realm – 186 of them in 1873 when the 'New Domesday' survey of landownership was taken. This survey made clear the immense concentration of English landownership, revealing that four-fifths of the country's total acreage was owned by fewer than 7,000 persons. But the hereditary peerage did not necessarily equate with the largest landed estates. In 1873 there were 360 owners of estates greater than 10,000 acres, of whom 58 were baronets and 116 untitled, and even of families with an income from land of more than £30,000 a year, one-quarter were commoners. Again, not all peers possessed estates yielding £10,000 a year, probably the minimum for maintaining a country seat and a London season, the two essential requirements for a landed aristocrat. £10,000 a year from land implied an estate in the region of 10,000 acres, and taking this as the test of a 'great estate', only just over half were owned by peers.

But although a substantial proportion of the greatest landed proprietors were commoners, it was only the peers who were the undisputed leaders, under the Crown, of taste and fashion, who controlled the affairs of the counties, held hereditary seats in the House of Lords and, until extensions of the franchise late in the century, dominated the House of Commons too. It was one of the virtues claimed for the English aristocracy that it was not an exclusive caste, but was always open to men of humble birth to be elevated into it: it was possible to point to a man like the banker, Lord Overstone, who was worth between £4 million and £5 million and owned 30,000 acres producing an annual rent of £60,000. The vast emoluments of a Lord Chancellor, reckoned in the early part of the century at £35,000 a year, might, with care, purchase the necessary estate, though with land at £20 to £30 an acre it would normally require 2 or 3 generations and as many advantageous marriages before an elevation was effected. Until the late nineteenth century new creations did little more than balance extinctions, and the elevation of a commoner like Alexander Baring, the financier, or Edward Strutt, the mill-owner, was still rare; but between 1880 and 1914 there were nearly 200 new peers, one-third of whom were industrialists, including the 'Beer Barons' Guinness, Allsopp and Bass. In its period of decline the health of the English peerage was at least partially revived by a transfusion of new blood.

There was no 'typical' peer and therefore no 'typical' peer's income. The range probably extended from a mere £3,000 a year to £50,000 or more, depending on the size of estates, the income from mineral resources or urban land, the profits of political or legal office and government sinecures. Marriage portions could add materially to capital and, hence, income. Lord Sefton, whose estates brought £8,500 a year, expected at least £60,000 for his son, and alliance with wealthy heiresses was a traditional means of augmenting income or reducing debts. From as early as 1836 partnerships between American wealth and English nobility had begun, to become much more common in the closing decades of the century. Thus, although £10,000 a year was a common income in the middle of the century, the Dukes of Bedford, Bridgwater, Devonshire and Northumberland could dispose of over £50,000, the Earl of Clarendon only £3,000; there were many gentry, and many more mere businessmen, who could command more income – though not more nobility – than this. In 1900 the Duke of Bedford, now with an annual income grown to around £100,000, declined a Cabinet office because of his interest in estate-management.

The fortunes of the landed aristocracy naturally depended to a critical extent on the prevailing state of the agriculture on which their wealth rested. Nearly all their estates, except for a small 'home farm' kept for pleasure and for fresh produce, were tenanted, and the ability of their tenants to pay rent rested on the demand for food and the prices it would command. Thus the period from 1790 to 1835 was generally one of great prosperity for landlords and their tenants, despite the rapid inflation that continued until 1812. The great rise in the price of wheat yielded substantially increased rents, which doubled on the Holkham and trebled on the Milton estates, besides accelerating the rate of enclosures, which were almost completed by the end of the period. This was a time for liquidating old debts and forming new savings, for improving tenants' holdings and undertaking capital works such as land drainage. With the fall in prices of the 1820s there were some losses, especially on the less profitable heavy clay soils, and in some places there were reductions of rent of around 10 per cent, but on the whole the landed interest gained substantially during the price-rise of the Napoleonic Wars and the heavy demand for food from a rapidly expanding population.

The Corn Laws, modified in 1815 to prohibit the import of foreign wheat when the English price was less than 80s. a quarter, probably had little effect on the fortunes of farmers, since European countries rarely had large surpluses and the costs of transport, before railways and steamships, would have raised their prices to the English level anyway. English agriculture continued to be reasonably prosperous in the years 1835 to 1880 mainly because of an increasing demand from a population whose purchasing power was also growing, and because of a fairly widespread adoption, at least on the larger estates, of more efficient methods of farming and estate management. But already by 1850 the return on farm capital was often only about 4 per cent a year, compared with the 8 or 9 per cent reckoned as the yield on commercial investment. Contrary to popular belief it seems that the middle years of the century were no 'Golden Age' for the territorial aristocracy unless they were fortunate enough to derive side-benefits from industrialization— from the sale of land to railway companies, from collieries or from the inflated values of urban property. One result of this was a growing division between these landowners, whose interests were increasingly allied to industry and commerce, and the purely rural gentry whose incomes expanded less than their outlays. A recent authority has summed up this period, 'Agricultural landowners more or less marked time while the wealth of the rest of the community surged forward.'

Nevertheless until the 1880s the landed interest largely retained its predominant economic, social and political leadership in the state. Within a few years that predominance was now quickly eroded by agricultural depression, by extensions of the franchise which brought into political competence first the urban, then the rural working classes, and by reforms of local government which established democratic institutions in place of organs formerly controlled by the gentry. The crucial factor was the fall in farm incomes caused by large-scale imports of food from the mid-seventies onwards which could, especially in the case of wheat, sell at prices at which the now unprotected English grower could not compete. A general price-index for English agricultural produce shows a fall from 104 in 1870 to 82 in 1913, but within this wheat fell from 101 to 59, prime beef and mutton only from 102 to 92. The depression hit the arable estates much more than the pastoral, the south and east of the country much more than the north and west. For nearly all landowners it meant considerable reductions in rent to their tenants and, hence, reduced incomes. On an average agricultural rents fell by one-quarter between 1870 and 1914, most of the fall being concentrated into the years 1875–90, but again its spread was very uneven. On some efficiently run pasture farms rents continued to hold their level: on some arable lands rent-reductions of 50 per cent were common, and in one extreme case 638 acres at Steeple, in Essex, which in 1873 paid £760 in rent, had to be dropped to a mere £1 a year between 1886 and 1891. In general there can be no doubt about the decline in profitability of farming during these years, which probably sunk to an average of only 2–3 per cent a year and on many estates disappeared altogether: moreover, the demand for land as an investment had virtually collapsed, so greatly depreciating the capital value of holdings. It was significant that many of the newly created peers of the late nineteenth century did not automatically buy great estates, as their predecessors would have done, and also significant that many old families embarked on policies of retrenchment or sought to recoup their losses on the Stock Exchange. By the end of the period one quarter of all peers had become company directors and a number had opened the doors of their ancestral homes to the paying public.

Much the same considerations applied to the lower levels of the landed interest. Beneath the peers, the gentry were also distinguished by the possession of broad acres, the enjoyment of a life of leisure, and political influence wielded, in their case, more at the local than the national level. In the middle of the nineteenth century £1,000 a year was probably the least income that could support the life of a 'gentleman', and this implied an estate typically of about 1,000 acres. The upper limit of gentry income was about £10,000 a year, at which point they generally merged into the aristocracy. Clearly this represented a wide range of wealth, and it was usual to subdivide the class into squires owning 1,000–3,000 acres and greater gentry owning 3,000–10,000 acres: at the time of the New Domesday Survey in 1873 there were 1,000 of the latter owning 17 per cent of English land, and 2,000 of the former owning 12½ per cent. These 3,000 families, together with the 300-odd peers, constituted 'landed society'. Not strictly part of it, though certainly part of the 'landed interest', were the yeomen (greater, with 300–1,000 acres, lesser, with 100–300) and the small proprietors (less than 100 acres) who, in total, owned the remaining 69 per cent of English land. Although the yeomen were traditionally supposed to be independent farmers, most of their lands, like those of the gentry, were now tenanted, and generally only the small proprietors now cultivated their own lands. The numbers of the gentry remained roughly constant through the century with extinctions balanced by new entrants: the smaller men tended to decline with the increasing concentration of landownership and the small profit margins of the later years: unlike the peers, they rarely had industrial or commercial interests to fall back on.

The pattern of expenditure on a great estate varied widely with the size and circumstances of the family, the number of houses to be maintained and children to be provided for, the scale of entertainment and recreation and so on. In general it can be said that the cost of living for the class grew continuously throughout the century without a compensatory rise in income, since the things on which their lives depended – servants, housing and recreation – all cost more as time went on. The biggest single expense of a noble lord would be on building if he were unfortunate enough to inherit property in need of repair or reconstruction, and since many peers had several country seats as well as a town house it was likely that some building would be going on in every generation. Astronomical expense could attend the building of an entirely new house, like Fonthill Abbey, which probably cost around £400,000 and whose tower collapsed shortly after completion. The days of cheap labour and cheap local materials which had made possible the building of Gothic cathedrals and Jacobean mansions were gone. The original Eaton Hall, remodelled twice later in the century, cost Lord Grosvenor £40,000, the Marquess of Ailesbury's Tottenham House, in Wiltshire, £250,000, and the reconstruction of Alnwick Castle for the Duke of Northumberland, carried out between 1852 and 1866 and employing up to 800 workmen, £320,000. This of course was the largest house in the possession of a private person, the 'Windsor of the North', and scarcely typical. The extension and improvement of Stratton Park, Sir Francis Baring's prudent purchase, cost a mere £25,000, and the Earl of Verulam doubled the size of Gorhambury House for £11,000. Many country seats underwent a Gothic or Tudor 'face-lift' in the early part of the century at the hands of such architects as Atkinson, George Dance and James Wyatt, who built a modest 'cottage ornée' for the Duke of Bedford at £70,000. Later in the century country houses needed central heating (Knole was warmed by steam as early as 1825), gas-lighting, hydraulic presses to lift coal to the kitchen ranges (as at Alnwick), even an indoor railway to convey hot muffins round to the guests in a vast drawing-room. Not all peers were as mad as the Duke of Portland, with his passion for tunnels and underground ballrooms, and the great age of heroic building was over by about 1870, but the upkeep and improvement of the domestic fabric continued to be one of the chief items of expense of any noble household.

The annual expenditure of such a family naturally depended on its income, size and style of life. A very wealthy peer like the Earl of Derby was still spending £50,000 a year in 1914, and when the King and Queen stayed at Knewsley for the Grand National, 40 guests and 120 servants were entertained. The Earl of Lonsdale, who turned out the Quorn Hunt to greet the Kaiser at Lowther in 1895, still kept a private band of 24 musicians as part of his permanent establishment, accompanying him also on visits abroad, while at Belvoir the medieval customs of a watchman calling the 'All's well' at hourly intervals through the night, and of meal-times announced by trumpeters, were kept up as late as the 1890s. But few peers could now afford the eccentricities of the fifth Duke of Portland, with his mile-long carriage tunnel which enabled him to reach his house unseen, his underground suite to which dinner was sent down in a heated truck running along 150 yards of rail, and his riding school illuminated by 4,000 gas jets: at his death in 1879 there were 94 horses attended by 50 grooms. Typically, in a modest household like that of Earl Fitzwilliam about £3,000 a year went on running expenses in the early part of the century – half on food and drink, a quarter on servants and another quarter on horses and carriages. At the end of the century the second Earl of Verulam was obliged by falling rents to cut total expenditure to £15,000 a year, of which £4,000 was devoted to living expenses: this was achieved by cutting the number of servants, reducing the consumption of liquor (590 bottles of sherry a year were reduced to 298, 255 of brandy to 75 and 161 of champagne to 126) and by giving up the hand-rearing of pheasants.

One essential requirement of the great household, as in former times, was the lavish provision of domestic service, and here, except perhaps in respect of transport, technology could effect little economy. The indoor and outdoor staff of a peer would number from about 20 up to perhaps 80 or 100, and there was a fairly widely accepted scale of provision according to income, defined by *The Complete Servant* (1825) as 4 females and 3 men at an income of £1,000 to £1,500 a year, rising to 11 females and 13 men at £4,000 to £5,000 a year. At the latter income it was suggested that servants should take £1,250 a year, or 25 per cent of income, household expenses £1,666 (33 per cent), clothes £1,250 and rent £625, the latter presumably for a town house for the season. These suggested numbers and proportions do not seem to have been too wide of the mark, for Lord Melbourne had 16 servants, the Duke of Argyll 28, the Dowager Lady Leigh 30 and Queen Victoria's household, in female staff alone, 80, 40 each at Windsor and Buckingham Palace. Servants were a major and increasing expense throughout the century, as wages rose and men, in particular, revolted against the long hours and drudgery of life 'below stairs'. Already in 1870 a writer was complaining that 'Servants are becoming scarce, wages are rising, and the work performed is not so well done as it used to be'. In the mid-eighteenth century a maid could be employed for £6 10s. to £10 a year, a footman for £15 and a valet for £25, but by the time of Mrs Beeton's 1888 edition a 'general' maid's wages were specified as £10 to £16, a cook's at £20 and a valet's at £35 plus. Upper servants in a large household could expect to do very much better still. William Taylor, a footman of 1837, describes in his diary earnings of 40 guineas a year, together with another £10 to £15 a year made up of gifts from visitors and tradesmen. Gastronomy commanded the highest prizes of all, Carême, chef to the Prince Regent, having £1,000 a year, and Ude, chef to the Earl of Sefton, 300 guineas. A top valet could earn £200 a year, and specialized outdoor staff could also do well – a head gamekeeper £100 or more and a head gardener £50 plus, both with free cottages. Charles Booth described footmen's wages in the 1890s as depending on height, for 5 feet 10 inches to 6 feet £32 to £40 a year, down to £20 to £22 for a 5 feet 6 inch second footman. For women servants the best occupation was that of housekeeper in a large establishment, where besides the nominal wage of around £26 a year there were handsome perquisites from guests: one old housekeeper left a will of £20,000. It must be remembered that the cost of keeping a servant was very much more than the wage, and that when board and uniform were included the cost was brought up to around £40 to £70 a year. Similarly, to maintain a single coach, with horses, grooms, footmen and postilions, could cost up to £400 a year.

These armies of retainers ministered to the wants of what was usually an extended family, often containing 3 generations and, not uncommonly, more distant relatives besides. Because of the strict rule of primogeniture, only the eldest legitimate male heir could succeed to the entire estate, widows and younger children receiving nothing unless specially provided for: nearly all estates were, therefore, entailed so that the heir enjoyed only a life interest, other members of the family receiving fixed annuities. These often constituted the largest single burden on the estate, and greatly reduced the available income at the disposal of the heir. A jointure for the widow, portions for sisters, capital sums for younger brothers as well as similar payments for his own children when they were married or came of age, could mean that the personal income of the life-tenant was only a half or quarter of the gross income of the estate. In marriages between equals a girl was expected to bring from £10,000 to £30,000, more if marrying into a higher rank, though not all families were as unfortunate as that of Ridley, who had to provide for 10 children at £10,000 each. Widows' jointures were typically fixed at about 10 per cent of the dowry brought into the marriage, say £2–3,000 a year.

Births, marriages, deaths and other family events all cost the incumbent of a great estate vast sums. Earl Fitzwilliam's funeral of state cost £1,000, the Countess of Darlington's £1,400, the undertakers' hearses and mourners taking 19 days on the journey from London to Raby Castle and back. Railways later reduced such costs considerably by providing special funeral trains. The celebration of coming-of-age was another expensive event, modestly met at Lord Milton's majority for £393, and much more handsomely at Belvoir where £5,500 was spent when the Duke of Rutland came of age in 1799; 3 days of feasting consumed, among many other things, 6 whole oxen, 12 sheep, 21 pigs, 23 turkeys, a hundredweight of cream cheese, 46 gallons of brandy and several thousand of beer. And before the heir reached his majority, it was increasingly likely that he had undergone a long and expensive education. After the Crimean War and Indian Mutiny in the 1850s had demonstrated the inefficiency of aristocratic leadership, public pressure for the opening-up of the army and the civil service to competition became irresistible, and the concept of leadership as a matter of breeding and birthright needed to be buttressed by educational superiority also. This usually began with private teaching at home by a tutor, often by a cleric of some intellectual eminence who regarded a spell of such service as an avenue to further advancement in the Church. Salaries of £150–£300 a year were not uncommon, and several former tutors ended their days with bishoprics – George Postyman at Winchester, Huntingford at Gloucester, Bethell at Bangor. The essentially private and personal system of tuition often continued when the tutor accompanied his charges to public schools, almost always Eton or Harrow, where board and tuition would cost from £175–£250 a year. A private boarding school at £100–£120 a year might instruct as efficiently, but did not carry the prestige which the reformed public schools of the mid-century were acquiring. The completion of education by a year or two at Oxford or Cambridge was now more usual than in earlier times, especially as the universities were beginning to lose their clerical preponderance under the curriculum changes of men like Jowitt at Balliol; but here too it was still common for a young aristocrat to be watched over by his own tutor, partly, perhaps, to guard against the 'sensual vice, gambling and extravagant expenditure' which a Royal Commission reported of Oxford in 1852. By the later years of the century it was not unknown for girls to join their brothers at university, where at Newnham, Cambridge she would need an allowance of £100–£150 a year and somewhat more at Girton. The men's colleges involved much the same cost as the major public schools. Thus the education of a family of 5 or 6 children, the average number, could easily involve some £1,500 a year, and was beginning to be regarded as one of the high but necessary costs the aristocracy had to pay for continued recognition and respect.

The hallmark of a gentleman was that he did not have to work, but could give himself up to a life of leisure. For a few, this meant active participation in affairs of state in Parliament and, perhaps, in government office: for some, it meant local affairs – the office of Lord-Lieutenant, the duties of magistracy at quarter sessions or the colonelcy of the local militia. There were some scholar-peers, a few artist-peers, and a fair number whose interest in the arts extended to enriching their picture galleries. A Gainsborough portrait was already fetching as much as £10,000, but for the knowledgeable there were bargains to be had like the da Vinci 'Madonna and Infant Child', sold in 1863 at Christie's for £209, or a Rembrandt for 220 guineas. But leisure essentially implied two things – fieldsports and the London season – the costs of both of which rose considerably during the period. A sporting peer who kept his own pack of hounds and a separate racing stable at Newmarket could easily spend thousands a year: even at the beginning of the century Lord Fitzwilliam's riding horses cost £2,000–£2,500 a year, his hounds £500 and his racing stables £1,500–£3,000. The increasing popularity of shooting added enormously to the game account on many estates – at Longleat, for example, the expenditure on the pheasants rose from £264 in 1790 to £3,000 a year by the 1890s, and at Savernake the £30 of the 1820s had risen to £1,500 by the later date. For such an outlay one could expect to slaughter between 1,000 and 2,000 birds in a season, carefully preserved and often hand-reared by the 3,000 game-keepers of England and Scotland. Fox-hunting also reached a peak of popularity in the 1860s, when there were 125 packs, many of them still in private hands like the Belvoir pack which cost £2,000 a year; additionally there would be a stable of 30 or more horses, a good hunter costing at least 120 guineas.

Wives and daughters no doubt suffered the boredom of life in the country in return for a 'season' of two or three months in London, where there would be a hectic round of balls and parties, shopping and entertainment which, for a girl, might well end in the announcement of an engagement. Such a season could again take several thousands a year. The costs of building a town 'house' – 'palace' would be more appropriate – were at least as great as a country seat, the Lambs spending £100,000 on Melbourne House (subsequently Albany), the Londonderrys £250,000 on Holdernesse House. When Northumberland House in the Strand was bought by the Metropolitan Board of Works in 1874 £497,000 was paid in compensation. Only the very wealthiest could, of course, afford such splendour, and Lord Verulam was content with a house in Grosvenor Square costing £13,000 in 1815. The majority of families merely rented a house, paying typically about £1,000 a year for a sizeable property in the West End. Thereafter the costs of a season – in food and drink, servants and all the paraphernalia of pleasure – could cost from £1,000 for a very modest peer to £20,000 for the Earl of Newcastle. A single 'rout' given by the wife of a West India planter, who was perhaps not quite respectable socially, was reputed to have cost £5,000–£6,000.

In one other respect, that of taxation, the cost of living for the nineteenth-century aristocracy was less favourable than it had been for their predecessors. Like all wealthy people they were affected by successive increases in income tax, which from its lowest point of 2d. in the £ in 1874 climbed slowly to 8d. by 1885 and 1s. 2d. in the last 4 years of peace down to 1914. Local rates were also an increasing burden, especially after 1888 when the new county councils were organized, the total raised increasing from £18 million in 1871 to £71 million in 1913. More important for the owner of land were the probate and estate duties, since these represented taxes on capital. From 1881 onwards estates of more than £1,000 paid a 3 per cent probate duty, and from 1894 there was a graduated estate duty, applicable to both real and personal property, which rose to 8 per cent on estates of £1 million or more: in 1907 this was steepened to 15 per cent on estates over £4 million. As yet, such taxes were not severe enough to threaten survival, but together with Lloyd George's budget of 1909 which introduced a super-tax on incomes over £5,000, they were portents of a new financial policy which was, in George's words, 'to tax the rich in the interests of the poor', and to level down those who for centuries past had enjoyed an 'unearned increment' from the land.

5

To many people, both then and since, the landed interest represented a traditional and anachronistic element in the social structure, irrelevant to the new sources of wealth and energy that were re-shaping English society. Disraeli's vision of government by an enlightened aristocracy had faded before the steady advance of a democracy to which he himself had contributed. Agriculture, the chief source of landed income, had been sacrificed to the demands for Free Trade from industrialists and workers alike; social policy came to be dependent on a fiscal system which demanded that the hereditary rich should 'pay ransom' to the community for the privileges they enjoyed. This mounting attack on aristocracy implied a fundamental shift in the balance of power in English society. The wealth on which Victorian England rested was the wealth built by merchants and industrialists, bankers, lawyers and shopkeepers, and it was these 'middle classes' who increasingly extended control over government, central and local, who manned and administered the institutions of British power at home and overseas, and who placed an indelible stamp on the culture and values of the 'age of improvement'.

They were equally the class which no one could define but to which everyone aspired to belong. What is reasonably certain is that in the middle of the nineteenth century they constituted considerably less than half of the 40 per cent of the community which most sociologists would credit them with today. On the basis of non-manual occupations, the number of adult males in the category in 1851 was about 1¼ million or 18 per cent of the total labour force; about half of these were in commercial occupations ranging from banking down to shopkeeping and clerking, a quarter were rent-paying farmers, and the remaining quarter professional, administrative and employing classes. Some of these occupations were already as old as the Middle Ages, others had only newly been called into existence by the Industrial Revolution. Industrialization demanded men who made and manipulated machines as well as men who manipulated capital; the rapid growth of towns which sprang as a direct consequence from it demanded builders and architects, surveyors and civil engineers, schoolteachers and shopkeepers, and at the lower levels, clerks, commercial travellers, agents, factors and petty tradespeople of all kinds. Out of this amalgam was gradually emerging not a single class, but a tier of classes and sub-classes, having as their only common characteristics a degree of literacy and an occupation requiring the exercise of mental rather than physical skill.

There were always more near the bottom of the class than near the top, more who fell back into manual labour than who penetrated into the privileged ranks of the gentry. In 1851 there were about 100,000 teachers and perhaps as many as 550,000 shopkeepers and street-sellers, only 44,000 commercial clerks and 86,000 'manufacturers employing capital in all branches'. It was this last group that constituted the dynamic, pace-making element of the class. Much of it was provincial – the Bells, Lambtons and Peases of Tyneside, ship-owners like the Booths, Holts and Rathbones, the great textile manufacturers like the Forsters and Baineses of Leeds – while in London there was already a strong Jewish element in the banking and finance families. Between these merchant and industrial princes and the petty bourgeoisie of tailors and milliners, chemists and elementary schoolteachers, there was little in common except a dislike of those below and a distrust of those above them. But the continued expansion of the class came mainly from the lower rather than the upper ranks, from the 'third rate men of business', the 'lesser professions', the governmental and clerical occupations. Between 1851 and 1881 alone those described under the head of 'dealing' increased by 69 per cent compared with an increase in population of 39 per cent, yet in 1909 there were still only 280,000 households in England and Wales with £700 or more a year. They, with their numerous offspring, constituted 1,400,000 persons out of a total population of 44½ million, though they drew to themselves one-third of the national income.

It would probably be right to designate these the 'upper' middle class, though some contemporaries regarded them as the only admissible members to the class as a whole – it was, for instance, clearly these that Arnold Bennett had in mind when he wrote

Their assured, curt voices, their carriage, their clothes, the similarity of their manners, all show that they belong to a caste. . . . It has been called the middle class, but it ought to be called the upper class, for nearly everything is below it. . . .

A few – the leading bankers, financiers and industrialists – were as wealthy as many of the landed aristocracy, with incomes of well over £10,000 a year and a style of life that had many of the outward trappings of gentility. A rising barrister of 1850 might have £5,000 a year, a doctor with a fairly fashionable practice £1,000–£2,000. Four Knight partners, owners and managers of a soap firm employing 150 men in mid-century, annually divided £15,000–£17,000 between them. Alfred Marshall, appointed Principal of Bristol University in the 1870s at a salary of £700 a year, kept two maids, managed to save £200 a year and to take a 2-months' holiday abroad: he assuredly was also in Bennett's limited 'middle' class, as were some headmasters of leading schools with stipends of £500–£1,000 a year.

Below such men with their obvious respectability lay the much broader band of the lower middle class. Where their incomes ended is not clear. The economic statistician L. C. Money in 1911 placed the lower limit at £160 a year, estimating the number of receivers, with their families, at 4,100,000. In 1858, the year when Acton's exposure of the extent of London prostitution had suggested that its incidence was largely due to the economic inability of young middle-class males to marry, *The Times* debated whether £300 a year was sufficient for a 'gentleman' to enter into wedlock. One correspondent disclosed that on this income he spent £25 a year on rent, £22 on meat, and £12 on a servant among other items, and still had a margin of £69 14s. Early in the twentieth century Rowntree used the concept of 'the servant-keeping class', which brought the level down well below this, and there were many families more who did not even aspire to a 'rough' girl but who enjoyed the relative security and esteem of a clerk's or cashier's wage. G. Kitson Clark has suggested that the lower limit for middle-class membership in 1850 might be placed at as little as £60 a year, and that even Dickens's Bob Cratchet with his 15s. a week might qualify for admission. In the offices of a Burnley cotton mill in 1852 wages for junior clerks were 8s. 7d. a week, for clerks 10s. 9d., and for senior clerks, after 15 years' service, 21s.; they were required to work from 7 a.m. to 6 p.m., to wear clothes 'of a sober nature' (though 'neck scarves and headwear may be worn in inclement weather') and each to bring 4 lb. of coal every day during the winter. Whether such poor slaves, working in what the management described as 'near Utopian conditions', regarded themselves, and were regarded by others, as middle-class, is doubtful.

Contemporary observers were impressed by the strides towards prosperity and comfort being taken by these men of 'moderate income'. Many of the price-changes of the period favoured them, imported foods, the ready-made clothing and furnishings of the department stores, travel, cooking and lighting all becoming cheaper as a result of technological developments. In a famous passage G. R. Porter, author of *The Progress of the Nation* (1847), wrote that

In nothing is the improvement ... more apparent than in the condition of the dwellings of the middle classes. As one instance, it is not necessary to go back much beyond half a century to arrive at the time when prosperous shopkeepers in the leading thoroughfares of London were without that now necessary article of furniture, a carpet, in their ordinary sitting-rooms. ... In the same houses we now see, not carpets merely, but many articles of furniture which were formerly in use only among the nobility and gentry: the walls are covered with paintings or engravings, and the apartments contain evidence that some among the inmates cultivate one or more of those elegant accomplishments which tend so delightfully to refine the minds of individuals and to sweeten the intercourse of families.

Porter's statistical mind went on to quantify this expanding wealth in terms of servants, horses, carriages and other material possessions. Already in 1841 – and the numbers were to continue to grow for the next 60 years – there were 110,000 male servants at an estimated annual cost of £6,650,000, together with 902,000 female servants costing £32 million: there were 28,000 4-wheeled carriages, the number having grown by 60 per cent in the last 2 decades, 42,000 2-wheeled carriages and another 35,000 let for hire, the total cost being £10,400,000. There were 176,000 horses kept for riding or drawing carriages, while 1,029,000 ounces of silver and 7,000 ounces of gold were annually retained for home consumption. All this was evidence of a steady accumulation of wealth in the hands of what was still a numerically small part of the population. It also seems likely that until the last decades of the century an increasing proportion of the national income was accruing to the middle classes, one estimate suggesting that between 1860 and 1880 the workers' share of the total fell from 47 per cent to 42 per cent.

A first-hand account of the costs of living of a modest middle-class family in the middle of the century is provided by the Carlyle household, where Thomas's thrifty Scottish wife Jane kept meticulous accounts. They had moved from Scotland to London in 1834 with £300, renting an 8-roomed Queen Anne house in what was then unfashionable Cheyne Row, Chelsea, for £35 a year. Carlyle's earnings from writing at this time were about £150 a year and Jane had a private income of the same amount: her household allowance for all purposes (she even paid the taxes and on one occasion triumphed over the Commissioners of Inland Revenue) was £200 a year, of which living expenses for 3 adults took about 30s. a week. One maid was employed (there were to be 40 changes in just over 30 years) at a wage which rose from £8 a year at the beginning to £16 by the 1860s: until a 'modernization' was carried out by the Carlyles in 1852, she cooked before an open fire in the dark basement where she was permitted to burn only 1 candle a day (10d.–1s. the lb.). The extensive alterations of 1852 included laying on running water in place of the basement pump, installing a new kitchen range which would cook and heat water (£7 3s.), and providing 2 gas jets, 1 over the front door and 1 in the kitchen: gas was still expensive, and the rest of the house continued to be lit by oil-lamps and candles (3 lb. every 9 days). In the 1850s Jane had to ask her husband for an increase in housekeeping, due to the rise in price of many foods: they were now using 2½ lb. of butter a week, 10½ lb. of meat, 10 lb. of potatoes at 1d. a lb., 12 tons of coal a year at 29s. a ton, 'bought judiciously, too'. In 1856 Carlyle was complaining to his brother in Canada that 'Everything is now changed and changing with furious rapidity in this country. A great increase of luxury is coming over all ranks: prices of everything very nearly doubled (13d. per pound for butter, 1d. each for eggs, and all in proportion) so that farmers prosper amazingly'. This was an exaggeration, reflecting the untypical conditions created by the Crimean War, but it was still true that some expenses had risen considerably. Taxes took £25 a year from this modest household, £11 a year for income tax and the rest for Poor Rate, Sewer Rate, Lighting, Pavement and Improvement Rate. Jane had a dress allowance of the same amount. Thomas had a horse given by an admirer on which in 10 minutes' trotting he could be in the country lanes of Clapham and Wandsworth, but had to give it up on discovering that its keep was costing nearly 4s. a day: for Jane, 'carriage exercise' consisted of going on the top of a horse omnibus to Richmond for 1s., until near the end of her life Thomas was able to buy her a brougham costing £60.

On an income of about £300 a year, the major items in the Carlyle budget were £75 on food, £35 for rent, £25 for taxes, £25 for Jane's clothes and £12–£16 for the servant: there were, of course, no children in the family. This may be compared with a suggested budget for £250 a year given by Mrs Rundell in her

New System of Domestic Economy (1825) for 'a gentleman, his lady, three children and a Maid-Servant', where food took £2 11s. 7d. a week, or £134 2s. 4d. a year. The biggest single item was 10s. 6d. a week for butcher's meat (18 lb. at 7d. a pound, or about ½ lb. each a day), followed by 7s. for beer and other liquors (Carlyle bought these himself), 6s. for bread, 3s. 6d. for 3½ lb. of butter, 3s. 6d. for fish, 3s. for sugar (4½ lb. at 8d. a lb.) and 2s. 6d. for tea (5 oz. at 8s. a pound). Two pounds of candles cost 1s. 2d. a week in 1825, coal and wood 3s. 9d. Rent and taxes were allowed at only £25 a year, clothes for 5 £36, the maid £16 and the education of 3 children £10 10s. There were small margins for recreation, medical expenses and savings, but although the family probably had more than enough food in total, it only devoted 3d. each a week to milk (2 pints) and 6d. each to fruit and vegetables. At an income of £1,000 a year Mrs Rundell's budget is quite different. There is now an establishment of 10, for besides the same-sized family there is a cook, a housemaid, a nursery-maid, a coachman and a footman, whose combined wages are £87 a year: there is also a 'Chariot, Coach, Phaeton or other four-wheel Carriage, and a Pair of Horses', costing £65 17s. a year in keep. The family consumes 52½ lb. of meat a week – a daily allowance of ¾ lb. for each person – there is now a guinea a week for drink, and ¾ lb. of butter for each person. The smallest items are still fruit and vegetables (9d. per person per week) and eggs and milk (4½d. per week).

In the £250 budget of 1825 the cost of food works out at 8s. 6d. per person per week. Eighty years later, at the beginning of the twentieth century, Mrs C. S. Peel estimated that 8s. 6d. a head would suffice for 'plain but sufficient living', 10s. for 'nice living', 15s. for 'good living' and £1 for 'very good living'. Although a good many items had changed in price or importance within these totals, their similarity over a long period of time is remarkable. Rowntree's lowest limit for his 'servant-keeping class' in 1901 went down to 5s. a head a week on food for a household of 3 adults and 3 children. Many of the foods they bought were now much cheaper than in Mrs Rundell's day – for instance, ½ lb. of tea only 1s., 3 lb. of treacle 9d., 4 lb. of sugar 3d., 6 oranges 6d., and 6 bananas 6d.; others, like the ¼ lb. of cocoa at 6d., the 4½ oz. of Benger's food at 7½d., the ½ lb. of marmalade at

2½d. and the 1½ lb. of self-raising flour at 3d., were new commercial products. There was a good deal of beefsteak eaten in the household (at 1s. a lb. it was not imported meat), halibut at 6½d. a lb., occasionally asparagus and potted shrimps (6d.).

At a considerably more elegant level is the budget of a young married couple without children, living in a London flat at the beginning of the twentieth century: out of an income of £700 a year, typical of a rising professional man, is spent:

	£	s	d
Rent, rates and taxes	100	0	0
Two maids (£22 and £20)	42	0	0
Food and cleaning materials for 4 at 10s. a head	104	0	0
Washing at 10s. week	26	0	0
Coal, 1 ton/month at £1 ton	12	0	0
Electric light	8	0	0
Wine	10	0	0
Office expenses, train fares and lunches at 12s. week	30	0	0
Insurance	25	0	0
Dress at £40 each	80	0	0
Savings	50	0	0
Total	487	0	0

There is still a surplus of over £200 here for additional household expenses, for holidays, entertaining and the other pleasant diversions of Edwardian life. However rigidly the virtues of thrift, sobriety and hard work had once been practised – and it seems likely that they were beginning to be abandoned from quite early in Queen Victoria's reign – there is little doubt that many of the Edwardian middle class did not even outwardly conform to these self-denying ordinances. Social imitation and ostentation became marked characteristics of the class from the 1880s onwards as the pressures for admission from below grew and the range of products and amusements to be enjoyed constantly expanded. With domestic service still abundant, with income tax rarely as much as 1s. in the £, oysters at 1s. the dozen, champagne at 6s. 6d. the bottle, a luxurious Mayfair flat for £200 a year, many more or less innocent vices could be indulged, without the social opprobrium that once attached to them. Probably the £700 a year newly marrieds were able to live more comfortably than they would ever do later in life: in 25 years' time they might find themselves like the established and successful man with £2,000 a year whose budget had to take account of 5 children, still the average family size early in the twentieth century. Here, rent, rates and taxes took £300 a year, wages for a manservant and 5 maids £157, besides another £300 for stable expenses and the wages of 2 more men, food for 14 persons at 12s. a week £437, and a governess and extra classes for the 3 girls £100. Washing for so many was a heavy expense (£104 a year), and there was no very great indulgence here on wine (£50 a year) or on dress and personal expenses (£100 each for husband and wife). Though there would be much solid comfort here, it required an income higher than this, or a family considerably smaller, to relish the full delights of Edwardian luxury.

It is clear from these budgets that food was the principal expenditure of the nineteenth-century middle class. Most of them liked to eat substantially, following the pattern set from above of three large meals a day and approaching it more or less nearly as income allowed. The principal social occasion for the class was the dinner-party, given weekly in a prosperous household and perhaps monthly in a modest one, where there would be 8 to 10 courses, served *à la Russe* rather than in 2 parts as in former days: this often involved additional help in the kitchen or dishes brought in from outside, so that the cost even of a modest meal for 8 persons would be 30s. to £2 10s., not including wines. A picnic for ten suggested by Mrs Beeton starts with 5 lb. of cold salmon (8s. 9d.), includes a quarter of lamb, 8 lb. of pickled brisket, a tongue, a galantine of veal and a chicken pie, which together with salads, cakes and 6 lb. of strawberries, totals £3 11s. 1d. Daily family meals were normally only of 4 courses – soup, fish, meat and dessert, and with the reduced prices of food after the 1870s and a widening range of home-produced and imported items, families of quite modest means could eat more interestingly than ever before. Mrs J. E. Panton's *From Kitchen to Garret: Hints for Young Householders*, was written in 1888 designedly for 'little people' with £300–£500 a year, employing 1 maid and not yet encumbered with children. At the lower income £2 a week will keep 'Angelina, Edwin and the model maid' in comfort, for everything is much cheaper and nicer than it used to be. . . . For example, when I was married [17 years before] sugar was 6d. a pound and now it is 2d.; and instead of paying 1s. 1d. a pound for legs of mutton, I give 7½d. for New Zealand meat, which is as good as the best English mutton that one can buy. Bread, too, is 5½d. . . . as against the 8d. and 9d. of seventeen years ago. . .

Out of the £2 a week on food meat takes 12s. (presumably about 18 lb. or nearly 1 lb. each a day), bread 4s., eggs 2s., milk 4s. (an unusually large amount, 32 pints), ½ lb. tea 2s. 6d., 1 lb. coffee 1s. 7d., 2 lb. of butter 3s., sugar 6d. and the remainder for fruit, fish, chickens and sundries. Edwin was sent off to work after a good breakfast – fruit, preserves, slices cut from a tongue (3s. 6d.) or a nice ham (8s. 6d.), sardines (6½d. a box), eggs, bacon, curried kidneys, mushrooms, a fresh sole, 'an occasional sausage'. From time to time money saved from the housekeeping might provide a little dinner-party for 6, a 9-course meal costing £1 1s. 4d. without wine (pheasant 2s. 6d. each, salmon 2s. 6d. a lb., turkey stuffed with chestnuts 8s. 6d., oysters 1d. each). This small family was devoting one-third of its income to food, and living very well. Mrs Rundell's £250 a year household of 1825 spent about half (£117 a year), though here there were 3 children: meat was again the biggest item (18 lb. costing 10s. 6d.), but bread cost 6s., 4½ lb. of sugar cost 3s. and only 1s. 6d. a week was allowed for milk. The diet of the 1880s was noticeably more varied, balanced and nutritious. In Mrs Rundell's £250 budget meat alone takes over one-tenth of total income, and in her £1,000 a year budget the 52½ lb. a week still take one-twelfth. In Mrs Panton's £300 budget of 1888 it also took one-tenth, though there was more of it, while in the Edwardian £2,000 a year budget food and drink take a quarter of total income, meat not being separately costed.

As incomes rose the proportion devoted to food fell, but the expenditure on servants increased and this, rather than accommodation, was the second largest item in many middle-class households. The number of domestic servants continued to grow throughout the period, reaching its maximum in 1911 at 1½ million, when they accounted for 1 in 7 of all employed persons and 1 in 3 of all girls in the country between the ages of 15 and 20. As in the nobility, there was a widely observed scale of servants according to income, set by Mrs Beeton's *Book of Household Management* at 1 maid-of-all-work at an income of £150–£300 a year, at £500 a year a cook and a maid, at £750 a cook, a maid and a boy, and at £1,000 a cook, upper- and under-housemaids and a man. A male servant was the first sign of affluence, and as incomes increased further there were butlers, coachmen, gardeners, footmen and stable-boys, besides a proliferation of housekeepers, lady's maids, housemaids and nursemaids, each with specialized functions and status in the hierarchical society of the servants' hall. Unlike the cost of food, which tended to fall over the period, the expense of keeping servants increased as alternative employment opportunities developed, especially for men, and as higher standards of maintenance came to be expected and received. In 1825 suggested wages for a butler were 50 guineas a year, coachman 28, footman 24, head gamekeeper 70 guineas plus cottage, gardener 40 guineas plus cottage, female housekeeper 24 guineas, lady's maid 20, upper housemaid 15 and nursery maid 7; 25 per cent of total income was expected to be devoted to servants and equipage, including horses, carriages and liveries. In a very modest household, like Mrs Rundell's £250 budget, or the Carlyle's £300, the employment of only 1 maid reduced the proportion to a mere one-fifteenth, though it has to be remembered that her keep would at least double this. But as soon as horses and a carriage appeared the proportion mounted rapidly. In Mrs Rundell's £1,000 a year budget the 5 servants cost £87 a year and the 2 horses £65, a combined fraction of nearly one-sixth. By Mrs Beeton's day a butler had at least £60 a year, and the head gardener as much as £120: the housekeeper rose to £50, the lady's maid to £25 and the cook to £45. By Edwardian times a butler might earn as much as £100 a year, a cook-housekeeper in a large establishment £80, a head housemaid £30 and an upper-footman £50. In the £2,000 a year budget of this period 6 servants cost £157 a year (manservant £50, cook £30, kitchen-maid £16, 2 housemaids £20 and £16, serving-maid £25), a governess for the 3 girls with additional classes £100. The garden and stable expenses, including the wages of 2 men and 1 boy and the keep of two cobs, added £300 – a total of £557 a year, or more than one quarter of income. Food and servants together seem always to have taken about one-half of earnings, the proportion of the first declining and of the second increasing with height in the social scale.

Housing and furnishing are not so easy to quantify for the class, since much depended on the part of the country, opportunities of inheritance and other factors. Again, it was more common for middle-class families to rent houses at a time before building societies had achieved their modern development, and it was often only in the country, or in the suburbs which began to grow up round the larger towns from the 1830s onwards, that houses were bought outright. In general, it is certain that building costs and rents increased substantially over the period, though much less than they have done subsequently. In many of the suggested middle-class budgets, one-tenth of income is allowed for rent, often including local rates. Thus Mrs Rundell suggests £25 out of a £250 a year budget, the Carlyles pay £35 out of about £300 a year, the Edwardian couple in their smart London flat devote £100 a year to rent, rates and taxes out of £700, and the established family man £300 out of his £2,000. A London villa, in mid-century, rented at £45 a year, has 2 drawing-rooms, breakfast-room, commodious kitchen and scullery, 3 large and 2 small bedrooms. Alfred Marshall's family house in Bristol, bought when he was appointed Principal of the University, cost £1,200, while Richard Cobden's large Manchester house, bought in 1832 for 3,000 guineas, was reckoned to be worth double 4 years later. At the beginning of the next century building costs were normally between 8d. and 10d. a cubic foot, putting a substantial, 4-bedroomed house at around £600–£700; in 1905 country cottages with living-room, scullery and 3 bedrooms were exhibited at £150 and were being patronized by the well-to-do seeking rural retreats. A large country house in Surrey, 'The Haven', cost £2,300, including stables and outbuildings: it had 5 reception rooms (including 'boudoir' and billiard-room), 8 bedrooms, 2 bathrooms and extensive kitchen quarters, being built around a central courtyard mainly in the Tudor style.

The Victorian and Edwardian middle classes also spent more on dress than their predecessors had done. This was not because clothes were dearer – rather the reverse – but because social life demanded frequent changes of fashion, for women at

THE NINETEENTH CENTURY

least, and because the range of desirable garments had greatly expanded under the influence of shops, advertisements and department stores. In 1825 Mrs Rundell allowed an expenditure on dress of £36 out of an income of £250 a year (husband £14, wife £12, 3 children £10), a fraction of one-seventh; in the Edwardian budget of £700 for 2 adults only, dress takes £80 (one-ninth), and in the £2,000 a year budget the husband and wife each have dress and personal allowances of £100, the 2 grown-up sons £50 each – this, with equivalents for the 3 girls, would suggest a fraction of about one-fifth, though not all of it would necessarily be spent on dress. Mechanization of the textile industries and, after the invention of the sewing-machine in 1851, of the garment trades, undoubtedly lowered the prices of ready-made clothes substantially in the later nineteenth century – garments suitable for a maid, for instance, included ribbed vests at 3¾d., broché corsets at 2s. 11d., a moirette petticoat 1s. 6¼d., and elastic-sided shoes 2s. 11d. Her mistress was unlikely to avail herself of such opportunities. Elegant silk dress-lengths would cost 16s. to £1 a yard, and Queen Victoria's lace wedding-dress was reputed to have cost £1,000: shawls in 1850 could be had from 1 guinea to 100 guineas, fans from 6d. to £300, a riding-habit made to measure, 10 guineas upwards. The growth of the great London and provincial department stores towards the end of the century still further widened the choice of women's clothes and accessories, making it possible for many families in modest circumstances to dress fashionably. Thus the bonnets worn by Princess Mary of Teck were reproduced in the 1890s at £2 8s., Harrods offered complete trousseaux at from £7 7s. 8d. to £33 18s., and the Irish Linen Company blouses at £2 9s. 6d. a dozen. At home the mistress and her maids could make dresses from one of Butterick's paper patterns (3d.–2s. in the 1880s) or knit from John Patton's *Universal Knitting Book* (1d. in 1899).

The Victorian middle classes were perhaps the most family-minded generation in English history, and the upbringing of children was a greater expense for them than it had been for their ancestors. Not only was it that as a result of medical and sanitary improvements more children survived than in the past (the average number of children per family reaching its maximum in 1871 at 5·6 and 1 in 5 of all families having 10 or more children), but as competitive pressures in industry and commerce developed, more formal education was needed than in the days when 'self-help' allied to natural aptitude could ensure business success. In 1865, it has been estimated, only 10 per cent of the leading steel manufacturers had been to public school, the vast majority having received their education on the job in an industrial or commercial apprenticeship. The figure would be different for the professions, and markedly different in the next generation, by which time Germany's rapid economic development was at last beginning to persuade Englishmen of the importance of education. By the end of the century the costs of raising children started with a nanny at £25–£50 a year, continued with a governess at £50–£100, followed by preparatory school for boys at 8 and public school at 13, where fees of £100–£150 a year were usual. At a lower income level there would be a grammar school or private day school and, increasingly for girls, one of the G.P.D.S.T. foundations. University education, or 'articled' training in one of the professions, would still further delay the onset of independence and would necessitate the payment of an allowance, at least to sons, until their middle or late twenties. Precise costs are clearly incalculable here, depending on individual circumstances, but the significant fact is that children were becoming dependent for a longer and longer time at the same time as their dependency was costing more in formal training. It is no coincidence that deliberate family limitation seems to have had its origin in this class in the 1870s and 1880s, and that the twentieth-century trend towards a smaller family size was initiated by the desire of late Victorian parents to launch a fewer number of children more successfully in life.

Shorter working hours, the development of new forms of recreation, the lengthening of the day by gas-light (3s. to 6s. the cubic foot) and improved transport facilities all meant that the Victorian middle classes did not share their Queen's predilection not to be amused. Indoors, reading had become much cheaper than ever before, with popular editions of books at 1s. and less, weekly journals aimed at family readership, which multiplied rapidly from the 1830s onwards, at 1d. and 2d. a copy (Charles

Dickens was first serialized in these) and, by the end of the century, the first of the 'popular press', the *Daily Mail*, the 'Penny Paper for a Halfpenny'. Scores of indoor games – one authority has counted nearly 300 – were marketed for family entertainment, many of them, like 'Virtue Rewarded and Vice Punished' (a kind of snakes-and-ladders game from Number 1 'The House of Correction' to Number 53 'Virtue') of a distinctly 'improving' kind. As a result of the application of mass-production methods the piano was gradually brought within the range of most middle-class homes – by mid-century Broadwood's made 5 sizes of instrument, the grand, semi-grand, the cabinet, the cottage and the square piano, while Robert Cocks and Company offered a 'semi-cottage' or 'piccolo' model at 30 guineas – and the necessary sheet-music to go with it became available for a few pence. Private subscription libraries like The Times and the London Library, available at about 2 guineas a year, were essentially middle-class institutions. But as travel about cities and about the country as a whole became easier, more leisure time was spent outside the home on day excursions and longer holidays. In London Cremorne Gardens were still open at 6d. for children and 1s. for adults in 1846, reached by a river omnibus service costing 4d.: the Zoological Gardens cost 1s., as did the Great Exhibition in Crystal Palace, Hyde Park, to which Thomas Cook's newly devised excursion trains brought millions of sight-seers. By the 1860s he was applying the same principle to foreign travel, and the middle classes were beginning to share the delights of Switzerland and Italy with the nobility, whose preserves they had once been: 'all-in' foreign holidays at £10 or less were common before the end of the century. For a family with small children it was more usual to rent a 'villa' in a south-coast resort for 6 to 8 weeks in the summer, taking the servants and allowing the husband to live in his club and join the others each weekend: between about 1830 and 1880 many watering-places passed through this period of middle-class predominance which has left indelible marks on them. Some husbands perhaps took advantage of this unaccustomed freedom to visit Covent Garden (boxes 2–6 guineas, stalls 21s., amphitheatre 2s. 6d. in 1862) or even a farce at the Lyceum (seats 5s. down to 1s.), and if the club meals were insufficiently exciting at

3s. to 4s., there was soon to be a range of glittering hotels and restaurants where some of the best food in the world could be had at moderate prices. Probably none could rival the Carlton, where a dinner for 2 in 1900 of 9 courses including oysters, truffled soup, sole, suprême de volaille, ortolans, champagne and liqueurs cost £2 19s. 6d., though an excellent 7-course meal at the Comedy Restaurant cost only 2s. 6d., and still included hors d'oeuvres variés, soup, sole Colbert, filet mignon and snipe, besides vegetables and dessert.

In many people's nostalgic view of the past, late Victorian and Edwardian England was a kind of 'Golden Age' for the middle classes from which peak of power and prosperity the twentieth century has seen a continuous decline. With a maid at £18 a year, 20 cigarettes for 6d., a bottle of whisky for 3s. 6d. and oysters at 1d. each, there was much in life to be enjoyed by those who had some margin of income over necessary expenditure, and in many respects the England of 1914 – whether it was in the clubs of Pall Mall, the suburban villas of Twickenham or on the sands of Bournemouth – was still 'England, their England'. Needless to say, this was not the view that contemporaries had of themselves. The last 2 or 3 decades of the old world were a period of questioning and doubt behind the apparent complacency, of abandonment of traditional political and religious beliefs, and of the adoption of new values in art and literature, and in domestic and social life. Among the business classes there was growing concern about 'ruinous competition' and declining profits at home and abroad, in the face of which the old, competitive structure of industry was coming to be modified by mergers, price-fixing and trade agreements. Among all classes there were complaints at the rising cost and inefficiency of domestic service and the increasing expense of house-rent and private education. Above all, it seemed to the middle classes that they were now bearing the brunt, through taxation, of the social reforms which were beginning to transform the lives of the poor but from which they themselves derived no material advantage. Private philanthropy was coming to be replaced by a public policy which involved a redistributive system of taxation, taking proportionately more from those who had more to give to those who had less. This shattering principle, although it had

had its origins earlier in the period, became fully manifest only in Lloyd George's 'People's Budget' of 1909, which raised income tax from 1s. to 1s. 2d. in the pound, introduced a super-tax of 6d. in the pound on incomes over £5,000 a year, and taxes on petrol and motor-car licences. The *Daily Mail* carried a portentous headline in its largest type 'Plundering the Middle Class'!

6

If Victorian England was, in many respects, the England of the middle classes, the standard of life that they enjoyed depended ultimately on the toil of a much larger section of society, the section that the eighteenth century usually designated the 'labouring poor' and the nineteenth the 'working class' or occasionally the 'proletariat'. Again, the singular noun was a quite inappropriate description for a group which comprised a vast range of skill and earnings, and between the various elements of which there was often little common attitude or purpose. The Victorian working classes had no more homogeneity than their social superiors, and it is safer to regard them as a series of sub-classes, ranging from élite workers whose habits and values were closely allied to those of the middle classes, down to the numerous categories of the poor, the deserving, the undeserving and the destitute.

Numerically, the working classes in the middle of the nineteenth century made up some 80 per cent of the whole community – rather more at the beginning of the century and rather less towards its end. Dudley Baxter in 1867 put them at 7·8 million out of a total of 10 million persons in England and Wales in receipt of independent incomes, not including dependants: of these, 1·1 million were the 'skilled labour class', 3·8 million the 'less skilled labour class' and 2·8 million 'agricultural workers and unskilled labour class'. For all these groups earnings were calculated at less than £100 a year. But the effect of continuing industrialization was to make important shifts within the 3 sections, to remove more from the lowest-paid manual operations and to promote them into the ranks of the machine-minding, the skilled and the clerical occupations. However distressing its immediate impact may have been on workers in traditional trades who were unable or unwilling to learn new ones, ultimately the Industrial Revolution offered greater rewards to a greater proportion of the population than was ever possible in the pre-industrial economy. This is not to argue that it raised the standards of all, that it eradicated poverty or equalized wealth in any spectacular way. At the end of our period, in 1911, L. C. Money estimated that one-third of the national income was enjoyed by an upper-class of 1·4 million, a second third by a middle class of 4·1 million, and the remaining third by a working-class of 39 million: society was still divided in much the same unequal way as it had been at the time of Dudley Baxter in 1867 or, for that matter, of Gregory King in 1688. In one highly important respect, however, the situation had changed radically for the better since 1688. In King's estimate half the entire population was in poverty, actually 'diminishing the wealth of the Kingdom' by consuming more than it produced: in 1900 the researches of Charles Booth, Seebohm Rowntree and other social investigators all confirmed that the fraction who were in this condition was now 'only' about one quarter. If both estimates are somewhere near the truth, and if they are comparable, they suggest one of the major social transformations in English history.

It is clear from Baxter's categories that agricultural and unskilled labour still made up one of the largest sections of society in mid-Victorian England. Agriculture provided in fact the largest single occupational group in 1851, followed by domestic service in second place, building and general labouring in fourth and fifth places: of the ten largest occupations at the time of the Great Exhibition only two – cotton and wool – had yet been radically transformed by mechanization. It was in the unrevolutionized trades that the lowest earnings and the greatest poverty lay, among the farm workers, the unskilled urban occupations like labouring, portering and navvying where work was often casual and seasonal, and among the still numerous hand-trades now in competition with factory-production like handloom-weaving, framework-knitting, silk-weaving and ribbon-making. No general statement about 'average wages' is likely to be realistic for such diverse groups whose earnings

THE NINETEENTH CENTURY

changed substantially in time and varied in different parts of the country. The descent of the handloom-weavers from prosperity to pauperism within half a century – the classic example of technological unemployment – is well-known. At the beginning of the century, before the adoption of power-looms, they were among the aristocrats of labour with wages of 30s.–35s. a week, sufficiently wealthy to collect their work by coach and to walk the streets with a £5-note displayed under their hat-bands: by the 1830s, as mechanical weaving took over, they had been reduced to a starvation wage of 1d. an hour or 6s. for a week of 72 hours' labour. At this time they still numbered almost 500,000 workers, though few survived the next generation. Comparable with them were the framework hosiery knitters of the Midland counties, earning an average of 5s. 3d. a week in 1833, the nail-makers of the Black Country, the silk-workers of Spitalfields and Macclesfield, the Coventry ribbon-makers, the lace-makers, shoemakers and seamstresses – a vast army of casualties of industrialization whose utmost labour in the middle of the century barely yielded the simplest kind of subsistence. Mercifully, many of them had disappeared from existence by the end of the period, their skill replaced by machines and factories which offered a new and more remunerative employment to their children. There remained, however, a substantial body of outworkers in the 'sweated' trades – mostly women working at home at ready-made tailoring and shirt-making, box-making and millinery trades – whose miserable lot excited widespread concern and some legislative action early in the twentieth century.

The sweated trades and their predecessors, the domestic textile industries, always contained a high proportion of women workers often supporting themselves as widows or contributing to a larger family budget of which they were not the sole support. The lowest earnings of any large body of adult male workers in the century were found among the agricultural labourers who, despite a substantial reduction in numbers (from 966,000 in 1851 to 643,000 in 1911), remained one of the largest occupational groups throughout the period. Their wages varied greatly from one year to another and between different areas, the north and north-west of England continuing to offer substantially higher earnings than the south and east, where there was less alternative industrial employment; there were also wide variations for skill, and between day-labourers and the more permanent yearly men. Again, much depended on the size and age of the family, whether wife and children were able to contribute by field or domestic employment, whether the family could grow any of its own food in garden, allotment or cow-pasture, and how much was given by the employer in the way of allowances or privileges for the purchase of food at farm prices. All these factors complicate calculations of the agricultural labourer's real earnings, and suggest that statistics of his weekly wages are valid mainly as indicating the direction of change. They show that the average wage in 1800 was about 10s. a week, from 1804–10 12s., in 1811, at the height of the wartime inflation, 13s. 9d., 9s. 4d. in 1824, 10s. 4d. in 1837, 11s. 7d. in 1860 and 13s. in 1866. Yet in 1824, when there was a Select Committee Report on the Rate of Agricultural Wages, they were as little as 3s. a week for a single man in some southern counties, 4s. 6d. for a married man, and even within different parts of Kent they varied from 6d. to 1s. 6d. a day. In Lancashire, on the other hand, a labourer could earn up to 12s. a week, and in Cumberland up to 15s. Sustained improvement came after the 1870s, as numbers on the land dwindled, and those who remained began to organize themselves into trade unions. In 1867–71 weekly wages varied between 10s. 6d. (Somerset, Cornwall, Devon, Dorset, Wiltshire) and 15s. 1d. (Cumberland, Westmorland, Northumberland, Durham, Yorkshire, Lancashire, Cheshire), while by 1914 the extremes were 14s. 3d. and 22s.: it is estimated that regular allowances of various kinds added another 2s. to 3s. a week.

The largest group of workers, however, and one that increased as the century went on, were the semi-skilled. They were substantially better off than the agricultural labourer, though separated from the skilled man by a differential which probably widened rather than narrowed: in the middle of the century, the ratio between skilled, semi-skilled and unskilled stood at about 5 : 3·3 : 2·4, putting the actual earnings of the semi-skilled at between £40 and £52 a year. Some were workers in old-established trades like building, mining and quarrying, others were new, public-service occupations like those of the policeman and postman: most characteristically, however, the semi-skilled were the machine-operators in the factories called into existence by the Industrial Revolution. To this extent they represented a largely new and highly significant element in the structure of the English working classes, where formerly there had existed virtually only skilled and unskilled men with little possibility of movement between them. The semi-skilled represented that third of the working classes whose earnings, according to the contemporary observer Samuel Laing, were just about sufficient for subsistence, in contrast to that other third 'plunged in extreme misery, and hovering on the verge of actual starvation'. Semi-skilled workers in the building trades earned, at the beginning of the century, about 2s. a day: by 1809 they had moved up to 29d. a day, and from 1810 to the middle of the century they hovered around 32d., or 16s. a week. As for the agricultural labourers, substantial increases came subsequently – to 42d. a day by 1872, 46d. in 1880, 50d. by the end of the century and 60d. (30s. a week) immediately before the outbreak of war. The earnings of coalminers were somewhat higher than this, though acutely subject to variations during trade fluctuations. At the beginning of the century a Northumberland miner had 2s. 6d. to 3s. a day, probably working an average of 4½ days a week; in 1834 he had 3s. 4d. to 4s. 5d. a day, with lower levels averaging 3s. 6d. a day during the slack years of the 1840s. Wage-increases came earlier to the miners than to the other groups, due partly to the rapid expansion of the industry after mid-century and partly to the effective organization of labour in the mines. Between 1850 and 1860 average weekly wages jumped from 19s. 6d. to 25s. 8d., rising little thereafter until the 1880s: by the end of the period 35s. a week was a common wage for what was by now an 8-hour day.

But the semi-skilled most characteristically found their employment in one of the new factory trades, the archetypes of which were the textile industries of Lancashire and Yorkshire. Here the position is complicated by the widespread employment of women and children as well as men, whole families sometimes working together in the mills as they had once worked at home. A clear distinction has to be made between individual earnings and the earnings of a family, which might include the wages of the husband as a spinner, the wife as a power-loom weaver and several children as piecers, doffers and scavengers. Even in the factory there were many gradations of skill and earnings, the highest-paid workers being spinners on fine counts who earned about 33s. a week at the beginning of the century and about 40s. in the 1840s: spinners on medium counts made about 20s. to 25s. at this time, and throstle-spinners only 7s. to 10s. 6d. Power-loom weavers' wages depended on the number of looms they attended, a minder of 2 looms in 1846 earning 10s. and a minder of 4 16s. Piecers' wages ranged from 3s. 6d. to 11s. in the 1840s, according to age and skill. Subsequent increases went largely to the weavers rather than the spinners, a weaver operating 2 looms earning 15s.–18s. a week by the 1880s, fine spinners' wages remaining at about 42s. In 1906 three-quarters of all fine spinners earned more than 40s. a week, and half more than 45s., putting these privileged workers in the ranks of the labour aristocrats rather than the semi-skilled.

To these wages – at least for the textile industries – have to be added the earnings of other members of the family. Since so much depended on individual family circumstances this would be quite impossible to quantify, though as a general measure it may be said that the earnings of a wife, a boy and a girl would together double the husband's wage. In her study of the textile industry in the early nineteenth century, Frances Collier collected many examples of actual family earnings which illustrate this point. Thus the Brooks family of 8, working at the Barr's Mill in 1802, had a combined weekly income of £2 8s. 2d., though the father's wage was only 14s.; the Stevens family employed by Grey and Sons in 1835 had 26s. a week, made up of 'John Stevens (labourer) aged 38, 12s., Elizabeth, aged 18, 6s., Rebeckah, aged 14, 3s. 6d., James, aged 12, 3s., and Mary, aged 10, 1s. 6d.'. By such means many families in Lancashire and Yorkshire made up their earnings, at least for a certain period of life, to something above subsistence level, or with greater skill, to comparative affluence. It is important to remember, however, that the textile industries were untypical in this respect. From other studies it appears that in the coal-fields and in the port towns it was exceptional for wives and very young children to work in the later part of the century: in Newcastle in 1851 only 5 per cent of wives worked, in Bristol about 15 per cent, while Booth's survey of London in the 1890s showed that among the better-paid workers the earnings of all other family members added only about 10 per cent to the father's wage. Generally, it seems, the function of family earnings was to bring the chief bread-winner's wage up to subsistence level where this was deficient, the assumption being that the husband's wage ought normally to be adequate for family support.

These two groups, the unskilled and the semi-skilled, accounted for the vast majority of the English working classes in the nineteenth century. In 1885 Sir Robert Giffen estimated that 59 per cent of all adult male workers earned less than 25s. a week, and in the next decade Charles Booth believed that there was another 30 per cent earning from 25s. to 35s. a week and enjoying 'solid working-class comfort'. These statistics omit a third, smaller group, the labour 'aristocracy' or élite, who probably composed between 10 and 15 per cent of the working class, increasing slightly in proportion towards the end of the period as mechanization continued to create demands for new and higher skills. The labour aristocracy were to be found in many industries and trades where skill was in short supply – in some old-established crafts like building, pottery, printing and book-binding, and in new ones like shipbuilding, engineering and steel-making. Their wage-base may be taken as 35s. a week, but most earned more than this and some much more, a compositor on daily newspapers averaging about 50s. a week in the 1880s, iron-puddlers and mill-men up to 20s. on piecework in a 12-hours' day. Many industries had a proportion of these highly skilled men. In 1865 Leone Levi found weekly wage-rates of 40s. or more among shipwrights, engine-drivers, book-binders, scientific instrument makers, cutlery-grinders, cabinet-makers, jewellers, forge-rollers, compositors, musical instrument makers, watch-makers, wood-carvers and pottery modellers and throwers: the significant point is that at this time so many of the élite workers were found among traditional hand-crafts little affected by mechanization. Forty years later the position had changed considerably. In the Earnings and Hours Inquiry (Wage Census) of 1906, the occupations with the highest proportions of 40s. a week wage-earners are listed as ship-building platers (82 per cent of workers), shipbuilding caulkers

(78 per cent), cotton spinners on 80 counts (78 per cent), railway engine drivers (72 per cent), shipbuilding riveters (70 per cent), engineering platers (68 per cent), steel coggers and rollers (62 per cent), turners (49 per cent) and fitters (48 per cent). The predominance of the metal industries among the labour aristocrats was now remarkable, while the skilled handcrafts of the mid-century had sunk relatively in importance and remuneration. Even highly skilled building craftsmen like masons, plasterers and joiners, with a daily wage-rate just before the outbreak of war of about 6s. 6d., now failed to qualify for admission into the privileged ranks.

These actual earnings must now be placed against prices to indicate changes in 'real wages' or the purchasing power of earnings. The difficulties of attempting this for earlier centuries have previously been discussed, and the problems of inadequacy of wage and retail price statistics are little easier for the nineteenth century. The wide variations in actual wages discussed above indicate that any 'average wage' for the period is a statistical abstraction, while other factors vital to the standard of living of the worker, such as the incidence of unemployment and short-time, also have to lie concealed in the averages. But although precise statements about real wages are of doubtful validity, it is possible to be more confident about the directions in which they moved at particular periods, a chart constructed by Professor A. L. Bowley being especially useful:

Period	Nominal wages	Prices	Real wages
1790–1810	Rising fast	Rising very fast	Falling slowly
1810–1830	Falling	Falling fast	Rising slowly
1830–1852	Nearly stationary	Falling slowly	Rising slowly
1852–1870	Rising fast	Rising	Rising considerably
1870–1873	Rising very fast	Rising fast	Rising fast
1873–1879	Falling fast	Falling fast	Nearly stationary
1879–1887	Nearly stationary	Falling	Rising
1887–1892	Rising	Rising and falling	Rising
1892–1897	Nearly stationary	Falling	Rising
1897–1900	Rising fast	Rising	Rising
1900–1914	Stationary	Rising	Falling slowly

Looking in more detail at some of the periods, it appears that there was little movement of real wages in either direction during the whole first half of the century. It certainly seems unlikely that they can have increased during the rapid inflation of the Napoleonic Wars, when from all accounts wages lagged badly behind the soaring prices, and there were widespread indications of growing poverty and destitution which the Speenhamland System of poor relief attempted to ameliorate. That there was no mass starvation was possibly due to fairly full employment during the war, and to improved economic organization and transport systems which meant that the available food supplies could, at least, be evenly distributed. It is also likely that some substitution – for example, of wheat bread by oats, barley and rye, or of bread by potatoes – took place, so that a price index weighted heavily in favour of wheat gives an unduly high reading for these years. When all allowances are made, however, there still seems no convincing evidence for a rise in average real wages during the war, or during the immediate post-war years 1815–20, when economic conditions were highly disturbed by adjustments to peacetime demands. On Professor Phelps Brown's index of the real wages of building workers there was a fall from 55 (1475–1500 = 100) in 1790 to 34 in 1801, the year of greatest scarcity, and 43 in 1813, followed by a small rise to 59 by 1820.

Between 1820 and 1840 wages were generally more stable, prices falling, and there is more likelihood of small gains in real earnings for those workers who were able to stay in reasonably full employment. In 1820 it is possible that the average real earnings of the working classes were no higher than they had been in the 1780s, but thereafter, as overseas markets recovered from the long wars, and the factory system accelerated, more workers began to find steadier employment at higher rates than they ever enjoyed in the pre-industrial age. The Phelps Brown index suggests a rise in real wages between 1820 and 1840 of 5 per cent, small enough in total, yet perhaps the first change in an upward direction since the 1760s, and the first indication of the very substantial gains that were to come later in the century.

The decade of the 1840s has been a favourite debating-ground for historians ever since Frederick Engels condemned the capitalist system in his *Condition of the Working Classes in England in 1844*. Here again, the wage-price data are inconclusive, showing on the Phelps Brown index a substantial rise in real wages from 62 points in 1840 to 79 in 1849. It has to be remembered, however, that 5 years of the decade (1840–2 and 1847–8) were years of acute cyclical depression with high unemployment, short time and wage-cuts in many industries: in 1842 the number of those in receipt of poor relief reached an all-time maximum of nearly 1½ million. On the other hand, the shift away from low-paid employments like agriculture and hand-loom-weaving to higher-paid and more regular factory trades was becoming distinctly more pronounced at this time, while the consumption-levels of such comparative luxuries as tea, sugar and tobacco, which had been practically stationary or falling since the beginning of the century, began to move upwards from about 1845. There is certainly no hard evidence that the 1840s as a decade were 'hungrier' than the 1830s or, probably, than the 1850s.

From the middle of the century the statistics are more abundant and the trends less in dispute. Although prices were rising after 1850, wages rose more rapidly as the economy moved into an era of rapid expansion and prosperity. By 1873 there had been a rise in real wages of 20 per cent over 1850 on the G. H. Wood index. This improvement came after some low levels in the mid-1850s, when the Crimean War resulted in a brief period of rapid inflation, and was mainly concentrated into the decade 1863–73, which could with some justice be regarded as a turning-point in working-class standards. From this time there were steady and substantial advances even for those sections of labour like the agricultural worker who had not previously shared in the benefits of industrialization.

The improvement was continued between 1873 and 1896 in a period of falling prices which contemporaries designated the 'Great Depression'. On the G. H. Wood scale (1850 = 100) average retail prices fell from 125 to 83, while money-wages remained almost stationary after some initial slight falls. The result was that real wages increased from 128 (1850 = 100) in 1873 to 176 in 1896, easily the biggest gain in the century. The poorer sections of the working class were now taking their first great strides out of that poverty which had been their lot for generations past, and it is significant that on the Phelps Brown index the year 1880 marks the time when average real wages at last returned to the level they had had at the end of the fifteenth century. The rise over the period on this index is even larger, from 84 points in 1873 to 132 in 1896.

For a few more years, until the beginning of the new century, real wages continued to grow, but thereafter there was a reversal of the trend which had persisted for the last 60 or 70 years. Between 1900 and 1914 wages in a number of industries were practically stationary, while retail prices increased by about 10 per cent: on the G. H. Wood scale the fall in real wages is from 183 in 1900 to 174 in 1914, on the Phelps Brown scale from 134 to 124. This fall was certainly not evenly shared, the wages of coal-miners, many cotton workers and public servants continuing to rise, while those of many building, engineering and railway workers rose less than prices. Although it was not a major reversal of the gains made during the previous half-century, this change in the direction of real wages largely accounts for the widespread social unrest and the militant labour politics which characterized the years immediately before the outbreak of the first world war.

In total, then, the whole period from 1790 to 1900 saw an increase in the real earnings of the average worker of some 2½ times, and probably a doubling within the considerably shorter period 1830–1900. This is comparable only with the doubling of real wages that occurred during the 60 or 70 years after the Black Death in the middle of the fourteenth century, though by 1914 the rise had gone to levels never previously experienced. Britain's productive resources had at last enabled her to realize a standard of life that was unique in time and in place, a standard which to many people seemed to stand as a monument to the capitalist imperialist system of which she was the prime exemplar. Because of this improvement, and because of the continuous up-grading of labour from less skilled to more skilled occupations, there can be little doubt that the worker had gained as much as – perhaps more than – other classes during the period of late Victorian prosperity. Many contemporaries, indeed, believed that he was now the principal beneficiary of economic progress, echoing the opinion of Giffen that nearly all the advances gained during the past half-century had gone to him, or of Professor Levi that 'In a large number of instances working men of 1857 have become middle-class ones of 1884'. It was against this background of optimism that the revelations of the extent of poverty by Charles Booth and Seebohm Rowntree at the end of the century came as such a disagreeable shock. By the standards of the most rigorous measures available to them – a subsistence level defined by reference to the smallest amount of food necessary to support mere physical efficiency – they came to an almost precisely similar conclusion, that 30·7 per cent of the population of London and 27·8 per cent of the population of York were existing in poverty. Within a few years other researchers had demonstrated a similar, or worse, story from cities old and new, from country villages as well as towns. In 1900, despite the undeniable progress of the past half-century, one-half of all the children of the working classes still grew up in poverty, 1 in 6 babies died before reaching their first year, and 1 in 5 of the population could still look forward to the indignity of a pauper's funeral from the workhouse in which they would end their days.

It remains to investigate the ways in which the working classes laid out their earnings. It will be clear by now that there was no 'typical' working-class wage or, therefore, pattern of consumption, and the following budgets can be regarded only as representative: they are, however, selected from examples of skilled, semi-skilled and unskilled earnings around 3 points in time – the beginning of the century, the mid-century and the end of the century – to give as wide a coverage as possible. First, however, it is interesting to look at what was probably the only attempt in the course of the century to estimate how wages as a whole were expended. The following calculation was made by a committee of the British Association for the Advancement of Science, and reported to its meeting in 1881:

	Total expenditure £m	Expenditure per head per day Pence
Bread	77,500,000	1·41
Potatoes	33,200,000	0·64
Vegetables	17,000,000	0·32

THE NINETEENTH CENTURY

	Total expenditure £m	Expenditure per head per day Pence	
Meat	99,800,000	1·87	
Fish	14,500,000	0·26	
Butter and cheese	36,000,000	0·67	
Milk and eggs	42,000,000	0·78	
Fruit	11,100,000	0·19	
Sugar	27,000,000	0·50	
Tea	15,300,000	0·29	
Coffee, etc.	3,000,000	0·05	
Beer	75,000,000	1·4	
Spirits	40,000,000	0·75	
Wines	9,000,000	0·16	
Total food and drink	£500,400,000	9·60	56·9%
Cotton	31,000,000	0·58	
Wool	63,000,000	1·18	
Linen	7,700,000	0·14	
Silk	17,600,000	0·32	
Leather etc.	23,500,000	0·44	
Total clothes	£142,800,000	2·66	16·8%
House-rent	77,000,000	1·44	
Furniture	11,000,000	0·20	
Coal	15,000,000	0·29	
Gas	13,700,000	0·25	
Water	5,000,000	0·09	
Total housing	£121,700,000	2·27	13·9%
Recreation and education	£60,000,000	1·33	7%
Taxes	£47,500,000	0·89	5·4%
	Total gross expenditure	16·63	100%

Turning now to actual budgets, we take first that of one of the most highly paid of all workers, a London compositor of 1810. He spends on himself, his wife and unusually small family of 2 children:

	£	s	d
Rent per week		6	0
Bread and flour, 5 quarters		6	9¼
Meat, 14 lb. at 9d.		10	6
Butter, 2 lb. at 1s. 4d.		2	8
Cheese, 1 lb.			11
Porter, 3 pints per day at 2½d.		4	4½
Candles		1	7½
Coals, 1 bushel		1	9
Soap, starch and blue			9
Tea, ¼ lb. at 7s.		1	9
Sugar, 2 lb. at 9d.		1	6
Vegetables		1	6
Milk			7
Pepper, salt, vinegar etc.			6
Clothing, shoes etc.		4	0
Schooling, books etc.		1	6
Benefit Society			10
	2	7	6¼

This suggests a level of consumption of almost middle-class standards but for the fact that no domestic servant is kept. The family lives exceptionally well, devoting 65 per cent of income to food and drink, and nearly 20 per cent to meat alone, which is the largest single food item. The dearness of rent in London, as of tea, sugar, coal and candles, is well illustrated, but this prosperous family is able to devote one-twelfth of income to dress, to have its children educated and to contribute to an insurance scheme, probably providing widowhood and burial benefits.

This may be compared with the budget of a Lancashire cotton spinner earning 25s. a week, something over a typical semi-skilled wage since this man works on fine counts. He had the average-sized family of 5 children, who were not yet working:

	s	d
Butter, 1½ lb.	1	3
Tea, 1½ oz.		4½
Bread baked at home	4	6
Oatmeal, ½ peck		6½
Bacon, 1½ lb.		9

	s	d
Potatoes, 40 lb.	1	4
Milk, 7 quarts	1	9
Meat, 1 lb. (Sundays)		7
Sugar, 1½ lb.		9
Pepper, mustard, salt etc.		3
Soap and candles	1	0
Coals, 1 bushel	1	6
Rent	3	6
Total	18	1

This careful budget left 6s. 11d. a week for clothing, schooling, sickness and miscellaneous items. It indicates the very different dietary pattern of the north of England, where bread was still often baked at home, and potatoes, oatmeal and milk played a much larger part than in the south, where many contemporaries considered the bakers' bread, the fresh meat and the beer extravagant. The lower house-rent and cheaper coal are other advantages of the north, but the major difference is that this frugal family devotes slightly under 50 per cent of income to food by cutting out joints of meat.

But earnings so high as this and the compositor's were still unusual at the beginning of the century. Far more numerous were agricultural labourers and unskilled workers, of which this carter, with wages of 12s. a week in 1795, may be taken as representative: the wife and 2 of the 5 children worked at roving cotton, nursing for neighbours and other odd jobs, bringing the family income up to 17s. a week. Even so, there was a deficiency between income and expenditure, made up by additional work by the husband or by occasional help from the parish. Like very many of the families described by Eden and Davies at the end of the eighteenth century, this one was either already pauperized or on the brink of becoming so, yet there were few agricultural labourers in 1795 who earned as much as this:

	s	d
Rent	2	0
Fuel		7
Oatmeal bread	5	0

	s	d
Meat, 3 lb.	1	6
Tea and sugar	1	3
Potatoes, 40 lb.	1	6
Milk, skimmed, 10 quarts	1	2
Butter, 1 lb.	1	0
Soap, candles, groceries	1	0
Clothes and other expenses	2	0
Cheese, 2 lb.	1	6
	18	6

This is another northern family, making good use of oatmeal, potatoes and skimmed milk which were either not available or not so valued in the south. Even so, there is little enough to eat and very little variety for a family of 7, although food takes 77 per cent of total expenditure and bread and potatoes, the great 'filler' foods, 36 per cent. Lower down the scale the clothes allowance, the meat, the milk and the cheese are all sacrificed, until there remain only bread, potatoes and tiny quantities of bacon and tea.

There is no significant change from this pattern in the budgets of the mid-century. Here first is an agricultural labourer of Lavenham, Suffolk, in 1843, whose family consists of a wife and 5 children, 3 of whom are at work.

Name	Age	Earnings s d	Expenditure	s d
Robert Crick	42	9 0	Bread	9 0
			Potatoes	1 0
Wife	40	9	Rent	1 2
			Tea	2
Boy	12	2 0	Sugar	3½
			Soap	3
ditto	11	1 0	Blue	½
			Thread etc.	2
ditto	8	1 0	Candles	3
			Salt	½
Girl	6	—	Coal and wood	9
			Butter	4½
Boy	4	—	Cheese	3
	Total Earnings	13 9	Total Expenditure	13 9

This family, with their above-average earnings, apparently never tasted meat. Bread and potatoes took over 70 per cent of their total income, and with tiny quantities of butter, cheese, tea and sugar made up their total diet. Any disturbance to this precarious balance of life, such as sickness or death, must have thrown them onto the mercies of public relief, which by now included the hated workhouse system.

The wage of an urban semi-skilled worker in regular employment in mid-century was around 15s. to £1 a week. This is a typical budget of such a man in 1841 for a family of 3 children, earning 15s.:

	s	d
5 4-lb. loaves at 8½d.	3	6½
5 lb. of meat at 5d.	2	1
7 pints of porter at 2d.	1	2
½ cwt coals		9½
40 lb. potatoes	1	4
3 oz. tea, 1 lb. sugar	1	6
1 lb. butter		9
½ lb. soap, ½ lb. candles		6½
Rent	2	6
Schooling		4
Sundries		5½
Total	15	0

There are a few 'luxuries' here – the cheap meat and the beer – though nothing for fresh vegetables or milk, sickness or insurance. The 2s. 6d. rent probably provided 2 rooms, the 4d. for schooling would pay for 2 children at a little dame school where they might learn the rudiments of reading and, perhaps, of number. Food takes 72 per cent of income, bread and potatoes 30 per cent. In a similar budget of the same date, that of a mechanic's assistant earning 16s. a week, bread, oatmeal and potatoes together take 44 per cent of earnings.

The 'comfort line' came at something over £1 a week, depending on the size of family. This is the budget of an overlooker in a Manchester cotton factory, whose family income is £1 14s. a week, several of the 6 children working: it is representative of a skilled worker's expenditure:

	£	s	d
Rent		5	0
Flour or bread		5	10
Meat, 7 lb. at 8d.		4	8
Bacon, ½ lb.			4
Butter, 2 lb.		2	0
Eggs (probably 18)		1	0
Milk, 8 pints		1	0
Potatoes, 40 lb.		1	8
Cheese, 1 lb.			9
Tea, ¼ lb.		1	0
Coffee, ¼ lb.			6
Sugar, 3 lb.		2	0
Soap, 1 lb.			6
Candles, 1 lb.			6
Coals, 2 cwt		1	2
Total	1	7	11

Here, the food bill took only 60 per cent of earnings, bread and potatoes a mere 20 per cent: for the first time the expenditure on meat is almost as much as that on bread, and although 5s. is quite a high rent for Manchester, probably representing a semi-detached rather than a back-to-back house, there is still a reasonable margin of about 6s. a week for clothing, education and occasional indulgence in tobacco (3d.–4½d. oz.) and beer.

Although the budgets so far discussed are all 'actual', they may still be atypical in that most working people in the nineteenth century did not record their income and expenditure. Those who did were either sufficiently educated to be literate, or sufficiently confident of their own rectitude to be willing to disclose their personal affairs to clergymen, doctors, Guardians of the Poor or whoever was collecting evidence. They tended to be those of 'sober and industrious habits' with nothing to conceal; their disclosures may have been made in order to excite sympathy, or to support a claim for higher wages. Where this is obvious, such budgets have been ignored, but there may still be a bias towards 'respectability' in some of those cited, especially in respect of the husband's indulgences in drink, gambling and other amusements, or the wife's commitment to debt. Even among the relatively well-paid iron-workers of Middlesbrough, Lady Bell found in 1907 that 125 out of 900 households investigated were 'absolutely poor', another 175 'so near the poverty-line that they are constantly passing over it', and that in many cases this was due not to inadequacy of income but to a quarter or a third of it being devoted to drink and gambling. At the other extreme was a careful housewife who on receiving her husband's wage of 18s. 6d. first set aside 5s. 6d. for rent, 2s. 4d. for coal, 1s. for clothing, 9d. for tobacco, 8d. for cleaning materials and 7d. for insurance, leaving herself only 7s. 5d. for food: the family was 'respectable' but under-nourished.

By the end of the century it is becoming possible for the first time to generalize individual budgets into national averages. Researches by private investigators like Booth and Rowntree and by government departments like the Board of Trade were increasingly concerned to quantify the income and expenditure of different sections of the population either for basic statistical purposes or with a view to assessing the extent of poverty and underfeeding which were now forcing themselves on public attention. In 1903–4 the Board of Trade carried out the first-ever cost of living inquiries, using a sample of several hundred agricultural labourers and urban workmen's budgets: in each case the average family was taken as husband, wife and 4 children. The summarized results are as in the table on p. 266.

Clearly, much had changed from the mid-century budgets previously discussed. Although food still took 75 per cent of the agricultural labourer's wages, he and his family ate very much better than they did half a century before. Meat for the first time takes a greater proportion of expenditure than bread and flour, and even in the low-wage counties of the south and west the 2 figures approach closely. There are now, on average, 7 lb. of meat a week in the labourer's diet, more than half of which is fresh 'butcher's meat' as opposed to bacon. Bread and potatoes have sunk relatively in quantity and in price, while the lower costs of tea and sugar have increased the consumption of these considerably; new products like margarine, jam and cocoa have appeared to add palatability, if not very much nutriment, to what had been a highly monotonous diet. When we add items occasionally purchased but not quantified in the survey – eggs,

	Agricultural labourers (average weekly wage 18s. 6d.)	Urban workmen (average weekly wage 29s. 10d.)	
Article	Consumption	Consumption	Cost
	lb. oz.	lb.	s d
Beef or mutton	3 6	6.5	5 5
Pork	1 2		
Bacon	2 11	1.4	11½
Cheese	1 3	0.8	6½
Bread	19 8	} 32	3 7
Flour	14 14		
Oatmeal, rice, tapioca	1 4	2.9	6
Potatoes	25 12	16.9	11
Tea	7½	0.6	1 1½
Coffee and cocoa	2½	0.2	3½
Butter	1 1	1.9	2 1½
Lard, margarine or dripping	1 0	Not known	—
Sugar	4 5	5.3	1 0
Syrup, treacle or jam	1 10		6½
Milk, new or skimmed	4½ pints or 9 pints	9.9 pints	1 3
Total cost of food	13s. 6d.		18s. 3d.
		Other food items	4 3
		Total cost of food	22s. 6d.

fish, tinned foods, currants, raisins and other groceries – and also the fruit and vegetables which increasing numbers of labourers were able to provide for themselves with the spread of the allotment system, there can be little doubt that standards of comfort had improved to an unprecedented extent during the previous 30 to 40 years. Among the urban workers, too, it may be said that the standards of the skilled of 1850 have become those of the average in 1900. Food here takes 75 per cent of total earnings, and meat almost twice as much as bread (6s. 5d.

compared with 3s. 7d.); butter is now in third place, milk in fourth. Although the consumption of such desirable foods as fish, fruit and green vegetables is still small, there had been a marked shift for many workers away from the cheapest carbohydrate foods towards more expensive protein sources.

Yet, despite so much evidence of improvement at the end of the century, it is important to remember that there were at the same time revelations of poverty that shook the confidence of Edwardian England. In particular, Seebohm Rowntree from his study of York in 1900 developed the concept of a 'poverty line' based upon what was then known of nutritional requirements (3,500 calories and 125 grams of protein a day for a man in moderate work, with adjustments for women and children) and costed an 'adequate' diet in terms of the cheapest possible food: his diet included no fresh meat, and was less generous than that provided in the York workhouse. For a man the cost worked out at 3s. 3d. a week, for a woman 2s. 9d., for children 8–16 2s. 7d., and 2s. 1d. for young children; with the least possible allowances for rent, clothing, fuel and sundries he arrived at a minimum of 21s. 8d. a week for a man, wife and 3 children, rising to 37s. 4d. for a family of 8 children. Anyone below these levels was defined as being in 'primary poverty', and in York in 1900 9·9 per cent of the whole population were in this category. In addition to this was a larger category of 'secondary poverty' – of people whose earnings would have been sufficient to maintain physical efficiency had not a proportion of them gone in other directions – legitimate, such as medical expenses or travel, illegitimate like drink and gambling. In York another 17·9 per cent came into this category, totalling 28 per cent who, for one reason or another, fell short of the standard of nutritional adequacy.

This submerged third of the population which Rowntree, Booth and other social investigators claimed to have discovered poses a problem for historians as it did for contemporaries. If standards were so low in 1900 after half a century of improvement, the natural inference is that they would have been substantially worse in 1850 if anyone had known how and where to look. In the view of the author this is almost certainly true, and some recent calculations by John Foster have shown that in Oldham in the 1840s, even in the best years, only about 15 per cent of the labour force can have been above the Rowntree poverty line, though without a comparable study for 1850 the question can never be resolved finally. Nevertheless, two things need to be said about Rowntree's pioneering work. In the light of modern knowledge of nutritional requirements, it seems likely that he somewhat over-estimated food needs – that, to be specific, his 3,500 calories a day for a man in moderate work should be placed at nearer 3,000, especially when it is remembered that average height was several inches shorter then than it is today. (Against this, it could be argued that hours of work were longer and that much work was more laborious or intensive than now.) A second arguable point is that some of the new products of food technology of Rowntree's day – the bleached, over-milled flour, the margarine, the condensed milk and sweet jams – were nutritionally inferior to their nineteenth-century predecessors, and that in this respect the diet of 1900 had suffered a deterioration. To substantiate this it would have to be shown that these new products were substitutes rather than additions to diet, which would be difficult except in the case of bread, and it also ignores the fact that food adulteration, often of a directly harmful kind, had been exceedingly widespread in the middle of the century but largely suppressed by 1900. In short, although the 30 per cent poverty figure of Rowntree and Booth should not be accepted uncritically, there is no hard evidence that it is widely in excess of the observed facts at the end of the century.

An investigation by the Board of Trade in 1904 of nearly 2,000 working-class households made it clear that there were still very wide differences between the consumption-patterns of skilled and unskilled workers. The poorest families in the survey (weekly income 21s. 4½d.) now devoted one-seventh of earnings to bread, compared with only one-twelfth by the best-paid group (weekly income 52s.); the latter spent twice as much as the former on meat, bacon and milk, 3 times as much on eggs, butter, vegetables and fruit. These differences were clearly reflected in the individual budgets that Rowntree analysed. Typical of a poorer-paid, though by no means the poorest, worker, was a lorry-driver earning 20s. a week: with occasional overtime, and the casual earnings of his wife at charring and plain sewing, the total income for 8 weeks was £8 14s. 6d. There was an unusually small family of only 2 children, aged 5 and 2 years. Their house, rented at 3s. a week, had 3 rooms, 1 on each storey: from the living-room stairs led to a bedroom and from that, a ladder to the attic above. There was a tap, but no sink, in the living-room, from which drippings fell on to an uneven brick floor partly covered with linoleum and rag mats. Furniture consisted of a table, 2 wooden easy chairs, a sofa covered with American cloth and an occasional table under the front window displaying family treasures such as a glass vase and a few photographs. This was existence in 1900 at 'round about £1 a week'. The income and expenditure of this family for a period of 8 weeks was as follows:

Statement of Income and Expenditure for Eight Weeks

INCOME	£	s	d
Eight weeks' wages at 20s.	8	0	0
Overtime		4	6
Mrs D.		10	0
	8	14	6

EXPENDITURE	£	s	d
Food, including beverages	3	19	0
Rent and rates	1	4	0
Coals and firewood	1	1	3
Oil, matches, candles		2	8
Soap etc.		1	5½
Sundries		2	3½
Sick Club		8	3
Life Insurance		6	5
Clothes		8	9½
Boots		5	10½
Doctor's Bill		9	9
Repayment of debt		5	0
	8	14	9
Deficit			3
	8	14	6

A HISTORY OF THE COST OF LIVING

Purchases during Week ending 22 February, 1901

FRIDAY. 2 bags of coal, 2s. 6d.; 1½ st. flour, 2s.; yeast, 1d.; 4 lb. sugar, 7d.; ¼ lb. tea, 4½d.; 1 lb. butter, 1s.; 3½ lb. bacon, 1s. 5d.; firewood, 2d.; ½ lb. lard, 2½d.; baking powder, 1d.; 6 eggs, 6d.; candles, 1d.; matches, ½d.; 1 lb. soap, 2d.; starch, 1d.; soda, 1d.

SATURDAY. Doctor's bill, 1s. 3d.; frying-pan, 6½d.; 2 teaspoons, 1d.; 1 tablespoon, 2d.; ½ st. potatoes, 5d.; cabbage, 2d.; 3 lb. pork, 1s. 7½d.; 1 lb. onions, 1d.; 1 qt. oil, 2½d.; ½ lb. rice, 1d.; milk, 1d.; ¼ lb. coffee, 3d.; kippers, 2d.; 2 tins condensed milk, 5d.

MONDAY. Insurance, 11d.; Club, 1s. 3d.; Doctor's bill, 1s.

TUESDAY. Debt, 1s.; 1 lb. figs, 5d.

Menu of Meals provided during Week ending 22 February, 1901

	Breakfast	Dinner	Tea	Supper
Friday	Bread, butter, tea.	Bread, butter, toast, tea.	Bread, butter, tea.	
Saturday	Bread, bacon, coffee.	Bacon, potatoes, pudding, tea.	Bread, butter, shortcake, tea.	Tea, bread, kippers.
Sunday	Bread, butter, shortcake, coffee.	Pork, onions, potatoes, Yorkshire pudding.	Bread, butter, shortcake, tea.	Bread and meat.
Monday	Bread, bacon, butter, tea.	Pork, potatoes, pudding, tea.	Bread, butter, tea.	One cup of tea.
Tuesday	Bread, bacon, butter, coffee.	Pork, bread, tea.	Bread, butter, boiled eggs, tea.	Bread, bacon, butter, tea.
Wednesday	Bread, bacon, butter, tea.	Bacon and eggs, potatoes, bread, tea.	Bread, butter, tea.	
Thursday	Bread, butter, coffee.	Bread, bacon, tea.	Bread, butter, tea.	

On this diet there was a deficiency of protein of 18 per cent and of calories of 9 per cent. Taking the average of all the families in Rowntree's 'Class 1' (earnings under 26s. a week), 51 per cent of income was devoted to food, 18 per cent to rent, 6 per cent to clothing, 9 per cent to fuel and light, 4 per cent to insurance and 3 per cent to repayment of debts.

The last family may be contrasted with that of a clerk earning 35s. a week who had a family of 3 children. The house, rented at 5s. 6d. a week, had 5 rooms and a scullery, a small flower-garden at the front and a fair-sized yard at the back; it was nicely and comfortably furnished. The wife was a good manager, made the children's clothes, curtains and fire-screens for the house, and so on. Their income and expenditure during 13 weeks was as follows:

Total Income and Expenditure during Thirteen Weeks

	£	s	d
INCOME			
Thirteen weeks' wages at 35s., less 'broken time'	22	0	9
EXPENDITURE			
Food, including beverages	12	6	7
Rent and rates	3	11	6
Coals etc.	1	8	7
Gas		8	0
Soap		2	1
Sundries		1	0
Insurance and medical aid	1	6	0
Shoes etc.		2	6
Tobacco		3	6
Balance	2	11	0
	22	0	9

Purchases during Week ending 20 May, 1900

FRIDAY. 2 sheep's hearts, 6d.; 1 mackerel, 4d.; 1 lb. tomato sausage, 9d.; ¼ lb. potted beef, 6d.; 1 lb. bacon, 7d.; week's milk 1s. 9d.; 1½ lb. butter, 1s. 9d.; 12 eggs, 1s.; 1 st. flour, 1s. 4d.; yeast, 2d.; 8 lb. sugar, 1s. 4d.; bread and tea-cakes, 1s.; 2 oz. tobacco, 6d.; ½ lb. tea, 1s. 2d.

SATURDAY. Vegetables, 1s.; 3 lb. pork, 2s.; 1½ lb. spare-rib of pork, 6d.; gas, 8d.; coals, 2s. 6d.; Insurance and medical clubs, 2s.

WEDNESDAY. 1½ lb. mutton, 1s.

THURSDAY. Tin luncheon tongue, 1s. 3d.; rent, 5s. 6d.

A HISTORY OF THE COST OF LIVING
Menu of Meals provided during Week ending 20 May, 1900

	Breakfast	Dinner	Tea	Supper
Friday	Fried eggs, bacon, bread, butter, tea.	Stuffed hearts, potatoes, bread, jam pudding.	Pickled mackerel, bread, butter, tea.	Porridge, bread, butter, cocoa.
Saturday	Potted meat, bread, butter, tea-cakes, tea.	Tomato sausages, potatoes, pastry, tea.	Boiled eggs, bread, butter, brown bread, cakes, tea.	Porridge, fried fish, bread, cocoa.
Sunday	Cold tomato sausages, boiled eggs, bread, butter, tea.	Stuffed pork, new potatoes, cauliflower, Yorkshire pudding, cakes, tea.	Bread, butter, tea-cakes, raspberry sandwich, tea.	Cold meat, pickled beetroot, bread, cocoa.
Monday	Fried bacon, brown bread, butter, cakes, tea.	Spare-rib pie, potatoes, Quaker oats pudding, tea.	Potted meat, bread, butter, tea-cakes, tea.	Porridge, cocoa.
Tuesday	Boiled eggs, bread, butter, tea.	Cold pork, mashed potatoes, jam roll, sauce.	Toast, butter, tea-cakes, tea.	Porridge, brown bread, butter, cocoa.
Wednesday	Fried bacon, eggs, bread, butter, tea.	Boiled mutton, onion sauce, potatoes, vegetables, pudding, tea.	Bread, butter, scones, tea-cakes, tea.	Porridge, fried fish, bread, cocoa.
Thursday	Boiled eggs, bread, butter, scones, tea.	Haricot mutton, lemon pudding, sauce, tea and cakes.	Lunch tongue, bread, butter, tea.	Porridge, cocoa.

THE NINETEENTH CENTURY

Here, as in most of the families in Class 2 (earnings over 26s. a week), the diet was just about adequate nutritionally: there was an excess of 8 per cent in calories though a deficit of 5 per cent of protein.

Much is revealed, or implied, about the quality of working-class life by the cold statistics of the budgets. It is obvious that food was still the major item of expenditure, taking from half total earnings among better-off families to three-quarters or more among the poorer. Until the closing decades of the century, bread or flour was easily the biggest food item, and for many the second was potatoes rather than meat; before the introduction of cheap, imported beef and mutton in the 1880s, 'meat' usually meant bacon or pork because these could be cut up small and made to go further as a flavouring for vegetables. The diet of agricultural labourers in mid-century, as of the poorest urban workers throughout the period, consisted essentially of bread – usually white rather than brown because this was more palatable without butter – potatoes, small quantities of tea, cheese and sugar, and meat perhaps once or twice a week. The meals of a Dorset labourer described by Dr Edward Smith in 1863 were:

Breakfast – water broth, bread, butter, tea with milk.
Dinner   – husband has bread and cheese: family take tea besides.
Supper   – hot fried bacon and cabbage, or bread and cheese.

This was practically indistinguishable from the poorest urban diets, though in the towns there were some advantages in the multiplicity of small shops, many of them prepared to give credit, the hawkers (13,000 of them in the London of the 1850s) and the street-markets where many working people bought their cheap joint of meat on Saturday night. The possibility of buying turnips or other vegetables by the pennyworth, sugar by the $\frac{1}{4}$ lb. and tea by the oz. were substantial benefits to the housewife whose available money was uncertain and who often had to buy by the day or even by the individual meal, while the purchase of 4 oysters for a penny from a street-stall, or of a piece of fried fish between slices of bread at a public-house, must have helped to enliven a drab and monotonous diet. That this was an extravagant way of housekeeping the middle classes never tired of pointing out, as they similarly condemned the poor for buying shop bread instead of baking their own or, better still, using oatmeal, stirabout and other 'messes'. The food of the poor was conditioned largely by the dearness of fuel, the lack of easily accessible water supplies, and the inadequacy of most kitchen ranges (gas cookers became common only towards the end of the century); Rowntree's calculations showed that, in general, the working classes got good value for money in terms of the number of calories and proteins per shilling spent. By this time, as we have seen, there had been notable improvement. The budgets of agricultural labourers at the end of the century indicate meat almost every day, more bacon and cheese, occasionally even a tin of salmon or sardines for Sunday tea. A Lancashire cotton operative of 1913 is described as having 'a breakfast of coffee or tea, bread, bacon and eggs – when eggs are cheap – a dinner of potatoes and beef, an evening meal of tea, bread and butter, cheap vegetables or fish, and a slight supper at moderate price'. This would have been very good fare, even for a skilled man, any time before 1870.

One of the principal causes of Rowntree's 'secondary poverty' was the extent of drinking among working people. It seems unfortunately true that the first effect of the growth of real earnings in the 1870s was to increase the consumption of beer and spirits to an all-time maximum of 34 gallons a year and 1·1 gallons a year respectively for every man, woman and child in the country: in 1871, out of 397,000 summary convictions in England and Wales, 131,000, or very nearly one-third, were for being drunk and disorderly. Subsequently, with the growth of education and the development of more rational means of recreation, consumption began a slow fall, though it remained at around 30 gallons a head until the end of the century. It was, of course, easy for 'respectable' Victorians to pass moral censure on 'the prevailing vice' of drink, to demonstrate the connexion between liquor, poverty, overcrowding and slums, and to show how indulgence led on the one hand to broken marriages or, on the other, to over-large families. The fact was that for men and women with limited spare time, and with limited opportunities for developing more constructive forms of leisure, the public-house offered a temporary relief from the anxieties of life in an atmosphere more comfortable and congenial than most homes were at the time. It is also fair to say that the government of the day had consciously set out to encourage beer consumption by the disastrous Beerhouse Act of 1830, which allowed any householder to sell beer merely on payment of a 2-guinea Excise licence free of magisterial control: by 1850 there were no fewer than 123,000 places for the sale of intoxicating liquor. The working man of 1870 was no more intemperate than his grandfather had been – probably he was less so – he was merely continuing to observe traditional consumption-patterns in an environment in which liquor had become financially and physically more accessible but more exposed to public criticism.

It remains nevertheless true that drink was one of the important factors that helped to make the poor poor. One estimate places the annual expenditure per head of the population on drink in 1850 at £2 18s. 10d., rising to £4 7s. 3d. in 1875; this would imply a family expenditure of £15–£20 a year out of an estimated average working-class income in 1880 of £80 a year, or a fraction of about one-fifth. At the end of the century Rowntree and Sherwell placed the weekly expenditure of the average working-class family at 6s. 11d., or somewhat over one-sixth of total family income. In London Booth found that drink had now declined substantially among the better-off, respectable families, but took up to one-quarter of the poor family's budget. Education and the spread of temperance had concentrated the problem into the lower strata of the working classes, while for those in the upper strata heavy drinking had become socially unacceptable. If the average statistics are anywhere near correct – and the close approximation of different sources suggests that they are – they mean that some families must have spent a third or even a half of all income on drink, for the temperance movement had been making steady progress ever since its introduction in 1830. For such families it clearly ranked as the second largest item of expenditure, and even for the 'average' it was paralleled only by that on accommodation. Together with betting and gambling, it was the price that many working people paid for a kind of relaxation and recreation, for the release from drudgery and the daily reawakening of hope, almost always unfulfilled, for a richer future.

The demon, drink, was avoidable for the more resolute, the more intelligent of the working classes: the expense of accommodation was not. Some farm labourers had a 'tied' cottage, or a cottage at a sub-economic rent, that went with the job, though this was frequently compensated for by a reduced wage, and a few factory workers, especially in areas of new development where there was no existing accommodation, had houses provided by the employer at a fairly nominal rent: thus, at Binns's Mill, Bury, at the beginning of the century employees were housed in 2-roomed back-to-backs at 1s. 3d. a week. But for the vast majority of working people accommodation meant the renting of a house, or of part of a house, at a cost which increased continuously throughout the century as the pressure on accommodation grew and the housing 'gap' widened. The possibility ever of owning property of their own was remote from their expectations, and it is significant that Rowntree found less than 6 per cent of working-class families in York in 1900 buying their houses, although building societies were well-established by this time, and patronized almost exclusively by the middle classes. Council housing began to make a small contribution to the accommodation of the working classes after 1890, though only 5 per cent of all houses built between then and 1914 were by local authorities, as did the charitable trusts like the Peabody, Waterlow and Guinness from the 1860s and 1870s onwards, but in total their contribution towards the solution of the problem was insignificant. In general the working classes paid economic rents to private landlords which were reckoned to repay capital costs (land, road and drainage charges and building) within about 20 years. As urban land values rose, building costs and, hence, rents, inevitably increased. In Leeds in the 1860s eligible building land cost from 2s. 6d. to 5s. per square yard freehold, a terraced cottage usually taking about 100 square yards. In the York of Rowntree's day, where land was reckoned to be cheap, it cost a minimum of 6s. a square yard, or £30 for a plot; making roads and drains added £16, and the building work for a cottage with sitting-room, kitchen, scullery and 2 bedrooms was about £140, making the total about £190. The rent of such a house was 5s. 6d. to 6s. 6d. a week. A larger house, with 3 bedrooms and on a 160 square yard plot, though still terraced and with only a small yard at the rear, cost £370 (rent and rates about 7s. 6d. a week). In the 1850s back-to-back cottages with a cellar, living-room, kitchen and 3 bedrooms had cost £120. These were substantial rises, though probably almost confined to the towns; in the country as late as 1900 a 'model' semi-detached cottage could be built for £150, having a living-room, scullery and 3 bedrooms.

This remained the ideal – rarely realized – of rural housing to 1914. There was, in fact, little new building of labourers' cottages, even by model landlords, after the economic setbacks of the 1870s, and the great majority of farm workers inhabited old cottages, some with walls still made of daub rather than brick, of one living-room, a scullery 'out-shot' and 1 or 2 bedrooms above. Many were damp, insanitary, and lacking in any kind of domestic conveniences except a fire-place; not uncommonly there was only a single bedroom for parents and grown-up children to sleep. The only compensation for such squalid living conditions was the comparative lowness of rents. As the Board of Trade Report of 1903 pointed out, the agricultural labourer on average devoted 13s. of his 18s. 6d. to food, leaving only 5s. 6d. a week for everything else. His rent was normally 1s. 6d. a week, varying little throughout the century since pressure on accommodation tended to fall with rural depopulation: rents of 'model' cottages were somewhat higher, though these were not expected to bear an economic level, and as late as the 1890s there were old West Country cottages rented at as little as 1s. a week. In the towns there could be no separate dwelling of any description at this sort of price. The poorest of all families, mostly of Irish and unskilled labourers, might take a single room or a cellar, let in Leeds and Bolton in mid-century at 1s. to 1s. 6d. a week; in London in 1852 lodging-house rents for single men were 2s. and for families 3s. upwards. The scarcity of urban land led to a considerable development of tenement building in the latter half of the century, particularly in London but also in the larger provincial towns, and these also offered the possibility of accommodation at something less than the cost of a whole house. In London in 1900 the average rent of County Council and Trust one-room tenements was 2s. 9d. a week, of 2-room tenements 4s. 9d., and of 3-room about 6s.; the rents of Peabody Trust rooms had increased by 24 per cent during the previous 25 years, and this was no doubt something less than the rise of unsupported rents. For whole houses rents naturally varied greatly with size, locality and amenities, and averages are again likely to be misleading. Of 28,000 working-class houses in Manchester in 1834–6, 6,900 were rented at more than 4s. a week, 4,900 at 2s. 6d. to 3s., 4,900 at 2s. to 2s. 6d., 3,600 at 1s. 6d. to 2s., and 3,100 at 3s. to 3s. 6d.; of 17,800 houses in Leeds in 1840 nearly half were rented at between 2s. and 4s. a week and a quarter at more than this. But by 1900 very few urban families could accommodate themselves at these levels. In York the lowest category of wage-earner (income under £1 a week) paid an average of 3s. 3d. and in London 5s. 3d. a week. Rowntree's calculation was that for the working classes as a whole, rent took 15 per cent of earnings, though striking differences in the proportion occurred with differences in income: thus, for the very poor, with average earnings under 18s. a week, rent took 29 per cent of income, for the 20s. to 25s. group 17 per cent, and for those earning over 60s. only 9 per cent. It also seems likely that the London-provincial 'gap' widened as time went on. For 2 rooms in London at the beginning of the twentieth century 6s. was the average compared with 3s. in the provinces, for 4 rooms 9s. compared with 5s.

Food and drink, fuel and rent, were the principal recurrent expenses of the working classes. Beyond these there were certainly other important items, but they occurred so irregularly as to make quantification extremely difficult. In total it is likely that clothes and shoes came into the fifth place, though only where budgets were kept for a year and more does this become evident. Many families contrived with gifts, cast-offs and second-hand garments and shoes: some bought through clothing clubs into which they paid from 6d. to 2s. a week until the price of a new garment had been saved. Many more bought on credit from the travelling Scotch drapers who supplied articles of clothing and later collected the price by instalments – 2s. to 7s.

THE NINETEENTH CENTURY

or 8s. every 3 weeks was said to be general in Stockport in the 1830s, where a half of the population was reputed to buy its clothes in this way. For the convenience of their hire-purchase service the Scotch drapers added anything from 50 to 100 per cent to the usual price. The pawning of best clothes was also extremely common, many poorer families regularly pawning their Sunday suit on Monday and redeeming it each Saturday. In his budget inquiries Rowntree calculated what should be the minimum clothing allowance for a family, and arrived at the figure of 6d. each for adults per week and 5d. for children, totalling 2s. 3d. a week for a family of 3 children, or 3s. 6d. for a not unusually large one of 6. Very few families realized these targets, for in the actual budgets investigated only 6·3 per cent of income was devoted to clothes. In one typical budget the husband during the course of a year bought 1 new pair of boots at 11s., 4 pairs of socks 9d. each, a second-hand coat 4s., a pair of trousers 7s. 6d., a second-hand overcoat, lasting 3 years, 15s., three shirts 1s. 4d. each, and a cap and scarf 1s. 3d. Agricultural labourers' families towards the end of the century typically spent about £3 to £4 a year on clothes and another £2 to £3 on boots, often paying for them out of harvest earnings or other extra work; not uncommonly, the farmer gave cast-off clothes and a roll of flannel or calico as Christmas presents, but boots and shoes remained an unavoidable expense for men in heavy work, and in large families it was not unknown for children to go barefoot even at the end of the century. The budgets collected by other observers at this time indicate a higher expenditure on clothing and footwear than Rowntree discovered in York, especially where the family contained a number of older children. Thus, a weaver with a wife and 3 children aged 7–11 years devoted 9 per cent of income to dress, but a mule-spinner with wife and 7 children 3–18 years as much as 21 per cent. It is also noticeable that while the proportion of expenditure on food fell with increasing income, that on clothing grew. In a study carried out in 1891 it was found that families with incomes under 20s. a week devoted 12 per cent of income to clothes while those with 40s. and over devoted 16 per cent.

When other, occasional expenses are added to these totals, it must have been the case that the budgets of many families rarely balanced, that they were constantly getting into and occasionally climbing out of debt – to the pawnbroker, the tally-man, the baker, anyone who could lend money or supply goods on credit. Rowntree calculated an average of 3 per cent of income for the repayment of debt, but there were clearly very wide variations and for the poorest it was much higher than this. One of the greatest causes of debt was the expense of burial, which could be a frequently recurring event in large Victorian families where the infant death-rate was still high; the cost of an adult burial, according to Chadwick, was at least £4 to £5, that of a child about half as much (Harrods in 1900 quoted from £2 10s. for children's funerals). Such an expense could pauperize a widow, or leave a family in debt for years. Medical expenses could also be overwhelming before the inception of school clinics in 1907 and health insurance in 1911. Often the doctor was only called in when the patient was already dead or dying: for the poor who could secure a patron's 'recommendation' there was a growing provision of infirmaries and out-patients departments, though in the middle of the century there were only 5,000 free hospital beds in the country. One in every 3 working people over 70 still died in the workhouse at the end of our period. For such old people, and for the chronically sick, little could be done, but the minor ailments of children, doctored increasingly by patent medicines at 6d. or 1s. the bottle, rather than by home-made recipes, could add seriously to the cost of living in large families. Ultimately, the answer was found in deliberate limitation of family size.

Compared with sickness and death, other domestic expenses were almost trivial. Most of the working man's furniture was bought second-hand, was passed down the family or given, and in any case was rarely worth more than a few shillings in total. Household inventories of the nineteenth century read very much like those of Tudor and Stuart times, the most valuable items still being beds and bedding and, for the rest, a table, a cupboard or two and a few chairs. The article that raised a family out of the poorest category was a clock, worth perhaps 10s. to £1, and that which distinguished the really comfortable working classes, a piano; in such a household there might be a carpet on the floor, a few pieces of mahogany furniture, framed prints on the walls and 1 or 2 Staffordshire figures (bought at a fair or from a pedlar at prices from 4d. to 2s. or 3s.) on the mantelpiece. For these fortunate families – and they grew as a proportion of the whole as the century advanced – late Victorian England probably offered greater opportunities of comfort and of decent domestic life than any previous time – a mass-produced bedroom suite of washstand, dressing-table, chest of drawers, towel-horse and chair for £3 4s., linoleum for the floors, curtains of casement cloth at 4¾d. a yard, a flock mattress for 10s. and a pair of York blankets for 6s. 6d. Technology benefited the same people by bringing piped water into their homes, gas-light and gas-cookers, sometimes even a fixed bath and a gas-geyser for hot water. They might have an annual holiday at the seaside – holidays with pay for long-service employees began in the 1880s – put money aside for insurance and sick clubs (an average of 4 per cent of income in York in 1900), save in the Post Office or through the Cooperative Society, travel, read and educate their children. These were the long-term benefits of industrialization to the working classes, not yet universally shared though discernible clearly enough as the portents of a future social revolution.

CHAPTER 5

The Last Fifty Years

I

FEW people who have lived through the last half-century would dispute the assertion that it has witnessed more far-reaching changes than any comparable period in modern times. Two world wars of an unimagined scale and cost in life and wealth, an international depression in trade which to some seemed to mark the beginning of the end of the capitalist economic system, continuous technological advance which has vastly enlarged man's power to control his environment – to enrich life and to destroy it – all these have changed the character of modern times in a way which seems to constitute a fundamental break with the past. Yet, in the historical perspective even of the few centuries outlined in this volume, 50 years is an insignificant period; the far-reaching and complex changes that have undoubtedly occurred constitute no sudden discontinuity with the past, but rather a development and a working-out of the forces that began to re-shape British society at least 2 centuries ago. The purpose of this final chapter is, therefore, not to attempt a chronological narrative of the period since 1914, but, from the standpoint of the present, to look back on what have been the main elements of change affecting the cost of living and the ways in which the consumer has responded to them.

The first aspect of change is in the population itself. After the very rapid growth in numbers that occurred in the nineteenth century, the rate has slackened noticeably in the twentieth, so that although numbers are still rising they have not outstripped the growth in productive capacity of the economy. The population of England and Wales, which had doubled from 18 million in 1851 to 36 million in 1911, increased only to 43·7 million in 1951 and 46 million in 1961. Thus, the decennial increase in recent years has been a mere 4–5 per cent, compared with the 11 per cent of the first decade of the century, and the 14 per cent of 1871–81. This change has been due to a continuous

THE LAST FIFTY YEARS

decline in the birth-rate from its peak of 36·3 in 1876 (i.e. 37 live births per thousand of the population) to its lowest point of 14·4 in 1933. This very low rate, which was barely above replacement level in the 1930s moved upwards during and after the second world war to reach 20·7 in 1947 and has remained above the pre-war level in recent years (currently c. 17), though it is still only about half that of the late nineteenth century. The increase in total size has, in fact, been achieved, not by a high birth-rate, but by a continued fall in the death-rate. The growth of medical knowledge and of health services have reduced mortality in this century more than in any previous period, and have increased the expectation of life in a dramatic way. In 1900 the death-rate stood at 18·2 (i.e. 18 deaths per thousand of the population) and the infant death-rate at 154 (i.e. 154 deaths per thousand of children under one year); in 1938 they were respectively 11·6 and 53, and at the present day 11·2 and 18·3. The chances of a baby surviving the first year of life are 8 times higher now than they were at the beginning of the century, while nearly 30 years have been added to the average expectation of life, from 45 to 72 years. Changes of such magnitude are, in themselves, worthy of the description 'revolutionary'.

With more children surviving, and remaining longer in education than ever before, and with more old people also living longer, there has followed a significant reduction in the proportion of the population of working age. In recent years additions to the working population have not kept pace with additions to the 'dependent' population outside it; between 1951 and 1961 young dependants under the age of 15 increased by 9 per cent, and aged dependants (men over 64, women over 59) by 14 per cent, while the working population grew by only 2 per cent. In Britain today a man-power potential of 33 million, made up of two-thirds males and one-third females, supports a dependent potential of 20 million, with every expectation that the latter group will continue to expand.

Already in 1914 England was an urban society, with 4 out of every 5 people living in towns. This particular change was, even by then, almost complete, and there has been no very significant alteration in the balance between town and country since then. Further growths in the industrial areas have been largely balanced by the drift of population to suburban and semi-rural areas made possible by improved communications and, above all, by the motor-car. But although the English people have, on the whole, continued to cluster into the great 'conurbations' of towns and cities, some marked changes have occurred within these groupings. London and the south-east have continued to exert that magnetic effect which they have had for centuries past, as has the West Midlands, once called the 'Black Country'; on the other hand, south-east Lancashire, west Yorkshire, Merseyside and Tyneside have grown much less rapidly than the rest in the last half-century, representing a reversal of that northerly movement of population that characterized the early stages of the Industrial Revolution. This change reflects the comparative prosperity which the south and Midlands enjoyed during the 1920s and 1930s when the staple industries of the north – coal, steel, cotton and shipbuilding – were hard hit by depression and unemployment, but the continued economic problems of some northern and Welsh regions have forced themselves upon public attention again even in recent years. The United Kingdom may still be divided into 'rich' and 'poor' regions, the latter having lower than average earnings, higher than average unemployment, outward migration and a contracting industrial structure. In 1964 the average weekly earnings of male manual workers in the U.K. were 364s. 3d., but in London and the south-eastern region they were 379s. 8d., compared with 302s. 2d. in N. Ireland and 335s. 3d. in Scotland. The gap in household earnings tends to be even wider, since there is a considerably smaller employment of women in the 'poor' regions. This again represents a reversal of the nineteenth-century trend, when individual earnings were higher in the north, and when there was also a higher employment of women than in the south.

But although there are still marked differences in the rates of unemployment in the regions (1964 rate for N. Ireland 6·6 per cent, Scotland 3·7 per cent, Wales 2·6 per cent, London, the south-east and the Midlands less than 1 per cent) post-war unemployment has been on a small scale compared with that of the pre-war period or, for that matter, of the nineteenth century. Between 1921 and 1938 unemployment was less than 10 per cent only in 4 years; in 1931 and 1932, at the height of the depression, it was 22 per cent and 23 per cent respectively, and even in 1938, with rearmament in full swing, it was 12 per cent. The period of nearly full employment, which has lasted from 1940 to the present, is a unique experience for Britain in modern times, and has been one of the main sources of social change.

Hardly less important has been the changed role of women in society. From the protected but under-privileged creatures of Victorian times who could own no property and take no part in the political life of the nation, they have emerged in the twentieth century with equal political and legal rights and a greatly enhanced economic and social status. Their participation in public life has been due to many factors – to increased educational opportunities, the growth of new fields of employment, the effects of two world wars – but for married women the major emancipation has been the release from continuous child-bearing consequent on the widespread adoption of deliberate birth control. This practice, which began among the middle classes in the closing decades of the last century, and gradually spread to almost all sections by the 1920s and 1930s, has had the effect of reducing the average size of the family from 6 children to 2. In 1900 half of all working-class wives had borne between 7 and 15 children by the time they were 40, and 1 in every 6 marriages produced 10 or more children. It has to be remembered, moreover, that with a still high infant mortality rate, many more than 6 pregnancies were necessary to produce 6 living children. Professor Titmuss has calculated that at the beginning of the century the average expectation of life of a woman aged 20 was 46 more years, of which one third, or 15 years, would be devoted to child-bearing; today, the expectation is almost 60 more years, of which only 4, about one-fifteenth, is spent in child-bearing. This reduction in family size is the most spectacular demographic change in modern times, having profound effects on the health of women, on their social status and on the extent of their participation in economic activity. Not only are more women in employment today than ever before, but the underpaid employments into which they formerly crowded, like domestic service, the sweated trades, millinery and laundry work, have been largely superseded by factory and distributive trades, clerical and professional occupations. Today, one third of the labour force of Britain is female, and of these slightly more than half are married: married women are vital to the national economy, and their contribution to the family budget is a major factor in the standard of living.

2

The British economy during the last 50 years seems to present a strange kind of paradox. Everyone knows – and this is not one of the myths of history – that the British people as a whole have been more prosperous than at any time in the past, have been able to achieve higher living standards, an improved diet, better housing and clothing, more leisure and more material possessions than ever before, and, indeed, more than almost any other nation in the world. Yet everyone also knows that the last half-century has included 2 enormously costly world wars and a major depression, that Britain has lost her role of world economic leadership to newer, richer nations, that she no longer enjoys her former share of world trade, that she has a recurrent balance-of-payments problem, that her economic growth is slower than that of many other industrial countries and that, especially since the end of the second world war, she has been particularly subject to the debilitating disease of inflation. This is not the place to attempt a detailed examination of these issues, though some comment on the major economic trends affecting the cost of living is inescapable.

One of the most salient features is that the British economy in its maturity has not continued to grow at the same rapid rate as it did in the nineteenth century. A convenient way of measuring industrial output, which does not suffer from the complication of changes in price trends, is the index of physical production (the Lomax Index), which takes total industrial production, including building, as 100 in 1924. On this scale, output during most of the inter-war years showed an absolute decline – from 90·5 in 1913 to 81·3 in 1919, and 73·5, the lowest point, in 1921. There were small rises after 1927, averaging 109 between 1929 and 1931, and more substantial increases after 1934 to reach a peak of 150·5 in 1937. The totals conceal many variations in the fortunes of particular industries, the traditional ones like coal, steel, shipbuilding and cotton suffering most in the 1920s and 1930s while newer industries like electricity, motor-cars and rayon expanded rapidly. It would be quite wrong to suppose that British industry as a whole had become stagnant or unadaptable to change, but one of the outstanding difficulties between the wars was that demand for our staple products had fallen off badly, and this had the effect of concentrating social problems, of which the most outstanding was unemployment, in a few areas of the country which were virtually dependent on a single industry. The total volume of world trade hardly increased between 1914 and 1939, and Britain's share of it fell; she never again enjoyed that third share of international trade she had had in 1913, and even in the best of the inter-war years, the volume of her exports was only 90 per cent of the years before the war. Not unexpectedly, there was an adverse balance of payments in a good many years, in 1920 and 1921, in 1926, between 1929 and 1932 and again in 1937.

Yet, despite these real difficulties, national income, income per head and the standard of living all continued to rise for most people between the wars. The national income recovered to its 1913 level by 1927, then rose to a peak in 1929 (132 compared with 120 in 1913 at 1900 prices, 1900 = 100); thereafter, it fell to 1932, and then rose to a new peak (155) in 1937. There was thus a very substantial growth in the national income of 17·7 per cent between 1929 and 1937. Income per head also increased, since population growth was now relatively slow, from 108 in 1913 to 119 in 1929 and 135 in 1937, a rise of 13·7 per cent between the two last years. Progress was clearly much faster in the 1930s than in the 1920s, and indeed, faster in the 1930s than it had been between 1907 and 1913 (3·8 per cent), and almost as fast as it had been in the 1890s (14·3 per cent). The other side of the picture is the 3 million unemployed of the early 1930s, the misery of the depressed areas and the inability of the economy to provide a reasonable standard of life for anywhere near the whole population. Sir John Boyd Orr could still discover in 1936, as Charles Booth had done 40 years earlier, that 30 per cent of the population who were able to devote less than 6s. a week to food were inadequately nourished. One recent writer has concluded with this judgement on the period –

No simple verdict is thus possible on the thirties. Probably a simple verdict distorts the truth for most decades. But the decade of the thirties was more mixed than usual. The overall standard of living rose: there were more houses, more cars, more wireless sets, food was cheaper and more abundant. But the average unemployment figure for the decade was about 2m. And this unemployment was particularly heavy in certain districts. And, especially in these districts, there was a lot of long term unemployment. In the Rhondda in 1936 over a quarter of those unemployed were long unemployed, and they had on the average been unemployed for no less than fifty-six months. No society, even with standards of living rising faster than they were in Britain in the thirties, could be satisfied or happy with a social problem and a personal tragedy of this character in its midst.

In historical retrospect it may well be that the 1940s will be seen as a turning-point in British economic and social history. Before the second world war it was not impossible to believe that the capitalist system in Britain and the U.S.A. was in decay, and that another major conflict would constitute its death sentence. By contrast, the last quarter-century has produced practically full employment and a standard of living that has risen faster than in any other equivalent recorded period. For this unexpected result there are a number of possible explanations. An immediate post-war boom in 1945 was predictable, as it was in 1919, due to the stored-up demand for goods which had been unobtainable for some years past. Since 1945 the continuation of a threat of war has necessitated stockpiling and the maintenance of armed forces, which have again given a boost to normal demand. More important, Britain, like some other developed industrial countries, has embarked on what some have called a 'new industrial revolution' based on such things as synthetic fibres, atomic power, jet engines, transistors, polymers and computers, which have considerably diversified the pre-war economy and provided valuable industrial and export outlets. Equally important, successive governments since the war have pursued conscious policies of full employment, redistributive taxation and public expenditure designed, partly at least, to maintain economic activity at a high level. Together with these have gone social and welfare policies which have injected a new measure of security into industrial life.

This is not to suggest that economic growth has been maintained at a satisfactory level or on an even keel during the last 25 years. We have seen that in the past the economy was subject to cyclical fluctuations averaging from 5 to 10 years between slump and slump, the most serious of all occurring between 1929 and 1932. Since 1945 the cycles have been shorter (4–5 years) and less severe, and have not been accompanied by the falls in gross domestic product that occurred before the war: the only recorded decline in output between 2 full years has been less than ½ per cent (compared with a fall of 9 per cent between 1929 and 1931) and the unemployment rate has fluctuated only between 1·1 per cent and 2·5 per cent. Three cycles are discernible in recent years – 1951–5 (trough 1952), 1955–60 (trough 1958) and 1960–65 (trough 1962): it is likely that in 1967/8 we are experiencing the trough of a fourth cycle which will move up towards the next peak in 1970. In recession years the average annual increase in gross domestic product has been only about half that of years of recovery (£420 million compared with £820 million), and overall the 'growth rate' of productive potential has been considerably less than in many other industrialized countries. Between 1953 and 1960 the growth in the gross domestic product per employee was only 1·8 per cent, and between 1960 and 1964 2·5 per cent: over the decade 1950–60 it was 1·9 per cent, compared with 5·3 per cent in Germany, 4·1 per cent in Italy, 3·8 per cent in France and 2·1 per cent in the United States. But with virtually full employment, and an actual scarcity of labour in some fields, wages and hence costs have tended to rise faster than total output, a condition in which no economy can thrive for an indefinite period. This is the background to the current prices and incomes policy, which will be discussed later. One indirect result of the problem has been Britain's poor showing in the export market and, hence, the unsatisfactory state of her balance-of-payments position. Although this is no new problem, going back to at least 1919, it has grown acute during recent years, while the volume of imports has been increasing faster than the volume of national product. Recurrent balance-of-payments crises have underlined the importance to Britain of stabilizing prices and increasing productivity in order to compete more effectively in world markets.

3

It requires no detailed historical knowledge to appreciate that the British people today earn their livings in ways very different from those of their ancestors. Occupational changes have followed upon changes in the economy as new employments have come into existence and old ones decayed or disappeared. In this way, technology has been one of the most potent of all the forces shaping modern society.

No very precise statement about the occupations of the people before the twentieth century is possible, since the early censuses either did not record occupations, or did so in ways which make direct comparison difficult, if not impossible. But it is undisputed that up to the middle of the eighteenth century – and from time immemorial before that – agriculture had occupied the great majority of the people. Perhaps, in 1750, farming and the numerous crafts associated with it accounted for three-quarters of occupied people. But from then onwards the advance of industrialization gradually changed Britain from a farming to a manufacturing economy. By 1881 the largest group of male occupations were those concerned with manufacturing (35 per cent), while agriculture took less than 1 in every 7: there were, in fact, considerably more women in domestic service than men in agriculture by that year.

Important changes have continued more recently. For example, between 1931 and 1951 those engaged in building and contracting increased by 20 per cent, those in professional and technical occupations by no less than 76 per cent; on the other hand, fishing and mining declined by 40 per cent, textile workers by 33 per cent and – a revealing social comment – the number of pawnbrokers from 13,000 in 1901 to 4,300 in 1931 and 1,500 by 1951. Women's employment has increasingly diversified from its former narrow limits. Manufacturing occupations took a substantially smaller proportion in 1951 than in 1931, but there was a 90 per cent increase in the number of women concerned with transport and communications, a 35 per cent increase of those in professional and technical occupations, and a huge increase of 122 per cent in the number of female clerks and typists: domestic servants (in hotels, institutions and private houses) fell from 1,333,000 to 724,000.

Between the two most recent census dates, 1951 and 1961, further occupational changes are noticeable. Today, 1 in every 3 married women is gainfully employed, and of all women workers slightly over half are married. Manufacturing industry took a slightly smaller proportion of the male labour force in 1961 (25 per cent) than in 1951 (26 per cent), but professional and technical occupations grew from 714,000 to 1,173,000, and clerical workers from 862,000 to 1,045,000. As 'white collar' occupations have continued to expand, traditional manual labour occupations such as mining, fishing, quarrying and agriculture have continued to contract. For women, there has been a further growth of clerical and typing occupations (from 1,270,000 to 1,780,000) and of professional and technical (523,000 to 707,000).

The modern industrial system, which had its origins in England in the later eighteenth century, has therefore passed through at least 4 phases, each of which has had significant effects on occupational structure. The first was marked by a rapid growth of factory production with the aid of power-driven machinery, particularly in the textile and metal industries, and created an industrialized, urbanized labour force in what had been a previously agricultural economy. The second phase was characterized by a revolution in communications by railways and steamships, and by the creation of new skills dependent on the development of precision engineering. Sharp differences in earnings and status now emerged between these skilled workers, often with powerful labour organizations, and the unskilled and 'sweated' trades which did not benefit from the spreading industrial system; there were also notable developments in the professions associated with commerce, distribution and finance which opened up new opportunities of wealth and social mobility. The third stage, beginning towards the end of the nineteenth century, witnessed the application of mass-production methods to industry on a large scale. This again caused structural changes – fewer heavy unskilled workers were now required, but more semi-skilled machine-minders, more technical and managerial staff and more clerical and distributive workers: the lines between wage-earners and salary-earners became more blurred, and hence that between 'working-class' and 'lower middle-class'. In the contemporary fourth stage, characterized by still more intensive mechanization and the development of industries based on new materials and sources of power, the proportion of the population engaged in direct production has tended to fall while that engaged in 'tertiary' occupations has risen. There are ever-increasing numbers of office workers and technicians, technologists, research workers, administrators and managers, but fewer engaged in the physical processes of manufacture. Also, in an economy which has now enjoyed practically full employment for 25 years, there has been some levelling-up from the bottom, some narrowing of wage differentials between degrees of skill as well as increased opportunities for a relatively small minority of highly skilled workers to earn considerably more than the rest.

Such changes in occupation have naturally had important consequences for the standard of living and on the class structure of modern Britain. Although it is unlikely that any 2 sociologists would ever agree about a definition of social class, there would be fairly widespread concurrence that Britain is still a 'class' society, that occupation is one of the major – perhaps the major – determinant of social class, and that British social structure has changed substantially during the last half-century, is changing, and is likely to continue to change. Specifically, the size of the middle class has expanded markedly, while that of the working class and of the traditional upper class (understood in the sense of a territorial aristocracy) has contracted. In the middle of last century, as we have seen, the middle classes comprised not more than 10–15 per cent of the whole population: Sir Arthur Bowley, the eminent statistician, placed them at 23 per cent in 1901, 25 per cent in 1911 and, slowed down by post-war depression, 26 per cent in 1931. In the 1950s G. D. H. Cole credited them with 30 per cent, increasing rapidly, and contemporary estimates vary around 35 per cent. The significant point here is not the precise accuracy of the statistics, which depend largely on the social categories to which particular occupations are ascribed, but the general effect which the changes have had on the shape of the social structure. All the earlier attempts to display British social stratification, from Gregory King in the late seventeenth century to Dudley Baxter in the late nineteenth, showed it as a tall pyramid with great wealth but small numbers at the top, large numbers and great poverty at the base. Today the social height has been lowered as if by pressure downwards on the point of the pyramid, and the shape of the social structure is now more like a pear or a Dutch cigar, tending towards an apple. The significant change is that for the first time the widest circumference no longer corresponds with the poorest stratum. Even in contemporary Britain, however, it remains important to distinguish between the distribution of income and the distribution of wealth. Although the division of income is now much more equal than in the past, landed property is still heavily concentrated in the hands of about 350 peers and some 1,500 gentry: little here has changed.

The census of 1951 identified 584 distinct occupations into which the population was posted. For convenience these are grouped into 7 occupational classes, 2 of which are sub-divided, as in the following table, which shows the changes, as percentages, between 1911 and 1951:

		Per cent of total in 1911	Per cent of total in 1951
Class 1A	Higher professional	4.05	7.78*
1B	Lower professional		
2A	Employers and proprietors	10.14	10.06*
2B	Managers and administrators		
3	Clerical workers	4.84	12.0*
4	Foremen, Inspectors, Supervisors	1.29	2.62
Manual workers			
5	Skilled	30.56	24.95
6	Semi-skilled	39.48	32.6
7	Unskilled	9.63	12.03

* Figures for 1959.

The most significant of these changes is the growth of the professional classes (1A rose from 184,000 to 434,000 and 1B from 560,000 to 1,059,000 between 1911 and 1951); but almost equally striking was the rise – nearly 3-fold – of Class 3, the clerical occupations. Class 2, on the other hand, has remained practically constant, since although managers and administrators have increased substantially with the growth of public companies, the number of individual employers and proprietors has fallen for the same reason. Class 4, consisting of foremen, inspectors and supervisors, has, however, doubled, and if these first 4 classes are combined to give an occupational 'middle class' the increase is from 20·3 per cent of the total in 1911 to 30·4 per cent in 1951. The totals of manual workers fell by the same amount – from 79·7 per cent to 69·6 per cent, the chief falls being in the proportions of skilled and semi-skilled: the proportion of unskilled is higher than it was in 1911, though lower than that of the 1920s (1911 9·63 per cent, 1921 14·17 per cent, 1951 12·03 per cent).

It is worth looking in rather greater detail at the most dramatic of the above changes, the growth of clerical occupations which today account for 1 in every 8 occupied persons. In part it is a result of the greater specialization and differentiation of industrial processes and of the growth of 'service' industries requiring greater communication between producers, retailers and consumers, in part a consequence of the mechanization of the media of communication (by typewriter, telephone, teleprinter and so on) and the opportunities thus opened up for the employment of women. In 1911 the census recognized only one category of clerk: 'female typewriters' were a novelty, and most correspondence was still done by copper-plate handwriting. In 1921 costing and estimating clerks were separately distinguished, in 1931 typists, in 1951 shorthand typists and office machine operators. Today, typists make up 24 per cent of the whole class, and book-keepers 21 per cent: machine operators make up only 4 per cent as yet, though increasing rapidly, leaving half of all those in the clerical category (1,219,000 of the 2,341,000) who do not fit into the major divisions. Today, 60 per cent of the class are female, 40 per cent male.

Probably the other most significant change, although the

numbers concerned are very much smaller, is in Class 1A, the higher professional. In 1911 it numbered only 184,000, and its biggest constituent was 54,000 ministers of religion: after them came 36,000 doctors and dentists, 26,000 lawyers and 25,000 professional engineers, while accountants numbered only 11,000 and scientists a mere 5,000. By 1951 the class had grown to 434,000, of which the biggest constituent was now engineers at 138,000: they have been continuing to grow in recent years at an annual rate of 7 per cent. The largest increase, however, has been in the scientists – from 5,000 to 49,000, an increase of 980 per cent in the 40 years: they, too, have an annual growth rate of $7\frac{1}{2}$ per cent – high, though not so high as many believe the economy requires. Ministers of religion have contracted by 4,000, lawyers increased by only 1,000: medicine has almost doubled, and accountancy risen by more than three times. Women have not penetrated into the higher professional class to anything like the same extent as they have all others: in 1911 they formed 6 per cent of the class, in 1951 still only 8 per cent, being best represented among doctors and dentists (15 per cent) and scientists (10 per cent).

Many other attempts have been made to define social class in terms other than occupation. In the view of some income is a major determinant, since this is a measurable quantity which affects a person's standard of life in a direct way: to others education is a main criterion, while others would also weight heavily such varied factors as speech and dress habits, house and its location, ownership of material objects such as cars and refrigerators, or leisure and cultural pursuits. For some years after the second world war the British Market Research Bureau produced a readership survey for the Hulton Press designed to provide information for advertisers on the extent to which newspapers and journals are read by different social classes: this allocated the population on the basis of a sample interview and the criteria of appearance, speech, occupation, type of house and district lived in. In the 1955 survey 5 social classes were identified with the following proportions:

Class A (Well-to-do, typical income over £1,300 p.a., typical occupations doctors, accountants, barristers, farmers on a large scale, administrative grade civil servants) 4 per cent.

Class B (Middle class, typical income £800–£1,300, typical occupations surveyors, qualified engineers, executive grade civil servants, medium-sized farmers) 8 per cent.

Class C (Lower middle class, typical incomes £450–£800, typical occupations bank clerks, teachers, commercial travellers, owners or managers of small business or shop, farmers on a small scale) 17 per cent.

Class D (Working class, typical income £250–£450, typical occupations bricklayers, plumbers, machine operators, miners, postmen, shop assistants) 64 per cent.

Class E (The Poor, typical income under £250, typical occupations labourers, charwomen, old-age pensioners living almost entirely on the pension) 7 per cent.

This survey therefore suggests a middle class (Classes A, B and C) of some 29 per cent, closely similar to the occupational class grouping: it has the disadvantage of concentrating a very large proportion of the population into the middle and lower middle groupings, though for the purpose of the readership survey this may be a justifiable over-simplification.

A more recent, and more detailed, classification has been developed by Dr Mark Abrams of Research Services Ltd, identifying 6 socio-economic grades. For 1961 they were:

Grade A (Upper middle class – higher managerial, professional or administrative, incomes, over £1,750) 4 per cent.

Grade B (Middle class – intermediate managerial, professional or administrative, incomes £950–£1,750) 8 per cent.

Grade C1 (Lower middle class – supervisors, clerical, junior managerial, professional or administrative, income under £950) 20 per cent.

Grade C2 (Skilled working class, incomes £650–£1,000) 35 per cent.

Grade D (Working class – semi-skilled and unskilled workers, incomes £350–£625) 25 per cent.

Grade E (Lowest grade workers, casuals, State pensioners, incomes under £340) 8 per cent.

The biggest difference is the high proportion ascribed to Grade C1, putting the middle class as a whole at 32 per cent. The incomes have been brought more into line with current changes (for 1964 the Grade A incomes were raised to £2,000 and over,

THE LAST FIFTY YEARS

the Grade E to under £416) and a survey of house- and car-ownership for 1964 showed that of all classes 43 per cent owned, or were in process of buying, their houses, while 42 per cent owned cars. Here too is evidence of a major economic and social change from the time, only half a century ago, when the majority of people died owning nothing or so little that it was not worthy of legal disposal.

The 'levelling-up-and-down' process which has been a characteristic of social class changes in the last half-century is reflected by – and is, in part, a consequence of – changes in relative levels of income. It is common knowledge that the numbers of the very rich, and, more importantly, of the very poor, have contracted since the beginning of the century: the economic height of society, like the social height, has been lowered, and the evidences both of great wealth and of great poverty are less obtrusive – and less acceptable – in the 1960s than at any time in modern history. In general, the main income changes between 1911 and 1961 can be summed up as a narrowing of differentials – between different social classes, between different components of a particular social class, between men and women and between juveniles and adults. Thus, in 1906 the median of all adult male manual earnings was 26s. 7d. a week, with 20s. 9d. in the lower quartile and 34s. 3d. in the upper – a range above or below the median of 51 per cent; in 1960 the median of 283s. 4d. (£14 3s. 4d.) varied by only 39 per cent between the lower and upper quartiles. It is now necessary, however, to look in more detail at the changes in earnings of different occupational classes, keeping in mind the changes in money values that have occurred in the last 50 years. The London and Cambridge Economic Service, taking 1911/12 as 100, gives a figure of 432 for 1958/9, and Professor Phelps Brown's index shows a rise from 984 points in 1911 to 3,825 in 1954: a factor of just over 4 times is therefore indicated.

In Class 1A (Higher Professional) earnings at the median have increased some 6 or 7 times – considerably ahead, that is, of price changes; in the upper quartile, however, they have risen only 4 times, and for the top tenth only 3 times, while those in the lower quartile have grown by nearly 9 times. The average earnings of some particular professions are as follows:

	1913/14	1922/4	1935/7	1955/6	1960	Per cent of 1913/14
	£	£	£	£	£	
Barristers	478	1,124	1,090	2,032	—	—
Doctors (GPs)	395	756	1,094	2,102	2,552	646
Clergy	206	332	370	582	582	283
Army officers	170	390	205	695	1,091	642
Engineers	292	468	—	1,497	1,973	676

Clearly, the fortunes of different professions have varied widely, and some have suffered a deterioration when changes in the value of money are taken into account. Thus, while the real income of the class increased some 40 per cent before tax over the period, that of the parochial clergy fell by 30 per cent. Relatively, bishops of the Church of England did worse still, their income, net of expenses, falling from £3,400 in 1913/14 to £3,200 in 1957, worth less than a quarter that at the earlier date. Similarly, the £5,000 p.a. of High Court Judges in 1933 did not change until after the second world war, and at £8,000 p.a. today they have added only 60 per cent instead of the 400 per cent necessary to keep up with the cost of living.

Some members of Class 2, the administrators and business managers, have done considerably better than the higher professional classes over the last half-century, the average pay of managers having risen as follows:

1913/14	1924/5	1938	1955/6	1960	Per cent of 1913/14
£200	£480	£440	£1,480	£1,850	925

On average, then, managers have about doubled their real incomes during the period, but their counterparts in the civil service have not done nearly so well: even with the very large increases they received between 1955 and 1960, only executive officers at the latter date had a real income higher than that of their 1913 equivalent, and the real income of principals had been almost halved. On the other hand, the highest-paid 1 per cent of company employees – directors and general managers – have maintained their relative position. Although there is a vast range of earnings in this category (the average pay of full-time directors of Turner and Newall in 1960 was £36,270, of Charrington's £3,073), the average salary of the 651 directors of the 100 largest companies, £14,000, was probably up to the pre-1914 average. These men, of course, fell into the 26,000 surtax-payers of 1960 whose earned incomes were more than £5,000 a year, and it is important to remember that at this level tax is now a decisive influence on real income: for instance, a married man with three children at £10,000 a year now gets, after tax, only £1,644 more than the same man at £5,000 a year.

We have noticed earlier that the largest of all occupational class increases in the last half-century is that of clerical workers. In general, clerks in business organizations have fared better than those in the Civil Service, and women clerical workers have improved their position relative to men, probably doubling their real earnings in the last 50 years:

	1911/13	1924	1935	1955	1960	Per cent of 1911/13
MEN	£	£	£	£	£	
C. S. clerical officers	116	284	260	503	661	570
In business	96	159	—	500	663	691
Railway clerks	76	221	224	559	751	988
Bank clerks	142	280	368	850	1,040	732
WOMEN						
C.S. shorthand-typists	79	179	162	367	491	662
In business	40	84	—	304	409	1,022

Despite their great growth in size, therefore, the clerical occupations, especially for women, have continued to bring rewards substantially above the rise in the cost of living, though it is fair to add that at the beginning of the century the leeway to be made up was a large one.

Class 4 (foremen, supervisors and inspectors) appear to have done even better than this. Although the wage statistics are not so full as for other categories, one estimate of foremen's earnings gives the following:

1906	1924	1935	1955	1960
£113	£268	£273	£784	£1,015

These figures indicate a 9-fold increase in earnings, and a doubling of real earnings, in the period. Foremen's rates have typically stood at around 40 per cent above those of skilled workers, so that the wages of the latter have also moved up in roughly the same proportion over the last half-century. Some typical earnings of Class 5 (skilled men) are as follows –

	1906	1924	1935	1955	1960	Per cent of 1906
	£	£	£	£	£	
Coalface workers	112	180	149	834	922	831
Fitters (time)	90	157	212	649	828	916
Carpenters	98	191	176	507	674	688
Railway engine drivers	119	276	258	622	863	725
Compositors	91	209	218	561	723	795
Weighted average	97	182	197	629	804	829

In general, then, the skilled worker has doubled his real earnings in the last 50 years, though the rank order of the skilled trades has changed noticeably: several of the 'aristocrats' of 1906 like pottery throwers, engine drivers and compositors have received increases considerably under the average, while engineering fitters, bakers and railway guards have improved their positions relative to the rest.

Semi-skilled workers on average more than doubled their real earnings in the period, reflecting the levelling-up process and the narrowing of differentials which has occurred in the last half-century:

	1906	1924	1935	1955	1960	Per cent of 1906
	£	£	£	£	£	
Semi-skilled pottery workers	77	171	173	—	585	760
Railway firemen	71	199	203	507	712	1,000
Bus and tram drivers (London)	107	190	218	476	546	510
Shop assistants	83	120	113	390	487	587
Postmen (London)	81	160	149	430	527	651
Agricultural labourers	48	82	89	423	512	1,067
Weighted average	68	136	144	506	627	923

Clearly, some particular semi-skilled groups who were formerly very depressed, like the agricultural workers and shop assistants, made very large gains, especially in the period 1935–55, while other groups such as the bus and tram drivers fared very much less well. One result of this is that the rank order of such occupations changed noticeably, bus and tram drivers being in first place in 1906 but only in ninth by 1960, engineering machine-men moving up from third to first place, and agricultural workers from the bottom to the fourth from the bottom. The increase in earnings for semi-skilled women has been somewhat less than for men – 737 rather than 923 points on the weighted average – though here again some poorly paid occupations have done relatively well – clothing machinists 1,276, laundry and dry-cleaning workers 1,033, and domestic servants less well at 633.

Finally, earnings of unskilled men have also increased more than the average, having risen 9·3 times between 1906 and 1960. Builders' labourers receiving an average of £63 a year in 1906 had £496 in 1960, railway porters £50 and £614, brewery labourers £50 and £583. Typically, the £1 a week of 1906 had become £10 by 1960, indicating one of the largest gains of all workers over the period.

If we summarize the performance of all occupational classes between 1913/14 and 1960, the largest increases have been scored by the small Class 2 – Managers (925 points) – and by the other small Class 4 – Foremen (989). Of the large groups, the unskilled have done best of all (849), followed by the semi-skilled (842) and the skilled (804): the smallest of all gains have gone to the professional occupations – Class 1B – Lower Professional (546) and Class 1A – Higher Professional (620). The other significant general comment is that women have performed better than men in every class except that of semi-skilled manual workers, and have increased their earnings as a proportion of men's from an average of 51 per cent in 1913/14 to 58 per cent in 1960. For this, the increases came almost entirely in the 2 war periods, in between which they merely held their own. It is also relevant to a study of the cost of living to note that the advances in real earnings of the last half-century have not occurred gradually and regularly, but have been largely concentrated into 3 periods – 1914–20, 1934–44 and 1951–55. The common characteristic of these 3 periods is their high rate of inflation, the average annual rise in the cost of living varying from 17 per cent from 1914–21 to 5 per cent from 1951–55. In the intervening periods, when differentials were either stable or widening, there was either deflation or a low rate of inflation (e.g. 1956–60 2·7 per cent per year). In terms, therefore, of recent history, inflation has tended to favour manual workers, and in particular those of a lesser degree of skill, while it has been to the disadvantage of professional workers whose relative superiority has been reduced.

This becomes even more pronounced when the tax changes of the last 50 years are taken into account and the net incomes of the more highly paid become still further lowered. This has been a consequence mainly of 2 vastly expensive world wars, occupying 10 years of the last 50, and of a greatly increased government expenditure on education, welfare and social services. In 1900 total government expenditure was a mere £281 million: in 1955 it was £6,143 million at current prices and £1,309 at 1900 prices, a real increase of about 5 times. This has been met principally by increased taxation – by additions to indirect taxes which now account for about 3s. 6d. on a 5s. packet of cigarettes and 37s. 6d. on a bottle of whisky, the basic cost of which is a mere 5s. 6d. and, more importantly, by additions to income tax and surtax which rise steeply with increased income. On the eve of the first world war the standard rate of income tax stood at 1s. 2d. in the £. By 1918 it had reached 5s., and remained at between 4s. and 5s. between the two wars. In 1940 it was raised to 7s., between 1941 and 1946 it stood at 10s., and since the end of the last war has only fallen back a little to around 8s. Although it is difficult to generalize the effect of this, since much depends on the extent of allowances for children and other expenses, it means typically that a married man in Class 1A with an income of £3,000–£4,000 a year and 1 or 2 children, pays up to one-third of this in direct taxation. Additionally, over £5,000 a year there is a surtax ranging from 2s. to 10s. in the £, and during the war years there was an Excess Profits Tax which began at 60 per cent and ultimately rose to 100 per cent. One consequence of this was that, whereas in 1938 7,000 people had incomes of £6,000 a year after tax, in 1948 the comparable figure was only 70. Post-war reliefs have tended to restore the balance somewhat, but the effects of taxation on the distribution of real incomes are still very substantial: in 1953 those in the income bracket £250–£499 a year retained 96·5 per cent of their gross income after direct taxation, those in the bracket £1,000–£1,499 83·2 per cent, £5,000–£9,999 45·5 per cent and over £10,000 only 30·4 per cent. Currently (1967) to double the take-home salary of a man earning £6,000 a year it would be necessary to raise his salary to more than £25,000 a year. Seven thousand people in Britain now have gross salaries of £10,000 or more a year, of which (assuming them to be married with 2 children) £4,027 is paid in taxation: Sir William Lyons, Managing Director of Jaguar Cars, pays £83,000 tax on his £100,000 a year, Sir Paul Chambers, head of I.C.I., £39,000 of his salary of £50,000.

If there has been some levelling-down of the top there has been some corresponding levelling-up of the lower strata of society, partly as a result of deliberate egalitarian policies, partly in consequence of the virtually full employment that has now prevailed for more than 25 years. As we have seen, the real earnings of the lowest-paid workers have been raised relatively more than those of other sections and, moreover, the differential between skilled and unskilled has narrowed substantially –

probably by about half since the 1880s. For centuries before then there had been almost no change. In 1500 the building craftsman had got half as much again as the labourer, 6d. a day against 4d.; in the 1890s he still got half as much again, 7½d. a hour to 5d. By 1954 the craftsman's rate was less than 15 per cent above that of the labourer – 445d. per 10-hour day compared with 390d. No doubt many influences have contributed to bring the change about – the spread of education since the end of the century, the growth of labour organizations for the unskilled, the effect of war, full employment and inflation. The important point here is that many of those poorly paid workers of 1900 who existed precariously at around £1 a week and who were often the first to suffer from the widespread unemployment of the 1920s and 1930s, have in the last quarter-century enjoyed a standard of security and comfort not very different from that of skilled men, and quite unique in the annals of labour.

How have these changes affected the extent of poverty in modern Britain? Until recently it was commonly believed that widespread poverty was a thing of the past, conquered by the rise in real wages and the post-war policies of social security. At the beginning of the century Booth, Rowntree and other social investigators had concluded that around 30 per cent of all the inhabitants of England were living in poverty, carefully defined to mean the minimum necessary for 'mere physical efficiency'. Rowntree lived long enough to repeat his survey of York on 2 further occasions – in 1936, when, using a more sophisticated measure, he concluded that 31 per cent of the inhabitants were still in poverty, and again in 1961 when he found that only 3 per cent were now in destitution. In 1899 the great cause of poverty had been insufficient wages, in 1936 unemployment, in 1961 neither of these great giants of the past but a new and feebler one – old age. Rowntree, like many optimistic politicians, believed that poverty had been all but eradicated by the social revolution of the 1940s, and that all that remained to be done was to raise the levels of the aged by appropriate pension provisions. Recently, a more pessimistic note has been struck by some researchers into social administration and, in particular, by the studies of Professors Abel Smith and Townsend, who believe that in the last few years there has been a large increase in both the proportions and the absolute number of people in Britain with low standards of living. Using as their definition of poverty those who live on less than 140 per cent of the basic National Assistance scale plus rent and/or other living costs, they have calculated that the proportion of people in poverty has increased from 7·8 per cent in 1953/4 to 14·2 per cent in 1960; although no absolute precision can be attached to the statistics, and although other investigators have argued that the standard has been set too high, they imply that perhaps some 7½ million people are in households with low levels of living. The principal suggested causes are, again, old age – an increasing incidence as the proportion of old people in the population continues to grow – and the increase in the proportion of large families in the population. Evidence from other directions is also disquieting. It has, for instance, been clear for several years from the annual food surveys that although, on average, all the major groups of the population receive an adequate intake of food nutrients, the proportion of nutrients declines sharply in households with more than 4 children or with more than 4 children and adolescents. In 1964 such households fell approximately 10 per cent below the recommended allowances for protein and calcium, and they constitute 48 per cent of the families with children in the sample. Even in families with only 1 child there is a lower intake of proteins, calcium and vitamin C today than in the austerely rationed days of 1950. But estimates of nutritional intake – and, indeed, of nutritional requirements – are notoriously uncertain and subject to error, and in the present state of knowledge it would be unwarrantable to conclude that any very large section of the community is suffering from serious malnutrition – some dieticians would even argue that more danger is likely to result from over-eating than from deprivation. Social class is no longer the prime determinant of nutritional adequacy as it was in the 1930s, when Sir John Boyd Orr discovered that half the population was below the required standard for one or more essential nutrients and 10 per cent below that for all nutrients. The 'nutritional gap' between rich and poor has greatly narrowed, partly because the poorest groups in the population have raised their consumption of such desirable foods as milk, eggs and cheese, partly because the wealthiest groups have lowered theirs of meat, butter and other items (in 1960 the richest 10 per cent ate 22 per cent less meat than in 1936). But the recent researches into poverty have at least demonstrated the persistence of a problem – perhaps, the emergence of a new problem related to new demographic trends – which, however difficult it may be to quantify precisely, casts a shadow on what we used to call 'the affluent society'.

4

The price-changes of the last 50 years have been of an altogether new order of magnitude. In the past, the period of greatest change was the Tudor era of inflation, when prices increased about 5 times within a century: since 1914 they have grown nearly as much – between 4 and 5 times, within the much shorter period of fifty years. The first half of the twentieth century has had to become accustomed to price fluctuations of an unprecedented scale and violence to the point where, for the first time in history, a prices and incomes policy has become a central issue of domestic politics.

Although price-material for the twentieth century is much fuller and more detailed than for earlier periods, it is no easier to handle. Ever since the outbreak of the first world war, when prices began to soar, there have been official collections of retail price data either in the form of a cost-of-living index (1914–47) or as an index of retail prices: there have been three of the latter since the end of the second world war (1947–56, 1956–62 and 1962 onwards), each based on different lists of commodities and each series starting afresh at the base year. The official statistics therefore cannot provide a continuous record of price-movements from 1914 onwards since they are not related to each other and since each has been made up of different components, differently weighted. In particular, many doubts have been expressed about the validity of the old cost-of-living index, which was based on a family budget inquiry made in 1904; although subsequently amended, it is particularly unsatisfactory for the inter-war years when patterns of expenditure were changing rapidly. It continued, for instance, to overweight the importance of candles long after they had been almost entirely replaced by gas and electricity. The current index of retail prices, although the weighting of its components is considerably more realistic, and is subject to annual revision, is specifically not a cost-of-living index, since it does not include mortgage repayments, national insurance or life insurance contributions, doctors' and dentists' fees, subscriptions to trade unions or hospital funds, income tax or the purchase of savings certificates.

Two independent cost-of-living series are therefore used here, based upon quite different sources, but both running continuously from 1906 so that comparison can be made. The first is that of Professor Guy Routh, using the series constructed by Professor A. L. Bowley to 1920 and the Ministry of Labour index of retail prices thereafter.

United Kingdom Cost of Living 1906–60
(Average for 1906–10 = 100)

1906	98	1920	266	1934	149	1948	287
1907	102	1921	241	1935	153	1949	295
1908	98	1922	194	1936	156	1950	305
1909	99	1923	184	1937	164	1951	333
1910	102	1924	185	1938	166	1952	362
1911	103	1925	186	1939	170	1953	373
1912	106	1926	182	1940	198	1954	381
1913	108	1927	177	1941	216	1955	397
1914	106	1928	175	1942	231	1956	417
1915	131	1929	173	1943	237	1957	432
1916	155	1930	167	1944	242	1958	445
1917	187	1931	156	1945	245	1959	449
1918	216	1932	152	1946	249	1960	454
1919	230	1933	148	1947	266		

The second is Professor E. H. Phelps Brown's estimate, which has been used throughout this book, of the cost of purchasing a finite 'bagful' of commodities – food, drink, fuel, light and clothing – over the whole period of 700 years. The conformity between the two series is striking enough to suggest a basic validity. This index is based on the price of a composite unit of consumables, 1451–75 = 100.

A HISTORY OF THE COST OF LIVING

1906	1016	1919	2254	1931	1146	1943	2145
1907	1031	1920	2591	1932	1065	1944	2216
1908	1043	1921	2048	1933	1107	1945	2282
1909	1058	1922	1672	1934	1097	1946	2364
1910	994	1923	1726	1935	1149	1947	2580
1911	984	1924	1740	1936	1211	1948	2781
1912	999	1925	1708	1937	1275	1949	3145
1913	1021	1926	1577	1938	1274	1950	3155
1914	1147	1927	1496	1939	1209	1951	3656
1915	1317	1928	1485	1940	1574	1952	3987
1916	1652	1929	1511	1941	1784	1953	3735
1917	1965	1930	1275	1942	2130	1954	3825
1918	2497						

In both indices, the rise in prices between 1906 and 1954 is 3·8 times; the Routh index, which continues to 1960, shows a rise to 4·5 times by the later date.

The 2 series also agree closely about the periods of price-change. The overall price-rise of the last half-century has not been a gradual and continuous process, but the product of several periods of inflation and deflation, frequently short and severe compared with earlier times. Immediately on the outbreak of the first world war prices began to move up sharply and continued to rise until the end of 1920; by then they had moved from 108 points (1913) on the Routh index to 266, and on the Phelps Brown scale from 1,021 to 2,591, in both cases an increase of about 2½ times in 7 years. Within 4 days of the declaration of war the Cost of Living Index had risen 15 per cent, though it subsequently fell back somewhat; the fastest annual rate of inflation was during 1916, when it was 29 per cent. A number of causes operated to bring this about. Although Britain officially remained on the gold standard during the war, gold practically ceased to be an important factor in the determination of price because of the issue of large quantities of paper currency to meet the huge volume of government transactions: nominally convertible at first into gold, this paper money soon became in practice inconvertible. Added to this was the fact that many goods and foodstuffs were in short supply because of military needs, yet there was a heavy demand for them from a population enjoying virtually full employment for the first time; although many prices were controlled, some foods rationed, and rents pegged to their pre-war level, scarcity and heavy demand brought about a price-rise that caused widespread industrial unrest and concern to the Government. As in most periods of rapid inflation, wages generally lagged behind the rise in prices, although there were many variations between different industries. It is likely that most wage-earners had caught up by the end of the war, and by 1920 some had made gains. In particular, the differential for skill had narrowed considerably – by 1920 the bricklayer's rate was 235 per cent that of 1914, his labourer's 300 per cent, while in engineering the advance of the unskilled was greater still. Salary-earners fared much less well, receiving their first major setback at this period. By the end of 1920 average salaries were approximately double their level of 1914 (civil service administrators only 67 per cent greater) while taxation was very much heavier than before; by contrast, average weekly wage-rates were 2·8 times greater for a working week that had been reduced from 48 to 60 hours a week to 44 to 48 hours.

After a brief economic boom at the end of the war, there followed a collapse in 1920 and a period of rapidly falling prices for the next 2 years. From their peak of 266 points in 1920 (Routh index) they fell to 241 in 1921 and 194 in 1922, a decline of one-third. The fall in wholesale prices was even greater, that for cotton textiles being only 30 per cent that of 1920. The cause of the price-fall was partly the deliberate policy of deflation undertaken by the government, which withdrew £70 million worth of currency notes from circulation, and thus considerably changed the ratio between currency and production. At the same time, many industries were embarking on programmes of expansion, employing new products, techniques and methods of cost-reduction which had the effect of increasing output at lower prices. Gold continued to have less influence on prices than it had had before the war. The inconvertible paper currency continued until the gold standard was restored in 1925, but even after that, gold could only be withdrawn from the Bank of England in certain circumstances, and in practice the currency remained inconvertible. Part of the economies in industry were achieved by wage-cuts which, in a period of

A HISTORY OF THE COST OF LIVING

falling prices, seemed defensible to many employers. The Ministry of Labour recorded an average decrease in 1921 of 17s. 6d. a week for 7·2 million workers, and a further 11s. in 1922 for 7·6 million: coal-miners did much worse than this, losing on average £2 a week in 1921 and another 10s. the next year. About half the wage-cuts in industry were made under sliding-scale agreements related to the cost of living, and since these were flat-rate reductions they tended to hurt lower-paid more than higher-paid workers, thus widening differentials again. But for workers who retained their jobs at this time wage-reductions were generally not quite so large as the fall in prices, so that real earnings stayed ahead: the real hardship was felt by the greatly increased proportion of unemployed (16·6 per cent of insured workers in 1921 and 14·1 per cent in 1922), and by those on short-time working. Professional earnings, which had risen less than wages up to 1920, now fell less. True, there were some cuts in civil service salaries (administrative class index fell from 167 points in 1920 to 134 in 1923, executive class from 264 to 197) but in private industry and the professions there was generally stability or even slight gains (barristers average 1921–2 £1,088 p.a., 1922–3 £1,309 p.a.). Deflation favoured those on salaries and fixed incomes and prejudiced particularly the lower-paid worker.

For the 10 years after 1923 there followed a much more moderate decline in prices which, after the rapid falls of the early 1920s, seems almost a period of price-stability. In fact, the fall was still almost as rapid as during the 'Great Depression' of the 1870s and 1880s. Wholesale prices fell more than the cost of living, which ended about 20 per cent lower than in 1923, and about 50 per cent above the 1906–10 level. (On the Routh index 1906–10 = 100, 1933 = 148.) The restoration of the gold standard in 1925 had the effect of over-valuing the pound relative to other currencies: on the other hand, wage-rates proved very resistant to change, and the policy of dear money tended to restrict initiative in British domestic industries without placing the export industries in a competitive position. High costs were one of the factors limiting the volume of our trade and, therefore, one of the reasons for the high level of unemployment which reached its peak in the world depression of 1929–32. Despite this, however, wage rates retained a remarkable general stability, falling on average only 6 per cent in the period, while actual earnings, as calculated by Professor A. L. Bowley, fell only 3 per cent between 1928 and 1931. Some professional earnings fell (teachers by 12 per cent between 1924 and 1934, for example) but, in general, these too held their levels to within 2 or 3 points. It seems likely, then, that for those who managed to stay in full-time employment in the 1920s and early 1930s standards of living rose significantly. Many food-prices fell more than the average – sugar by as much as 50 per cent, frozen meat 17 per cent, flour 14 per cent – and other things which do not appear in the index, like transport and entertainment, also fell considerably. No generalization about the 'average' standard of life is likely to be very helpful, since there are always as many people below it as above it. Much depended on the particular industry and its extent of unemployment, on locality and on the degree of skill of the worker. Probably it would be true to say that the unskilled worker in a 'sheltered' industry (i.e. one catering primarily for the home market) and in full employment was considerably better off than before the war, the skilled worker in a similar industry also better off though slightly less than the unskilled, labourers in export industries about the same as in 1914, and skilled 'unsheltered' workers almost certainly worse off. It will be shown that average standards of food consumption improved notably at this period and that the whole range of comforts in such things as domestic furnishings and appliances, entertainment and leisure activities, expanded for many people. Such generalizations in no way apply to the 3 million unemployed and their families of 1932, whose standards were often barely above survival level.

From the trough of 1933–4 prices now moved up slowly to the outbreak of the second world war in 1939. The rise was not sufficient to make up the ground lost during the depression – on the Routh index, for example, the 1928 cost-of-living number stood at 175, 1933 at 148 and 1939 at 170. By 1939, then, the cost of living stood about two-thirds higher than it had been before the first world war. This was a period of renewed economic activity in which unemployment, although well over a million even in 1939, fell by half. One reason for the British recovery was, undoubtedly, the abandonment of the gold standard in 1931, which had the effect of depreciating the pound sterling, reducing the cost of British goods and so stimulating exports. It also meant that the bank rate did not have to be manipulated in order to induce an influx of gold, but could be dropped to the low level of 2 per cent. Interest rates followed, and Britain moved into a period of cheap money which was a direct incentive to business enterprise: on the other hand, she continued to have the advantage of cheap imports of food and raw material from primary producing countries which had been even worse hit by depression. The previous falls in manual earnings were now halted; by 1935 the level of 1928 had been regained, and thereafter there was a rise of around 8 per cent to 1939. Professional earnings and salaries, on the other hand, remained almost static in these years, resulting in a further narrowing of differentials. Ironically, the employed worker was the principal beneficiary of the economically most disturbed period 1918–1939, increasing his real earnings between one third and one half.

During the second world war (1939–45) prices rose much less rapidly than after 1914. On the official Cost-of-Living Index (July 1914 = 100) the rise was from 155 in 1939 to 196 in 1941 and 202 in 1945, on the Routh index (1906–10 = 100) it was from 170 in 1939 to 216 in 1941 and 245 in 1945. A rise of little more than one-third during a period of 6 years of full employment and increasing earnings was a remarkable achievement compared with the doubling in the cost of living during the first world war, and was a direct result of deliberate government policy to stabilize prices at a time of national emergency. This was achieved by the control of many wholesale and retail prices by administrative order, by rationing of food, clothing and other necessities, and by the state subsidization of some producers contributing directly to the war effort. In particular the cost of food, which had soared during the first world war as a result of scarcity, was held down in a highly successful way by rationing and price control, the official index number for food rising only from 155 to 168 points. This is not to say that there was always enough of the kinds of food people wished to eat, or that many people did not dislike forcible change to an unfamiliar dietary pattern, but it did mean that there was always enough food to ensure nutritional adequacy at prices all people could afford. Further, there is reliable evidence that nutritional standards, and the standard of living generally, actually improved substantially for the population as a whole during the war years – so much so that the dark days of the 1940s can justifiably be regarded as a turning-point in the social conditions of the working classes. With millions of men in the forces and the need for greatly increased output, it was natural that there should now be a premium on labour, and particularly on the manual labour needed in shipbuilding, coal-mining and a score of other essential industries. As in other periods of inflation, manual earnings moved upwards at an accelerating rate, salaries much less quickly. The consequent erosion of differentials (between manual and non-manual, between skilled and unskilled, and between men and women) was one of the egalitarian characteristics bred by the war and largely accepted in the immediate post-war years of reconstruction. During the war, and especially during its earlier years, a major shift in income in favour of manual workers appears to have taken place. Manual earnings rose by 30 per cent between 1938 and 1940, and by another 34 per cent between 1940 and 1945; by contrast, the administrative class civil servants' salary index, which stood at 100 in 1938, was only 108 in 1945, and the executive class index rose only from 100 to 116. The 'decline of the middle classes', which became a favourite post-war slogan, had its origins at this time.

Again, unlike the situation after the first world war and the Napoleonic War, the second world war was not succeeded by a period of deflation and high unemployment. Under the post-war Labour Government many forms of rationing, price and investment control were continued and developed, and despite world shortage of many commodities the level of economic activity and of employment remained unusually high for peacetime. The government, however, was not able to prevent rapid rises in prices which developed in the late 1940s and early 1950s. Between 1945 and 1950 retail prices rose 26 per cent, and between 1950 and 1955 by another 30 per cent; on the Routh cost-of-living index the increase in the decade is from 245 to 397 points (1906–10 = 100), a rise of almost three-fifths. Already by the early 1950s inflation was coming to be recognized as an outstanding economic problem, but the means of curbing it while maintaining full employment and expanding output continued to elude successive governments. Public expenditure at a prodigiously high level for peacetime was necessary to finance the vast extension of social services after 1945, and heavy taxation of an almost wartime degree of severity was also a way of 'mopping up' excess purchasing power. Changes in bank rate and hire-purchase restrictions were also designed to have the same effect. The power of organized labour was now greater than ever before, and substantial increases in earnings in general kept ahead of price-rises, average wage-rates rising by slightly more than two-thirds during the decade. There was a continued narrowing of differentials between professional and manual workers: comparing 1949 with 1955/6 manual earnings rose in the proportion of 100–160, while professional salaries moved only from 100–136. The chief beneficiaries of Labour's policy of 'fair shares' were the working classes, cushioned to some extent against inflation by the extension of social services, local authority housing, controlled rents and the continuance of food rationing in some forms until 1954.

Inflation has continued in the most recent decade, 1954–64, to the extent of 30 per cent on consumer goods and services, or an annual average rise of 2·6 per cent. Different cost-indices have risen at markedly differing rates – exports of goods and services by only 16 per cent, imports of goods and services a mere 9 per cent, but government expenditure on goods and services by as much as 62 per cent. The final price-rise for the decade, 31 per cent, is therefore somewhat less than for 1945–55, although in total it means that retail prices have doubled since the end of the war. The breakdown of the 31 per cent rise is instructive. Import costs contributed only 4 points, but higher employment incomes accounted for 18 points and increases in profit, rent and indirect tax components for the remaining 9. Employment income (wages and salaries) per head has risen on average 6 per cent each year in the last decade, varying from 4·3 per cent in 1958–9 to 8·4 per cent in 1955–6 (1964–5 7 per cent). It seems likely that differentials have tended to widen again, especially between 1955 and 1960, with a relative decline for semi-skilled and unskilled workers and for women manual workers. Average wages in 1956 represented 68 per cent of average salaries; in 1960 they represented 64·8 per cent. In recent years, it seems, professionals have won back a little of the lost ground of the last half-century.

Clearly, there can be no simple explanation of the causes of post-war inflation. One of the main influences on price must be the pressure of demand, and this in turn is influenced by the level of earnings, by the bargaining power of trade unions and, probably, by independent social forces. Price-changes may also be affected by cost-changes, which include changes in import prices and long-term changes in productivity. Most economists would accept that recent inflation has been caused by a mixture of demand and cost influences. The pressure of demand, it seems, has had little direct effect on prices, but it does have direct effects on earnings which then lead to price-increases by the process known as 'cost-push': price-increases then lead to renewed wage-increases by a process of 'cost-of-living push'. In popular language, this is the wages and prices spiral.

The price-indices that have been used here suggest an average rise in the cost of living of about 5 times since 1914 and 3 times since 1939. It will be obvious to anyone who remembers recent times that this rise has been spread very unevenly, that some commodities and services have increased very much more than 5 times since the first world war, others in about that proportion and some less than this. In a half-century of extremely rapid economic and social change, during which spending patterns have changed radically, it is impossible to make a direct comparison of 1914 with the present; many articles which we take for granted today were either then unknown or highly priced luxuries, while some things in common use then have almost disappeared today. The rapid advance of technology has been one of the principal instruments of change, and any complete price-index would need to take account of the great cheapening of new products since their first appearance which has been made possible by mass-production – of television sets which were rare luxuries in the 1930s and are now in 4 out of every 5 households in the country, of washing-machines, vacuum-cleaners and refrigerators, of frozen foods and of ballpoint pens (which on their appearance in 1946 cost 35s. and can now be bought for 6d.). These and a hundred other items enter into the cost of living today, but did not in 1914.

If we restrict the comparison to things that have remained largely unchanged over the period it becomes more meaningful, though even here it is necessary to take account of changes in habits of expenditure. For example, bread which in 1914 generally cost 6d. for a 4-lb. loaf now costs about 3s. for an equivalent quantity, but whereas in 1914 bread accounted for about one-sixth of total expenditure on food, today it is less than one-sixteenth. Food-prices in general have kept fairly close to the average 5-fold increase, and because of substantially higher real earnings are therefore relatively lower than they were; one result of this is that food now takes a substantially smaller proportion of total consumers' expenditure than it did. Other prices have, of course, risen considerably more than the average – from about 25s.–30s. a ton for best house-coal in London in 1914 to about £15 a ton currently – though, again, the development of more economical methods of heating means that fuel bills as a proportion of total expenditure have not necessarily increased. The most important single price-change in the period is, no doubt, in housing where, whether rent or freehold prices are considered, the factor of 5 must be doubled or trebled to put into present-day terms. Much of the rise here has occurred since the second world war, for even in 1939 new semi-detached houses in the outer London area sold at around £600 and in the provinces at £450, which today cost up to ten times as much. Council-house rents have risen on average about 6 times since the 1930s, though wide regional differences, and substantial changes in the amenities provided, make direct comparison difficult.

We need to remember also that expenditure patterns have changed in recent years. In 1913 total consumers' expenditure stood at £2,058 million, of which food was the largest single item at £693 million (34 per cent); next came housing at £230 million (11 per cent), clothing £210 million (10 per cent), alcoholic drink £175 million (8 per cent), transport and communications £124 million (6 per cent), fuel and light £79 million (4 per cent), durable household goods £76 million (4 per cent) and tobacco £40 million (2 per cent). 'Other goods and services' (which include books and stationery, entertainment, toys, domestic service, medicines, insurance and other services) accounted for £431 million (21 per cent). For 15 years, between 1939 and 1954, traditional expenditure patterns were disturbed by shortages, rationing and price-controls; we therefore take 1955, by which time a more normal pattern was returning, for comparison. In that year, of the total consumers' expenditure of £5,248 million, food took 31 per cent, housing 11 per cent, transport and communications 10 per cent, clothing 9 per cent, durable household goods 6 per cent, alcoholic drink 6 per cent, fuel and light 5 per cent and tobacco 4 per cent; 'other goods and services' accounted for the remaining 17 per cent. Already there were some significant changes. Expenditure on food had fallen; more important, that on transport had moved up to third place with the increased use of motor-cars and of travelling for work and pleasure. Alcoholic drink had fallen noticeably, though tobacco had doubled to keep the combined proportion at 10 per cent in both years. But the beginning of the 'consumer revolution' was noticeable in the 5 per cent rise in durable household goods, which cover furnishings and domestic appliances generally. Ten years later, in 1966, these trends have become much more marked. Food now accounts for only 4s. 5d. in every £ of household expenditure, compared with 5s. 6d. a decade ago. On the other hand, pressure on accommodation has raised the amount spent on housing, fuel and light to 3s. 3d. in the £ instead of 2s. 7d., and the proportion devoted to private cars has doubled from 9d. to 1s. 6d. in every £.

More complete details of household expenditure are given in the Family Expenditure Survey, the latest report of which refers to 1965. The average household today consists of 2·9 persons, and spends on all purposes, including taxes, insurance, and savings, £27 a week. Food accounts for £5 19s. per household (22 per cent), housing for £3 12s. (13 per cent), fuel, light and power for 27s. (5 per cent), alcoholic drink 16s. (3 per cent), tobacco 24s. (4 per cent), clothing and footwear 41s. (8 per cent), durable household goods 27s. (5 per cent), other goods (e.g. books, stationery, toys, fancy and sports goods, photographic equipment, medicines, seeds and plants) 30s. (6 per cent), transport and vehicles 53s. (10 per cent), and services (e.g. postage, cinemas, theatres, radio and television, domestic help, hairdressing, laundry, holiday expenses) 38s. (7 per cent). Income tax and surtax take an average of 45s. a week (8 per cent), insurance (including national and private insurance) 37s. (7 per cent) and other forms of saving 12s. (2 per cent). In the supposedly affluent society we spend half as much on moving about as we do on food, and slightly more on our homes (combining housing, fuel, light and durable household goods) than on what we eat. We devote very little to direct forms of saving, though if we combine this with insurance and mortgage repayment the fraction is 13 per cent – rather more than the traditional 10 per cent calculated by Victorian domestic economists. Each household spends on average £2 a week on the purchase and maintenance of motor vehicles compared with 11s. a week on bus and train fares, 13s. a week on holidays and hotel expenses, 8s. 6d. a week on radio and television, 3s. a week on toys and 2s. on animals and pets. Other points are also of interest: expenditure on bread and flour is now a mere $1\frac{1}{2}$ per cent of average household expenditure. We spend almost as much on soft drinks as on tea – 2s. a week compared with 3s. Women now spend substantially more on their own dress than do men – 14s. a week (not including hats, gloves and shoes) compared with 9s. 6d. – a clear reversal of the former pattern: cosmetics and toilet requisites (not including medicines) take another 4s. 3d.

All this points clearly enough to the fact that much of today's expenditure is on what earlier generations would have described as 'luxuries'. Compared with the Victorian and pre-Victorian household budgets we have discussed in earlier chapters, when food alone often took half and more of total expenditure and the rest went on other basic necessities like shelter and warmth, these now constitute a minority of expenditure in the average household. Far more than ever before goes on services and entertainment, taxation and the various forms of saving, less on the traditional luxuries, drink and tobacco, but much more on 'conspicuous expenditure' – dress, personal possessions and adornment of the home. With the exceptions of domestic help and private educational expenses, which now take a mere 2s. 6d. and 2s. a week respectively in the average household, it would be a fair generalization to say that contemporary spending habits have moved towards what was formerly regarded as the typically middle-class pattern and away from the traditional working-class pattern.

The question remains to be asked how far the 'average' household expenditure described above approximates to the very real differences in income that still exist in English society. Rich and poor were formerly sharply distinguished by the ways in which they spent their money, the former devoting a much higher proportion to luxuries and personal services, the latter obliged to spend almost everything on basic necessities of life. It has been argued earlier in this chapter that the general trend in the last 50 years has been to reduce earnings differentials and that, in particular, the effect of the social revolution of the 1940s has been to raise substantially the standards of what was formerly a submerged third of society. It remains true, however, that wealth is still very unequally divided and that a problem of poverty, of uncertain size, persists in the midst of general plenty. The following statistics from the Family Expenditure Survey for 1965 show the differing consumption patterns of 3 economic groups – the £15–£20 a week household typical of a manual worker, the £5–£10 a week household typical of the lowest-paid workers and of pensioners, and the over-£50 a week household representative of the higher professional class. It should be noted that the average size of the household differs importantly in the 3 groups, from 1·5 persons in the poorest to 4 in the wealthiest.

The pattern is predictable in some respects, though not in all. The proportion of expenditure on food falls with increasing income, as it has always done, though even for the poorest group represented here it is still only one-third of total expenditure. On the other hand housing, fuel and light is revealed as an exactly equal burden for this group, occupying a much larger place than it did historically: for the over-£50 a week group the equally heavy 18 per cent on housing is accounted for by mortgage repayments, amounting to three-quarters of the total. Items which are roughly equal for all classes are clothing,

Family Expenditure 1965

Weekly income of household	£5–£10	£15–£20	Over £50
No. of persons per household	1·5	3·0	4·0
Per cent of weekly expenditure	%	%	%
Housing	19	12	18
Fuel, light and power	12	6	2·5
Food	31	25	15
Alcoholic drink	2	3	3·5
Tobacco	4	5	3
Clothing and footwear	6	7	7
Durable household goods	3	7	3
Other goods	7	6	5
Transport and vehicles	3	8	9
Services	9	7	9
Income tax and surtax	1	5	16
Insurance	2	7	6
Savings	0·5	1	3
Betting payments	0·5	1	—

tobacco and services, though the composition of the last differs noticeably between the groups: in the poorest radio and television licences and rental are the largest single component; in the wealthiest hotel and holiday expenses, subscriptions and donations (41s. 6d. a week) followed by educational expenses (17s. a week) and domestic help (15s. a week). Expenditure on transport, income tax and surtax and savings all increase with income, but the largest proportionate outlay on goods occurs in the middle group, where there is presumably greater leeway in consumer articles still to be made up.

5

The control of rapid and violent price-changes has now for long been an object of government policy. Earlier chapters have discussed the abortive attempt to check inflation after the Black Death in the middle of the fourteenth century and the somewhat greater success with which wages were pegged in 1563 during the great price-rise of Tudor times. In the eighteenth and nineteenth centuries, however, laissez-faire governments would have considered it injudicious – and almost immoral – to attempt to regulate prices, an object that would have involved intervention in the inexorable, and necessarily just, laws of supply and demand. Fortunately for the classical economists, the price-changes of their time were not of a magnitude sufficient to disturb the equanimity with which this view was generally accepted.

But in the present century, price-movements have been of an altogether new order of severity. A gradual, though significant, rise from 1896 to 1914 was translated by the first world war into rampant inflation lasting until 1920; then followed a catastrophic collapse of prices all over the world, culminating in the international depression of 1929–32, when currencies in many countries became almost worthless; since the second world war we have experienced another 20 years of inflation of an unprecedented rate. Price-changes in the past, as this book has attempted to show, have never been disastrous to the community as a whole. Periods of inflation and deflation have brought gains and losses to different sections – manufacturers, merchants and entrepreneurs generally benefiting from inflation, wage-earners generally gaining from price-falls. Inflation, and the expectation of larger profits, has often in the past stimulated new industrial enterprise, while deflation has sometimes forced more economic methods of managing existing industries. What is new in the post-war situation is the fact that, because of a high level of economic activity and employment, and because of powerful and effectively led labour organizations, wages have generally kept up with – and have sometimes gone ahead of – price-rises, thus causing the well-known spiralling effect on costs. This, in itself, would not be serious if productivity had increased commensurately, but this has not been the case; indeed, in 1966 the gross national product increased, in real terms, by only $1\frac{1}{2}$ per cent (though by 4 per cent in money terms) over 1965. The competitiveness of our costs intimately affects our ability to export, and our success or failure here is the key to the balance-of-payments situation.

Inflation 50 years ago was thought of in terms of its harmful effects on individuals – the denuding of savings and pensions, the disastrous consequences which sudden price-increases could have on the frail budgets of the poor. The great economist Marshall propounded that under an ideal currency system prices should fall at such a rate that those in receipt of fixed incomes should secure a fair proportion of man's increasing control over his environment – that is, the purchasing power of a fixed income should increase with successive improvements in the means of production: he had in mind a fall of the order of about 1 per cent a year. But in the middle of the twentieth century price-control has come to be seen in the larger and more urgent context of national survival, and it is no exaggeration to say that, after the maintenance of peace, it represents the greatest concern of contemporary governments.

In the years immediately before the first world war, when rising prices were seen as one of the major causes of the growing labour disputes of the period, 2 main types of remedy were proposed for the disease. One, which received its fullest development in the work of the economist Jevons, was that all incomes and contract prices should be made to vary in order to offset movements in prices. Wages, debts, rents and so on would be fixed in terms of purchasing power, and the amount of money paid would vary in accordance with the movements of an index number of prices. The administrative problems involved in such a system would obviously be immense, even supposing that there could be any general agreement about an acceptable index number. The first world war did, however, make the public much more familiar with the idea of index numbers than ever before, and before its end manual earnings in a considerable number of industries were being fixed, and varied, in accordance with changes in the cost of living. But after 1920, when prices turned downwards, labour opinion reacted sharply against the consequent reductions in wages, and many of the agreements had to be abandoned. There appeared to be a natural unwillingness of wage-earners to think of their income in terms of the goods and services it would purchase rather than in terms of the monetary units it comprised, at least when reductions in income were involved. Despite often bitter experiences of the effects of changes in value, we continue naïvely to believe in the intrinsic worth of money.

The alternative to varying incomes and other payments in accordance with variations in the value of money is, obviously, to remove the variations themselves. One such method was proposed by the American economist Professor Irving Fisher before the first world war, when international currencies were still based on the gold standard, by which the gold content of the dollar (or the pound sterling) would be varied in order to offset price-movements. If, for example, prices rose by 1 per cent, the weight of gold exchanging for a dollar would be raised by 1 per cent; this would reduce the price of gold proportionately, would obviate the need for a general rise in the price-level, and correct that which had already occurred. This would happen because the central bank (Bank of England), finding its gold reserve at a lower valuation, would have to contract credit and initiate a fall in prices. Such a plan, if successful at all, would clearly only work with currencies linked to the gold standard, and it would have the grave defect that central banks or governments would find themselves with constant losses or gains as the monetary value of their stocks was revised. But although the 'compensated dollar' plan was only adopted for a brief experiment of a few weeks by the United States Government in 1933, it at least gave impetus to the general idea of a 'managed currency'.

British anti-inflationary measures in recent years have been concerned mainly to reduce demand and hence the pressure on costs. Other aspects of government economic policy – the encouragement of higher rates of growth of productivity, the reduction of restrictive practices and the curbing of monopolies – have also been anti-inflationary, at least in part, since their object is to lower costs of production and distribution, but most attention has been focused on directly deflationary policies. These have taken various well-known and unpopular forms such as credit 'squeezes', restrictions on borrowing and hire-purchase, import restrictions, increases in indirect taxation, manipulation of the bank rate, and devaluation of the pound. Most economists who agree that the remedy is to run the economy at a lower pressure of demand accept as inevitable a higher rate of unemployment than we have enjoyed in recent years. It has been said that an unemployment rate of 2–2½ per cent 'would make a major difference to the rate of rise in prices', and Professor Paish's calculation is that unemployment of 2¼ per cent would permit an annual wage-increase of about the same size as the rise in output per man.

Any deliberate generation of unemployment by government policy is likely to provoke a very sharp reaction from labour, as was demonstrated in the 1967 Trades Union Congress. 'Full employment' has become a tenet of faith as sacrosanct as the welfare state and the right of free speech, and it is unlikely that any government would long survive which actively pursued a policy of deliberately putting a substantial number of people out of work. In any case, it is by no means certain that a rise in unemployment of the order suggested above would have the desired effect on prices: between 1960 and 1964 unemployment averaged 1·9 per cent but final prices rose at an average rate of 2½ per cent a year, and it may well be that real price-stability could only be achieved by a return to what we have come to think of as 'mass unemployment' of the order of 1 million or more people. In the winter of 1967–8 the (unfulfilled) prospect of a rise to three-quarters of a million caused deep concern.

The alternative remedy for inflation, less undesirable socially though more difficult administratively than unemployment, is to restrain wage and price increases by direct government intervention. An incomes policy of sorts goes back 20 years – to the 'wage-freeze' of 1947, which broke down under the Korean War boom – to be followed by a 'pay pause' in 1961 and a 'guiding light' principle of 2½ per cent for wage-increases in 1962. The Labour Government has since greatly extended control by establishing the National Prices and Incomes Board in 1965 with the avowed cooperation of the T.U.C., so that now for the first time in history there is a public body whose sole responsibility is to watch over changes in the levels of earnings and prices. Since then, the major problem has been to arm the Board with teeth. The new 'guiding light' of 3–3½ per cent has been exceeded by a number of trade unions, and, indeed, the average increase in hourly wage-rates from January 1965 to January 1966 was double this amount, 7 per cent. 'Voluntary restraint' was shown to be insufficient, and in 1966 the government reconstituted the Board on a statutory basis, instituting the compulsory 'early warning system' under which firms intending to raise prices and unions intending to make wage-claims are obliged to report their intentions to the government. They are then obliged, under penalty, to wait until the Board has reviewed and reported on the proposed increases. In the middle of 1966 the government introduced a 6-months' general standstill on prices and charges, followed by a further period of six months of 'severe restraint', the White Paper commenting that 'the country needs a breathing space of twelve months in which productivity can catch up with the excessive increases in incomes which have been taking place'. Coupled with this, the government was given power to make orders directing that specified prices or charges should not be increased without ministerial consent, thus for the first time giving statutory power of price-fixing.

The intention of the policy is clear enough – that 'total money incomes should rise in line with the growth of real national output', and that 'increases in wages and salaries above the norm should be confined to cases in which exceptional treatment can be shown to be in the national interest'. If wage-increases can be kept to the 'norm' of $3-3\frac{1}{2}$ per cent based on expected productivity increases, firms will be able to absorb the labour-cost increases and will not be required either to raise prices or reduce their profits. Further than this, where profits contain a monopolistic element, it is the intention of the Board that existing prices should actually be lowered, although there is no intention to squeeze normal profits.

The implementation of such a policy is obviously a matter of enormous difficulty. It might easily work unfairly, since the Board has limited time and might, consciously or unconsciously, be selective in its investigations and recommendations. More fundamentally, its success depends on productivity-increases keeping in step with wage-increases – an expectation that may well prove to be optimistic – and on continued public acceptance of the necessity for an incomes policy over a period of years rather than months. Research has shown that there are quite long time-lags between a lowering of the pressure of demand and a reduction in the rate of earnings increase, and also between lower earnings and lower prices. It is too early yet to judge whether present policies will succeed, but it seems certain that if they do not they will have to be replaced by even more stringent ones.

6

In the first chapter of this book we discussed the medieval concept of the 'just price' – the idea that there was some fair remuneration for services and some equitable price for goods determined, not according to market conditions, but by reference to some external principle of natural justice which assured the producer a comfortable livelihood and the seller a reasonable profit. In pursuance of such beliefs, the prices of some necessary goods were fixed nationally, and the wages of many classes of workers regulated by local or gild ordinances; at particular times of inflationary crisis, like 1351 and 1563, the government stepped in directly in attempts to peg wages and prices at their former levels. Such policies assumed that excessive earnings and prices were in some fundamental way wrong – that they were both contrary to the moral law enjoined by the Church, and to the prejudice of the order and good government of society.

There followed a period of perhaps 4 centuries during which such concepts were gradually abandoned in favour of the free operation of market forces. In the heyday of economic individualism in the eighteenth and nineteenth centuries it came to be believed that any interference with the free play of supply and demand was not only unnecessary but unwarrantable, that the wage-earner should be free to sell his labour in the dearest market and the employer equally free to hire his in the cheapest, that the seller should be allowed to demand whatever price he could get for goods of whatever quality he could sell, and that the interests of the consumer would be best served by encouraging the maximum degree of competition. Such views had been followed by all the great economists from Adam Smith to John Stuart Mill, who himself had said that 'Laissez-faire ought to be the general rule. Any departure from it, unless justified by some great good, is a certain evil.'

During the last 100 years the free market economy has been substantially eroded. Competition between producers has been modified by the development of monopolistic structures in industry, by mergers, cartels and trade associations which attempt to regulate and standardize prices over a wide sector of the economy. Similarly, the individual worker now rarely sells his labour in the open market, but through the negotiating machinery of his trade union with a particular employer or, more often, a whole industry. More significantly still, the state has intervened in innumerable ways between employer and employee and between buyer and seller – by legislation affecting, for instance, the contractual relationship between master and servant, the hours and conditions of work, the quality and description of goods. In some instances it has established machinery for the determination of minimum rates of pay, while through the Monopolies Commission it exercises the right openly to condemn those manufacturers who abuse their power by exploiting the public.

In the prices and incomes policy we are now witnessing a major extension in the apparatus of collective control. There is much in the current debate that is reminiscent of the medieval concept of the just price, for although the argument may be couched in the language of the economist, the social and even the moral overtones are audible enough. Social policy in Britain has hitherto been concerned mainly to establish 'minimum standards' in, for example, welfare or housing, and, more debatedly, 'equality of opportunity' in health and education. It may now be moving, perhaps unwittingly, into a much less defined area where the considerations are in reality about 'equity' and 'social justice'. In the Middle Ages the Church could offer its own definition of the principles of economic justice, as can the State in contemporary communist societies: what they should be in Britain in the second half of the twentieth century few have yet ventured to speculate. What seems clear in the present situation is a widespread determination not to return to 'free-for-all' conditions, and a recognition that some form of control over incomes and prices is a legitimate concern of the state. The real importance of the policies of the last few years is that they mark a radical departure from the past, and that for the first time in modern history we are attempting to control the monetary monster that we have created. We may yet be its victim, or its master.

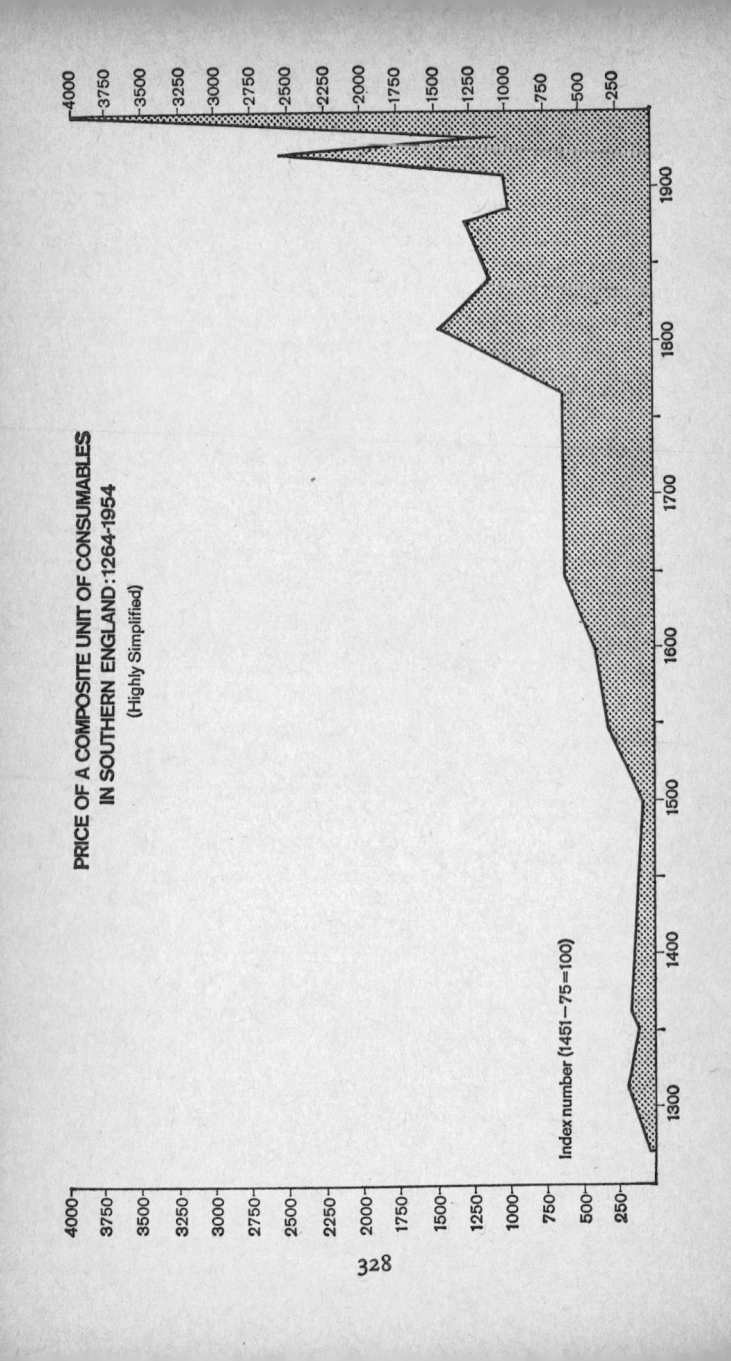

PRICE OF A COMPOSITE UNIT OF CONSUMABLES IN SOUTHERN ENGLAND: 1264-1954

(Highly Simplified)

Index number (1451-75=100)

Note on Further Reading

INNUMERABLE references to prices and the cost of living are scattered throughout literature, contemporary and modern. Original sources include manorial and estate accounts, household budgets, price courants and market reports, letters, diaries, autobiographies and reminiscences: parliamentary papers are, on the whole, lacking until quite recent times, although there are price regulations and ordinances, national and local, throughout the whole period. Secondary sources include the attempts that have been made, mainly during the last 100 years, to collect and interpret historical price data, as well as the many works on economic and social history which frequently include some discussion of changes in prices over a limited period.

The following is a selection only from what could be an extremely long list of authorities. 'General' references are to works which cover the whole, or most of, the period dealt with by this book: others are listed under the chapters to which they most appropriately belong. Many of the works cited contain extensive bibliographies.

GENERAL

Beveridge, Sir William, and others: *Prices and Wages in England*. Vol. I (1939)

Brown, E. H. Phelps, and Hopkins, Sheila V.: 'Seven Centuries of Building Wages', *Economica*, New Series, Vol. XXII, No. 87 (1955)

Brown, E. H. Phelps, and Hopkins, Sheila V.: 'Seven Centuries of the Prices of Consumables, Compared with Builders' Wage-Rates', *Economica*, New Series, Vol. XXIII, No. 92 (1956)

Davis, Dorothy: *A History of Shopping*, (1966)

Drummond, J. C., and Wilbraham, Anne: *The Englishman's Food. A History of Five Centuries of English Diet* (1939)

Fussell, G. E.: *The English Rural Labourer. His Home, Furniture, Clothing and Food from Tudor to Victorian Times* (1949)

Hamilton, Henry: *History of the Homeland* (1947)

Hasbach, W.: *A History of the English Agricultural Labourer*. Translated by Ruth Kenyon (1920)

Marshall, Dorothy: *The English Domestic Servant in History*. Historical Association General Series (1949)

Mitchell, B. R., and Deane, Phyllis (Eds.): *Abstract of British Historical Statistics* (1962)

Morgan, E. V.: *A History of Money* (1965)
Morgan, E. V.: *The Study of Prices* (1950)
Rogers, James E. Thorold: *A History of Agriculture and Prices in England*. 7 vols. (1866–1902)
Rogers, James E. Thorold: *Six Centuries of Work and Wages. The History of English Labour.* 2 vols. (1884)
Trevelyan, G. M.: *English Social History* (1944)

CHAPTER 1: THE MIDDLE AGES

Abram, A., etc.: *English Life and Manners in the Later Middle Ages* (1913)
Archaeologia: Miscellaneous Tracts (1844)
Barraclough, Geoffrey (Ed.): *Social Life in Early England* (1960)
Bennett, H. S.: *The Pastons and Their England. Studies in an Age of Transition* (1922)
Bennett, H. S.: *Life on the English Manor* (1956)
Collier, J. Payne (Ed.): *Household Books of John, Duke of Norfolk and Thomas, Earl of Surrey, 1481–1490*. The Roxburghe Club (1844)
Coulton, G. G.: *Social Life in Britain from the Conquest to the Reformation* (1918)
Farmer, D. L.: 'Some Grain Price Movements in Thirteenth Century England,' *Economic History Review*, Second Series, Vol. X (1957–8)
Hunt, Percival: *Fifteenth Century England* (1962)
Knoop, Douglas, and Jones, G. P.: *The Medieval Mason* (1933)
Labarge, Margaret Wade: *A Baronial Household of the Thirteenth Century* (1965)
Lipson, E.: *The Economic History of England*. Vol. I, *The Middle Ages*. 10th edition (1949)
Power, Eileen: *Medieval People*. 2nd edition (1925)
Riley, H. T. (Ed.): *Liber Albus* (Rolls Series, 1859–62)
Turner, H. T. (Ed.): *Manners and Household Expenses of England in the Thirteenth and Fifteenth Centuries*. The Roxburghe Club (1841)

CHAPTER 2: TUDOR AND STUART ENGLAND

Barley, M. W.: 'Farmhouses and Cottages, 1550–1725', *Economic History Review* (1954–5)
Barton, Elizabeth: *The Elizabethans at Home* (1958)
Bindoff, S. T.: *Tudor England* (1950)
Black, J. B.: *The Reign of Elizabeth* (1936)
Byrne, M. st. Clare: *Elizabethan Life in Town and Country* (1954)

NOTE ON FURTHER READING

Clapham, Sir John: *A Concise Economic History of Britain* (1957)
Cornwall, J.: 'The Early Tudor Gentry', *Economic History Review*, Vol. XVII, No. 3 (1965)
Emmison, F. G.: *Tudor Food and Pastimes* (1964)
Fisher, F. J.: 'Influenza and Inflation in Tudor England', *Economic History Review*, Essays in Economic History presented to Professor M. M. Postan, Vol. XVIII, No. 1 (1965)
Garside, B.: *People and Homes in Hampton-on-Thames in the Sixteenth and Seventeenth Centuries* (1956)
Gould, J. D.: 'The Price Revolution Reconsidered', *Economic History Review*, Vol. XVII, No. 2 (1964)
Harrison, M., and Royston, O. M. (Eds.): *How They Lived*. Vol. II, *An Anthology of Original Accounts written between 1485 and 1700* (1963)
Hartley, D., and Eliot, M. M.: *Life and Work of the People of England: The Seventeenth Century* (1928)
'Household Book of Edward Stafford, Duke of Buckingham', *Archaeologia*, Vol. XXV (1834)
'Household and Privy Purse Accounts of the Lestranges of Hunstanton, 1519–1578', *Archaeologia*, Vol. XXV (1834)
Hovinden, M. A. (Ed.): *Household and Farm Inventories in Oxfordshire, 1550–90*. (Historical Manuscripts Commission, JP 10, 1965)
Knoop, Douglas, and Jones, G. P.: *The Medieval Mason* (1933)
Mathew, David: *The Social Structure of Caroline England* (1948)
Quennell, M. and C. H. B.: *A History of Everyday Things in England*. Vol. II (1919)
Ramsay, Peter: *Tudor Economic Problems* (1963)
Richardson, W. C.: 'Some Financial Expedients of Henry VIII', *Economic History Review* (1954–5)
Rowse, A. L.: *The England of Elizabeth* (1950)
Simpson, Alan: *The Wealth of the Gentry, 1540–1660* (1961)
Stone, Lawrence: *Social Change and Revolution in England, 1540–1640* (1965)
Tawney, R. H., and Power, Eileen: *Tudor Economic Documents* (1924)
Thomson, Gladys Scott: *Life in a Noble Household, 1641–1700* (1937)

CHAPTER 3: THE EIGHTEENTH CENTURY

Ashley, W. J.: *The Bread of our Forefathers* (1928)
Ashton, T. S.: *Economic Fluctuations in England, 1700–1800* (1959)
Ashton, T. S.: *Changes in Standards of Comfort in Eighteenth Century England* (The Raleigh Lecture on History, British Academy, 1955)

A HISTORY OF THE COST OF LIVING

Blundell, Margaret (Ed.): *Blundell's Diary and Letter-Book, 1702–1728* (1952)
Chambers, J. D., and Mingay, G. E.: *The Agricultural Revolution, 1750–1880* (1966)
Davies, Rev. David: *The Case of the Labourers in Husbandry* (1795)
Deane, Phyllis: *The First Industrial Revolution* (1965)
Eden, Sir Frederic: *The State of the Poor* (1797)
George, Dorothy: *England in Johnson's Day* (1928)
Gilboy, E. W.: *Wages in Eighteenth Century England* (1934)
Hammond, J. L. and Barbara: *The Village Labourer* (1948)
Hammond, J. L. and Barbara: *The Town Labourer* (1948)
Hammond, J. L. and Barbara: *The Skilled Labourer* (1948)
Hutton, William: *The Life of William Hutton* (1816)
Lackington, James: *The Memoirs of James Lackington* (1792)
Mingay, G. E.: *English Landed Society in the Eighteenth Century* (1963)
Neale, R. S.: 'The Standard of Living, 1780–1844: A Regional and Class Study', *Economic History Review*, Vol. XIX, No. 3 (1966)
Plumb, J. H.: *England in the Eighteenth Century* (1951)
Plumb, J. H. (Ed.): *Studies in Social History* (1955)
Pressnell, L. S. (Ed.): *Studies in the Industrial Revolution* (1960)
Prior, James: *The Life of Oliver Goldsmith* (1837)
Stuart, D. M.: *The English Abigail* (1946)
Turberville, A. S. (Ed.): *Johnson's England* (1933)
Turner, Florence Maris (Ed.): *The Diary of Thomas Turner, 1754–1765* (1925)
Williams, J. E.: 'The British Standard of Living, 1750–1850', *Economic History Review*, Vol. XIX, No. 3 (1966)

CHAPTER 4: THE NINETEENTH CENTURY

Adburgham, Alison: *Shops and Shopping, 1800–1914* (1964)
Ashworth, W.: *Economic History of England, 1870–1939* (1960)
Barker, T. C., McKenzie, J. C. and Yudkin, John (Eds.): *Our Changing Fare: Two Hundred Years of British Food Habits* (1966)
Booth, Charles: *Life and Labour of the People in London* (1902)
Briggs, Asa, and Saville, John (Eds.): *Essays in Labour History, In Memory of G. D. H. Cole* (1960)
British Association for the Advancement of Science: *Report of 51st Meeting* (1882). Report of the Committee ... on the Present Appropriation of Wages [in the] United Kingdom
Burnett, John: *Plenty and Want. A Social History of Diet in England from 1815 to the Present Day* (1966)

NOTE ON FURTHER READING

Checkland, S. G.: *The Rise of Industrial Society in England, 1815–1885* (1964)

Clapham, J. H.: *An Economic History of Modern Britain*. 3 vols. (1939)

Clark, G. Kitson: *The Making of Victorian England* (1962)

Collier, Frances: *The Family Economy of the Working Classes in the Cotton Industry, 1784–1833* (1964)

Deane, Phyllis: *The First Industrial Revolution* (1965)

Eden, Sir Frederic: *The State of the Poor*. 3 vols. (1797)

Ffrench, Yvonne (Ed.): *News from the Past, 1805–1887. The Autobiography of the Nineteenth Century* (n.d.)

Gayer, A. D., Rostow, W. W. and Schwartz, A. J.: *The Growth and Fluctuations of the British Economy, 1790–1850* (1953)

Hobsbawm, E. J.: *Labouring Men. Studies in the History of Labour* (1964)

Hole, James: *The Homes of the Working Classes, With Suggestions for their Improvement* (1866)

Holme, Thea: *The Carlyles at Home* (1965)

Home Comforts: *A Book of Useful Hints for Housekeepers* (n.d.)

Laslett, Peter: *The World we have Lost* (1965)

Layton, Sir Walter T. and Crowther, Geoffrey: *The Study of Prices*. 3rd edition (1938)

Levi, Sir Leone: *Wages and Earnings of the Working Classes* (1885)

Lockhead, Marion: *The Victorian Household* (1964)

Mackinness, E. D.: *A Social History of English Music* (1964)

Marwick, Arthur: *The Deluge: British Society and the First World War* (1965)

Masterman, C. F. G.: *The Condition of England* (1909)

Memoranda: *Statistical Tables and Charts prepared in the Board of Trade etc* (Cd. 1761, 1903)

Memoranda, 2nd Series: *Statistical Tables etc* (Cd. 2337, 1904)

Mogg, Edward: *New Picture of London, or Stranger's Guide to the British Metropolis*. 4th edition (1841)

Nowell-Smith, Simon (Ed.): *Edwardian England, 1901–1914* (1964)

Pardon, George Frederick: *Routledge's Popular Guide to London and its Suburbs* (1862)

Pimlott, J. A. R.: *The Englishman's Holiday: A Social History* (1947)

Porter, G. R.: *The Progress of the Nation* (1847 edition)

Reader, W. J.: *Life in Victorian England* (1964)

Reeves, Mrs P.: *Round About a Pound a Week* (1913)

Rowe, Richard: *How our Working People Live* (n.d.)

Rowntree, B. Seebohm: *Poverty. A Study of Town Life* (1901)

Rowntree, B. Seebohm and Kendall, May: *How the Labourer Lives. A Study of the Rural Labour Problem* (1913)

A HISTORY OF THE COST OF LIVING

Smelser, Neil J.: *Social Change in the Industrial Revolution* (1959)
The Victorian Poor: *Fourth Conference Report of the Victorian Society* (1966)
Thompson, F. M. L.: *English Landed Society in the Nineteenth Century* (1962)
Wise, Dorothy (Ed.): *The Diary of William Tayler, Footman, 1837* (1962)

CHAPTER 5: THE LAST FIFTY YEARS

Ashworth, W.: *An Economic History of England, 1870–1939* (1960)
Burnett, John: *Plenty and Want. A Social History of Diet in England from 1815 to the Present Day* (1966)
Cole, G. D. H.: *Studies in Class Structure* (1955)
Cole, G. D. H. and Postgate, Raymond: *The Common People, 1746–1938* (1938)
Family Expenditure Survey: Report for 1957–9 (Ministry of Labour, 1961)
Family Expenditure Survey: Report for 1965 (Ministry of Labour, 1966)
Graves, Robert and Hodge, Alan: *The Long Weekend. A Social History of Great Britain, 1918–39* (1940)
Jefferys, James B.: *Retail Trading in Britain, 1850–1950* (1954)
Laslett, Peter: *The World we have Lost* (1965)
Layton, Sir Walter T. and Crowther, Geoffrey: *An Introduction to the Study of Prices* (1938)
Lewis, R. and Maude, A.: *The English Middle Classes* (1949)
Malnutrition in the 1960s: Office of Health Economics (1967)
Marsh, David C.: *The Changing Social Structure of England and Wales, 1871–1961* (1965)
Marwick, Arthur: *The Explosion of British Society, 1914–1961* (1963)
Method of Construction and Calculation of the Index of Retail Prices (Ministry of Labour, 1964)
National Income & Expenditure 1966 (The Blue Book, 1967)
Prest, A. R. (Ed.): *The U.K. Economy. A Manual of Applied Economics* (1966)
Prices and Incomes Policy (Cd. 2639, 1965)
Prices and Incomes Standstill (Cd. 3073, 1966)
Routh, Guy: *Occupation and Pay in Great Britain, 1906–1960* (1965)
Sampson, Anthony: *Anatomy of Britain Today* (1965)
Youngson, A. J.: *The British Economy, 1920–1957* (1960)

Index

Aberdeen, population in nineteenth century, 195

Abrams, Dr Mark, socio-economic grades, 296

Academies, nonconformist, fees and curriculum, 158

Acton, William, and prostitution in London, 234

Acts of Parliament: Beerhouse (1830), 212, 275; Companies (1861), 203; Navigation (1651), 82; Reform (1867), 205; Septennial (1716), 148

Adam, Robert (1728–92), 143

Agriculture: its practice in England, 10, 15, 55, 58, 101, 128, 138, 190, 290; payment for imported articles, 16; profit motive, 17, 20; obligations of villeins, 18–19; effect of Black Death, 19–20, 24, 41; inroads into great forests, 55; effects of inflation, 70–71; surplus productions in eighteenth century, 129; demands of increased population, 130, 139, 192; scientific improvements, 130, 192; effect of low prices, 134; the 'agrarian revolution', 192; declining economic importance, 193; demands of war, 202, 222; effect of Free Trade, 204; aristocratic dependence on, 221–2; conditions in nineteenth century, 222, 223. *See also* Farming

Ale: *see* Drinks

Allotment system, and improved diet, 266

America: emigration to, 187; food exports, 192; marriage with heiresses, 221

America, North, grain exports, 208

America, South: civil war, 202; food exports, 210, 211

Apprenticeship, as page in royal and noble houses, 38, 91

Architects: fees in Middle Ages, 41–2; become professional, 84; nineteenth-century, 225

Aristocracy: in Tudor and Stuart social structure, 72, 99; changing size and composition, 72–3; ownership of land, 73; average incomes and estates, 73–4; expenditure on servicing the household, 74–9, 80, 82–3, 142–4; practice of hospitality, 74; clothing, 74–5, 145–6; effect of price rises, 75, 139, 150; failure to adjust to change, 75–6, 99; industrial development, 76, 131; maintenance of social status, 76; construction of new houses, 83–4; social structure in eighteenth century, 139 ff.; territorial pinnacle, 140; new creations, 140–41, 221; numbers of peers, 141, 220; characteristics, 141, 220; great houses, 141; estate maintenance, 142–4; life of luxury and comfort, 144–5, 229–30; cost of furnishings, 146–7; education, 147, 228–9; recreations, 148–9, 229; cost of season in London, 155; position in nineteenth century, 195, 219–20, 223; claims to non-exclusiveness, 220; elevation of commoners, 221; range of incomes, 221; sidebenefits, 221, 222; marriage, 221; dependence on agriculture, 221–3, 231; erosion of predominance of,

INDEX

Aristocracy – *cont.*
223, 228, 231; high finance, 223; provision of domestic servants, 226–7; rule of primogeniture-227; provision for dependants, 227–8; cost of family events, 228; effect of taxation, 230–31; mounting attack on, 231; twentieth-century, 292, 293

Army: cost of (1588–1603), 67; soldiers' daily rations, 125; as a career, 154; opened up to competition, 228

Artisans: wage-rates, 22, 118–19, 122, 180–81; methods of retaining, 22–3; conditions of work, 23; Black Death and, 24; effects of inflation, 118; additional earnings, 121; diet in sixteenth and seventeenth centuries, 126–7; rising standards in eighteenth century, 139, 180–81

Artists, payment of, 27, 88, 146

Arundel, Earl of, debts to tailors in seventeenth century, 74

Ashbrooke, Robert, mercer, 102

Assizes: and food prices, 45, 53; of bread, 30, 138, 209; repeal of, 211

Atkinson, Thomas W. (1799–1861), 225

Australia: export of foodstuffs, 192, 210; use of refrigeration, 211; wool exports, 214

Bacon, Sir Nicholas (1509–79), Lord Keeper: purchase of land, 75, 101; cost of Queen's visit, 96; rise to prosperity, 101

Bailey, Captain, hackney coach, 97

Balance of payments: recurrent problem, 286, 287, 289; importance of increasing productivity, 290; affected by ability to export, 321

Bank of England, 172; suspension of cash payments, 202, 309; changes in bank rate, 314, 323

Banking and finance: developments in Tudor and Stuart age, 67; in eighteenth century, 138, 141; in nineteenth century, 190, 194, 202, 203; Jewish element, 233; opportunities of wealth and social mobility, 291

Baronets: social position in Tudor and Stuart age, 72; in eighteenth century, 141, 149; value of estates, 74

Bath, 149; labourers' wages in, 181–2

Baxter, Dudley, 293; division of national income, 219–20; numbers and wages of working classes, 247

Baxter, Richard (1615–91), on labourers' diet, 126

Beaumaris Castle, 23, 27; building workers employed, 25

Bedford, William Russell, Duke of (1613–1700): household expenses, 74, 78, 82–3; funeral expenses, 75, 78, 90; income, 78; coronation expenditure, 78; household staff, 78–9; tapestries, 86; re-equipping London house, 87; payments for portraits, 88; clothing expenditure, 80; education, 91, 92; grand tour, 93; cost of stabling, kennels, etc., 94, 97; expenditure on tobacco, 95; transport costs, 97–8; visit to Cambridge, 98; medical expenses, 99, 116; legal expenses, 115

Bedford family: Covent Garden development, 76, 78; wealth in eighteenth and nineteenth centuries, 140, 141, 221, 225; kitchen accounts, 143

Beer: *see* Drinks

Beeton, Mrs Isabella Mary (1836–65): picnic menus, 239; domestic servants, 241; *Book of Household Management*, 227

Berkeley estate, servants employed, 74

INDEX

Beveridge, W. H. Beveridge, Lord (1879–1963): Price and Wage History Research group, 7; prices paid by institutions, 61, 63

Bicester Church, fourteenth-century fees, 42

Birmingham: population figures, 171, 195; improved conditions, 187; Canal, 217

Birth control: in nineteenth century, 191, 285; effect on position and life of women, 285

Birth-rate, 191, 283

Black Death: inflation caused by, 19–20; effect on population, 19, 56; and wages and prices, 23–4, 51, 69, 127, 257, 320; precipitates a monetary economy, 24, 52

Blundell, Nicholas, Diary and Letter-Book, 152, 153, 181, 184

Board of Trade: cost of living inquiries, 265; consumption-patterns of skilled and unskilled workers, 268, 277

Books: cost of, in Middle Ages, 39; in Tudor and Stuart age, 91: used in tutoring, 91; popular editions, 244

Booksellers, eighteenth-century, 174–5

Booth, Charles (1840–1916): on footmen's wages, 227; family earnings, 253; working-class wages, 253; extent of poverty, 248, 258, 265, 275, 304

Bordars, 19

Bowley, A. L., 307; direction of wages in nineteenth and twentieth centuries, 254; and middle-class numbers, 292

Boyd Orr, Sir John Boyd Orr, Lord (b. 1880): undernourishment in the 1930s, 287–8, 305

Bradford, 171, 195

Bread: composition of, 10, 30, 48, 57, 105, 125, 177; index number, 12; cost of, in Middle Ages, 21; staple diet in all households, 30, 206; price-fixing, 45, 53, 209; price increases in sixteenth and seventeenth centuries, 62, 126; in wealthy households, 80; yeoman, 105, 108, 125; use of white flour in towns, 117–18, 125, 126, 177, 180; eaten by labouring class, 120, 125, 126; in the eighteenth century, 129, 135, 136, 138, 139; popularity of toast, 177; professional bakers, 208; size variations with price of wheat, 209; in working class diet, 273; changed expenditure on, 316

Brewing, 18; cost of, 21; and price stability, 211–12; competition in retail trade, 212

Bridgeman, Charles (d. 1738), and Houghton, 142–3

Bridgewater, Francis Egerton, Duke of (1736–1803), his Canal, 217

Brighton, 149, 216

Bristol: population in 1545, 56; labourers' wages in, 165; industries, 171; employment of women, 252–3

British Association for the Advancement of Science, wages inquiry (1881), 258–9

British Market Research Bureau, identification of social class, 295–6

Brown, E. H. Phelps: price-index, 7, 51–2, 60–61, 132–3, 307–8; index of wage-rates for building workers, 71, 255; real wages, 255, 256, 257, 297

Brummel, George Bryan (1778–1840), 149

Buckingham, Edward Stafford, Duke of (1478–1521): Christmas entertainment and consumption, 74; household accounts, 80–81

Buckinghamshire: landowners, 73; gentry, 101, 102, 151

Building industry: organization on capitalist basis, 26; cost of under-

337

INDEX

Building Industry – *cont.*
takings, 26–7; payments to builders, 44; craftsmen's wage-rates, 71; employment of Italian and German artists, 83; labour costs in sixteenth and seventeenth centuries, 84, 86; wage-rates, 118–20; in eighteenth century, 181, 183; decline in masons' standards of living, 120; housing investment, 218; increased costs in nineteenth century, 242; fall in real wages, 255; increased numbers in twentieth century, 290; lowering of wage differentials, 304

Buildings: medieval expenditure on, 25–6; cost of upkeep, 26; use of brick and stone, 84, 160; cost of materials, 84; by private individuals, 85; eighteenth-century, 129, 187

Burghley, William Cecil, Lord (1520–98): and the currency, 66; income, 73; palaces, 74; cost of Queen's visits, 96

Bury House of Correction, dietary, 125

Busby, Richard (1606–95), headmaster of Westminster, 92

Caernarvon Castle, 22; cost of building, 26
Caister Castle, 28, 29–30
Cambridge, 98
Cambridge University: medieval fees, 38; journey from London, 46; expansion in sixteenth and seventeenth centuries, 85; cost of attending, 92, 147; aristocracy and, 229; Caius College, 85; King's College, 119; St John's College, 85; Trinity College, 85
Canals: development in eighteenth century, 131, 158, 177, 190; in nineteenth century, 215–16; transport of coal by, 217
Candles, 35–6, 43, 307; price of, 77–8, 104

Canning, introduction of corned beef, 210
Canterbury, medieval rents, 45
Capitalism: medieval building trade and, 26; replaces cooperation, 57, 59; Tudor price-rise and, 68–9; gentry and, 100; trade cycles, 198; nineteenth-century manufacturers, 232; twentieth-century, 288
Carême, Antoine (1784–1833), wages as chef, 227
Carlyle, Thomas (1795–1881) and Jane (1801–66), income and household expenses, 235–6, 241, 242
Carrier service, 97
Caxton, William (?1422–91), 39
Ceylon tea, 213
Chadwick, Sir Edwin (1801–90), 280
Chandos, James Brydges, Duke of (1673–1744), 140, 147; his wealth, 150–51
Charity: in Middle Ages, 40, 46; by merchant class, 110–11; dependence of poor on, 123
Charles II (1630–85), 87; coronation, 78, 90; dress, 88
Chartist Movement, 205, 207
Chaucer, Geoffrey (?1340–1400): income as building administrator, 42; his pilgrims, 45–6, 49; his Poor Widow, 47, 48
Cheese Riots, 136
Cheshire, agricultural wages, 250
Chester, wage-assessments in 1590s, 122
Chester, Sir Thomas, of Knole Park, 154
Chichester Cathedral, cost of windows, 27
Child, Sir Josiah (1630–99), his wealth, 109
Child, Robert, his house and goods in 1582, 107
Child-birth, cost of, 174, 187
Children: wage-rates in Middle Ages, 18, 22; toys, 38; clothing in sixteenth and seventeenth cen-

338

INDEX

turies, 90; increased employment, 121, 122; position in eighteenth century, 142; earnings at farm tasks, 166; employment in 'sweated' trades, 179; cost of boarding paupers, 185; family size in nineteenth century, 239, 243–4; cost of bringing up, 243, 244; employment in textile trade, 251, 252; numbers in poverty, 258; as wage-earners, 262, 263; cost of burial, 280; increased survival rate, 283; diet deficiencies in large families, 305. *See also* Education

China, tea, 213

Chippendale, Thomas (d. 1779), 146

Chocolate: *see* Drinks

Church: festival holidays, 23, 50; expenditure on buildings,; 25 education in Middle Ages, 38; taxation by, 39, 40; charity, 40; road to preferment, 41, 42; fees for offices, 42–3; code of mercantile ethics, 52–3, 326, 327; breach with Rome, 58, 83; decline of charitable bequests, 111; social status, 114; wealth of bishoprics in eighteenth century, 140; as a career, 150, 172; increasing rewards, 172; fall in value of real incomes, 298

Churchyard, Thomas (?1520–1604), 62

Cider: *see* Drinks

City of London: Court of Aldermen and price of meat, 81; Companies, 110, 111; attempts to specify wages (1538), 119

Civil service: opened up to competition, 228; real income in, 228; salary cuts, 310

Clare, Bogo de, pluralist cleric, 37, 40

Clarendon Place, Wilts., repair of, 26

Clark, G. Kitson, *Making of Victorian England*, 234

Clarke, Dr John (1582–1653), 97

Clarke, Sir William Bee, his goods, 103

Clergy: stipends and livings, 42, 114, 150, 172, 298; a professional class, 114; standard of living, 114; typical vicarage, 114–15; pluralism, 150, 172; eighteenth-century parsonages, 160, 172; curates' pay, 172; as private tutors, 228; decreased numbers, 295; fall in real income, 298

Clerical occupations: increased numbers employed, 291, 293, 294, 299; causes of growth, 294; variations in earnings, 299

Clerk of works, 26–7; income in Middle Ages, 41, 42

Cloth: export of, 23, 57; purchase of, 28; imports, 34; financial rewards, 41; price control, 53; flourishing industry, 58; variations in size and quality, 63; price increases, 63; increased trade in Tudor period, 66

Cloth of gold, 34

Clothing: cost of, in Middle Ages, 21, 33–5, 49; in eighteenth century, 145–6; and social status, 33, 34; use of fur, 34; employment of tailors and seamstresses, 34; expenditure on, 43; of medieval peasant, 48–9; scale of quality, 49; materials used, 49, 89–90, 145; of the nobility, 49, 89, 90; elaboration in Tudor times, 57, 74–5; wealth and extravagance in sixteenth and seventeenth centuries, 88–9; of the gentry, 103, 151; of yeomen, 107; of working classes, 125, 136, 186–7, 278–9; cost of, in eighteenth century, 145–6; new tastes, 129, 145; of agricultural labourers, 169; regional variations, 169; 'ready-made' shops, 173, 243; use of 'slop-shops', 186; fall in price in nineteenth century, 214–15, 243; use of cotton, 214–15; middle-class expenditure, 242–3; effect of mechanization,

339

INDEX

Clothing – *cont.*
243; bought on credit, 278–9; price of articles, 279

Clothing villages, 59

Coal: increased use by industry, 64, 217; for household heating, 77, 104, 135; price of, 135, 217–18; effect of weather on supply, 138; in working-class budgets, 186; increased production, 191; universal fuel, 217, 218; transport of, 217; duty on sea-borne, 217

Coalminers: increased wages, 251, 257; declining numbers, 290; wage-cuts, 1921–2, 310

Coalmining: development in seventeenth century, 56, 59; in eighteenth century, 135, 165; in nineteenth century, 251; and agricultural wages, 165; declining productivity, 218; employment of women and children, 252; depression and unemployment in twentieth century, 284, 287

Coffee: *see* Drinks

Cogan, Thomas (?1545–1607), at Oxford, 93

Coinage: medieval, 17; debasement, 52, 65–6, 67; clippers and counterfeiters, 66; introduction of milling, 66; recoinage in seventeenth century, 66–7; the mark, 17; pound, 17, 66; shilling, 17; silver penny, 17, 65–6

Coke, Thomas William, Earl of Leicester (1752–1842), Norfolk estates, 130

College of Physicians, foundation, 42

Colonialism: beginnings of, 58–9; in eighteenth century, 138; acquisitions, 190

Common lands: *see* Enclosure

Communications: in Middle Ages, 16, 28; developments in nineteenth century, 190–91, 196, 215–16, 291; mechanization, 294

Companies, joint-stock, 203

Company employees: increase in real wages, 298–9; range of earnings, 299

Complete Servant (1825), 226

Consumer goods: price-index for Middle Ages, 51–2; increasing demand for, 56, 191; increase in range in eighteenth century, 132; eighteenth and nineteenth centuries price-indices, 133, 198, 199, 200–201; quantity and price changes, 202; short supply in second world war, 308–9; changed pattern of expenditure, 316–19

Conway Castle, cost of building, 26

Cook, Thomas (1808–92), and foreign travel, 245

Copyholders: acquisition of demesnes, 20; 'fine' or 'gressom' on entry, 63; rent increases, 64

Cork, Earl of, expenditure on interior decoration, 86

Corn: price fluctuations in Middle Ages, 50–51; in fifteenth and sixteenth centuries, 67, 68; export control, 69; relation between its price and wages, 71

Corn Laws: repeal of (1846), 192; and price of wheat, 207–8, 209; and farmers, 222

Cost of living: universal concern, 9–10; and occupational changes, 10–11; index numbers and, 13; effect of Black Death, 20; in Middle Ages, 20–21; in sixteenth and seventeenth centuries, 60–62, 82; eighteenth-century, 132, 178; nineteenth-century, 214, 235, 239–40; twentieth-century, 60, 61, 311, 315–16; increases due to expenditure changes, 132; increase in, for great estates, 224–5; elements affecting, 282, 286; and inflation, 302; table of indices since 1906, 306–8, 311–14; fall in wholesale prices and, 310; wage variations and, 322

340

INDEX

Cottars, 19

Court, the: aristocracy and, 72; medical attendants, 98

Coventry, its destitute, 123

Cowper, William (1731–1800), 156

Crabbe, George (1754–1832), 159

Craftsmen: exclusion from medieval middle class, 41; code of ethics, 52–3; and price-rises, 118; wage-rates, 119, 304; in eighteenth century, 180–81; survival into nineteenth, 193; working-class élite, 253

Credit: relationship to prices, 202, 203; government restrictions, 323

Crimean War, 228, 236, 256

Cromwell, Oliver (1599–1658), 80; Navigation Act, 82

Cromwell, Thomas, Earl of Essex (?1485–1540), 72; income, 73

Crown, the: sources of revenue, 39–40, 65–6, 67; renounces privilege of coining, 66; monopolies, 67; aristocracy and, 72; building work, 84–5; royal visits, 96, 225; the gentry and office under, 100, 104

Cullum, Sir Thomas (?1587–1664); rise to prosperity, 111; household expenses, 111–12

Cumberland, agricultural wages, 250

Cumberland, George Clifford, Earl of (1558–1605), privateering by, 76

Currency: effect of changes on prices, 11, 66; debasement by Henry VIII, 66; devaluation, 66; reissue, 66; hoarding of gold, 202; its volume and price changes, 202, 203; issue of paper money, 308, 309; government withdrawal, 309; devaluation of pound, 323

Customs duties: to maintain armed forces, 67; on spirits, 129; French wines, 145; due to Napoleonic Wars, 202

Cuxham, Oxon., 17–18, 43

Dance, George (1741–1825), 225

Davies, Rev. David (d. ?1819): on changes in food prices, 1750–94, 137; and the poor, 163, 186; agricultural income, 165, 167; labourers' budgets, 167, 186–7

Death-rate: *see* Mortality rates

Deer: preservation of, 55; break up of parks, 94, 148

Deflation, 302; and price-rises, 308; government policy against price-fall, 309; favours salaries and fixed incomes, 310, 321

Defoe, Daniel (?1661–1731), 177; on vails, 122; English poor, 163; shopkeeping, 173–4

Derby estate: household expenses, 1561, 74; expenditure in 1914, 225

Derbyshire, agricultural wages, 164

Devonshire, Dukes of, 155, 221

Diet: of medieval poor and prosperous, 45, 47; deficiencies in town diet, 117; relationship to family size, 305; social class and, 305

Doddington, George Bubb, Baron Melcombe (1691–1762), 140; purchase of Eastbury, 142; income and expenses, 142; election expenses, 148

Dorset, Duke of, staff at Knole in fifteenth century, 143

Dover Castle, 41; wine ration during siege, 32

Doylye, Mrs Katherine, her wealth, 102–3

Drink: expenditure on and family budgets, 264–5, 267; and poverty, 274

Drinks: *Ale*: variations in price, 31; price-fixing, 45, 53; in working-class diet, 48, 135; in yeomen's diet, 108.

Beer: increased consumption in seventeenth century, 82, 83; in eighteenth century, 139, 180; in working-class diets, 135, 180, 274; prices in nineteenth century, 211,

341

INDEX

Drinks—*cont.*
212; declining demand, 211; adulteration, 212; retail competition, 212; as recreational drink, 212.

Chocolate, 82.

Cider: prices in Middle Ages, 31; in working-class diet, 48; in aristocratic houses, 83; in yeomen's diet, 108.

Coffee, 79, 82; price of, 83; use of in eighteenth century, 129, 132.

Spirits: customs duty on, 129; gin-drinking, 129, 179–80; consumption in eighteenth and nineteenth centuries, 139, 274.

Tea, 10, 79; social habits and, 14, 82, 212; price of in seventeenth century, 82, 83; in nineteenth century, 204, 212–13; use of in eighteenth century, 129, 132, 135, 145, 163–4, 180, 212; retail trade, 173, 174; in competition with beer, 211, 212; drunk by all classes, 212; duty on, 212–13; new sources of supply, 213; world price-war, 213; branded packets, 213–14.

Wine: purchase of in Middle Ages, 28; drunk by all classes, 31–2; import of, 32, 79; variation in prices, 32, 82; at banquets, 33; in aristocratic households, 83, 145; appearance of champagne, port and brandy, 83; cost of, 113; consumption in eighteenth century, 145

Drunkenness: in eighteenth century, 152, 156, 158–9, 163; 'gin-mania' in London, 179; among nineteenth-century working classes, 274; cause of 'secondary' poverty, 274

Dunning, Richard, and labourers' wages, 162–3

Durham Priory, food consumption in Middle Ages, 32

Earnings: changes in spending habits, 10–11; setback in real value in twentieth century, 205; lowest group in nineteenth century, 205; differences in skilled and unskilled workers, 291; changes of value for different occupational classes, 297–302, 303; common factors in periodic increases, 302; narrowing of differentials between skilled and unskilled, 303–4; effect of pressure of demand, 315. *See also* Wages

Earnings and Hours Inquiry (Wage Census), 1906, 253–4

East, the: import of silks from, 34 89; sea routes to, 82; trade with 109

East Anglia: 'clothing villages', 59; broadcloth, 63; farming, 156; agricultural wages, 164

East India Company, 172; foundation, 58–9; import of tea, 82, 212; interest payments, 109

Eating and drinking: by eighteenth-century aristocracy, 144–5; the gentry, 153–4; nineteenth-century middle classes, 239; in hotels and restaurants, 246. *See also* Drink, Food, Meals

Eden, Sir Frederick Morton (1766–1809), and state of the poor, 163, 164, 167, 169, 186–7, 212

Education: in Middle Ages, 38–9; endowments, 46; cost of school uniforms, 90; cost of materials, 91; of noblemen's children, 90–92; in eighteenth century, 142, 147; of girls, 148; of the gentry, 154; in nineteenth century, 228, 244; and drinking, 275; and social class, 295; increased expenditure on, 302; spread of, 304

Edward, Prince (later Edward I) (1239–1307), yearly income, 25

Edward III (1312–77): Household Ordinances, 33; falconers, 37; revenue, 40

INDEX

Edward IV (1442–83), Black Book, 33

Edward VI (1537–53), 106–7; Prayer for Landlords, 63

Egerton, Sir Thomas, Lord Ellesmere (?1540–1617), cost of Queen's visit, 96

Eldon, John Scott, Earl of (1751–1838), fees as Lord Chancellor, 140

Elizabeth I (1533–1603), 73; trade recession, 65; issue of new currency, 66; prices and incomes policy, 69; expenditure at Court, 80; extravagant clothes, 88, 89; cost of royal visits, 96; travelling retinue, 96

Emigration, cost of, 187

Enclosure: movement, 58, 63; yeoman farmers and, 106; increase in eighteenth century, 130, 140; connexion with rising grain prices, 134; and land ownership, 140; gentry and, 150; loss to commoners, 166; dispossession by, 169–70; completion in nineteenth century, 192, 222

Engels, Friedrich (1820–95), 75; and working-class clothing, 215; condemns capitalism, 255–6; *Working Classes in England in 1844*, 256

England: *Edwardian*: middle-class expenditure, 238; its luxuries, 239; employment of domestic servants, 240; rents, 242; expenditure on dress, 242; movement of 'real' wages, 255, 257; period of stationary wages and rising prices, 257; widespread social unrest, 257; revelations of poverty, 267.

Eighteenth-century: a society in transition, 128; extremes of wealth and poverty, 128, 185; increase in national income, 128–9; flourishing economy, 129–31; price-indices, 132–3; end in poverty and famine, 133, 138, 188; rise in food prices, 137; causes of price fluctuations, 138; social structure, 139 ff.; improvement in manners, 153, 156, 180; growth of shops, 173; terraced housing, 176; narrowing wage differentials, 183.

Medieval: occupations and expenditure, 10; 'natural' economy, 15; manorial system, 15–16; currency, 17, 52; land values, 17; incidence of Black Death, 19–20, 23–4; public expenditure on building, 25–7; use of creative artists, 27; feasting and banqueting, 33; methods of travelling, 36, 45–6; rise of middle classes, 45 ff.; variations in standard of life, 45; living conditions of peasants, 46–50, 54; slow rise in prices, 50 ff.; economic regulations, 53; comparison with modern life, 54; concept of a 'just price', 69, 326, 327; price- and wage-fixing, 326.

Nineteenth-century: inheritance of social evils, 179; reliance on overseas producers, 190, 192; industrialization, 190; revolutionary developments, 190–91; price-indices, 198; first setback to industrial predominance, 203–4; cost of education, 244; movement of real wages, 255–6; 'Great Depression', 256, 310; increase in real earnings, 257; development of mass production, 292.

Northern: effect of Industrial Revolution, 131, 183, 195, 284; rising wage-rates, 183; diet in eighteenth century, 186; agricultural wages, 250; lower cost of living, 261–2; depression and unemployment, 284.

Tudor and Stuart, 15; the manor house, 27; medieva. characteristics, 55; pursuit of farming, 55; division by river Trent, 56; increasing population, 56; belief in spending wealth, 57, 67, 69, 74;

INDEX

England – *cont.*

economic changes, 57; its 'industrial revolution', 59; inflation, 60–62, 65, 67, 68, 69, 306; contemporary comments on, 62; rent increases, 63–4; causes and results of price rises, 64, 65–9, 72; alleged acquisition of gold, 65; results of inflation, 69, 70–71, 127; wage-assessments, 70; social structure, 72 ff.; reputation for good food, 79–80; indoor and urban pastimes, 94–6; new mobility, 97; yeomen, 105, 107; rise of middle classes, 109; housing improvements, 113; unemployment problems, 123; destitution, 127.

Twentieth-century: rise in cost of living, 60, 61; price changes, 204; social and industrial unrest, 205, 246–7; middle-class expenditure, 238, 239; abandonment of self-denial, 238; expenditure on domestic servants, 240; and the smaller family, 244; far-reaching changes, 282; becomes an urban society, 283–4; attraction of London and south-east, 284; state of prosperity, 286; slowing down of industrial development, 286–7; changes in social structure, 290 ff.; numbers in poverty (1900), 304; scale of price fluctuations, 306 ff.; existing differences in incomes, 319; importance of price-control, 322.

Victorian: material and technological advancement, 53–4; foundations of her pre-eminence, 189; power of middle classes, 194; problems of town-dwellers, 195–6; height of her power, 203; social structure, 219; basis of wealth, 231–2; family-mindedness, 243–4; beginnings of family limitations, 244; social unrest and doubt, 246; working class, 247; movement of real wages, 255; years of acute depression, 256

Entertainment: indoor, 37–8; in sixteenth and seventeenth centuries, 94–6. *See also* Recreation and sport

Eresby, Lord of, household in Middle Ages, 28

Essex, Robert Devereux, Earl of (1566–1601), at Cambridge, 93

Estates: *Ecclesiastical*: marketing of goods, 16; sale of by Henry VIII, 58, 67.

Landed: marketing of goods, 16; their accounts, 17; equipping and running in Middle Ages, 17–18; effect of Black Death, 19–20, 41; complex administration, 28; wool tax, 40; decrease in private parks, 55; basis of social privilege, 72, 73; average value, 73; provisioning and servicing in sixteenth and seventeenth centuries, 74; self-sufficiency, 79, 80, 104, 117, 144; the gentry and, 100, 224; acquisition by merchants, 110; cost of domestic servants, 117; value in eighteenth century, 141; expenditure on purchases, etc., 142–3; cost of staffing, 143–4; effects of industrialization, 195; dependence on rent, 221; improved management, 222; fall in income, 223; varying patterns of expenditure, 224, 225 ff.; rule of primogeniture, 227–8; burden of dependent relatives, 227–8; probate and estate duties, 231

Europe: inflation in sixteenth century, 60; shortage of precious metals, 65; business houses, 109; import of wheat from England, 129; Grand Tour of, 147; demands on industry in nineteenth century, 202; middle-class travel and, 245

Exeter: population in 1545, 56;

INDEX

rebuilding the Guildhall, 85; its destitute, 123

Expenditure: variations between past and present, 10–11; relationship to cost of living, 132; class variations in patterns, 219, 224; apportionment according to income, 226; changing patterns today, 316–19; increase in 'luxuries', 318; movement towards middle-class patterns, 319; variations between 'rich' and 'poor', 319–20

Exports: value in 1565, 57; increased by cheap money, 66; expansion in eighteenth and nineteenth centuries, 129, 191; in twentieth century, 287, 289; dependence on competitive costs, 321

Factory system: home in the North, 134; replaces home industries, 178; effect on hand-trades, 248; acceleration in nineteenth century, 255, 291

Factory-workers: rising standards in eighteenth century, 139; semi-skilled workers, 251; individual and family earnings, 251–3; hierarchy of skills and wages, 252; increases in nineteenth century, 256; housing, 276

Falconry: cost of, 37, 94; gives place to shooting, 94

Family Expenditure Survey: household accounts, 1965, 317–18; differing patterns of consumption by income-group, 319–20

Famines, 47–8, 51, 135, 138

Farmers: tenant, income in Middle Ages, 20–21; cost of living, 21–2; rise of middle classes, 41; rent increases, 63; yeoman class, 105–7, 155; range of acreage and incomes, 155–6; progress towards gentility, 156–7, 160; travel, 157; standard of life, 158 ff.; housing improvements, 159–60; separation from servants, 159; furnishings, 160; daily life, 161; average income, 162; aristocratic dependence on, 221–2

Farming: cost of in Middle Ages, 18; unchanging characteristics, 55; pursuit for individual gain, 55; wool prices and, 63; inflation and, 101; effect of Enclosure Acts, 130; prosperity in eighteenth century, 130, 140; effect of low prices, 134; new techniques, 140, 192, 222; movement of cattle to market, 177, 210; world-wide reputation, 192; regional variations in decline, 223; changing importance of, 290. *See also* Agriculture

Fastolf, Sir John (?1378–1459): at Caister Castle, 28; cloth of gold gowns, 34; tapestries, 36

Fens, drainage of, 55–6, 76, 78

Feudal system: market towns and, 16; after Black Death, 20; taxation under, 39; its decline, 55

Fielding, Henry (1707–54), his Squire Weston, 152

Fielding, Sir John (d. 1780), and 'gin-mania', 179

Fiennes, Celia, on an apothecary's house, 116

Firebrace, Sir Harry, inventory of goods (1543), 103

Fiscal policy, and the hereditary rich, 231

Fisher, Irving, 'compensated dollar' plan, 323

Fishing industry, decline in numbers, 290

Fitzwilliam, Earl: expenditure in nineteenth century, 226; funeral, 228; stabling, 230

Food: salting in Middle Ages, 31; expenditure in middle-class budgets, 43, 177–8, 235–8, 239–40; professional specialists, 45, 67; price-fixing, 45, 69, 81, 312; rise

H.C.L.—16

345

INDEX

Food – *cont.*

in price, 62, 120; expenditure in aristocratic households, 79, 80, 82–3, 143–5; increase in luxuries, 79–80, 83, 256; expense of importing, 81; and social status, 82; the gentry and, 104–5, 153–4; of yeoman class, 108; the townsman and, 117; increasing refinement 118; Free Trade and, 192; new tastes in eighteenth century, 129; cheap and plentiful, 133; price of and standard of living, 137; dependence on weather, 138; of farmers, 159, 161; of labourers' families, 167; of the poor, 167, 185–6; regional variations, 167–8, 186; adoption of French cooking, 177–8; price changes in nineteenth century, 203, 204, 205, 237–8; expenditure in twentieth century, 237, 238; working classes and, 260–64, 265; adulteration, 268; diet deficiencies, 271; price-fall during depression, 311; changed pattern of expenditure, 316, 317, 318, 319–20.

Dairy produce, 82, 83, 136, 138; transport by rail, 216.

Eggs: consumption in Middle Ages, 29, 31, 48; in working-class diets, 136.

Fish: Lenten consumption, 29, 30; purchase of, 29; in diet of poor, 45, 48; in aristocratic houses, 79, 80, 83, 144, 145.

Fruit: consumption in Middle Ages, 29, 31, 45; in aristocratic houses, 81, 82, 83; import in eighteenth century, 136, 145.

Meat: cost of, in Middle Ages, 21, 30; in eighteenth century, 133, 136, 138; in nineteenth century, 204, 210; salting of, 30; working classes and, 48, 126, 136, 210; in Tudor England, 79; in aristocratic houses, 80, 81, 82, 83; yeomen and, 108; consumption in eighteenth century, 177, 178, 185; lack of standard price, 209–10; cost of transport, 210; import of, 210–11; effect of refrigeration, 211; middle-class expenditure, 240; working-class expenditure, 260–64, 265, 273.

Poultry, 30, 45, 48, 80, 81, 82, 83, 108.

Salt, 29, 45.

Spices, 29–30, 31, 33, 45, 79.

Sugar, 13, 31, 33, 79, 81, 82, 144, 180, 204.

Vegetables, 48, 82, 125, 135, 136, 138, 144, 178

Forests, depletion by agriculture and industry, 55, 64, 148

Fountains Abbey, purchase of, 85, 100

France: wars with, 23–4, 58, 198; imports from, 32, 34; sixteenth-century population, 56; state of inflation, 60; her 'noblesse', 72; tapestries from, 86; eighteenth-century labouring classes, 129; increase in gross domestic product, 289

Franchise, extension of, 222

Free Trade, 191, 210, 326; demands from industrialists, 231; erosion of its principles, 326–7

Freeholders: yeomen, 106, 155; voting rights, 155; land ownership and numbers, 155; household goods, 160

Froissart, Jean (*c.* 1333–*c.* 1405), *Chronicles*, 91

Furniture: in medieval houses, 35–6; beds, 35, 36, 50, 87, 113, 117; of the peasantry, 49–50, 169; in great mansions, 85–8, 146; of the gentry, 102–3, 151, 154; farmhouse, 107, 160; merchant class, 112, 113; of the poor, 124; new elegance in eighteenth century 129, 145, 146; use of mahogany,

INDEX

129; working-class, 136, 280–81; price of, 146; retail trade in, 173; middle-class, 176–7, 242

Gainsborough, Thomas (1727–88), 146, 229
Game Laws, strengthened, 94
Gaming and gambling: in fifteenth and sixteenth centuries, 95, 179; losses from, 148; working-class budgets and, 264, 265, 267, 275
Gardiner, Stephen (?1483–1555), Bishop of Winchester, 101
Gentry, landowners, 73, 75, 76, 101, 102, 149, 150; increased income, 76, 150; cost of servicing the household, 77; shift of power to, 99–100; basis of social claims, 100; methods of acquiring wealth, 100, 104, 150–51; division between Court and country, 100; range of wealth, 102, 149–50, 224; value of estates, 101–2; numbers, 102, 149, 224; possession of chattels, 102–3; contrasts within the class, 103–5, 149; in the eighteenth century, 141, 149; use of grammar schools, 147, 154; diverse origins, 149; characteristics, 149, 224; source of unearned income, 149; social position, 149; effect of price changes on, 150; choice of profession, 150; administration of their estates, 151–2; uncultured survivals, 152; improved manners, 152–3; housing improvements, 153; education, 154; twentieth-century land ownership, 293
George, Duke of Clarence (1449–78), 36; riding household, 37
Germany, 65; rising power in nineteenth century, 204, 244; adopts gold standard, 204; increase in gross domestic product, 289
Gibbon, Edward (1737–94), 147
Giffen, Sir Robert (1837–1910), 204; working-class wages and advancement, 253, 258
Gilds: taxation of members, 39; control of boroughs, 41; wages and prices, 53, 326; decay of, 59; apprenticeship premium, 110
Girdlestone, Canon Edward (1805–84), 170
Gladstone, William Ewart (1809–98), and tea prices, 213
Glasgow, population in nineteenth century, 195
Glass: price in Middle Ages, 27, 44, 47; increased use of, 44, 84, 113
Glasse, Hannah (*fl.* 1747), 144–5
Gloucestershire, agricultural wages, 164
Gold: supplies from New World, 65; inflation in Tudor times, 65; relationship to price changes, 202; restriction in world supplies, 202; discoveries in California and Australia, 203; demand outstrips supply, 204; dwindling output, 204; increased supply from South Africa, 204–5
Gold standard, 11; departure from and restoration, 202, 309, 310, 312; adopted by Germany, 204; first world war and, 308; international currencies and, 323
Goldsmith, Oliver (1728–74), 145
Gould, J. D., 'The Price Revolution Reconsidered', 61
Governments: concern with cost of living, 9; attempts to freeze wages, 19–20; and course of wages and prices, 52, 68; demands in nineteenth-century war years, 202; control by middle classes, 231–2; successive post-war policies, 288; expenditure on social services, 302, 314; stabilize prices, 312, 320–21, 322; anti-inflationary measures, 323–6; restraint on wages and prices, 324–6

347

INDEX

Grand Tour: private tutors and, 93, 116; cost of, 147

Great Britain: change from agricultural to an industrial society, 190, 192; increase in productivity, 191; ceases to be self-sufficient, 192; trade cycle in nineteenth century, 196; set-back to industrial predominance, 203–4; loss of world trade, 204, 287; standard of living in 1900, 257; increased numbers of dependants, 283; 'rich' and 'poor' regions, 284; change in population movements, 284; state of full employment, 285; paradoxical economy, 286; loss of leadership, 286; position in 1930s, 287–8; 'new industrial revolution', 288; poor export figures, 289; change to a manufacturing economy, 290; four phases in her industrial system, 291–2; 'class' society, 292; changing social structure, 292 ff.; extent of contemporary poverty, 304; period of cheap money, 312

Gresham, Sir Richard (?1485–1549), 100

Gresham, Sir Thomas (?1519–79): his wealth, 103, 110; College foundation, 111

Greville, Sir Fulke (1554–1628), at Shrewsbury, 91

Grosvenor, Lord, expenditure on horse-racing, 148–9

Halfpenny, William (d. 1752), *Useful Architecture*, 160

Hamilton, Henry, 68

Hampton Court: building costs, 85; labourers' wages, 118

Hanway, Jonas (1712–86): and tea-drinking, 163–4; food of the poor, 167, 185

Hargreaves, James (d. 1778), spinning-jenny, 182

Harington, Sir John (1561–1612), water-closet, 84

Harlech Castle, cost of building, 26

Harrison, William (1534–93), *Description of England*, 57, 79, 89; on yeomen, 106; merchant class, 109; composition of bread, 125

Harrogate, in eighteenth century, 149

Harvests, 133; and price movements, 138, 196, 201; and wages, 164, 182

Health insurance, 280

Henley-on-Thames, 18, 41

Henry III (1207–72), 21, 34

Henry IV (1367–1413), 37, 44

Henry V (1387–1422), 34

Henry VI (1421–71), 34

Henry VII (1457–1509), 33

Henry VIII (1491–1547): acquisition of monastic wealth, 58; debasement of coinage, 65–6; supplying his palaces, 78; building programme, 85

Hepplewhite, George (d. 1786), 146

Hertfordshire: wage-assessments, 70; agricultural wages, 164

Heyward, Rowland, sixteenth-century estate, 110

Hire purchase system: and clothing, 278–9; post-war restrictions, 314, 323

Hogarth, William (1697–1764), 146

Holidays: medieval, 23; working-class, 281

Holland, Henry Fox, Lord (1705–74), 151

Holland, Robert (d. 1568), day labourer, household goods, 124–5

Holme, Randle (1627–99), on furnishings, 87–8

Horse: used by all classes, 36, 45–6; cost of maintenance, 36, 37, 78, 94, 229–30; and war, 37; replaced by coach-travel, 96–7; middle classes and, 235, 236, 237, 241

Horse-racing, cost of, 148, 229–30

Hospitals: building of, 187; pro-

348

INDEX

vision of infirmaries, 280; outpatients departments, 280; Bethlehem, 215; Chelsea, 215; St Thomas's, 216

House of Commons: election costs, 148; gentry and, 149; peers and, 220

House of Lords, monopolized by peers, 141, 148, 220

Housing: increase in comfort and elegance, 44; variations in rent, 44; demands on forests, 55; development in sixteenth and seventeenth centuries, 83 ff.; changes in internal construction, 84; cost of building materials, 84; for the clergy, 114–15; developments in eighteenth century, 129, 153, 159; urban overcrowding, 179; in nineteenth-century towns, 195, 218; shortages, 218–19; charitable trusts, 218, 276, 278; increased cost since second world war, 316, 319

Howard, Sir John (later Duke of Norfolk) (?1430–85): purchase of cattle, 28; food consumption, 32–3; cost of clothing materials, 34; recreation expenses, 37–8; clothing gifts, 49

Howard, Lord William (1563–1640), household expenses, 76–7

Hull, population in eighteenth century, 171

Hunting, cost of, 37, 93–4, 148, 229, 230

Husbandmen: distinguished from yeomen, 105, 107; price-rise and, 107; clothing, 125

Hutton, Catherine (1756–1846), 154

Hutton, Matthew (1529–1606), Archbishop of York, at Cambridge, 92–3

Hutton, William, 175, 185

Ibstone, Bucks., 18–19

Imports: increase in nineteenth century, 192, 208, 210; enemy blockade and, 201; and farm prices, 223; and volume of national product, 289–90; restrictions, 323; foodstuffs, 129, 208, 210, 223; paper, 39; silks, 34; wine, 32; wool, 214

Income: price level and, 9, 20; rise in eighteenth century, 138; growth of 'moderate' sector, 220; and number of servants, 241; a determinant of social class, 295–7; narrowing of differentials, 297, 313; effects of taxation, 302–3; manual workers, 313; contemporary variations and expenditure patterns, 319–20

Income tax: increases in, 231, 303; middle class, 236, 238; 'People's Budget' (1909) and, 247; and income levels, 303

India, imports from, 208, 213

Individualism, 57, 326

Industrial Revolution, 129; origins of, 131, 190; and low prices, 134; working-class standards, 179, 189; creation of factory-worker, 180; productivity, 189, 191; an evolutionary process, 190; and population increase, 192; social changes due to, 192, 194–5; trade cycles, 197; new occupations, 232, 251; ultimate benefits from, 248, 255; northward movement of population, 284

Industrialists: acquisition of land, 140, 223; elevation to peerage, 221

Industrialization: movement towards, 138; and agricultural wages, 165–6; and working-class standards, 178–9, 189; effect on occupational structure, 193, 290; and working-class skills and earnings, 194–6; effect on food supplies, 196; trade cycles, 196–7; social structure, 219, 247; new

INDEX

Industrialization – *cont.*
  demands on manpower, 232; its casualties, 249; wage-rates, 255
Industries: domestic, 120, 178; development of, 121; wage-rates, 182; in textile trade, 251
Industry: competition for labour, 22, 193; depletion of forests, 55; search for wealth in, 57–8; development in Tudor and Stuart age, 58, 109; use of coal, 64; Tudor price-rise and, 68–9; investment in, 76, 106, 130–31; surplus production, 129; technical innovations, 131; working-class standards, 178; eighteenth-century wage-rates, 181; Victorian pre-eminence, 189; response to mechanization, 190; Continental demand, 202–3; 'Great Depression' (1874), 203–4; pre-first world war expansion, 205; working-class élite, 253; areas of high wages, 253–4, 257; twentieth-century depression, 284, 289; measurement of output (Lomax Index), 286–7; new post-war outlets, 288; effect of mass production, 292; new discoveries, 292; increased specialization, 294; unrest caused by high prices, 309, 322; programme of expansion, 309; wage-cuts agreements, 310
Infant mortality: decline in, 128, 191, 280; percentage in 1900, 25; in twentieth century, 283
Inflation: caused by Black Death, 19–20, 326; in sixteenth and seventeenth centuries, 60–62, 65, 67, 68, 69; effects of, 69–71, 127; urban wage-earners, 71, 118–19; food prices, 81; yeoman, 106–7; merchants 109; domestic service, 121; effect of wars, 202, 255; in twentieth century, 208, 286, 302, 308, 314, 321; classes favoured by, 302; and price-rises, 308, 309; failure to solve, 314; causes of, 315; government efforts to check, 320, 323; and the individual, 322; and national survival, 322; suggested remedies, 322–4
Inns: provision of meals, 98, 157; small turnover and high profits, 113; cost of food and lodgings, 157, 178; use of by middle classes, 178
Inns of Court, 115, 147
Inventories, evidence from, 110, 112, 124, 160, 168, 280
Ireland, Northern, wage-rates, 284
Iron and steel industry, 55; new processes, 59; use of coal, 64; aristocracy and, 76; technological advances, 131; prevalence of labour élite, 254; poverty among workers, 265; depression and unemployment, 284, 287
Isabella de Fortibus, income, 25
Italy, 34; population in sixteenth century, 56; increase in gross domestic product, 289

Jenkyns, Soame (1704–87), 188
Jevons, William Stanley (1835–82), and price-control, 322
Jewel, John (1522–71), Bishop of Salisbury, 62
Jewellery, 34, 90, 146
Jews, and banking and finance, 233
John of Evesham, wages in 1359, 23
John of Gaunt, Duke of Lancaster (1340–99), almsgiving, 40
Johnson, Samuel (1709–84), 184; London house, 176; taste in food, 178
Jones, Inigo (1573–1652), 84; and Woburn Abbey, 86

Kemble, Sarah (1755–1831), 184
Kenilworth Castle, 28; cost of, 85
Kent: enclosed farms, 55; broadcloth, 63; agricultural wages, 164, 165, 250
Kent, Nathaniel (1737–1810), mode cottages, 170

350

INDEX

Kent, William (1684–1748), and Houghton, 143

Keynes, John Maynard, Lord (1883–1946), on Tudor price-rise, 69

King, Sir Edmund (1629–1709), Court physician, 115–16

King, Gregory (1648–1712): estimates of peerage, 72–3, 74; the gentry, 102, 149; yeomen, 106; trading class, 114; paupers, 123, 162, 163, 248; temporal and spiritual lords, 140; freeholders, 155; labouring people, 162; classification of population, 1688, 171

Kingston, Duke of: Grand Tour 147; London stay, 155

Kneller, Sir Godfrey (1646–1723,) 88

Knoop, Douglas: price-index for food, 1500–1702, 61–2; *The Medieval Mason*, 120

La Rochefoucauld, Francois de, and English manners, 152–3

Labour: deterioration in economic position, 68; concept of a 'just price', 69, 326; low cost in sixteenth century, 84, 86; failure to keep up with price-rise, 118; 'Golden Age' in eighteenth century, 132; mercantilist interest in cheapness, 162; areas of poverty, 180; range of earnings and culture, 180–83; increased specialization, 193; social mobility, 257; scarcity in some fields in 1940s, 289; change from manual to 'white-collar' occupations, 291, 294; effect of mass production on, 292; redistribution between 1911 and 1951, 293–4; collective bargaining, 327

Labourers: *Agricultural*: under manorial system, 15–16; fines for non-attendance, 19, 38; effect of Black Death, 19–20, 24; methods of retaining, 22–3; in a bargaining position, 24; emoluments, 119; additional earnings, 120, 121, 160, 261; diet in sixteenth and seventeenth centuries, 125–6; effect of enclosures, 130, 166, 168; price fluctuations, 139; percentage of population, 162, 248, 249; average income, 162; uncertain standard of life, 163, 164–5; varying standards of comfort, 165–8; housing, 166, 167–70, 276, 277; household budgets, 167, 261–3; indebtedness, 167, 168; possessions, 168–9; factors influencing real earnings, 250; cost of living estimates, 265, 266; improved diet, 265–6, 274; preponderance of bread, 273; increase in real earnings, 1906–60, 301.

Semi-skilled: increasing numbers, 250; wages and areas of work, 250–53; household budget, 250–51, 263; increase in real earnings, 300–301; changes in rank and order, 301.

Skilled: wage-assessments and, 70; wage-rates, 118–19, 180–81, 253; working class élite, 253, 300; changed occupations in twentieth century, 253–4; household budgets, 259–60, 263–4; varying patterns of expenditure, 268; opportunities for higher grades, 292; increase in real earnings, 1906–60, 300, 302; changes in rank and order, 300; narrowing differentials, 309.

Unskilled: wage-rates, 21–2, 118, 181–3; and poverty, 180; occupational groups, 248, 253; social mobility, 257; household budgets, 261–2; varying patterns of expenditure, 268–9; menu of meals, 270; diet deficiencies, 271; increase in real earnings, 1906–60, 301, 302; improved security, 304

Lackington, James (1742–1815), 174–5, 185

INDEX

Lancashire: wage-rates, 165, 181, 250; textile industry, 25, 252; household budget, 260–61; rate of growth, 284

Land: uncleared state, 16; values in Middle Ages, 17; new attitude towards ownership, 55, 57, 58; rising values, 67, 72, 140, 142; basis of aristocratic privilege, 73, 141; and the acquisition of wealth, 100, 140; the gentry and, 101–2, 104, 149–50; accumulation by yeomen, 106; improved cultivation, 130; increased rents, 130; concentration in fewer hands, 140, 141, 150, 155, 195, 220; and social status, 141; middle-class cultivation, 155; ownership in Victorian period, 220; in twentieth century, 293; fall in investment in, 223; rise in urban value, 276, 277

Landlords: complaints against, 63–4; imposition of 'fines', 64; failure to raise money for war, 64; inflation and, 70, 100–101; Enclosure Acts and, 130; investment in industry, 130; effect of industrialization, 195, 222

Lane, William, merchant, value of goods (1522), 102

Langland, William (?1330–?1440) on the medieval peasant, 48

Latimer, Hugh (?1485–1555), sermon' of the plough', 106–7

Law: sure road to wealth, 41, 115, 140, 220; and Tudor food prices, 69; and wage-rates, 70; capitalist techniques, 100; a professional class, 114; status, 115; as a career, 115, 150; in eighteenth century, 171, 172; increase in real value of incomes, 298

Leases: 'fine' or 'gressom' for renewal, 63; adjustment to price changes, 64

Leeds: population, 171, 195; textile manufacturers, 232; cost of building land, 276; housing rents, 277, 278

Leicester, medieval rents, 45

Leicester, Earl of (c. 1532–88): income, 25; household, 28; feeding and provisioning, 29, 31; consumption of wine, 32; bed covers, 35; almsgiving, 40; archers' clothing, 49; clothing costs, 74; funeral costs, 75; entertaining the Queen, 80, 96

Lely, Sir Peter (1618–80), 88

Lestrange family (sixteenth-century): wax candles, 77–8; household accounts, 81; clothing expenditure, 89; guests, 96

Levi, Leone (1821–88): and weekly wage-rates, 253; working-class mobility, 258

Lighting: by candles, 35–6, 43, 77–8; of baronial rooms, 77; gas, 244

Lincolnshire, 107, 124

Lipton, Sir Thomas (1850–1931), 213–14

Literature: Tudor and Stuart reading, 91–2; farmers and, 156; in Victorian age, 244–5; subscription libraries, 245

Liverpool: population, 171; improved conditions, 187

Llanrwst Wood, cost of felling, 27

Lloyd-George, David Lloyd George, Earl (1863–1945), 1909 budget, 231, 247

Local authorities, and housing, 218, 219, 276, 278, 314

Local government: county elections, 155; nineteenth-century reforms, 223; gentry and, 229; rates, 231; organization of county councils, 231

Loder, Robert, farm accounts 1610–20, 106

Lomax Index of physical production, 286–7

Lombe, Sir Thomas (1685–1739), fortune, 171, 175

352

INDEX

London: a market town, 16, 156; wage-rates, 22, 118, 119, 120, 181, 182–3, 284; population, 25, 56, 110, 170; 'farm rent', 39; medieval housing, 44; housing rents, 44–5, 176, 186, 242, 277, 278; medieval endowments, 46; growth in importance, 56, 109, 110; effect on economy of south-east, 58; redevelopment after Great Fire, 77, 85; travelling in, 97; inns, 98, 113; wealth of merchants, 109; destitute population, 123; gin-drinking, 129; food prices, 136; social and political life in eighteenth century, 141, 148; commission agents, 151; cost of accommodation, 152, 154, 230; shopkeepers, 172; middle-class housing, 175–6; food supplies, 177, 210, 216; new buildings, 187; development of suburbs, 216, 242; coal supplies, 217; nineteenth-century slums, 218–19; its season, 230; Victorian amusements, 245; numbers in poverty, 258; magnetic effect on labour, 284. *See also* City of London

Lonsdale, Earl of (1857–1944), 225–6

Lord of the manor, 19, 20

Luke de Lucca (*fl.* 1256), Henry III and, 34

Manchester: 'new towns', 171; textile wages, 182; improved conditions, 187–8; population growth, 195; Engels and, 215; slums, 218; rents, 264, 278

Manor houses: in Middle Ages, 27–8; complex administration, 28; feeding and provisioning, 28–31; consumption of fish, 30–31; home-produced food, 31; sample menus, 32; furnishings, 35–6; lighting, 35–6; wall-hangings, 36; gold and silver plate, 36; stabling 36; recreations and sports, 36–8;

fall in aristocratic ownership, 76; conversion into grander homes, 83; new designs, 84; improvements, 153

Manorial system: its 'natural' economy, 15; regional variations, 15; position of labourers, 15–16; target of self-sufficiency, 16; 'imported' goods, 16; marketing of goods, 16; profit-motive, 17–18; tenants' obligations, 18–19; use of money, 19; effect of Black Death, 19–20, 24

Mansions, town and country: in sixteenth and seventeenth centuries, 83–4, 85–7; furnishings and decorations, 85–8, 146–7; entertainment of guests, 96; servants' wages, 121; in eighteenth century, 129; open to public, 223; cost of building, 225, 230; improvements to, 225; essential domestic servants, 226; Audley End, 74, 84, 85, 143; Bedford House, 87; Belvoir, 87, 226, 230; Eaton Hall, 225; Fonthill Abbey, 225; Gorhambury House, 225; Haddon Hall, 84; Hellesdon House, 36; Holdernesse House, 230; Holkham, 222; Houghton, 142–3; Ingatestone, 77, 86, 94–5, 119, 121; Kenilworth, 225; Kirby Muxloe, 27; Knewsley, 225; Knole, 143, 225; Longleat, 84, 230; Lowther, 225–6; Melbourne House, 230; Milton, 222; Montacute, 84; Penshurst, 83; Redgrave Hall, 85; Somerset House, 85; Stratton Park, 225; Syon House, 74, 85, 143; Theobalds, 96; Tottenham House, 225; Verulam, 85. *See also* Woburn Abbey

Manufacturers and manufacturing: beginnings of capitalism, 59; 'outwork' system, 59; inflation and, 71; lowered cost of goods, 133; rise to wealth, 171, 232;

353

INDEX

Manufacturers and manufacturing – *cont.*
  advantage from lowered prices, 203; Britain's labour force, 193; largest occupation, 290; decreased numbers employed, 290–91, 292

Marriage: acquisition of wealth through, 141, 142, 152, 221; dowries for, 228; lower middle classes and, 234; working women, 291

Marshall, Alfred (1842–1924): salary at Bristol University, 233; family house, 242; and fall in prices, 322

Marx, Karl (1818–83), 75, 189

Mary, Princess (later Queen) (1516–58), and gaming, 95

Mass production, 134; of furniture, 136, 245, 281; cotton cloth, 215; application to industry, 292; instrument of change, 315–16

Massie, Joseph (d. 1784), 163

Mayhew, Henry (1812–87), 210

Meals: in noble households, 80–81, 144–5; townsmen and countrymen, 117; of gentry, 153; middle class, 239–40; working class, 270, 272, 273; breakfast, 48, 118, 144, 153, 185; dinner (midday), 48, 105, 118, 144, 153–4, 185; (evening), 118, 239; supper, 48, 105, 144, 153, 185; tea, 177

Mechanization: and clothing manufacturing, 215; creates an urbanized society, 291

Medical profession: status and fees, 42, 98–9, 108, 172, 187; payments to apothecaries, 98, 99, 108, 116, 172; lack of standard of competence, 116; as a career, 150; cost to working class, 280; numbers, 1911–51, 295

Merchants: rise of, 109; range of incomes, 109–10, 112, 141, 171–2; houses, 110, 112, 113; control of civic life, 110; separation from trading class, 110; entrance requirements, 110; charitable bequests, 110–11; acquisition of wealth, 111–12; value of personal goods, 112, 113; clothing, 114; land, 140

Micklethwaite, Sir Joseph (1612–82), physician, 116

Middle classes: beginnings of, 41–3; expenditure, 43; tea-drinking, 82; rapid rise, 109, 171; in Victorian England, 194, 195, 231–2; numbers and occupations, 232, 233; tier of classes, 232–3; social mobility, 233, 238; range of incomes, 233; lower limits, 234; effect of technology, 234–5; household budgets, 235–8; social orientation and imitation, 238; expense of domestic servants, 240–41; dress, 242–3; family-mindedness, 243–4; education, 234; beginnings of discontent, 246; dependence on working class, 247; condemnation of poor, 274; contemporary size, 292, 294; origin of 'decline', 313.

  Rural, 155–62; characteristics, 155; land ownership, 155; range of properties and incomes, 155–6; travel, 157–8; standard of life, 158–62; domestic servants, 183–4.

  Urban: wealth, 171; range of earnings, 171–2; social mobility, 172, 174–5; growth of shopkeepers, 173–4; household budget, 174; eating habits, 177–8; effects of Industrial Revolution, 194

Middlesex, 164, 183

Midlands: effect of Industrial Revolution, 131, 178, 195; coal-fields, 135, 171; its western region, 284

Mill, John Stuart (1806–73), and laissez-faire, 326

Monasteries: medieval buildings, 25; meals, 32; schools, 38; alms-giving, 40; dissolution, 58; sale of lands, 58, 67

INDEX

Money: effect on prices, 11; lack of abstract value, 13; in Middle Ages, 15, 46; commutation of labour for, 19, 20; growth of foreign trade and, 23–4; effect of Black Death, 24; medieval peasant and, 46, 47; becomes basis of economy, 52, 65; agricultural labourer and, 166; changes in value in twentieth century, 297; effect of dear and cheap money on industry, 310, 312; belief in intrinsic value, 322–3; modern effort to control, 327

Money, L.C.: and national income, 220, 248; lower middle-class income, 234

Monopolies Commission, 327

Moody, Sir Henry, Bt, 74

Moore, Rev. Giles, cost of bed (1656), 117

More, Sir Thomas (1478–1535), 91

More, Sir William, and Loseley Hall, 85

Morison, Fynes, 97

Moritz, Karl (1756–93), in England, 157–8, 178

Mortality rates: from 'sweating sickness', 68; decline, 128, 191–2, 243, 283; of children, 179; exceed births, 185. *See also* Infant mortality

Motor-car: and suburban development, 284; expansion in industry, 287

Motoring: expenditure on, 10, 317; beginnings of, 217

Municipalities: and endowments, 46; and course of wages and prices, 52, 53; public buildings, 85

Music: development in Tudor and Stuart England, 94–5; cost of instruments, 95; mass production and, 245

Musicians and minstrels, payment of, 37–8, 94–5

Napoleonic Wars: fall in prices after, 197, 198, 201; economic results, 202, 255; and landed interest, 222; inflation during, 255

National economy, 183; increased productivity in nineteenth century, 190–91; slowing down in twentieth, 286–7, 321; cyclical fluctuations, 289; increase in gross domestic product, 289; change from agricultural to urbanized labour force, 291; state of nearly full employment, 292, 303, 321

National income: distribution among classes, 219–20, 233, 235, 248; inter-wars rise in, 287; rise in value per head, 287; greater equality in division, 293

National Prices and Incomes Board: duties, 324; 'early warning system', 325; policy, 325–6

Navy: expenditure, 1588–1603, 67; position of surgeon, 116; Victualling Dept, 125

Nef, J. U., 59; and Tudor price-rise, 69

Netherlands: and England's cloth trade, 66; tapestries from, 86

Neville, Richard, Earl of Warwick (1428–71), cost of page's apprenticeship, 38

New Doomesday Survey (1873), 220, 224

New Zealand, import of foodstuffs from, 210, 211

Newcastle, Duke of, wealth in eighteenth century, 140

Newcastle upon Tyne: 'sea-coal', 64, 77, 135, 138; colliers' wages, 181; and London's coal, 217; coal prices, 217; shipowners, 232; employment of women in coal-mining, 252; rate of growth, 284

Newgate Gaol, 40; building of, 22

Newspapers: increased circulation, 156; popular press, 245

Nobility: incomes in Middle Ages, 24–5; clothing materials, 34, 49;

INDEX

Nobility – *cont.*
stabling, 36–7; taxation, 39–40; almsgiving, 40; Strand palaces, 57; position in Tudor and Stuart social structure, 72, 100; changing composition and number, 72–3; average value of estates, 73; cost of servicing households, 76–7; church building, 85; town and country mansions, 85–8; silver plate, 86; children's education, 90–92; patrons of literature, 91; universities, 92–3; transport problems, 97; medical expenses, 98–9; distinguishing characteristics, 100; eighteenth-century peerage, 141; expenditure on building, 224–5; leisure, 229; town houses, 230. *See also* Aristocracy

Northampton, population, 171

Northamptonshire, agricultural wages, 164

Northumberland, wages, 250, 251

Northumberland, Algernon Percy, Duke of: nineteenth-century fortune, 221; cost of reconstructing Alnwick Castle, 225

Northumberland, Henry Percy, Duke of (1502–37), household expenses, 76

Northumberland Household Book, 32

Norwich: medieval rents, 45; population (1545), 56; building operatives, 121; destitute population, 123; market centre, 171

Norwich, Earl of, small estate, 73

Nottingham, 46; Wollaton Hall accounts, 81; working-class diet, 135, 136; cheese riots, 136; wage-rates, 182; population, 171

Nottingham, Daniel Finch, Earl of (1647–1730), purchase of estate, 142

Nottinghamshire: yeomen, 107; inventories, 124

Occupations: changes in, 10; changed structure due to industrialization, 193–5, 232; grouping by numbers and earnings, 248; in contemporary Britain, 290–92; major determinant of social class, 292; at 1911 and 1951 censuses, 293–4; largest increases in earnings, 301–2

Ogilby, John (1600–1676), *Book of the Coronation*, 91

Ogle of Catherlough, Viscount, small estate, 73

Oldham, percentage above poverty line, 268

Ordinance of the Cooks, and food prices, 45

Overstone, Lord, wealth in nineteenth century, 220

Oxford, 113; carrier service, 97; labourers' wages, 165

Oxford University: cost of Merton bell-tower, 26; medieval fees, 38; fines, 38; income of Fellows of Oriel, 42; expanding colleges, 85; cost of, 92, 147; foundation of St John's College, 111; Wadham College (masons' wages), 119; aristocracy and, 229

Oxfordshire: household inventories, 102, 124; shopkeepers, 113–14

Panton, Mrs J. E., *From Kitchen to Garret*, 239–40

Paper, cost of, 39

Parker, Matthew (1504–75), Archbishop of Canterbury, income and expenditure, 75

Parliament: and use of gold cloth, 34; and Game Laws, 94; lengthened life (1716), 148; entrance by pocket boroughs, 148; right to report proceedings, 156–7; participation by gentlemen, 229

Paston, William (1378–1444), rise to fame, 25

Paston family, 25, 27, 29, 36; at

356

INDEX

Oxford, 1470, 39; match-making, 41

Pawnbrokers, for clothing, 279

Peasants' Revolt (1381), 20; provoked by poll tax, 40

Peel, Mrs C. S., middle-class budgets, 237

Pepys, Samuel (1633–1703), 95; breakfast and dinner dishes, 118

Percival, Thomas (1740–1804), on Manchester, 187–8

Peter the Mason, worker in alabaster, 27

Petre, Sir William (?1505–72), 78, 87, 91, 92; household staff, 77, 104; daughter's clothing, 89; hawking, 94; payments to entertainers, 94–5; guests, 96; cost of a royal visit, 96; medical expenses, 98–9; style of living, 104–5

Pharmacy, 98–9, 116, 172

Philippa of Hainault, Queen (?1314–69), her bed, 36

Pitt, William (1759–1806), creation of peers, 141

Place, Francis (1771–1854), and working-class standards, 180

Politics: aristocratic monopoly, 139, 141, 220; possession of land and, 140; cost of entering, 148; the gentry, 149, 150; extension to working class, 223; militant Labour and, 257

Poor: clothing in Middle Ages, 33; educational facilities, 38; diet, 45, 125–6, 164; new category, 71–2; at public schools, 92; relief of by charity, 111, 123; low standard of life, 123–7; and fluctuating prices, 138, 139; rural numbers, 162; calculations concerning, 162–3; percentage of total population, 163; rising standards in eighteenth century, 180; conservative habits, 185–6; 'economic' rents, 218; beginnings of social reform, 246–7; Speenhamland System of relief, 256; factors governing diet, 274; public houses, 275; changed numbers in twentieth century, 293; contraction in lowest levels, 297; improved diet, 305–6

Poor Law: necessity for, 123; sums disbursed, 123; in eighteenth century, 162, 167, 187

Population: effect on supply of currency, 11, 52; distribution and increase in Stuart period, 56, 67; pressure on resources, 67, 122–3, 196, 201–2; cause of price revolution, 67–8; and unemployment, 122–3; increase in eighteenth century, 128, 130, 133, 139, 191; rapid expansion in nineteenth century, 191–2; influx into towns, 195; increase in twentieth century, 282–3; reduction in working age group, 283; disposition between town and country, 283–4; change in proportion between direct production and 'tertiary' occupations, 292; changes in age groups, 305

Porter, G. R., expanding wealth of middle classes, 234–5

Portland, William Cavendish, Duke of (1800–1879), wealth and eccentricity, 225, 226

Portman, Sir William, Bt, 74

Postal service, 216

Postyman, George, Bishop of Winchester, 228

Poverty: increased incidence, 71, 255; public attitude to, 72; due to low wage-rates, 122, 123, 127; in eighteenth century, 133, 185; concentration in certain classes, 180; areas of greatest numbers, 248, 251; outward movement of working classes, 256–7; numbers existing in, 258; revelations of extent, 267; 'primary' and 'secondary' levels, 267, 274; problem of submerged third, 267–8; part

357

INDEX

Poverty – *cont.*
played by drink, 275; extent in contemporary Britain, 304–6, 319; caused by old age, 304, 305; increase in large families, 305. *See also* Poor

Prices: effect of changes in level, 9; regional variations, 12, 13; effect of Black Death, 19, 20, 23–4, 51, 52; rise in Middle Ages, 50, 51, 52; construction of price-index, 51–2; stability in fifteenth century, 59–60, 65, 69; rapid rise in sixteenth and seventeenth centuries, 60–64, 65, 118, 119, 306; outstrip wages, 67, 118, 127; policy of relating wages to, 69–71; relative stability in eighteenth century, 131–3, 136, 137–9; relationship to Industrial Revolution, 134; fluctuations in nineteenth century, 196–9, 201–5; determined by volume of gold and goods to be bought, 202; relationship to social discontent, 205; effect of changes on real wages, 254, 255–7; contemporary importance, 290, 322; rise since 1914, 306 ff.; periods of change, 308, 311–13; outstrip wages during inflation, 309; fall during depression, 309, 311; wage-cuts, 309–10; breakdown of price-rise for 1954–64, 314; main influences on, 315; government control of, 320, 324–5; movements in this century, 321; influence of unemployment, 324; attempts to regulate, 327

Prices and incomes policy, 9; under Elizabeth I, 69; background of present policy, 289; main issue in domestic politics, 306; social and moral considerations, 327

Professional classes: entry to 'bourgeoisie', 41; payment of, 41–4; membership, 114–17; demands of industrialization, 193, 194; use of public schools, 244; in twentieth century, 290, 291, 294, 295; opportunities in wealth and social mobility, 291; changed order of constituents, 294–5; increase in real earnings, 297, 302; average earnings, 297–8; variations in fortune, 298–9; fall in earnings, 310

Public institutions: diets provided by, 125, 126–7, 168; prices paid by, 133–4, 214–15; prisoners' clothing, 186

Public office: and acquisition of wealth, 100, 104, 140, 142, 150, 171, 172, 175; demands of administrative side, 193–4

Puritans, and Court expenditure, 80

Railways: and unification of social life, 97, 190; development in nineteenth century, 190, 197, 203, 208; food and passenger transport, 210, 216; funeral trains, 228; effects on communications, 291

Recreations and sport: in Middle Ages, 37–8, 94; of the peasantry, 50; of wealthy in sixteenth and seventeenth centuries, 93–6; card playing, 95; in eighteenth century, 148–9, 157; of nineteenth-century 'gentlemen', 229; the London season, 229, 230; of Victorian middle class, 244–6; the public house, 275. *See also* Entertainment

Refrigeration, and import of meat, 211

Rent: *Housing*: for agricultural workers, 166; middle-class, 175–6; working-class, 186, 218, 269, 276, 277–8; in nineteenth century, 218–19, 242, 276; proportion of gross national income, 219; in London, 260; regional variations, 277–8, 316; post-war, 316.

INDEX

Land: yields in Middle Ages, 17–18, 19, 130; payment by villeins, 19; regional and amenity variations, 44–5; in sixteenth and seventeenth centuries, 62, 63–4, 101; in eighteenth century, 130, 141

Reynolds, Sir Joshua (1723–92), 146

Rich, Barnaby (?1540–1617), and tobacco trade, 95

Richard II (1367–1400), 37

Richard, Earl of Cornwall (1209–72), income, 24

Richardson, Samuel (1689–1761), on extravagant women, 132

Richmond and Lennox, Duke of, his estate, 73

Roads, 27, 36, 96; improvements due to Industrial Revolution, 131; in eighteenth century, 157, 177, 190

Rogers, James E. Thorold (1823–90), 7, 61, 63, 126; and medieval peasant, 48; his 'Golden Age', 53; and urbanization, 54; relationship between food and wages, 120; labourers' wages, 164

Rotherham, Thomas (1423–1500), Archbishop of Canterbury, school foundation, 43

Routh, Guy, 7; cost of living index, 1906–60, 307, 308, 309, 310, 311, 313–14

Rowntree, Seebohm (1871–1954): concept of 'servant-keeping' class, 234, 237; and numbers in poverty, 248, 258, 265, 304; 'poverty line', 267–8; expenditure on drink, 275; working-class rents, 278; clothing allowance, 279; credit, 280

Rundle, Mrs Maria (1745–1828), middle-class budgets, 236–7, 240, 241, 242, 243

Rural population: and spending, 11; in sixteenth and seventeenth centuries, 55; degree of self-sufficiency, 117; diet, 117; day wage-rates, 119; payment in kind, 119; in eighteenth century, 156–62; nineteenth-century housing and rents, 277; decline, 277, 283–4

Russell, John, Earl of Bedford (?1486–1555), drainage scheme, 56

Rutland, landowners, 101, 102

Rutland, Duke of, cost of coming of age, 1799, 228

Rysbrach, John Michael (?1693–1770), and Houghton, 143

St Albans, Francis Bacon, Viscount (1566–1626), cost of Verulam, 85

St Augustine's Abbey, Canterbury, cost of lead roof, 27

St Swithin's monastery, food consumption, 32

Savernak, William, household expenditure, 43

Savery, Thomas (?1650–1715), use of steam power, 59

Schoolmasters: status, 116; salaries, 116–17, 172; second employment, 172

Schools: *Boarding*: for girls, 147; fees in eighteenth century, 158; lack of prestige, 229.

Grammar: foundation, 111; masters' salaries, 116, 172; gentry and, 147, 154; middle classes and, 158, 244; curriculum, 158.

'*Petty*', 92.

Private: wider curriculum, 158; middle classes and, 244.

Public: new foundations, 92; aristocracy and, 147; reformation in nineteenth century, 229; middle classes and, 244; Charterhouse, 114; Eton, 2, 84, 93, 116–17, 142, 147, 229; Harrow, 92, 229; Merchant Taylors, 92; Oundle, 116; Repton, 92; Rugby, 92; Shrewsbury, 91; Uppingham, 92; Westminster, 64, 77, 90, 92, 135, 154; Winchester, 38, 42, 63, 78, 84, 92, 121

INDEX

Scotland: effect of Industrial Revolution, 195; wage- and unemployment-rates, 284

Seaside resorts: development of, 149; railways and, 216; middle-class predominance, 245; working-class holidays, 281

Select Committee Report on the Rate of Agricultural Wages (1824), 250

Serfs: under manorial system, 15, 36; become rent-paying copyholders, 20; payment for manumission, 39

Servants, domestic: in Middle Ages, 23; furniture for, 35; clothing, 49, 89, 90, 121; for estates in sixteenth and seventeenth centuries, 74; roles and remunerations, 76, 77, 78–9, 121; cost of maintaining, 79, 227, 241; town and rural numbers, 117; emoluments, 121, 144, 184; wages, 121, 183–4, 227, 236, 241; tipping, 121–2, 184; advantages of, 122, 184–5; in eighteenth century, 143, 144, 153, 159; middle-class accommodation, 176, 184; complaints against, 184, 227; dependence of great houses on, 226; scarcity of, 227; middle classes and, 234–40 *passim*, 260; hierarchical society, 241; second largest occupational group, 248; status, 260; fall in numbers in twentieth century, 291

Sheffield: population, 171, 195; wages, 181

Sheraton, Thomas (1756–1806), 146

Shipbuilding: and great forests, 55; wage-rates, 253, 254; depression and unemployment, 284, 287

Shooting: replaces hawking, 94, 148; game accounts in nineteenth century, 230

Shopkeepers: precarious existence, 112, 114; in eighteenth century, 171, 172; range of luxury specialists, 173; capital required, 173–4; rents, 175; rise of multiple stores, 214; increase in real earnings, 301

Shrewsbury, Elizabeth Talbot, Countess of (1518–1608), wealth, 73, 74

Sidney, Sir Philip (1554–86), at Shrewsbury, 91

Silver: basis of medieval currency, 17, 52; increased demand for, 52; alleged influx from Spain, 65; reduction in fineness, 66

Slingsby, Sir Henry (1602–58), establishment, 104

Slums, urban, 218

Smiles, Samuel (1812–1904), *Self Help*, 194, 216

Smith, Adam (1723–90): and taxation, 136–7; and free exchange, 190, 326

Smith, B. Abel, and contemporary poverty, 304–5

Smollett, Tobias (1721–71), a London cook shop, 185

Soap, 78, 133, 139, 187

Social services: middle classes and, 246; aimed at industrial security, 289; increased expenditure, 302, 314; and working classes, 314

Social status: clothing and, 33, 34; maintenance of an establishment and, 76; gentry, 100, 102; yeomen, 105; of merchant class, 110; of shopkeepers, 112, 173; and possession of land, 140; position of women, 285; determined by occupation, 292; other determinants, 295; research surveys, 295–7; 'levelling-up-and-down', 297, 300, 303; and nutritional adequacy, 305–6

Social structure: price changes and, 9, 68; Tudor and Stuart England, 72; effect Tudor price-rise, 121; eighteenth-century, 128, 139 ff.; effect of Industrial Revolution, 131, 192, 194 ff., 219, 231, 251; Victorian England, 219, 231; changes wrought by full employ-

INDEX

ment, 285; position of women in twentieth century, 285–6; mass production and, 292; occupational changes and, 292; changed shape today, 293

Somerset, Edward Seymour, Duke of (?1506–52): and the coinage, 65–6; cost of London house, 85

Southey, Robert (1774–1843), Yorkshire farmhouse, 159–60

Spain: inflation, 60; alleged influx of bullion from, 65; expenditure on Armada war against, 67

Spas and watering places, 148, 149

Spensers of Althorp, enrichment, 76

Sport: *see* Recreations and sport

Spring, Thomas, of Lavenham, 110

Standard of living, 14; variations in Middle Ages, 45; comparisons with other times and places, 54, 57; stability in fifteenth century, 59–60; of the gentry in sixteenth and seventeenth centuries, 103, 104–5; of the clergy, 114–15; for wage-earners, 119–21, 127; in eighteenth century, 129, 133, 139; of rural middle classes, 156, 158; regional variations for labourers, 165–7; or urban working class, 178–82; factors influencing, 182–3, 205; its many elements, 189; in Britain, 1900, 257; rise between wars, 287–8; post-war rise, 288; definition of poverty, 305; during depression, 311; in second world war, 313

Staphorst, Abraham, 88

Statute of Artificers (1563), 69–70

Statute of Labourers (1351), 19–20, 24, 53

Stavordale, Lord, losses at Almack's, 148

Steam power, 59, 131; development of steamships, 190, 208, 291

Sterling: origin of term, 17; reduced by Henry VIII, 65–6; restoration by Cecil, 66

Stow, John (?1525–1605), 62

Strikes, 205

Stubbes, Philip (*fl.* 1583–91): on the poor, 72; and English gluttony, 79–80; and English clothing, 88–9

Stumpe, William, purchase of Malmesbury Abbey, 110

Suffolk, rent rises, 64

Sumptuary laws (1363), 33

Surrey, wage-rates, 183

'Sweating sickness', outbreak of 1556–8, 68

Tailoring, 34, 89, 145–6, 151; appearance of 'ready-made' shops, 173; wage-rates, 181

Tawney, R. H., and aristocracy, 75-6, 99–100

Taxation: in Middle Ages, 39–40; for armed forces, 67; for war, 150; development in nineteenth century, 190; redistributive, 288; decisive influence on real income, 299, 302, 303; changes of last fifty years, 302–3, 314; average expenditure on, 1965, 318; capital, 231; coal, 85; Danegeld, 39; excess profits, 303; 'farm-rent', 39; indirect, 302, 323; motor-car, 247; petrol, 247; poll, 40; spirits, 180; super, 231, 247; surtax, 299, 303; 'tenths and fifteenths', 39–40; wine, 113; wool, 40

Taylor, Thomas, of Witney (d. 1583), household goods, 107–8

Tea: *see* Drinks

Technology: advances in eighteenth century, 131; nineteenth-century trade cycles, 197; and middle-class improvements, 234; creation of unemployment, 249; and nutritional inferiority, 268; benefits to working class, 281; advances in twentieth century, 282; influence on occupational changes, 290; instrument of change, 315–16

Telgraph system, 216

INDEX

Temperance Movement, 211, 212, 275

Temple, William, and treatment of labourers, 164

Textile industry: women's wages, 181; of domestic workers, 182; effect of industrialization, 182; cotton, 186, 191, 214, 215, 284, 287; effect of mechanization, 190, 243, 248–9; mechanical weaving, 214, 249; poverty of hand-loomers, 249; semi-skilled labour, 251; employment of women and children, 251–2; individual and family earning, 252–3; wage movements in twentieth century, 257; expansion of rayon, 287; decline in employment, 290

Thames, as a highway, 97–8

Thanet, Earl of, his wealth, 73

Thatchers, 21, 24, 47

Theatre, the, 95, 145

Thingden, manor of, 64

Thornton, John, tutor, 91

Tips (vails), 121–2

Tobacco, smoking of, 95, 130, 139; cost of 95; expenditure on, 317, 318, 320

Towns: liberties under Royal Charter, 39, 41; trading sanctions, 53; growth of, 56, 67, 109; carrier service, 97; growing influx, 128; social conditions in eighteenth century, 128, 170 ff., 178, 179, 185, 187–8; source of economic advances, 171; food supply, 177; social evils, 179; wage-rates, 180–84; high proportion of poor, 185; new problems, 195; new demands on labour, 232; development of suburbs, 242, 284; availability of small shops etc., 273; exodus from country to, 283–4

Townsend, P., 305

Townsmen: rise of middle classes, 41; specialized diet, 46; endowments by, 46; effect of inflation, 71; entertainments for, 95; dependence on professional producers, 117; economy in domestic servants, 117; and economic advances, 171; acquisition of wealth, 187

Trade, 23; financial rewards, 41; code of ethics, 52–3; search for wealth in, 57–8; depression of 1551, 58, 65; development in sixteenth and seventeenth centuries, 58–9, 100, 109; and social mobility, 110, 174–5, 291; developments in nineteenth century, 190–91, 193; fluctuations in cycle, 196–7; demand from the Continent, 202; twentieth-century depression, 282, 285.

Overseas: development of, 58–9, 65, 109, 190–91, 255; Britain's reduced share, 286, 287.

Retail: slow turnover and high profits, 112–13, 114; use of multiple stores, 213–14, 215; competition in, 215; official collections of price data, 306

Trade unions, 250, 291; increased power, 314; wage increases, 324

Trades Union Congress, 324

Transport, 27, 36–7, 81, 84; in seventeenth century, 97–8; Industrial Revolution and, 131, 158; effect on prices, 138; new international systems, 208; lowered cost in nineteenth century, 215–16; railways and, 216; invention of bicycle, 217; changed pattern of expenditure, 317; passenger, 97, 157–8, 187, 216–17

Travel: use of the horse, 36, 45–6; developments in sixteenth and seventeenth centuries, 96 ff.; in eighteenth century, 157–8, 187; in Victorian age, 245; changed pattern of expenditure, 317, 318

Trevor-Roper, Hugh, on the gentry, 100

INDEX

Tusser, Thomas (?1524–80), on yeomen's food, 108

Tutors, private: noble families and, 91, 116, 147; for the Grand Tour, 93, 116; for the gentry, 154; for nineteenth-century aristocracy, 228; at public schools and universities, 229

Twici, William, wages as huntsman to Edward II, 23

Unemployment: in sixteenth and seventeenth centuries, 123; in nineteenth century, 256, 284–5; regional variations in twentieth century, 284, 288; decline since 1945, 284–5, 289; in the depression, 285, 287–8, 310, 311; caused by high costs, 310; acceptance of higher rate, 323–4; price stability and, 324

United States: rising power, 204; gold standard, 204; exports to Britain, 208, 210–11; increase in gross domestic product, 289; 'compensated dollar' plan, 323

Universities: *see* Cambridge University, Oxford University

Unton, Sir Henry (?1557–96), furniture at Wodley, 87

Usury, legal control under Tudors, 69

Vale Royal Abbey, Yorks., 22, 23, 25–6

Verulam, Earl of, expenditure in nineteenth century, 226

Villeinage, variations in, 15; rights under, 16; tenants' obligations, 18–19; commutation of labour services, 19, 20; disappearance of, 20; taxes, 39; payment for manumission, 39; diet, 48

Violence, in rioting, 182, 205

Wage-earners: replace craftsmen, 59; victims of inflation, 71, 118, 121, 127; lack of bargaining associations, 118; fall in standard of living, 119–21; draw nearer to salary-earners, 292, 309; attitude to reductions, 322

Wages: of agricultural labourers, 18, 21, 119, 161, 162, 164, 167, 168, 249–50, 251; rise in after Black Death, 19, 23–4, 52, 59; payment in kind, 21, 22, 119; regional variations, 22, 164–5, 182, 284; yearly contracts, 22, 23, 119; diversity in identical occupations, 22; seasonal variations, 23; outstripped by prices, 67, 119; related to prices, 69–71; attempts to fix in London (1538), 119; narrowing gap between skilled and unskilled, 119; effect of price-rises on 'nominal' and 'real', 254–7; analysis of expenditure per head per day, 258–9; rise faster than total output, 289; narrowing of differentials, 292, 309, 313, 314; cuts during falling prices, 309–10; effect of spiralling on costs, 321; government efforts to control, 324–5; 3½% norm increase, 325

Waldegrave, Sir William, claim to gentility, 102

Wales, unemployment rates, 284

Walpole, Sir Robert, Earl of Orford (1676–1745), palace at Houghton, 142–3

Walter of Henley, 18, 23

Walter of Hereford, salary as King's architect, 41

War: obligations of villeins, 19; use of the horse, 37; taxation, 39, 150, 302; price fluctuations, 138, 201–2

Ware, Isaac (d. 1766): on London housing, 176; *Architecture*, 160

Warrington: medieval rents, 45; nonconformist academy, 158

Wars of the Roses, and the aristocracy, 72, 75

Wealth: distribution in seventeenth century, 56; belief in its expendi-

INDEX

Wealth – *cont.*
 ture, 57; desire for in Tudor and Stuart society, 57–8; and membership of aristocracy, 73; acquisition by the gentry, 100; unequal distribution in eighteenth century, 128, 138; rapid increase in, 128–9; changes in sources and distribution in nineteenth century, 194; at outbreak of 1914 war, 220; new opportunities for its acquisition, 291; continuing unequal division, 319

Wedgwood, Josiah (1730–95), 154; London showroom, 173

Welfare services, 302

West Country: enclosed farms, 55; clothing villages, 59; broadcloth, 63; labourers' possessions, 169; decay of cloth trade, 182; wage-rates, 183, 250

West Indies, imports from, 129, 135

Westminister Abbey, cost of nave, 26

Westmorland, 168, 250

Westmorland, Earl of, wealth, 73

Wheat, 12: price variations, 13, 29, 51, 62, 83, 133–5, 204, 206–9, 222; export in eighteenth century, 129; and price of bread, 209

White, Sir Thomas (1492–1567), 111

Whittington, Richard (d. 1423), endowments, 46

William, Brother, daily allowance, 21

Wills, evidence from, 107–8, 110, 112, 124

Wilson, Thomas (*fl.* 1600), estimate of yeoman's wealth, 106

Wiltshire: prevalence of long leases, 64; wage-rates, 164, 182

Winchcombe, John (d. 1520), clothier, 109

Winchester Cathedral, 42

Windows, 44, 47, 84, 113

Wine: *see* Drinks

Witney blanket trade, 108

Woburn Abbey: cost of servicing and maintaining, 78–9; household accounts, 82–3, 90; reconstruction, 86; internal decorations, 86; cost of stabling etc., 94; transport costs, 97; wage-rates, 122

Wolsey, Thomas (?1475–1530), 72, 101; wealth, 73; cost of Hampton Court, 85

Women: wage-rates in Middle Ages, 18, 21–2; cost of accoutrements, 34, 146; wives of peasants, 48; dress, 88, 89–90, 145, 169, 242–3, 318; method of travel, 97, 98; employment in domestic industry, 121, 122, 166, 249; dowries, 142, 152; as additional wage-earners, 166, 167; domestic service, 184, 194, 227, 290; Sunday dresses, 186; new careers open to, 194; university education, 229; London season, 230; employment in 'sweated' trades, 249; in factories, 251–2; in ports and coal-mines, 252–3; employment in poor regions, 284; changed role in modern society, 285; increased expectation of life, 285; percentage of labour force, 285–6; diversified employment in twentieth century, 290–1; clerical occupations, 294, 299; higher professions, 295; increased earnings compared with men, 301, 302

Wood, G. H., wage scales, 256, 257

Wood, John (?1705–54), on labourers' cottages, 170

Woodforde, Parson (1740–1803), daily life and meals, 161

Wool: export of, 23, 57; cost of, 49, 58, 62–3, 135, 214; replaced by cotton, 186; poverty of hand loomers, 249

Workhouses, 263, 280

Working classes: diet, 47–8, 125–7, 133, 135, 136, 181, 184–5, 265–7; clothing, 48–9, 125, 214, 215, 278–9; furniture, 49–50, 124,

INDEX

280–81; life of toil, 50, 55, 123–7; state of poverty, 71, 121–7; rise in standard of living, 139, 178, 180; effect of industrialization, 178–9, 189; wage-rates, 180–82; expenditure, 186–7; additional earnings, 187; contingencies in budgets, 187; illness, 187; recruitment into white-collar work, 193; new demands on skill, 194; insecurity brought by trade cycles, 197; effect of price changes, 205; causes of discontent, 205; tea-drinking, 212, 213; transport to work, 217; political competence, 223; range of skills and earnings, 247, 253; social mobility, 247, 257; advancing standards, 256; movement out of poverty, 256–7; beneficiaries of Victorian prosperity, 257–8; household budgets, 259–64; cost of living estimates, 265, 266; improved diet, 265–7; consumption patterns in skilled and unskilled, 268–73; credit, 273, 280; drinking, 274, 275; expense of accommodation, 276–8; indebtedness, 280; cost of funerals, 280; medical expenses, 280; family limitation, 280; contraction in size, 292; Labour's policy and, 314

World war, first, 282, 302, 308

World war, second, 282, 302; price rises, 312; improved standard of living, 313; wage differentials, 313

Wyatt, James (1746–1813), 225

Wykeham, William of (1324–1404), Bishop of Winchester, 41–2

Wyllyby, John, barber-surgeon of Banbury, 116

Yeomen: economic and social status, 105; characteristics, 105–6, 155; accumulation of land, 106, 107; investment in industry, 106; favoured by price-rise, 106; accumulation of goods, 107–8; urban counterpart, 109; part of 'landed' interest, 224

York, 123; Booth's surveys on poverty, 258, 267, 304; value of land, 276; housing costs and rents, 276–7, 278

Yorkshire: clothing villages, 59, 182; broadcloth, 63; wage-rates, 165, 181, 250; textile industry, 251, 252; rate of growth, 284

Young, Arthur (1741–1820): on land rents, 130; cheap food, 136; his ideal farmer, 156, 159; and poor families, 163, 166; agricultural wages, 164–5; clothing of labourers, 169; urban wages, 181, 182

MORE ABOUT PENGUINS
AND PELICANS

Penguinews, which appears every month, contains details of all the new books issued by Penguins as they are published. From time to time it is supplemented by *Penguins in Print* – a complete list of all our available titles. (There are well over three thousand of these.)

A specimen copy of *Penguinews* will be sent to you free on request, and you can become a subscriber for the price of the postage – 4s. for a year's issues (including the complete lists). Just write to Dept EP, Penguin Books Ltd, Harmondsworth, Middlesex, enclosing a cheque or postal order, and your name will be added to the mailing list.

Another Pelican by John Burnett is described overleaf.

Note: *Penguinews* and *Penguins in Print*
are not available in the U.S.A. or Canada

Also by John Burnett

Plenty and Want

A Social History of Diet in England from 1815 to the Present Day

Our great-grandparents' food was far less pure and wholesome than our own.

Throughout the industrial revolution most town workers ate better than countrymen.

The 'Hungry Forties' were no hungrier than earlier decades of the nineteenth century.

Our overall standard of living has risen faster in periods of national crisis, such as the Great Depression and two world wars.

These are some of the surprising conclusions of *Plenty and Want*, an engaging survey of British dietary and social change in the nineteenth and twentieth centuries. John Burnett's sources range from royal menus and dinner-party etiquette to reports on starvation and the lot of the labouring poor; and he is keenly aware of the extremes of destitution and penury which lurk behind bland statistical averages. His book shows how the Victorians coped with the vast logistic problems of feeding their new super-cities; how until the eighteen-seventies many foods were adulterated with poisonous substances; and how under the pressures of war and social unrest national nutritional planning gradually became accepted as an essential part of the Welfare State. The book ends with an account of our changing eating habits since the war.

NOT FOR SALE IN THE U.S.A.